"Sacraments are at the heart of Catholic spirituality and liturgical life. They are celebrated in the context of the proclamation of God's Word. This excellent series will help Catholics appreciate more and more both the relationship between Word and Sacrament and how the sacraments are grounded in the riches of Scripture."

—**Thomas D. Stegman, SJ,** Boston College School of Theology and Ministry

"This series shows tremendous promise and ambition in laying out the multiple living connections between the Scriptures and the sacramental life of the Church. Taken together, these books could accomplish what Jean Daniélou's *The Bible and the Liturgy* accomplished for a previous generation of biblical and theological scholarship. And like that work, this series gives to students of the Bible a deeply enriched view of the mesh of relationships within and between biblical texts that are brought to light by the liturgy of the sacraments."

—**Jennifer Grillo,** University of Notre Dame

"In recent years, theological exegesis—biblical commentary by theologians—has made a significant contribution. This series turns the tables: explicitly theological reflection by biblical scholars. The result is a breakthrough. Theologically trained, exegetically astute biblical scholars here explore the foundations of Catholic sacramental theology, along paths that will change the theological conversation. This series points the way to the theological and exegetical future."

—**Matthew Levering,** Mundelein Seminary

"The sacraments come to us clothed in images that carry their mystery and propose it to our hearts. These images come from Scripture and are inspired by the Holy Spirit, who wills to transfigure us each into the full measure of Christ. The books in this series, by situating the sacraments within the scriptural imagery proper to each, will over time surely prove themselves to be agents in this work of the Spirit."

—**John C. Cavadini,** McGrath Institute for Church Life, University of Notre Dame

A CATHOLIC BIBLICAL THEOLOGY OF THE SACRAMENTS

SERIES EDITORS

Timothy C. Gray
John Sehorn

ALSO IN THE SERIES

The Bible and Baptism: The Fountain of Salvation
Isaac Augustine Morales, OP

THE BIBLE
and THE
PRIESTHOOD

*Priestly Participation
in the One Sacrifice for Sins*

———————◆———————

ANTHONY GIAMBRONE, OP

𝕭
BakerAcademic
a division of Baker Publishing Group
Grand Rapids, Michigan

Published by Baker Academic
a division of Baker Publishing Group
PO Box 6287, Grand Rapids, MI 49516-6287
www.bakeracademic.com

Printed in the United States of America

Library of Congress Cataloging-in-Publication Data
Names: Giambrone, Anthony, 1977– author.
Title: The Bible and the priesthood : priestly participation in the one sacrifice for sins / Anthony Giambrone, OP.
Description: Grand Rapids, Michigan : Baker Academic, a division of Baker Publishing Group, [2022] | Series: A Catholic biblical theology of the sacraments | Includes bibliographical references and index.
Identifiers: LCCN 2022009314 | ISBN 9781540961860 (paperback) | ISBN 9781540966087 (casebound) | ISBN 9781493438020 (ebook) | ISBN 9781493438037 (pdf)
Subjects: LCSH: Priesthood—Biblical teaching. | Priesthood—Catholic Church. | Catholic Church—Doctrines.
Classification: LCC BS680.P66 G53 2022 | DDC 232/.8—dc23/eng/20220404
LC record available at https://lccn.loc.gov/2022009314

Imprimi potest:
Fr. Gerard Francisco Timoner III
Magister Ordinis
February 8, 2022

22   23   24   25   26   27   28   7   6   5   4   3   2   1

To Benedict XVI

Contents

PART 3 **"The Order of Melchizedek"**

Sidebars

Series Preface

> But one of the soldiers pierced his side with a spear, and at once there came out blood and water.
>
> —John 19:34 (ESV)

The arresting image of Jesus's pierced side has fed the spiritual imagination of countless believers over the centuries. The evangelist tells us that it "took place that the Scripture might be fulfilled" (John 19:36 ESV). Extending this line of thought, St. Thomas Aquinas goes so far as to compare the opened heart of Christ to the Scriptures as a whole, for the passion reveals the secret depths of God's trinitarian love latent in the Word, both written and incarnate. The Fathers of the Church—Latin, Greek, and Syriac alike—also saw in the flow of blood and water a symbol of the sacraments of Christian worship. From the side of Christ, dead on the cross, divine life has been dispensed to humanity. The side of Christ is the fount of the divine life that believers receive, by God's grace, through the humble, human signs of both Word and Sacrament.

Recognition of the life-giving symbiosis between Scripture and Sacrament, so richly attested in the teaching of the Fathers of the Church, has proved difficult to maintain in the modern world. However much the Church has insisted upon the unity of Word and Sacrament, "the faithful are not always conscious of this connection," so "there is great need for a deeper investigation of the relationship between word and sacrament in the Church's pastoral activity and in theological reflection" (Benedict XVI, *Verbum Domini* 53). This series seeks to contribute to that "deeper investigation" by offering a biblical theology of each of the seven sacraments.

One classic definition of theology is "faith seeking understanding." Catholic theology operates with the conviction that the deposit of faith—that which theology seeks to understand—has been brought to completion in Jesus Christ, is reliably transmitted in Scripture and Tradition, and is authentically interpreted by the Church's teaching office (see *Dei Verbum* 7–10). Accordingly, the teaching of the Catholic Church is the *initium fidei* or starting point of faith for theological reflection. The series does not aim primarily to demonstrate the truth of Catholic sacramental doctrine but to understand it more deeply. The purpose of the series, in short, is to foster a deeper appreciation of God's gifts and call in the sacraments through a renewed encounter with his Word in Scripture.

The volumes in the series therefore explore the sacraments' deep roots in the revelation of the Old and New Testaments. Since the study of Scripture should *always* be "the soul of sacred theology" (*Dei Verbum* 24), the expression "biblical theology" is used to indicate that the series engages in a theological reading of the Bible in order to enliven our understanding of the sacraments. The guidelines for such theological interpretation of Scripture are specified in *Catechism of the Catholic Church* 112–14 (cf. *Dei Verbum* 12): attention (1) to the entire content and unity of Scripture, (2) to the living Tradition of the whole Church, and (3) to the analogy of faith. A few words on each of these criteria are in order.

In keeping with the series' character as "biblical theology," the content and unity of Scripture is the criterion that largely governs the structure of each volume. The *Catechism* provides a helpful summary of the series' approach to this criterion. Following "the divine pedagogy of salvation," the volumes attempt to illuminate how the meaning of the seven sacraments, like that of all liturgical signs and symbols, "is rooted in the work of creation and in human culture, specified by the events of the Old Covenant and fully revealed in the person and work of Christ" (*CCC* 1145). Each volume explores (a) the Old Testament threads (including but not limited to discrete types of the sacraments) that (b) culminate in the ministry and above all in the paschal mystery of the incarnate Christ.

The series' acceptance of the Church's sacramental teaching ensures that the Church's Tradition plays an integral role in the volumes' engagement with the Bible. More directly, sidebars offer specific illustrations selected from the teaching and practice of the postbiblical Church, showing the sometimes surprising ways in which Tradition embodies the Church's ongoing reception of the biblical Word.

In the case of the sacraments, attention to the analogy of faith means, among other things, keeping always in mind their origin and end in the eternal life of the Blessed Trinity, their relationship to the missions of the Son and the Spirit, their ecclesial context, their doxological character, their soteriological purpose, their vocational entailments, and their eschatological horizon.

The series' intended readership is broad. While the primary audience is Catholics of the Roman Rite, it is hoped that others will find much to appreciate, particularly Catholics of the non-Roman rites as well as Eastern Christians who are not in full communion with the Bishop of Rome but whose sacramental theory and practice are very close. Protestant Christians, of course, vary widely in their views of sacramental worship, and their reception of the series is likely to vary similarly. It is our hope that, at the very least, the series will help Protestant believers better understand how Catholic sacramental teaching is born of Scripture and animated by it.

We pray that all those who read these volumes will together delight in the rich food of God's Word (cf. Isa. 55:2), seeking the unity in faith and charity to which we are called by our common baptism into the life of the Blessed Trinity. To God be the glory.

Timothy C. Gray
John Sehorn

Preface

The Bible has more to say about the priesthood than about any of the other mysteries of grace that Catholics have called the seven sacraments for a thousand years. This abundance of revealed truth about such a profound gift—indeed the wellspring of so many further gifts of Christ to his Church—is a true embarrassment of riches. With that abundance comes a proportionate burden: a burden evident in its great theological depth to any sensitive Christian mind and visible in its extreme interpretative complexity to any trained exegetical eye. The present work accordingly makes no pretense whatsoever to offer anything approaching a comprehensive or definitive "biblical theology of the priesthood." It is instead presented in the loose spirit of an introduction in the interpersonal sense, not a manual or German-style *Einführung*. This book is one personal rendition out of an immense variety of possible, profitable, theologically engaged readings of the scriptural witness to the Christian priesthood.

Rather than straining to survey all the rich material with a right to be heard, I have opted to select a few illustrative passages and treat them with greater patience and delectation. This method of more narrow focus should not obscure the grand theological arc I mean to trace, however. Three chapters on the Old Testament, which tell their own integral but open-ended story, are followed by two chapters exposing New Testament variations on the Old Testament themes. There is a clear canonical form implicit in this layout: Pentateuch, Prophets, and Writings; Gospels and the Apostolic corpus. It is true that in this arrangement the Writings get short shrift indeed, with the notable exception of Ben Sira, to whom a final recapitulative word is given, as well as some modest attention, off the main track, paid to Chronicles and the Psalms. (Ezra and Nehemiah also poke in their heads but get no concentrated treatment.) Plenty of worthy material is certainly missed, but overall the distribution accurately reflects the nature of the texts in my opinion. The three-pointed shape of the opening Old Testament section accordingly also follows, at a deeper level, what we might call the contours of the biblical plot, seen typologically and prophetically in advance, while the New Testament presentation reflects the ecclesial structure of head and mystical members—that is, Jesus and the Church. A series of ten short excursuses is also included, two connected with each exegetical chapter. These are not meant as superfluous or optional in any way. They belong to the argument, so to speak. The compact format of the excursus was chosen simply as an expedient for maintaining control over an overwhelming body of relevant data while assuring illustrative variety as well as the handling of essential but supporting themes.

This little experiment—for that is what it is—is certainly stamped by the training and interest of a modern biblical scholar. Still, it strains to be pedagogic rather than pedantic and to observe throughout the correct theological proportions. It is consciously envisioned for lay consumption—that is, it should be readable without a special initiation into the vast professional exegetical literature, even if at times it may feel like an initiation in its own right.

The opening, introductory chapter with its appended "Hermeneutical Interlude" is no technical treatise, but it is obliged, nonetheless, to lay out a certain number of preexegetical premises in order to assure a responsible (if experimental) ecclesial reading. Skipping this in whole or part is a respectable option. The "Interlude," in particular, may be circumvented. It will be useful above all for those who wish to see laid out clearly and in advance the concrete Catholic framework and interpretative orientation otherwise inductively evident.

After this preparatory discussion, the work remains focused on the business of reading the Bible. The emphasis throughout is consciously placed on the Scriptures, not on academic debates (though such debates play their role and are not ignored). For ease of digestion the inevitably detailed exegetical chapters all conclude with a succinct "Summary of Key Points," which might also freely be read in advance without penalty or shame. These lists should be pedagogically helpful. Should it still become a wearisome challenge for certain readers to push dutifully through these pages, they are welcome to jump selectively from Scripture to Scripture, navigating the floating chunks of Bible that make a kind of archipelago of quotation islands across the text—perhaps even throwing open their Bibles at home to see them in context. Such verse-hopping should be pleasant sport. The loquacious ocean of words surrounding these God-given texts is obviously only my own effort to wrap them together in a sort of interpretative synthesis and to present both honestly and simply what I take for defensible scholarly positions.

As with an ocean, the surface covers unseen creatures in the deep: some of fantastic beauty, others ugly monsters. For this reason, while trying to steer a steady and calm course in making my presentation, I have also tried to include a judicious number of footnotes, where the curious are invited to dive down and plumb the depths at their own peril and pleasure. I am conscious of a certain unevenness in what may appear a scattershot annotation, but this must be judged as a function of the winds and waves, which sometimes make the ride a little choppy. Those familiar with the conventions of contemporary exegetical writing will easily forgive whatever may here and there appear an excess of zeal in my manner of offering notes. They will recognize how temperate, in fact, has been my footnoting, on the whole. The measure of temperance involved actually owes more to my editor than to any native moderation; for on your behalf, dear reader, he removed half the citations that I already thought quite admirably restrained and embarrassingly scarce. (A good deal of Hebrew and Greek in transliteration, many polysyllabic words, some semi-learned allusions, and a touch of clever banter were also removed.) As much as possible, I have attempted to cite literature available in English. Bible translations, unless otherwise noted, are taken from the NRSV. Only my squawking, academic super-ego knows (together with colleagues who might dip into these pages) how many countless times, to keep on course, I had to jettison points worthy of greater discussion and how many academic debts are here sadly unpaid. But that is all fitting to the nature of a project such as this—and in its own way it is also rather freeing, for the author as much as the reader.

For reasons related to the COVID-19 pandemic, which long exiled me from Jerusalem and our dear library at the *École biblique*, this manuscript was written in an unexemplary way in the compressed period of August and September 2020, at which point I was obliged to wrap it up and begin a research year in another country, focused on a different project. The subject deserves more mature musing than it here receives. This would be true, however, even had I the leisure to give it two years or two lives. May the Lord remedy its defects and bless the use of this humble study, which I offer to the Church with deepest gratitude for the gift of God's Son's holy priesthood.

Anthony Giambrone, OP
École biblique de Jérusalem
Feast of St. Jerome—September 30, 2020

Abbreviations

1 Apol.	Justin Martyr, *First Apology*	AT	author's translation
1 Clem.	*1 Clement*	AYB	Anchor Yale Bible
1 En.	*1 Enoch*	*Barn.*	*Epistle of Barnabas*
1QS	*Rule of the Community* (Dead Sea Scrolls)	*b. B. Bat.*	Babylonian Talmud tractate *Bava Batra*
4Q175	*Testimonia* (Dead Sea Scrolls)	BETL	Bibliotheca Ephemeridum Theologicarum Lovaniensium
AB	Anchor Bible		
ABR	*Australian Biblical Review*	*BibInt*	*Biblical Interpretation*
AIL	Ancient Israel and Its Literature	BN	*Biblische Notizen*
		b. Ned.	Babylonian Talmud tractate *Nedarim*
AJA	*American Journal of Archaeology*	*b. Pesah.*	Babylonian Talmud tractate *Pesahim*
ALD	*Aramaic Levi Document*	*b. Rosh Hash.*	Babylonian Talmud tractate *Rosh Hashanah*
AnB	Analecta Biblica		
AncJud	*Ancient Judaism*	*b. Sanh.*	Babylonian Talmud tractate *Sanhedrin*
ANEM	Ancient Near East Monographs		
ANEP	*The Ancient Near East in Pictures Relating to the Old Testament.* Edited by James B. Pritchard. 2nd ed. Princeton: Princeton University Press, 1994.	*b. Shabb.*	Babylonian Talmud tractate *Shabbat*
		b. Sotah	Babylonian Talmud tractate *Sotah*
		b. Yoma	Babylonian Talmud tractate *Yoma*
ANET	*Ancient Near Eastern Texts Relating to the Old Testament.* Edited by James B. Pritchard. 3rd ed. Princeton: Princeton University Press, 1969.	BZAW	Beihefte zur Zeitschrift für die alttestamentliche Wissenschaft
		b. Zebah.	Babylonian Talmud tractate *Zebahim*
Ant.	Josephus, *Jewish Antiquities*	BZNW	Beihefte zur Zeitschrift für die neutestamentliche Wissenschaft
As. Mos.	*Assumption of Moses*		

ca. *circa*, approximately
CBQ *Catholic Biblical Quarterly*
CBQMS Catholic Biblical Quarterly Monograph Series
CBR *Currents in Biblical Research*
CD Cairo Genizah copy of the *Damascus Document*
cf. *confer*, compare
chap(s). chapter(s)
CTH *Catalogue des textes hittites.* Emmanuel Laroche. Paris: Klincksieck, 1971.
CTM *Concordia Theological Monthly*
CTQ *Concordia Theological Quarterly*
d. c. died circa
DCLS Deuterocanonical and Cognate Literature Studies
Denzinger Denzinger, Heinrich. *Compendium of Creeds, Definitions, and Declarations on Matters of Faith and Morals.* Edited by Peter Hünermann, Robert Fastiggi, and Anne Englund Nash. 43rd ed. San Francisco: Ignatius, 2012.
Did. *Didache*
Dion. Nonnus of Panopolis, *Dionysiaca*
DSD *Dead Sea Discoveries*
EJL Early Judaism and Its Literature
esp. especially
FAT Forschungen zum Alten Testament
FC Fathers of the Church
Gen. Rab. *Genesis Rabbah*
GRBS *Greek, Roman, and Byzantine Studies*
HBAI *Hebrew Bible and Ancient Israel*
HCOT Historical Commentary on the Old Testament

HSM Harvard Semitic Monographs
HTR *Harvard Theological Review*
ICC International Critical Commentary
IEJ *Israel Exploration Journal*
IPriene *Die Inschriften von Priene*
ITQ *Irish Theological Quarterly*
JANER *Journal of Ancient Near Eastern Religions*
JBL *Journal of Biblical Literature*
JHebS *Journal of Hebrew Scriptures*
JHMTh/ ZNThG *Journal for the History of Modern Theology / Zeitschrift für Neuere Theologiegeschichte*
JJS *Journal of Jewish Studies*
JSJ *Journal for the Study of Judaism*
JSJSup Supplements to the Journal for the Study of Judaism
JSNT *Journal for the Study of the New Testament*
JSOT *Journal for the Study of the Old Testament*
JSOTSup Journal for the Study of the Old Testament Supplement Series
JSP *Journal for the Study of the Pseudepigrapha*
JSQ *Jewish Studies Quarterly*
JTS *Journal of Theological Studies*
Jub. *Jubilees*
J.W. Josephus, *Jewish War*
KBo *Keilschrifttexte aus Boghazköi.* Leipzig: Hinrichs, 1916–23; Berlin: Gebr. Mann, 1954–.
L.A.B. Pseudo-Philo, *Liber Antiquitatum Biblicarum (Biblical Antiquities)*
LCL Loeb Classical Library
Lev. Rab. *Leviticus Rabbah*
LG *Lumen Gentium*

LHBOTS	Library of Hebrew Bible / Old Testament Studies	RBS	Resources for Biblical Study
LW	*Luther's Works* (American edition). Edited by Jaroslav Pelikan and Helmut T. Lehmann. 55 vols. Philadelphia: Fortress; St. Louis: Concordia, 1955–86. New series, vols. 56–82. St. Louis: Concordia, 2009–.	*RevQ*	*Revue de Qumran*
		RSV	Revised Standard Version
		RTR	*Reformed Theological Review*
		SCG	Thomas Aquinas, *Summa contra Gentiles*
		SNTSMS	Society for New Testament Studies Monograph Series
LXX	Septuagint	*ST*	Thomas Aquinas, *Summa Theologiae*
m. Demai	Mishnah tractate *Demai*	STDJ	Studies on the Texts of the Desert of Judah
m. Ma'as.	Mishnah tractate *Ma'aserot*		
Mos.	Philo, *On the Life of Moses*	SVTP	Studia in Veteris Testamenti Pseudepigraphica
m. Pe'ah	Mishnah tractate *Pe'ah*		
MT	Masoretic Text	TBN	Themes in Biblical Narrative
m. Yoma	Mishnah tractate *Yoma*	*Test. Dan*	*Testament of Dan*
NETS	New English Translation of the Septuagint	*Test. Gad*	*Testament of Gad*
		Test. Jos.	*Testament of Joseph*
NPNF¹	*Nicene and Post-Nicene Fathers*, Series 1	*Test. Jud.*	*Testament of Judah*
		Test. Levi	*Testament of Levi*
NRSV	New Revised Standard Version	*Test. Reub.*	*Testament of Reuben*
		Tg. Ps.-J.	*Targum Pseudo-Jonathan*
NTS	*New Testament Studies*	*Tg. Yer. I*	*Targum Yerushalmi I*
OTL	Old Testament Library	*t. Menaḥ.*	Tosefta tractate *Menaḥot*
OTP	*The Old Testament Pseudepigrapha*. Edited by James H. Charlesworth. 2 vols. New York: Doubleday, 1983–85.	Tob.	Tobit
		t. Soṭah	Tosefta tractate *Soṭah*
		VC	*Vigiliae Christianae*
		VT	*Vetus Testamentum*
Pesiq. Rab Kah.	*Pesiqta de Rab Kahana*	WA	*D. Martin Luthers Werke* (Weimarer Ausgabe). 136 vols. Weimar: Böhlau, 1883–2009.
PFES	Publications of the Finnish Exegetical Society		
		WBC	Word Biblical Commentary
PG	Patrologia Graeca [= *Patrologiae Cursus Completus. Series Graeca*]. Edited by Jacques-Paul Migne. 162 vols. Paris, 1857–86.	*WTJ*	*Westminster Theological Journal*
		WUNT	Wissenschaftliche Untersuchungen zum Neuen Testament
Pirqe R. El.	*Pirqe Rabbi Eliezer*	*y. Yoma*	Jerusalem Talmud tractate *Yoma*
PL	Patrologia Latina [= *Patrologiae Cursus Completus. Series Latina*]. Edited by Jacques-Paul Migne. 217 vols. Paris, 1844–64.	*ZAW*	*Zeitschrift für die alttestamentliche Wissenschaft*
RB	*Revue Biblique*	*ZNW*	*Zeitschrift für die neutestamentliche Wissenschaft*

PART 1

INTRODUCTION

1

Priesthood and the Project of Catholic Exegesis

At the very opening of his exceptional reflection "The Catholic Priesthood," spoken with profound personal feeling from out of the silence of his retreat, the former pontiff Benedict XVI identifies with disarming clarity the precise exegetical malpractice that has undermined the sacrament of Holy Orders in our day.

> Given the lasting crisis that the priesthood has been going through for many years, it seemed to me necessary to get to the deep roots of the problem. . . .
>
> At the foundation of the serious situation in which the priesthood finds itself today, we find a methodological flaw in the reception of Scripture as the Word of God.
>
> The abandonment of the Christological interpretation of the Old Testament led many contemporary exegetes to a deficient theology of worship. They did not understand that Jesus, far from abolishing the worship and adoration owed to God, took them upon himself and accomplished them in the loving act of his sacrifice. As a result, some went so far as to reject the necessity of an authentically cultic priesthood in the New Covenant.[1]

The present work is offered as a meditation on these words and as an attempt to begin the work of addressing "the deep roots of the problem." The mystery of priestly life in the Church is here examined through an encounter with *Scripture as the Word of God*—approached in contemplation of Jesus' perfect sacrifice of love.

1. Benedict XVI and Robert Cardinal Sarah, *From the Depths of Our Hearts: Priesthood, Celibacy, and the Crisis of the Catholic Church* (San Francisco: Ignatius, 2019), 25.

Seen from a biblical angle, of course, the "crisis" of the priesthood, of which Benedict speaks, is a "lasting" thing indeed and actually anything but new. Like the monarchy, the priesthood is both glorious and contemptible in the Bible. One might even say that a crisis of priestly sin and its supernatural resolution stands at the very center of the priestly mystery as it is revealed in the Scriptures. A failed institution of mediation with God, a beautiful but broken covenantal and cultic aspiration, stands re-created in the holiness of Jesus Christ, the one mediator of a new and "better" covenant and cult.

It would be an error, of course, to imagine that the sort of reflection and *ressourcement* offered here is an entirely new initiative. In the wake of Vatican II, a huge swell of scriptural reflection flooded into the Catholic bloodstream. This powerfully affected long-held perceptions of priestly service. Even if the biblical renewal ultimately engendered the fatal "methodological flaw" that Benedict evokes, this derailing of a vast intellectual and spiritual movement of true reform in the Church must not lead to full retreat or hardened opposition. This must be insisted upon in the face of the manifest theological sterility of so much modern exegetical writing, which frequently renders the living and effective Word of God quite dead and inert. Understandably, given such shortcomings, there is a strong sense among many theologians and students today that alternative patristic or dogmatic approaches are simply "safer" and more fruitful than direct engagement with the biblical text. This is a theologically untenable situation. The "abandonment of the Christological interpretation of the Old Testament" cannot be made right by a simple about-face in interpretative fashion, abandoning modern exegetical methods in favor of older models. The challenges confronting an exegetical *sanatio in radice*, a healing of certain diseased hermeneutical roots, are considerable and will be addressed below. It is clear, however, what must be attempted. Like scribes trained for the kingdom of heaven, we must draw forth from the treasure both the new and the old (Matt. 13:52).

The openly ecclesial orientation of a study such as this is obvious and unavoidable. This orientation must be more markedly *Catholic* than a similar study on baptism would be, moreover, for sacramental priesthood is a prominent point of ecumenical disagreement. It would clearly be irresponsible in this context merely to ignore the monumental, earnest, and unambiguous objection raised against the entire Catholic viewpoint represented by the Protestant position. "Of this sacrament [Holy Orders] the Church of Christ knows nothing; it was invented by the pope's church," said Martin Luther. "Not only is no promise of grace attached to it anywhere in the scriptures; not a single word is devoted to it in the entire New Testament."[2] Without en-

2. Martin Luther, *Babylonian Captivity of the Church* 7.1 (AT).

tering into "controversial theology" in the older sense of Catholic-Protestant exchange, I will thus take account of certain key points of interpretative divergence, with the indirect hope that some explanations might be useful also to non-Catholic Christian readers.

Whatever ecumenical and ecclesial audiences it may in the end actually find, this book largely targets Catholic seminarians preparing for initiation into the mysteries here described. For this reason, with a pedagogical interest in mind, following the example of a far greater teacher of Catholic truth in his magisterial instruction of beginners, I hope to avoid "the multiplication of useless questions" that only bring "weariness and confusion to the minds of readers."[3] Exegetical literature is often a noteworthy offender on this front, capable of stultifying extremities of detail. It is no less a "methodological flaw," however, when dogmatic theology rests content (as it too often does) to skim superficially over the scriptural witness, abstracting a few key, syllogistically susceptible thoughts, with no real patience for the exegetical tool kit required to actually study and savor the Bible. What is proposed here is accordingly offered as a sort of reading guide for thinking scripturally about Holy Orders: introductory, incomplete, and schematic, yet with sufficient landmarks staked out to permit the unhurried navigation of a few essential themes as I see them.

Holy Scripture is the first of Melchior Cano's ten *loci theologici*, and it will be the focus of all the chapters that follow. No exegesis ever is free of the influence of the other legitimate sources of theological reflection, however. It is therefore fitting here at the outset to make some acknowledgment of the general understanding of the sacrament of Holy Orders that informs this experiment in biblical theology.

Doctrinal Definitions

Authoritative Catholic dogma is most conveniently concentrated in exercises of the magisterium. Although several pronouncements reaching back to the twelfth century number Orders in lists of the seven sacraments (Denzinger §§718, 860, 1310, 1326), the Council of Trent was the first (and only) Church council required to make a solemn and lengthy statement about the nature of Holy Orders per se, so as "to condemn the errors of our time," as the decree says (§1763). Three basic teachings are offered.

(1) To begin, the existence of a sacrificial priesthood is affirmed. Trent's doctrinal summary is compact and makes broad appeal to Scripture and Tradition, without offering any specific discussion.

3. Thomas Aquinas, *Summa Theologica*, Preface. See https://www.newadvent.org/summa/.

Sacrifice and priesthood are, by the ordinance of God, so united that both have existed under every law. Since, therefore, in the New Testament the Catholic Church has received from the institution of Christ the holy, visible sacrifice of the Eucharist, it must also be acknowledged that there exists in the Church a new, visible and external priesthood into which the old one was changed [cf. Heb. 7:12]. Moreover the Sacred Scriptures make it clear and the tradition of the Catholic Church has always taught that this priesthood was instituted by the same Lord and Savior and that the power of consecrating, offering, and administering his Body and Blood, and likewise of remitting and retaining sins, was given to the apostles and to their successors in the priesthood. (Denzinger §1764)

The Council's view here is very tightly bound to the sacrificial character of the Eucharist, already taught in the previous session (Denzinger §§1739–40). Canon 2 of that previous session codifies the traditional understanding of a coincident institution of both priesthood and the Eucharist together at the Last Supper: "If anyone says that by the words 'Do this in memory of me' [Luke 22:19; 1 Cor. 11:24] Christ did not establish [*instituisse*] the Apostles as priests or that he did not order that they and other priests should offer his body and blood, let him be anathema" (Denzinger §1752).

(2) Next, a more developed statement on the specifically sacramental nature of Orders expands this doctrine. The Council again appeals to the authoritative sources of this teaching in a hermeneutical spiral of *auctoritas*:

Since from the testimony of Scripture, apostolic tradition, and the unanimous agreement of the Fathers it is clear that grace is conferred by sacred ordination, which is performed by words and outwards signs, so one ought not to doubt that orders is truly and properly one of the seven sacraments of Holy Church. For the apostle says: "I remind you to rekindle the gift of God that is within you through the laying on of my hands: for God did not give us a spirit of timidity, but a spirit of power and love and self-control" [2 Tim. 1:6]. (Denzinger §1766)

It is added (echoing the bull *Exultate Deo* published in 1439) that, as an effect of this grace, "in the sacrament of orders, as also in baptism and confirmation, a character is imprinted [*character imprimatur*] that can neither be erased nor taken away" (Denzinger §1767; cf. §1774).

(3) Finally, as an important point of correction, the Pauline doctrine of the mystical body is invoked to insist upon the hierarchical nature of the Church against false conceptions of the baptismal priesthood.

If Christians should assert that all Christians are without distinction priests of the New Testament or that all are equally endowed with the same spiritual power, they seem to be doing nothing else than upsetting the ecclesiastical hierarchy, which is like "an army set in array" [Song 6:3, 9], as if, contrary to the teaching of St. Paul, all were apostles, all prophets, all evangelists, all pastors, all doctors [cf. 1 Cor. 12:29; Eph. 4:11]. (Denzinger §1767)

The specific grades of clerical hierarchy were recognized from ancient usage to include all seven traditional orders, but only priests and deacons were acknowledged as openly mentioned in the Sacred Scriptures (Denzinger §1765; cf. Acts 6:5; 21:8; 1 Tim. 3:8–13; Phil. 1:1). Bishops, of course, are also present in the Scriptures; and "priests" in this context plainly includes both bishops and presbyters.

The Second Vatican Council amplified at length Trent's teaching on the hierarchical nature of the Church, emphasizing the communion between head and members and giving great attention to the office of bishop, in which the "fullness of the sacrament of Orders is conferred" (*LG* 21, 18–29; cf. Denzinger §4354). Vatican II also clarified that the ministerial and common priesthoods, though interrelated as shares in the one priesthood of Christ, differ in essence, not just degree (*LG* 10). Pius XII, in the encyclical *Mediator Dei* (1947), prepared for this statement when he specified that, while the baptized do "offer the divine Victim" in a special sense, they do this by virtue of their intention, not their ministry. Accordingly, the ordained minister, who offers the sacrifice *in the person* of Christ, is "inferior to Christ, but superior to the people," who "are not the conciliator between themselves and God" and can "in no way enjoy the sacerdotal power" (Denzinger §§3849–50).

The essential sum of these pronouncements is simple and pointed. In accord with Scripture and Tradition, the Church recognizes a hierarchical priesthood, elevated by a special grace above the baptismal dignity and entrusted with offering the eucharistic sacrifice in the person of Christ, to be a sacramental reality established by Jesus himself. This dense yet minimal framework gives articulate expression to the universal *sensus fidei* and defines the doctrinal space of Catholic orthodoxy. It hardly exhausts what theology might explore or say about Holy Orders, however.

Disputed Questions

These basic teachings of Trent are naturally vehemently contested from the Protestant side. Honesty thus requires not only some attention to objections that are raised but also an interest in the live questions that Catholic theology itself, as a work of faith seeking understanding, poses about these definitions. Each of the three dogmatic emphases above can be taken as the starting point for a short discussion that will help situate the chapters to follow.

1. Institution of the Priesthood

Baptism and celebration of the Holy Eucharist are the two most obvious sacramental rituals endorsed by the New Testament witness. Not only are these rites' grounding in the life of Christ and in the liturgical experience of the primitive Christian community both quite clear, but the supernatural grace conferred by each ritual is also expressly revealed: rebirth, remission of sins, adoption as sons (John 3; cf. Rom. 6–8); remission of sins, participation in the death of the Lord (Matt. 26:26–28; cf. 1 Cor. 10:16–17). It occasions little surprise, then, that during the Reformation it was often only these two major sacraments that survived—at least in some mitigated ritual form. They are the easiest to recognize and justify on the basis of Scripture alone.[4]

A Church conformed to the testimony of the Holy Scriptures is not exclusively the desire of Protestant Christians, nor in any way a false demand on their part—even if *sola scriptura* is a premise that cannot be shared. Catholic efforts to ground the Church's full sacramental system in the Gospels must, nevertheless, be admitted as being frequently a tenuous apologetic undertaking, grounded upon naïve biblical hermeneutics and enshrined in a mediocre manual tradition. More searching, late post-Tridentine theology ultimately acknowledged the depth of the problem. In his *questio disputata* on the sacraments, written on the very eve of the Second Vatican Council, Karl Rahner frankly stated the difficulty.

> We must ask how it is possible to demonstrate in an historically credible way the sacramentality of matrimony, holy order, extreme unction and confirmation, that is to say, here, their institution by Christ, which is, of course, a dogma. We have no sayings of Jesus about these sacraments. The authorization given to the apostles to celebrate the Lord's supper is not the institution of a sacramental rite which confers ministry and office. For no one can deny that in the new covenant there are official powers by divine law, and the transmission of such powers, which are not sacraments. One has only to think of Peter and his successors [i.e., the papal office]. The sacrament of order does not therefore follow from the *anamnesis* precept, the command to commemorate. Consequently, for four sacraments we have no words of institution from Jesus Christ himself.[5]

Rahner, who is clearly interested to stay within the bounds of defined Catholic dogma, nevertheless poses an open challenge to the canon cited above on

---

4. Penance, which is not without a strong biblical base, lost ritual standing in part because of Martin Luther's discovery that the Greek *metanoia* had quite a different sense than the Vulgate's *penitentiam agite* had acquired. The medieval Church's practice of sacramental penance, of course, stood at the very center of Luther's protest. See Luther's 1519 treatise on penance (LW 35:9–22).

5. Karl Rahner, *The Church and the Sacraments* (New York: Herder & Herder, 1963), 41–42. The original German edition was published a few years earlier (1960).

the institution of the priesthood. The concern, as he sees it, is historical, and he is right that the problem here should not be underestimated. Finding a "historically credible" approach will be a preoccupation in much of what follows. Is it possible to bind Jesus convincingly to the institution of a new eschatological priesthood?

Given many scholarly reconstructions of Jesus as a millenarian prophet who was ultimately mistaken in his expectation of the imminent end of the world, the more basic question is perhaps whether Jesus could have envisioned an institutional Church at all (a theme taken up and discussed below in chap. 7). In this connection, Rahner's own rigorously ecclesiological attempts to address the sacramental concern as he perceived it, which obviously took the form of abstract dogmatic reflection, not historical investigation or biblical exegesis, certainly has much merit. Jesus founded the Church itself, the primordial sacrament, which fully actualizes and manifests its own properly sacramental nature in a range of seven discretely efficacious acts, all somehow belonging to divine law yet tied to diverse historical conditions.

Invoking divine law calls attention to the sacraments' decisive material forms, which find their basis in something deeper than the human decisions of canon law. To this degree, insofar as the Church itself is not ultimately only an *institution* but a corporate union with Christ in the Spirit, the very language in which the sacramental question is posed is seen to be misleading. To claim that Jesus "instituted" (*instituisse*) the priesthood must mean something more than institutional stipulations governing the Church's future leadership class, though the essential elements of this are not excluded. It must indicate, ultimately, a living reality of union, by which God's perfect law reigns among men and Christ is made present.

If the ecclesiological turn is thus foundational and compelling, an evolutionist solution, excessively detached from Christ's own living actions, clearly poses intolerable risks.[6] Still, whatever questions Rahner's broader premises and private speculations might raise, he points in the right direction. Applied to the Church's hierarchical construction in sacred ranks of bishops, priests, and deacons, empowered to exercise those fundamental kerygmatic and eucharistic actions by which the Church is continually constituted, the situation is clear. The deepest essence of the *ekklēsia* as Christ's living body is profoundly engaged, thus sacramentally implicated in these consecrated grades. Indeed, in a real way the Church is never more herself than when the headship of Christ is made sacramentally present in this hierarchically constituted form. (Yves Congar's critique of so-called hierarchiology, an overly juridical simulacrum

6. The following Modernist thesis was condemned by Pius X in *Lamentabili* 49: "When the Christian supper gradually assumed the nature of a liturgical action, those who customarily presided over the supper acquired the sacerdotal character."

of ecclesiology, can be acknowledged here but for the moment set aside.[7]) In a word, the Church experiences and recognizes herself present in the living sign and grace of Holy Orders. The existence of the sacramental priesthood is as real and revealing as the very existence of Christ's Church.

THE PRIESTHOOD OF CHRIST

In our post-Reformation and modern democratic context, appeals to the Church's intuitive self-understanding quickly become problematic, of course. A hierarchical constitution and sacrificial cult are no longer obvious first principles of Christian social experience. The essential *holiness* of the Church (*sine macula et ruga*), on the other hand, is one defining mark that at least classically commands firm ecumenical agreement[8]—ironically enough, despite what might easily appear to be formidable counterevidence.

In manifold ways, the scars of evil tragically mar ecclesial life—a fact that has long preoccupied reformers, both Protestant and Catholic. The Donatist crisis was the first frontal confrontation with the considerable challenge posed by this obvious sinfulness in the Church's members—and notably her ordained ministers. The authoritative answer that emerged at an early date is very clear, however. Sacramental action itself is the locus of indefectible ecclesial holiness. This has been unambiguously maintained at least since Optatus of Milevis, who preceded Augustine as the Church's voice during the early period of the Donatist fight.[9] Augustine subsequently applied the principle with memorable precision:

> It was said of the Lord before He suffered, that He baptized more than John; then it was added: "Howbeit, Jesus Himself baptized not, but his disciples" [John 4:1–2]. He, and not He: He by power, they by ministry; they performed the service of baptizing, the power of baptizing remained in Christ. His disciples, then, baptized, and Judas was still among his disciples. . . . Those whom Judas baptized, Christ baptized. In like manner, then, they whom a drunkard baptized, those whom a murderer baptized, those whom an adulterer baptized, if it was the baptism of Christ, were baptized by Christ.[10]

Chrysostom, in a different context independent of Augustine's formulations, articulates a similar perspective on the untarnished dignity of priestly office.[11]

---

7. See Yves Congar, *Lay People in the Church* (Westminster, MD: Newman, 1965).

8. In the treatise *Von den Konziliis und Kirchen* (On the Councils and the Church) in 1539, for instance, Luther saw the Spirit sanctifying believers through the Word as the most important mark of the Church.

9. Optatus of Milevis, *On the Donatist Schism* 5.4 (PL 11:1053).

10. Augustine, *Tractates on the Gospel of John* 5.18 (PL 35:1423). Translation from *NPNF*[1] 7:38.

11. "If you see an unworthy priest, do not criticise the priesthood: one should not criticise the office—just the one exercising a good office badly, since Judas also proved a traitor, yet this

There is at once a sober realism and a buoyant hope in this unbroken teaching of the Church. It recalls an all-important article in Aquinas's *Summa Contra Gentiles*: "That the sacraments may be administered through [*per*] wicked ministers" (4.77). Thomas reasons very succinctly: "It would be unfitting for one to place the hope of his salvation in the goodness of a mere man, for it is said in Jeremiah 17:5, 'Cursed is the man who puts his trust in man.' . . . In order then that we might place the hope of our salvation in Christ, who is God and man, it is to be confessed that the sacraments work salvation by the power of Christ [*ex virtute Christe*], whether they be administered by good or evil ministers."[12] The exercise of theological hope actually depends upon faith in this doctrine of the true source of saving virtue.

An alternative and not incompatible foundation for the superstructure of sacramental theology is accordingly to begin not with the Church's members (as Rahner's paradigm might suggest) but, rather, with *the priesthood of Christ*—that is to say, Christ's supreme headship: a conception of the Church's sacramental economy as his own eschatologically triumphant, high priestly *opus operatum*.[13] This christological recentering accentuates the direct agency of God in the sacramental order and recalibrates "hierarchy" as more than a simple accidental and external sociological status. Contemplated in the elevation of the head, hierarchy instead becomes the recapitulative (*in capite*) manner in which Christ holds all things together (Col. 1:17–18), just as the head of the body exercises an immediate energy and life-giving power of movement within all the members. In this vein, hierarchy within the *totus Christus* is reconceived as a cascade of capital grace touching the whole: the original, integrative Dionysian sense of "hierarchy" as the "perfect total of all [the Church's] sacred constituents" (*Ecclesiastical Hierarchy* 1.3 [373C]).[14]

A view of sacramental life centered upon the high priesthood of Christ boasts a solid biblical warrant in the Epistle to the Hebrews (and elsewhere).

---

was a fault not of apostleship but of his free will, not a charge against priesthood but against the evil of free will" (John Chrysostom, *I Have Seen the Lord*, quoted in *St. John Chrysostom: Old Testament Homilies; Volume Two, Homilies on Isaiah and Jeremiah*, trans. Robert Charles Hill [Brookline, MA: Holy Cross Orthodox Press, 2003], homily 4.4–5, p. 89 [PG 56:126]; cf. *On Priesthood* 3.10 [PG 48:646–47]; *Homilies on the Epistle to Titus* [PG 62:672]).

12. "Nothing can act in what exceeds its own competence [*in id quod eius facultatem excedit*] unless it receives the power from another. . . . But what is done in the sacraments exceeds human competence, as is clear from the premise. Therefore no one may dispense the sacraments, no matter how good he is, unless he receives the power of dispensing. Now malice and sin are the opposite of goodness. Therefore neither is he hindered by sin from the administration of the sacraments who has received the power to do so" (Thomas Aquinas, *SCG* 4.77 [AT]).

13. See, e.g., Colman E. O'Neill, *Meeting Christ in the Sacraments* (New York: Alba House, 1990 [1964]). See also O'Neill, *Sacramental Realism* (Wilmington, DE: Michael Glazier, 1983).

14. Translation by Colm Luibheid, *Pseudo-Dionysius: The Complete Works* (New York: Paulist Press, 1987), 197.

Luther's disregard for this letter did not help enable an adequate doctrine of Holy Orders within the Lutheran context. Yet Catholic dogmatic reflection has also, unfortunately, left Christ's priesthood rather underdeveloped, as a recent survey of the subject notes with regret.[15] The most general scan of Hebrews yields an immediately useful framework, however. The priesthood of Christ recasts with saving power the prefiguring rituals of the old order and mediates the efficacious and "better" (*kreittōn*) rites of a "better" covenant (Heb. 7:22; 8:6; cf. 6:9; 7:19; 9:23; 10:34; 11:16). Jesus is the great high priest whose one supreme sacrifice attains the "perfection" (*teleoisis*, Heb. 7:11), that supreme aspiration and reality (*res*) that the old regime of offerings could not effect and yet somehow desired: atonement for sins and union with God. The Gospel of John, in which Jesus' high priesthood is again at play, if in a considerably less pronounced fashion, programmatically pursues a similar "grace in place of grace" motif, indicating how Jesus' heavenly gifts (*anōthen*) effect a systematic replacement of Jewish ritual life.

There are ample grounds to attribute to Christ himself a self-identification with the messianic priest of the order of Melchizedek addressed in Psalm 110 and celebrated in the Letter to the Hebrews. As our study advances, vistas will also open on Jesus' own aims for the inauguration of a new eschatological cult and a new temple. Rahner is thus ultimately right to move our research away from too narrow a focus upon precise words of institution and to seek instead to integrate Christ's institution of the priesthood into the wider constitution of the Church (though Rahner's take on Peter is profoundly unhelpful, as I will suggest in chap. 5). This does not mean leaving all to later, ecclesially sanctioned innovations—of which there are plenty. The epochal institution of a New Covenant belongs strictly to Christ's own personal priestly action, formally announced in the context of the Last Supper: "This cup is the new covenant in my blood" (1 Cor. 11:25; cf. Luke 22:20).

The broad replacement framework suggested here obviously cannot be pressed as a simple one-to-one mapping of the Church's seven sacraments onto some preexisting Jewish array of seven mystical rites. Certain sacraments of the New Law, eschatological reconfigurations of the Old—for example, baptism for circumcision—do nevertheless suggest themselves and find clear expression in the tradition. The question of a similar eschatological correspondence between the priestly hierarchies in the old and the new dispensations is in many ways the central problem that any biblical theology of Holy Orders must address. Are there spiritual Levites in eschatological Israel? In what concrete way has Christ replaced the old priestly order?

---

15. See Gerald O'Collins and Michael Keenan Jones, *Jesus Our Priest: A Christian Approach to the Priesthood of Christ* (Oxford: Oxford University Press, 2010).

2. The Grace of the Sacrament

Grounded upon a wide base of New Testament data, it was the common opinion of the medieval schools that, "because the Old Law merely instructed, its sacraments were only signs of grace; whereas because the New Law both instructs and justifies, its sacraments are both the sign and the cause of grace."[16] Sacramental theology in the latter part of the twentieth century, by contrast, frequently unmoored itself from this scholastic paradigm of signs and instrumental causality, adopting instead an alternative account oriented around *symbols* and attentive to anthropological/cultural and linguistic considerations, more than to metaphysics.[17]

While room can be easily found in the traditional paradigm for the evocative dimensions stressed in newer models, it is also important to appreciate what is at stake in maintaining that the sacraments of the New Law are a cause (and not just a sign) of grace. Ironically, despite the classic Protestant charge that Catholic sacramental praxis is somehow stunted in a "fleshly" Old Testament framework, it is precisely in this doctrine of the causality of the sacraments where the Church most clearly asserts the specific *newness* of the New Law: the powerful work of grace. From this vantage point, the failure to appreciate the grace of the gospel is not the danger of so-called Catholic "magic" but, rather, the risk run by so much Protestant theology, which still sees in the Catholic Church's ritual life the empty shadows that characterized Israel's cult of mere signs. What precise sense does the ritual performance of a Calvinist "Lord's Supper" have on its own terms, after all? It makes no claims to transmit Christ's grace; such ceremonies thus stall in a strange pre-though-post-gospel twilight. If Protestant thought is ultimately preoccupied by a concern to ensure that Christian existence be centered on faith, Catholic doctrine has long been perfectly transparent that the sacraments are always *sacramenta fidei*.[18]

A second reason for insisting upon the causality of the sacraments may be added beyond this epochal metaphysical marking of the border distinguishing the Old and the New. Emphasis on instrumentality safeguards the full, realistic force of the biblical language. It does not proceed from an obtuse

16. Thomas Aquinas, *De veritate* q. 27, a. 4.

17. See Bernhard Blankenhorn, "The Instrumental Causality of the Sacraments: Thomas Aquinas and Louis-Marie Chauvet," *Nova et Vetera* 4 (2006): 255–94. Signs stand for some other thing and are more limited in their meaning than symbols. For a seminal treatment, see Karl Rahner, "Theology of Symbol," in *Theological Investigations IV* (New York: Seabury, 1973), 221–52. See also C. Annice Callahan, "Karl Rahner's Theology of Symbol: Basis for His Theology of the Church and Sacraments," *ITQ* 49 (1982): 195–205.

18. A marvelously succinct and lucid account of this primacy of faith in the sacramental order appears in the first chapter of Abbot Vonier's classic *A Key to the Doctrine of the Eucharist* (Bethesda, MD: Zaccheus, 2003), 1–6.

interest in employing Aristotelian categories for the pure philosophical fun
of it. Scripture plainly attributes to Christ's humanity a genuine instrumental
power in the work of making people holy. For instance: "It is by God's will
that we have been sanctified *through* [*dia*] the offering [*tēs prosphoras*] of the
body of Jesus Christ once for all" (Heb. 10:10). This is not merely an exem-
plary, occasional, or disposing causality but a true perfective causality, as the
teleios word group in Hebrews underlines. It is cast in the unmistakable form
of Christ's priestly work. He "sanctifies" us by means of his unique sacrificial
"offering." The application of this same biblical language and principle of
Christ's own high priestly causation in the case of baptism—"*Christ* [not Peter
or Judas or any other administering agent] saved us through [*dia*] a bath of
regeneration" (Titus 3:5 AT)—enabled theologians to see its extension across
the entire sacramental field. In each of the sacraments, and in a way proper
to each sacrament, through the action of Christ's priesthood something supernatural *happens*: specifically, we are supernaturally sanctified.

The Council of Florence (Denzinger §1326), closely following St. Thomas's
De articulis fidei et ecclesiae sacramentis, defined that the effect of the sacrament of Orders is "an increase in grace so that one may be made a suitable
minister of Christ." This surge of holiness that transforms a weak human
into Christ's own sanctifying agent is described as an ineffaceable character.
It essentially charges the priest, with an instrumental mission of his own,
to be himself a font of sacramental causation (cf. *ST* III, q. 63, a. 2). It was
fitting, says St. Thomas, that God in his goodness thus not only established
spiritual ministries but also joined those ministries to the grace necessary for
their proper exercise (*SCG* 4.74). For Bonaventure, this was not just suitable
but required (*In quartum librum Sent. dist.* 24, *pars* 1, a. 2 q. 2). Matthias
Scheeben spoke about sacramental character as "the signature"—the author's
personal mark of attestation—by which members of the mystical body show
their belonging to the divine-human head through an organic link. It is Jesus'
own living version of Paul's promise of authenticity, when he writes with his
own hand (Gal. 6:11; 2 Thess. 3:17). In the case of Orders, this signature of the
God-man somehow underwrites and validates the whole sacramental system
as a source of grace. Priestly character is a divine seal upon and a sanctification of the ordering principle that stands at the root of the *ordo salutis* itself.

Can priests really be so personally accredited by God? A deep suspicion
of metaphysics and lingering doubt about the grace-enabled "suitability" of
patently unholy priestly ministers has presented a challenge to this teaching
from the time of the Reformation down to this day. Some recent scholars
thus confidently reduce the entire doctrine of sacramental grace to a mere
rhetorical power-play by clerical elites. Ultimately, however, as Walter Kasper
notes, the doctrine of an ontological infusion of stable grace is a source of

consolation not only for priests, burdened with the immense weight of their impossible task, but for the community as well.[19]

If the metaphysical arguments stand ultimately in service of the biblical data, the grace of the sacrament in its biblical formulation has several highly evocative expressions. Ontological change defends the force of the revealed prophetic promise of a priestly minister who decisively acts "according to God's heart" (see chap. 4). This need not and does not mean that every New Covenant priest burns with the shepherd's heart of a Curé d'Ars, any more than all the baptized, who also bear the mark of God's divine sign, live lives even remotely worthy of the gift they have received. It signals, rather, that God's intentions are fulfilled in a new and definitive way in this dispensation. A sort of inviolability is conferred by which the eschatological priesthood itself accomplishes God's purpose of salvation, in virtue of Christ and irrespective of individual priests. At the same time, at the individual level, just as in the letters of Paul the baptized are often seen to live in fundamental contradiction with their deeper identity as persons sharing in the common priesthood, and must therefore be reminded to be what they nevertheless are, so too from time to time it appears necessary to "rekindle" (*anazōpyrein*) "the gift of God" (*to charisma tou theou*) that comes through the laying on of hands (2 Tim. 1:6)—not to *ignite* this grace from scratch, as though it could somehow die out (cf. Ignatius, *To the Ephesians* 1.1).

The open question from the Catholic view is not whether there is a sacramental character given in Orders but, rather, how to understand the internal differentiation of this grace. This must be acknowledged as a murky domain. The high scholastics discerned a sevenfold arrangement following the Church's ancient ranks of major and minor orders. The biblical temple hierarchy knows a very similar, if less neatly ranged, series of grades. There is high priest, priest, and Levite, with the Levites further divided into cantors (lectors), those responsible for the liturgical vessels (acolytes), and the gatekeepers (porters). The Levites—being a priestly tribe but also a distinctly subpriestly rank, with more menial functions and dignity—are a very complicated group in the Bible (see excursus 2). The extreme historical blurriness that surrounds them might be considered a sort of scriptural version of the doctrinal questions about the diaconate in its relation to the episcopate and presbyterate.

Despite the utopian Marxist dream of a perfectly classless state, the natural tendency of human societies—like communities of cows or chickens—to establish internal order and rankings makes perfectly clear that, as with all the sacraments, Holy Orders is a case of grace elevating and transforming

19. Walter Kasper, "Ministry in the Church: Taking Issue with Edward Schillebeeckx," *Communio* 10 (1983): 185–95.

nature. In this regard and in harmony with the newer paradigm in sacramental theology, but without the reductionist temptation, it is fruitful to consider priesthood as a phenomenon of religious anthropology. Israel and the Church are hardly alone, after all, in harboring at their heart a priestly caste.

Without offering a survey of pagan priesthood, which is obviously enormously diverse, it is very useful to observe two passing anthropological points. First, priestly colleges and individuals are, at least within the cultural world of the Bible, without fail connected to a sanctuary. This essential juncture of priest and temple will take on a particular configuration in the New Testament, where the temple will no longer be a localized material holding. Here we encounter in a particularly striking way the *novum* of grace that both builds on nature and replaces an older grace. Second, the Old Testament Levites were a dynastic institution, whereas Roman priesthood, to take a contrasting example, was an official function, often gained by election and unconnected (at least in principle) to lineal descent, in nearly all cases being a service of temporary duration. In the New Testament, we encounter a momentous break with the deeply ethnic matrix of the Levitical order. This is of high theological import and is not unrelated to the point about the temple just made. Both of these points of anthropological readjustment will be carefully explored in chapter 6.

The nature of the New Testament priesthood, though acquiring something of the character of an elected or appointed office, ultimately differs from the Greco-Roman model in the lifelong character it presumes. In its own way, this transformation into a nondynastic yet life-consuming form of priesthood is a cultural expression of the ontological force of the Christian conception. The Christian pastor's entire life is required of him in the form of a self-sacrifice, on behalf of the flock and in union with Christ: a form of total claim not unlike the baptismal condition (dying with Christ) for being born anew of supernatural stock. The ecclesiological reorientation of sacramental reflection thus comes once again into view in this graced fusion of anthropology and personal biography in priestly existence, so reminiscent of Christian baptism. The priest of Jesus Christ subsists as a foundational part of the structure of a people supernaturally constituted as Christ's living body. Priestly ministry accordingly represents an extraordinary witness to what Joseph Ratzinger's *communio* theology of the Church understands as "the people of God living from the body of Christ."

3. Baptismal and Hierarchical Priesthood

At least since 1520 and Luther's *Appeal to the German Nobility*—a revolutionary and passionate call to raze what he called "the three walls" by which the "Romanists" preserved their clerical privilege—the Church's centuries-long understanding of hierarchical priesthood has been actively assailed. The supposed superiority of the spiritual over the temporal power, an enforced interpretative monopoly on the Word of God, and the pretended rights of the popes over councils were what Luther specifically saw as these "walls of straw and paper," but it was against the first that his largest siege engines were brought forward. As a demonstration that the notion of an elevated spiritual status was the cleric's own self-serving "pure invention," Luther affirms the community's adequacy simply to depute and thus to create bishops from its own baptismal priestly power. His proof is that the early Church elected its leaders by simple acclamation. This, like much in Luther's polemics, is far too hasty.

Dom Gregory Dix, the great Anglican liturgical scholar of the mid-twentieth century, offers the following balanced assessment:

> A multitude of passages can be cited which emphasize the extreme importance attached in pre-Nicene times to the bishop's proper and free election. . . . A genuine election by his own Church and the free acceptance by all its members as their bishop (symbolized by the kiss of peace given him immediately after his consecration) . . . were as much a *sine qua non* for the episcopate as consecration itself. (I do not think this puts the matter too strongly.) Yet the election and acceptance did not and could not of themselves make a man a bishop. Only God could do that. No man can stand for his fellow sinners before God, still less stand for God before them, simply by their own choice of him. Only God's choice and empowering of him can make him a mediator in that fashion. Hence the insistence in the [consecration] prayer that it is God Himself who has "chosen this Thy servant for the episcopate" . . . just as it is God himself who is prayed "now to pour forth that power which is from Thee upon him to equip him for the task."[20]

In a word, God, not the people, makes the priest. The Church's ancient understanding of ministerial service is thus rightly captured in the declaration "No one takes this honor for himself, but only when called by God" (Heb. 5:4 ESV). Church history here is illustrative of an inherited understanding that reaches back as far as we can possibly hope to see. In the very first ministerial succession, in the days still before Pentecost, when the community "proposed" Joseph Barsabbas and Justus Matthias but then cast lots in order to divine God's own choice—the Lord alone knows the hearts of all—the essential pattern of God's own special election is already unmistakably observed (Acts 1:23–26). Both men were already fully disciples from the time

20. Dom Gregory Dix, "Ministry in the Early Church," in *The Apostolic Ministry: Essays on the History and the Doctrine of Episcopacy*, ed. Kenneth Kirk (London: Hodder & Stoughton, 1957), 198–99.

of John's baptism; this was a condition of their elevation. Yet God himself
had to intervene to establish the elect one in Judas's "office" (*episkopē*, Acts
1:20 RSV; Ps. 109:8 LXX). It is not enough for the community simply to will
it for them to create a new bishop (*episkopos*).

To (literally) "give lots" (*edōkan klerous*), a Levitical practice from which
the word "cleric" (*klēros*) ultimately derives, in the end offers an unusually
weighty hint of the primitive community's specifically priestly understanding
of this apostolic office and succession. It is interesting to note that, during the
First Jewish War, roughly contemporaneous with Acts, Josephus recounts the
rebels identifying a new high priest by exactly this method. The phrase "to
give lots" continues as a technical expression meaning "to ordain priests" in
the earliest and most explicit Christian evidence preserved—namely, the late
second-century *Apostolic Tradition* of Hippolytus.

Admittedly, Matthias in Acts is never called a priest; and on the surface,
the Bible can seem openly to advance quite the opposite view from what the
Catholic Church proposes. The incontestable fact that the Greek word for
priest, *hiereus*, is conspicuously never used for Christian pastors or ministers
in the New Testament is quite striking (see the discussions in excursus 8 and
chap. 6). In fact, Jesus alone and the Christian community as a whole are the
exclusive parties (apart from Jewish leaders) openly described as "priests"
in the New Testament. Luther was obviously keen to cite exactly these key
"nation of priests" texts. Coupled with a strong anticlerical sentiment, stoked
by real, late medieval clerics deserving real anticlerical ire, a negative conclusion was accordingly drawn on the Protestant side from this "perspicuous"
doctrine of baptismal priesthood. In the New Covenant, there is no longer
any hierarchical structure proper to God's priestly people.

This purely negative, egalitarian conclusion moves (like Luther) far too
quickly, of course. It must either disregard or otherwise explain the quite pat-
ent (even *perspicuous*) fact that being a corporate "nation of priests" (Exod.
19:6) is not actually new to the New Covenant. In the Old Covenant, Israel's
commonly shared priestly status as a people was perfectly compatible with
an elaborately hierarchical priestly service. Why should the common and
hierarchical priesthoods not be equally compatible under the New Law as
well? The answer would seem to be bound up with a pronounced and characteristically Lutheran dialectical opposition between law and gospel—that
is, the supposition of radical discontinuity between Israel and the Church:
in this case expressed in the full abolition of the ministerial priesthood. The
Catholic understanding of the grace that Christ brings, by contrast, envisions
an eschatologically profound but also much less radically disjunctive transformation of Israel's priestly experience, which was at once both ministerial
and common.

The common or baptismal priesthood is one of multiple Reformation-era motifs that prospered in the more irenic mood of the twentieth century and was significantly embraced at Vatican II. A terminological gesture in this direction, seriously masked in most English translations, is the Council's epochal shift in its language of reference for Holy Orders so as to better harmonize with the New Testament discourse, moving from *sacerdos* (priest) to *presbyter* (elder)—namely, from a cultic official who offers sacrifice to a community leader of moral probity and proven wisdom. While important aspects of New Testament ministry are obviously retrieved by this move, the consequent obscuring of the Old Testament language must not be wrongly read as a dialectical opposition of absolute discontinuity. Though the priestly lexicon of the New Testament has its own peculiarities suited to the situation of the primitive Church, the Catholic hermeneutic, in adopting a wider biblical terminology, has not simply reverted to the Old Covenant dispensation.

THE ORDER OF MELCHIZEDEK

How shall Christian theology view the transformation of the Levitical estate under the power of grace? Hebrews again provides a direct reply and an indispensable index for addressing this question in Melchizedek's priestly model. The significance of this motif cannot here be even remotely exhausted, but one startling and deeply suggestive circumstance can be mentioned.

Melchizedek was a pagan priest—albeit a pagan priest of *El Elyon*, "God Most High," a biblical title also given to YHWH. Implicit in adopting Melchizedek as a model of the transformed New Testament priesthood is thus a radical break with the genealogical, fleshly principle that restricted priestly honor not only to the biological family of Aaron but to ethnic Israel itself. The implications extend far beyond simply addressing the difficulty posed by Jesus' Judahite lineage. Priesthood according to the order of Melchizedek means (i) somehow being "without father, without mother, without genealogy" and (ii) possessing an eternal sacerdotal office (Heb. 7:3), according to the oath of Psalm 110:4, "You are a priest forever according to the order of Melchizedek." Summed up in a word: Christ became "a priest, not through a legal requirement concerning physical descent, but through the power of indestructible life" (Heb. 7:16). Thus, Hebrews describes a new mode of priestly status "resembling the Son of God" (7:3)—that is to say, conformed to Jesus' divine sonship and eternal life in heaven.

Appealing to the figure of Melchizedek to articulate Christ's new filial possession of the priesthood is a way of asserting a primordial continuity within the unbroken plan of God, as attested in the Scriptures. Indeed, as Melchizedek is prior even to the Mosaic law, he functions in Hebrews very similarly to the way Abraham functions in the argumentation of Paul in

Galatians and Romans. Still more: as the sole agent so elevated that he can bless even Abraham himself—"See how great he is!" (Heb. 7:4)—Melchizedek implicitly represents the priestly instrument of God Most High's own foundational promise: to make the patriarch a blessing (Gen. 12:1–3). In this sense, the eschatological fulfillment of God's promise in the radical equality of all who, like Abraham, are justified by faith—"There is no distinction" (Rom. 3:22); "There is no longer Jew or Greek . . . slave or free . . . male and female" (Gal. 3:28)—is a radical baptismal equality that ultimately depends upon a hierarchical distinction. Without the sacerdotal role of Melchizedek (i.e., Christ), who stands above even Abraham (i.e., those justified by faith), there can be no mediation of the divine blessing.

The case of baptism, which also entails a sacramental share on the part of Christ's members in his own divine sonship (Rom. 8), permits one further important remark. Namely, an objection is answered; for the clear possibility emerges here of a sacramental share in the distinctly sacerdotal aspect of Christ's sonship. That is to say, a gracious seal (*signum*) of priestly character, conforming a man to Jesus' filial headship, cannot be any more excluded on the grounds of Christ's unique possession of the Church's high priesthood than baptized believers can be prevented from crying out *Abba* in the Spirit of their adopted sonship on the grounds that Christ alone is the unique Son of God. Christ's members participate in his divine life with the Father.

The pointed question thus arises: Is there scriptural evidence that such a distinctive participation in the eternal Son's mediating humanity, somehow different from the normal baptismal portion in this dying and rising (Rom. 8), is indeed shared with a special priestly class in the New Testament Church? A great deal obviously depends on the answer given to this question. In the Old Testament, priestly office is the undergirding matrix of Israel's worship, the very medium of her whole ritual life. To this degree—as the history of theology can confirm—the Church's entire sacramental system also substantially stands or falls with one's conceptualization of New Testament priesthood.

The Shape of Biblical Theology: *Semper Reformanda*

Before at last launching out upon the biblical sea, it is important to consider why the Protestant Reformers, who were so keenly attentive to the scriptural data, drew conclusions so different from what will be proposed in the following pages. In other words, why has the very thought of a biblical theology of the priesthood been openly rejected by a massive sector of the Christian world?

Historically, but theoretically as well, it is impossible to address the Protestant position by ignoring the glaring problem of clerical sin, a problem so towering that it must openly configure any proposed biblical perspective on the priesthood—as it here will. Late medieval abuses—hypocrisy, ignorance, corruption, luxury and license, avarice, simony, unchastity, and so on—are the essential context of the formative Protestant hermeneutic. The problem is not exclusively late medieval, of course, as I have already said, but endemic in its own way to the priestly caste (not that the wider human race is immune from sin). The point in emphasizing this unflattering clerical context is merely to highlight two simple things.

First, the Protestant account of the biblical witness gives great attention to an important, largely prophetic, and highly polemical anticlerical tradition in the Scriptures. Blistering critiques of the cult and its ministers do indeed form a significant part of the relevant data, for misbehaving priests are a very old problem. Useful as these texts have proved to be as polemical ammunition and as a pastoral point of orientation, it is, nevertheless, wrong to give them disproportionate weight. Other, much more positive perspectives on priests are also found in the Bible. Unfortunately, the literature stemming from the so-called Priestly school is very difficult to approach for a variety of reasons, which has resulted in its effective marginalization and even vilification. Joseph Blenkinsopp understates the case when he remarks that "the Israelite priesthood and its literary productions have not had a good press in Christian Old Testament scholarship since the Enlightenment."[21] Instinctive distrust of "priestcraft" has been a staple of modernity, and the prejudices remain so deep that, remarkably, after more than two centuries of concentrated historical research, it is still possible to say that "the study of the cult and priesthood in ancient Israel is still very much in its infancy."[22] This points indirectly to the second Reformation tendency.

The Protestant position was articulated in opposition to a perceived clerical claim to have a monopoly on divine truth (the second of Luther's "three walls"). Only the priests were theological doctors (like the specialists behind the Bible's highly technical Priestly writings), so this elitist wall of separation also had to be torn down. The ultimate result was the hermeneutical adoption of a more or less explicit doctrine of the "perspicuity of Scripture" (*perspicuitas*; e.g., Westminster Confession I.7): namely, an insistence that every believer gifted with the Holy Spirit, even the unlearned, can apprehend in an unmediated way all necessary biblical doctrine, as though what is essential in the Bible is always inevitably easily accessible to faith.

From the Catholic perspective, this hermeneutical view not only gravely underestimates the challenge of understanding texts written millennia ago

21. Joseph Blenkinsopp, *Sage, Priest, Prophet: Religious and Intellectual Leadership in Ancient Israel* (Louisville: Westminster John Knox, 1995), 66–67.

22. Gary Anderson and Saul M. Olyan, *Priesthood and Cult in Ancient Israel*, JSOTSup 125 (Sheffield: Sheffield Academic, 1991), 7.

in very different languages and cultures than our own, but it would exclude the teaching service of a living magisterium altogether. St. Augustine, in the preface to his important treatise on the rules of biblical interpretation, *On Christian Instruction*, openly rejects the claims of those who would thus "talk vauntingly of divine grace and boast that they understand and can explain scripture" without aid, supposing that understanding the Scriptures is best served "by the unassisted grace of God." Accordingly, if we lay special emphasis here on certain privileged scriptural deposits, notably the Priestly literature and the Letter to the Hebrews, this is not because the profound doctrinal richness of these texts concerning the mystery of priesthood is always transparent. It is not. It is only perceptible, in fact, with laborious study and within an ecclesial air hospitable to what Aidan Nichols calls the "hermeneutic of recognition."[23] Christian sacramental priesthood is no more facilely present in the Bible than is the "Trinity" itself. But like this creedal cornerstone, it is vital to the very structure of Christian existence.

The Reformers' energetic protest, however unbalanced from a Catholic viewpoint, is nevertheless salutary for a Church that is indeed *semper reformanda*. On the one hand, the huge biblical accent laid upon clerical sin guards against complacent and exaggerated constructions of the priestly ministry. On the other hand, the stress on exegetical transparency rightly holds the clarity of the Church's scriptural teaching to account.

---

23. See Aidan Nichols, *Holy Order: Apostolic Priesthood from the New Testament to the Second Vatican Council* (Eugene, OR: Wipf & Stock, 1990), 4:

> If we accept the notion of a development of doctrine, whereby some features of Catholic faith, ethics and worship are regarded as legitimate outgrowths from New Testament origins, then we commit ourselves to what may be termed a "hermeneutic of recognition," whereby we who share the developed consciousness of the later Church come to the evidences of the earliest Church in positive expectation of finding the seeds from which the great tree of the *Catholica* has grown. This is not a value-free or presuppositionless enquiry, even were such things possible. It is Scripture read in Tradition. Indeed, Tradition is, for the most part, nothing other than the reading of Scripture by the Church's eyes of faith—which organs alone are fully adequate to their wonderous object.

A Catholic Alternative

How shall Catholics honestly approach the scriptural foundations of the New Covenant priesthood? Is there indeed no historically credible way to link Jesus to its inception? How shall the Church say something fittingly biblical about the mystery of priestly grace?

The enterprise of elaborating a sound biblical theology of the sacramental priesthood (or elaborating a "biblical theology" of anything, for that matter) faces an immediate challenge: the successful integration of all the elements enumerated in *Dei Verbum* 12 as necessary for a correct interpretation of the biblical text. These include (1) the meaning intended by the sacred writers in their historical context; (2) the content and unity of all Scripture; (3) the living Tradition of the whole Church; and (4) the analogy of faith. This seamless fusion of historical perspectives within a single canon, somehow attentive to the living Tradition and balanced by the inner proportions of the revealed data, is not a process easily subjected to a formula or a simple method. This explains, in part, why Vatican II's envisioned synthesis still remains largely untried, with contemporary study generally stagnated in the discussion of historical context.

Successfully weaving an exegetically responsible, theological vision out of these four hermeneutical strands inescapably invites a certain measure of personal intuition and experiment. The mind of the Church as expressed in *Dei Verbum* must, nevertheless, operate as a framework and control. The recognized standards of judgment regarding research into the historical context have long been sufficiently well established to secure a basic objectivity for that dimension of the project. Historical-critical investigation is thus assumed and followed throughout. It remains, in order to stand accountable, to offer some explanation of how the latter three criteria will here be understood and applied.

1. The Unity of Christian Scripture

The "unity" of the canonical Scriptures as intended by the Council is a dog-matic proposition, originally articulated in the face of the Marcionite threat. Through the working of the Holy Spirit, God is the "author" of both Testa-ments. This means that God is the single, ultimate source both of Scripture's inspired words and of the realities to which those inspired words point. The unity of Scripture is thus a divine work and is expressive of the one God's own unity as manifested in the unbroken oneness of his eternal plan: that all humankind should have access to the Father through the incarnate Son in the Holy Spirit. In this light, it is important to see that the unity of the two written Testaments, Old and New, which together comprise the single book of Christian Scripture, mirrors the profound inner accord between two epochal regimes of God's grace actively uniting humanity to himself, first in Israel and finally in Christ.[1]

Jesus' high priestly prayer, "That [*hina*] they may be one, as we are one" (John 17:11), represents the great purpose clause governing this whole econ-omy of salvation and ordering of all things under a single divine unity of design and direction. Christ's own priesthood, captured in this prayer for union and expressed in his unique high priestly role of mediation (1 Tim. 2:5; Heb. 8:6; 9:15; cf. *ST* III, q. 22; q. 26, a. 1–2), thus stands in a special way at the very heart of the great dispensational unity of God's saving plan. Indeed, this plan of human sharing in God's triune oneness is the most final of all the remote causes of the priesthood. The specific, unifying oneness of Christ's priestly work is itself grounded upon the oneness of the incarnate Son's perfect sacrifice, offered once for all (Heb. 10:12; 1 Pet. 3:18), yet shared with men sacramentally joined to him to offer that one selfsame sacrifice and participate in his own "ministry of reconciliation" (2 Cor. 5:18–20).

As a mystery uniquely localized at the unity of God and man in Christ, priestly ministry in the Church is inevitably central to the hermeneutical unity of the Scriptures. Accordingly, the Christian Bible's twofold inner division into the Old and New Testaments—the first and primary partition (*divisio textus*) of the unified biblical whole—entails an architectonic asymmetry not simply in the text but in the reality of the priestly work of uniting God and man

---

1. See further Anthony Giambrone, "Revelation in Christian Scripture," in *The Oxford Handbook of Divine Revelation*, ed. Balázs M. Mezei, Francesca Aran Murphy, and Kenneth Oakes (Oxford: Oxford University Press, 2021).

that is there revealed. The single sacrament of Orders is thus itself configured through a double internal movement—law and gospel—"enjoining by commandments and aiding by the gift of grace."[2] There is an Old Covenant and a New Covenant priesthood, somehow unified as one within God's higher plan.

It is vital to recognize this higher plan in Christ's one priesthood. For if the division between law and gospel, between the old priesthood and the new, is not rightly parsed, a theologically deadly duality can emerge: an irreconcilable, dialectical opposition. This explains the huge significance of correctly understanding Paul's intricate teaching about the law, its *telos* in Christ, and its eschatological perfection in the Spirit. Reformation readings of Paul, however distant they may appear to the immediate questions of the present study, are thus central to the larger theological operation. The specific risk in Protestant controversial thought is, namely, to create an absolute antagonism of the *spiritual-and-inward* against the *merely ritual*. This touches directly upon the "methodological flaw" that Benedict XVI identifies (see chap. 1).

From the Catholic standpoint, the distinction between the sacraments of the Old Law and the sacraments of the New presents a clear case of continuity in discontinuity. Ritual acquires a new interior power; it is not radically abrogated. Thus, Augustine, echoing Matthew 5:17, says that the sacraments of the Old Law were retired, not because they were somehow fundamentally errant and misleading, but because they were incomplete and had been fulfilled in Christ. The new sacraments, he said echoing Hebrews, are more efficacious and more useful—also less cumbersome and not so excessively numerous (*Reply to Faustus* 19.13). With compact precision, the Decree for the Armenians of the Council of Florence teaches that the sacraments of the Old Law did not confer grace by their own power; yet they did prefigure the grace that was to be given by the passion of Christ. For Aquinas, this meant that rites like circumcision occasioned that grace by reason of the faith in Christ that they represented (*ex fide significata*, ST I–II, q. 102, a. 5)—which is to say, the change in sacramental regime from the Old Covenant to the New is a change from the principle of *ex opere operantis* to *ex opere operato*. In short, the validating minister in the New Testament sacraments is now Christ.

As a hermeneutical point, this Catholic commitment to the division yet internal unity of God's single plan of grace legitimates, among other interpretative moves, the typological instinct. Old Testament rituals in truth signify what New Testament realities in truth accomplish. Holocausts, sin offerings, and peace offerings, for instance, in which nothing of the giver's is reserved, *do* really point to that most perfect sacrifice offered by Christ, just as the Fathers and medieval doctors taught. This interpretative perspective derives from a

2. Thomas Aquinas, *Hic est Liber*, pars 2.

unity of scriptural subject—namely, the Church's firm self-understanding that it occupies the place of Israel. The *totus Christus* thus finds itself reflected in Israel's experiences as in a mirror—or rather in a *typos*, to use the language of St. Paul (1 Cor. 10:6). An honored instrument in the Church's traditional exegetical tool kit, typology has been too long neglected in modern attempts at doing biblical theology. Its controlled adoption here (notably in chap. 2) represents an important element in this present effort at *ressourcement*.

At the same time, a more comprehensive and complex intertestamental unity is considered as a controlling dimension of this project. For "at the heart of the problem of Biblical Theology lies the issue of doing full justice to the subtle canonical relationship of the two testaments within the one Christian Bible."[3] Brevard Childs is profoundly correct on this point. I add only a strong intonation upon the key adjective "subtle" and note that growing appeals to Childs's so-called canonical reading of Scripture frequently misconstrue his proposal as a naïve, synchronic, purely narrative, Genesis-to-Revelation, "salvation history" sort of exposition, rather than an engaged diachronic manner of reading, deeply concerned with discerning the right theological balance of the historically layered elements comprising the canonical whole. The broad canonical shape of the present study was already mentioned in the preface: Pentateuch, Prophets, and Writings; Gospels and the Apostolic corpus. Appropriate attention to the subtleties interweaving this arrangement of corpora interior to the Church's unified canon will be an aspiration against which the following chapters may be judged.[4]

2. The Living Tradition

It is obvious that the shape of Catholic exegesis, as outlined in *Dei Verbum*, is not confined by the dogma of *sola scriptura*. To this extent, Catholic exegesis is closely attuned to the shape of Christian life itself. Yves Congar is the recognized spokesman for this dimension of the Church's existence.

> Christianity, I repeat, is a reality. It was given to us as a life to be received and practiced and not simply a text to be consulted. As a transmitted, lived reality,

3. Brevard Childs, *Biblical Theology of the Old and New Testaments: Theological Reflection on the Christian Bible* (Minneapolis: Fortress, 2011), 78. Childs continues in another place: "The problem of the early church was not what to do with the Old Testament in the light of the gospel, which was Luther's concern, but rather the reverse. In the light of the Jewish scriptures which were acknowledged to be the true oracles of God, how were Christians to understand the good news of Jesus Christ?" (227).

4. As an illustrative point of methodological contrast, the present study may be compared to the approach of John Bergsma, *Jesus and the Old Testament Roots of the Priesthood* (Steubenville, OH: Emmaus Road, 2021).

Christianity completely transcends what we are able to say about it. . . . In their haste to rebel against the Church and their impatience to find fault in order to justify their rebellion, the reformers failed to understand that these kinds of Christian realities are *handed over* more than they are *proclaimed*. Among these Christian realities are the sacraments, the lives of the saints, and the Church itself.[5]

Congar's exposition of the theme of Tradition was groundbreaking a generation ago and is now already classic. It is hardly necessary here to belabor the theme. The essential point is that the sacrament of Orders and indeed the whole liturgical life of believers belongs to this extratextual sphere of Tradition, just as episcopal office was handed over in apostolic succession.

In application to this biblical theology of the priesthood, it is clear that we must indulge a respect not only for nonbiblical expressions of sacramental and priestly life (as found preeminently in the writings of the Fathers and other monuments) but also for all the instruments of *Traditio*: liturgical books and the acts of the martyrs, for example—even archaeology in its own way. Tradition also concerns what I mentioned above with Aidan Nichols's phrase: a "hermeneutic of recognition."[6] This is not a concocted exegetical method based on an ideological theory, like the so-called hermeneutic of suspicion. It is the simple operation of a supernatural instinct, the *sensus fidei*. Without this application of Christian supernatural life to the work of biblical interpretation, moreover, the winds and rains of historical-critical methods will inevitably prevail and cast every ecclesial community built on the sand of *sola scriptura* into a permanent identity crisis. In his *Symbolism*, Möhler writes: "Without doubt, if the Church were a historical or antiquarian society, if she had no self-concept, no knowledge of her origin, of her essence and her mission," then it would be necessary for her to search with the exegetes to find her identity in the Scriptures. "She would be like someone who, by researching documents he himself has written, tries to discover whether he really exists!"[7]

"Christ is the same yesterday and today and forever" (Heb. 13:8). His body, too, the Church, exists as a living subject, always contemporaneous with itself. For this reason, every age of the Church holds the faith in its entirety, even when it is not explicitly formulated equally in every age. It is accordingly in the supernatural synergy of the *sensus fidei* together with the testimony of the

5. Yves Congar, *True and False Reform in the Church* (Collegeville, MN: Liturgical Press, 2011), 274.

6. See Aidan Nichols, *Holy Order: Apostolic Priesthood from the New Testament to the Second Vatican Council* (Eugene, OR: Wipf & Stock, 1990), 4.

7. Johann Adam Möhler, *Symbolism: Exposition of the Doctrinal Differences between Catholics and Protestants as Evidenced by Their Symbolic Writings* (New York: Herder & Herder, 1997), 296.

Fathers that we discover the real meaning of the famous Vincentian Canon: *quod semper, quod ubique, quod ab omnibus creditum est* (What is believed always, everywhere, and by everyone). The Canon is not an absolute, positivistic rule for recognizing what is and *what is not* Tradition; rather, it is to be applied positively, not negatively. Thus, that which has not been *explicitly* believed always, everywhere, and by everyone is not thereby automatically barred from Catholic doctrine. This would be incompatible with a living growth in doctrinal insight and would squelch any authentic *sensus fidelium communis*, supplementing the silence of the Fathers on many matters. It is noteworthy in embracing this precise understanding of the Vincentian Canon that, although the Oxford Movement had applied it in a negative fashion, John Henry Newman himself eventually came to revise his understanding of the dynamics of the Church's living Tradition under the influence of the great Roman School Jesuit Giovanni Perrone, whose work on the development of doctrine argued for this positive sense and so prepared for the proclamation of the dogma of the Immaculate Conception.[8]

The doctrine of the sacrament of Orders, like the Marian dogmas, must be approached with this double attention to the testimony of the ancient Church and to the living instinct of the faithful. In this mode, while obviously always alert to anachronism, contemporary Catholic exegesis will have little difficulty seeing the pages of Scripture ripe with indications of the Church's familiar sacramental life, just as the Fathers also easily saw this. Joined with them, we gain a vision of the priestly mystery wider and truer than any vision supposedly based upon Scripture alone. Even the entirely negative datum of the New Testament's lack of the explicit word "priest" for early Christian officeholders will, for instance, do little to discourage this sure recognition of the well-known reality (see excursus 8). The hermeneutic of recognition adopted here is not the Church's narrow effort to pull itself up by its own exegetical bootstraps, by main force of *sola scriptura*, but rather the confident vision of a living community of readers that knows itself to be in solid possession of the broad interpretative keys for understanding its very own books. Living Tradition in *Dei Verbum*'s proposal is this envelope of ecclesial life by which the Bible is delivered to us as an intelligible Christian text.

3. The Analogy of Faith

The final member in *Dei Verbum*'s list, the *analogia fidei*, is in many ways the most elusive but also the most critical for holding the integral project together.

---

8. See C. Michael Shea, "Father Giovanni Perrone and Doctrinal Development in Rome: An Overlooked Legacy of Newman's *Essay on Development*," *JHMTh/ZNThG* 20 (2013): 85–116.

It somehow assimilates (or blurs into) both the unity of Scripture and the living Tradition and enmeshes them in the *ordo salutis*.

The phrase "analogy of faith" is a biblical expression, originally indicating that prophetic charisms are somehow normed by the gift of faith (Rom. 12:6); yet as a theological category it first emerged as an explicit principle during the Reformation era.[9] Both Luther and (especially) Calvin discerned in the prophetic grace not only the forecasting of future events but above all the interpretation of Scripture, recognized as the preeminent Spirit-led ministry of the Word (cf. 1 Cor. 14).[10] Paul's normative "analogy of faith" was accordingly the supreme criterion of all exegesis, and thus of all preaching and theology in the Church.

Luther, for his part, pinned between radical, sectarian enthusiasts on the one side and papists on the other, each camp appealing equally to the Bible, determined that the regulative *fides* in question was not and could not be the *fides qua*, the subjective faith of individual believers, but rather the common and objective deposit of truth: the articles of faith or *fides quae*. This deposit of faith was emphatically not located in inherited traditions, however, but rather in Scripture itself and more precisely in the "gospel" of justification *sola fide*. Interpretation "according to the analogy of faith" was thus reading in agreement with the central salvific truth of biblical revelation: exegesis normed by *faith in faith alone*.

While Luther's outright rejection of Tradition is obviously unacceptable as such (and already addressed in the preceding criterion), the existence of a certain exegetical norm somehow interior to the Bible is not problematic in itself. It essentially means that interpretative priority must be given to the most developed and explicit scriptural ideas, with less obvious materials understood only in that clearer light. This principle of "Scripture interprets Scripture" was not an invention (only an emphasis) of Protestant hermeneutics. In the work of St. Thomas and medieval theology more generally, for instance, nothing may be theologically demonstrated by the spiritual sense that is not elsewhere attested more plainly in the *sensus literalis*. The rabbis also, well before this,

---

9. See, e.g., Luther, *Marburg Colloquy*; Calvin, *Prefatory Address*; Westminster Confession I.9. See also Otto Hof, "Luther's Exegetical Principle of the Analogy of Faith," *CTM* 38 (1967): 242–57; and David Starling, "The Analogy of Faith in the Theology of Luther and Calvin," *RTR* 72 (2013): 5–19.

10. Luther: "To interpret Scripture, that is the noblest, highest, and greatest gift of prophecy" (WA 17 II, 39 l. 26); "Prophesying does not mean [to speak] as the prophets once did of future things but to interpret the Prophets, the Psalms, as we have done here in Wittenberg; we are prophets" (WA 34 I, 104, 16 [AT]). Calvin: "Prophesying at this day amongst Christians is almost nothing else than a right understanding of the Scripture, and singular gift of expounding the same, since all the old prophecies and oracles of God have been finished in Christ and his gospel" (John Calvin, *Commentary upon the Epistle of Saint Paul to the Romans* [Edinburgh: Calvin Translation Society, 1844], 460).

had their own carefully formulated rules for a related hermeneutical idea. Modern study, indeed, especially since the work of Michael Fishbane, recognizes even a prerabbinical form of intrabiblical interpretation: expressions of self-exegesis native and entirely interior to the Bible. In multiple ways these various expressions of this "Scripture interprets Scripture" phenomenon will play a significant role in this study.

The analogy of faith is more complex than just a "canon in the canon," however. On account of its history of polemical use, appreciative Catholic appeals to the *analogia fidei* first began in the nineteenth century, when, especially in the work of the Roman School, the phrase took on an Augustinian sense of agreement between the Old and New Testaments. Leo XIII in *Providentissimus Deus* (1893) subsequently introduced the term into magisterial teaching as a hermeneutical rule for the ecclesial reading of Scripture. The sense here is arguably quite similar to its earlier usage: a harmony between the Old and New Testaments. Thereafter the term became a settled but unexplained feature of biblical interpretation *ad mentem ecclesiae*. Reflection upon the idea developed considerably in the twentieth century, however, after Karl Barth adopted *analogia fidei* as his counterproposal to the Catholic metaphysical notion of the *analogia entis*.

Gottlieb Söhngen, the *Doktorvater* and mentor of Joseph Ratzinger, in responding to Barth (evidently to Barth's own surprised satisfaction), formulated an intricate series of meanings in his brilliant but dense two-part essay on the *analogia fidei*. In the first place, there is the Catholic version of the principle that Scripture is a self-interpreting whole.

> The analogy of faith is the *oeconomia Scripturae*, the economy of Scripture: the words of Scripture are interpreted by corresponding words in Scripture. The Catholic exposition of Scripture also works under the assumption that the Word of God is its own interpreter. The Word of God set down in Scripture presents a divine economy in which everything is related to everything else—testament to testament, book to book, word to word—in an analogy that dispels any apparent contradictions.[11]

This unified internal ordering and proportion among all the intricate parts of Scripture—between prophetic attacks on the clerical establishment and priestly perspectives on cultic life, or between the Levitical and New Testament priesthoods, for instance—stands in harmony, however, with another term: the rule of faith (*regula fidei*). This echoes Luther's attention to the *fides quae*, yet also pertains to a Catholic conception of the basic character

11. Gottlieb Söhngen, "The Analogy of Faith: Likeness to God from Faith Alone?" and "The Analogy of Faith: Unity in the Science of Faith," *Pro Ecclesia* 21 (2012): 56–76, 169–94 (here 171).

of the theological act, which is never so simple as a mere interpretative act of reading. The result is a hermeneutical spiral relating dogmatic to exegetical truth; and here a conundrum arises: "We are spinning within a vicious circle of a Catholic variety."[12] Scripture somehow both governs and is governed by the rule of faith.

The *regula fidei* as it is applied in authors like Tertullian and Irenaeus appears to be something like the sum content of apostolic doctrine, functioning as a governing framework within which the Scriptures must be read. Thus, for Irenaeus this canon or rule contrasts with the alternative, pseudo-apostolic Gnostic systems in and through which the same biblical data might also be (mis)interpreted. In the classical Catholic understanding, this governing deposit and apostolic interpretative space comes to special self-expression in doctrinal formulae such as creeds and in other authoritative acts of the magisterial *ecclesia docens*.

Dei Verbum's extraordinarily strong claim about the exclusive rights of the Church's teaching office to interpret the Word of God in an authentic manner should here be recalled.

> The task of authentically interpreting the word of God, whether written or handed on, has been entrusted exclusively to the living teaching office of the Church, whose authority is exercised in the name of Jesus Christ. This teaching office is not above the word of God, but serves it, teaching only what has been handed on, listening to it devoutly, guarding it scrupulously and explaining it faithfully in accord with a divine commission and with the help of the Holy Spirit, it draws from this one deposit of faith everything which it presents for belief as divinely revealed. (*Dei Verbum* 10)

The Council thus recognizes the "vicious circle of a Catholic variety" that Söhngen mentions: Scripture norming the teaching office norming Scripture, and so on. This intrusion of the episcopal structure into the exegetical dynamic represents an ongoing scandal to Protestant observers, despite a version of circularity all their own. It is quite plain that Catholic hermeneutics belong soundly within an ecclesiology that openly *presumes* the hierarchical reality of Holy Orders. In this sense, Luther's aggressive attack simultaneously upon both the clergy as such and the clergy's claimed rights over authoritative interpretation rightly saw and targeted a critical knot. The entire project of Catholic biblical theology as such is inextricably tied to the existence of a priestly ministry.

The bishops' unique custody of the authentic Christ-given apostolic *munus* of teaching has never excluded having non-episcopal coworkers, of course,

12. Söhngen, "Analogy of Faith," 175.

both clerical and lay. This book is an expression of such collaboration from the side of the lower clergy, from a member also, as it so happens, of the *ordo praedicatorum*, enjoying a special share in the teaching charism of the episcopal office, and one who is, finally, concretely deputed by the Apostolic See for a special mission of biblical study and teaching. This naturally carries a certain measure of official authority, beyond whatever credentials I may enjoy as a private scholar. Nevertheless, the positions presented in this book cannot honestly be presented as a Catholic interpretation of Scripture in the fullest sense of that word, except to the extent that they coincide with apostolic teaching, both embracing and embraced by the bishops' universal magisterial *munus*.

In describing the magisterium's reverent docility to the Word, *Dei Verbum* rightly adverts to the help of the Holy Spirit. For Söhngen, this pneumatic solution ultimately eases the tension teasing the relation of the *analogia* and the *regula fidei*.

> How does the Catholic account of the rule of faith mesh with the Catholic claim that the Word of God is its own interpreter? Are we not bringing a second, external standard to the Word of God and to Scripture? Not at all! This claim about Scripture remains true and vigorously true; it is only rendered more personal. The Holy Spirit, the primary author of Holy Scripture, is and remains its own proclaimer and interpreter through his work in the formation of the doctrine of the Church of Jesus Christ.[13]

Interpretation of the sacred text in the prophetic Spirit in which it was written (*Dei Verbum* 12) is what ultimately prevents the Catholic account from simply objectifying the *depositum fidei* as a lifeless letter that stands above and kills the pneumatic *actualitas* of the Word of God. And yet this active attunement of ecclesial interpretation to the living Spirit remains, in the Catholic vision, also greatly concerned, as Söhngen says, that "the substance of the Word and faith cannot turn into a fleeting reality," an actualized will-o'-the-wisp, an interpretation moved by the *Zeitgeist*—a word, in short, that fades like the proverbial flower of the field. For the Word of God is both "living *and abiding*" (1 Pet. 1:23 ESV; cf. Isa. 40:8).[14]

In the end, therefore, pursuing this pneumatic understanding of the intertwining ecclesial exegesis and doctrine, Söhngen presents a typically *both-and* Catholic view, quite a bit bolder than Luther.

> The rule of faith, the Apostles' Creed, is certainly *fides quae creditur*, that is, the content of the faith that is believed. But is not the rule of faith in the

13. Söhngen, "Analogy of Faith," 176.
14. Söhngen, "Analogy of Faith," 177.

analogy under consideration simultaneously active as *fides qua creditur*, not in the usual sense of the act of faith in which the content of faith is believed but also as *fides qua intelligitur Scriptura ad credendum verbum Dei?* . . . Does our understanding of Scripture, if our theology is genuinely theological, which can only mean biblical, not point to the understanding of faith?[15]

The faith at stake in the analogy of faith is at once *fides quae* and *fides qua*. To this extent, all Christians possessed of the Spirit can equally participate as interpreters of the Word, in proportion to the understanding of their own faith as in Romans 12:6. This understanding of faith boils down, of course, to having the *mind of Christ*—namely, the real union of members of the one body, in the one Spirit, with Christ the one head. The analogy of faith, in this charismatic and ecclesially unitive sense, is thus another expression for the same premise of coworking unity with the episcopal office just described. Yet it also presents a coordinate measure of the bishops' own individual submission in faith to the governing Word.

Following Söhngen, one final aspect of the analogy of faith must be considered. There is the twofold meaning already broached of (1) the whole range of internal connections within Scripture and (2) this connection between the understanding of Scripture and the rule of faith. Now there also arises a kind of proportion between the "economy of Scripture" and the economy of salvation: the living *nexus mysteriorum*.[16] This nexus is often taken as a kind of dogmatic map, the hierarchy of truths, against which a given motif must be plotted. Priestly ministry, for instance, bears a close inner relation to specific doctrinal landmarks: the incarnation, the atonement, Christ's ascension to God's right hand, the saving character of the Church, and eternal life in the presence of the triune God. More unexpected, perhaps, but a special contribution of this study, will be the attention that is paid here to Christ's transfiguration as a mystery of distinctly priestly meaning.

The economy of salvation is more than an occasion for doctrinal orienteering, however. It ultimately evokes the vital power of the saving realities that Church doctrine describes. Taken in this way, as the living *ordo salutis*, scriptural reflection can never be a purely academic and abstract exercise. The Bible's witness to Holy Orders accordingly appears not only at the intersection of key Old and New Testament texts and in connection with certain important Church teachings. *Contemplation of the revelation of the priesthood of Christ and the gift of that priesthood to his Church is itself a participation*

15. Söhngen, "Analogy of Faith," 178.

16. The succinct definition of the "analogy of faith" offered in the *Catechism of the Catholic Church* §114 evokes this basic sense of the phrase: "By analogy of faith we mean the coherence of the truths among themselves and within the whole plan of Revelation."

in this same priesthood's very action. Sacred Scripture inserts us directly within the celestial hierarchy and its cascade of supernatural light. For the Bible itself is handed down to us through chosen mediators of God's saving truth, ecclesial hierarchs in the strongest Dionysian sense: priestly writers, entrusted with the rites of the Mosaic covenant; prophets, illumined to lead God's people on the paths of salvation; apostles, bathed in the light of Christ.

A kind of theurgy thus governs the interpretation of the Church's Scriptures. And this brings us at last back around to the original biblical datum. The analogy of faith in Romans 12:6 is the control placed upon a prophetic gift of the Spirit. The similar discussion in 1 Corinthians 14 makes the proper place of the *analogia fidei* within a liturgical setting perfectly clear. This setting is fitting as a hermeneutical rule, moreover, for the Bible belongs firmly to the cult of the Church. Indeed, the Church, the *ecclesia*, is itself one enormous cosmic liturgy, a great assembly, in which the prophetic Scriptures resound and surround the offering of Christ our Pasch. "To interpret the Scriptures in the same Spirit in which they were written" (*Dei Verbum* 12) is thus, in the end, nothing else than to be attuned to a prophetic grace that sounds out in this vast liturgy bridging heaven and earth: a liturgy that far excels some brute anthropological fact, as this would be viewed from the vantage point of "ritual studies." A heavenly high priest, triumphantly interceding at God's right hand, presides as the eternal head of a cult spanning the cosmos. Heaven and earth intersect and are united precisely in this great high priest's one sacrifice for sins.

What does this imply for our reading of Scripture and its presentation of this selfsame priestly act? Since the destruction of the temple and the end of Israel's Mosaic economy of sacrifice, pious Jews celebrate the Feast of Yom Kippur, not through the actual offering of blood by the high priest within the holy of holies, but by devoutly reading and studying the priestly ritual described in Leviticus 16. Scripture functions both as a surrogate and also as a mediation and medium of real participation in the truth of what it describes. Post-temple Jewish *avodah* in the form of Torah study corresponds in this way rather closely to what Catholics would understand as a spiritual communion. In the Christian economy, for which the Mosaic system of sacrifice is also definitively ended, the same study of the same text, but with a different gift of divine light, unites the mind with the more elevated heavenly sacrifice that the earthly Day of Atonement foreshadowed. Here too there is true worship and a spiritual communion.[17] The inspired oracles to which

17. St. Thomas writes, "Since every word of wisdom is derived from the Only Begotten Word of God—'The fountain of wisdom is the Only Begotten of God' (Sir 1:5)—this Word of God is especially called the bread of life. Thus Christ says, 'I am the bread of life'" (*St. Thomas Aquinas: Commentary on the Gospel of John, Chapters 6–12*, trans. Fabian Larcher and James A.

we are now ready to turn initiate us in mind into an inner sanctum reserved for the highest priestly action. Our exposition will, to this extent, carry the character of a mystagogy: an exegetical ascent from prophetic shadows to the reality of better things, yet an exposition that presumes the consummation of the high priestly ministry that it describes.

The project of scriptural study that now opens before us must be pursued in a resolutely contemplative and ecclesial frame of mind. It is substantially grounded upon a firm faith in the very truth that it seeks to understand and uncover. The circular character of this hermeneutic of recognition is manifest from multiple directions, as we have seen. Believers will perceive this ecclesial epistemology, however, as a participation of the faith-filled mind in the mystery of the infinite God. Taking *Dei Verbum* 12 as the comprehensive norm for genuine Catholic biblical theology, our study must thus be moved by the same supernatural Spirit who animates the assembly of the elect. This means—to make one final but critical point—that we must, for the duration of at least the next five chapters, be coworkers in an ecclesial charism of priestly teaching. And that demands no less docility to the action of divine grace on the part of this little book's readers than it requires of its author.

Weisheipl [Washington, DC: Catholic University of America Press, 2010], chap. 6, *lectio* 4, no. 914 [p. 25]).

PART 2

"The Sons of Aaron in Their Splendor"

2

"The Glory of the LORD Appeared" (Lev. 9:23)

Priesthood as Theophany

The Priestly document, or P source, is a foundational theological strand prominently woven into the fabric of the Pentateuch: a vital source, naturally, in exploring the biblical theology of the priesthood. Literarily, historically, and theologically, these P traditions reach to the very origins of the priestly ministry among God's people. Clearly, the technical austerity and complexity of this material often make it a great challenge to understand and enjoy. Julius Wellhausen morbidly characterized P as "legalistic, restrictive, and servile, . . . destructive of spontaneity and the religion of the heart."[1] This is not a glowing (or fair) endorsement, and it has had its effect. Still, it is impossible to gain a correct perspective on the essential contours of the sacrament of Orders as it has been revealed in the Scriptures without intelligently engaging this fundamental corpus.

In Medias Res: Leviticus 8–10

In the traditional rabbinic cursus, a child's learning begins with the book of Leviticus—just where Christian reading of the Old Testament too often

1. Joseph Blenkinsopp, *Sage, Priest, Prophet: Religious and Intellectual Leadership in Ancient Israel* (Louisville: Westminster John Knox, 1995), 66–67.

ends. Small surprise then if, like Paul's converts in Corinth, much Christian theology is feeding on milk, not solid meat (1 Cor. 3:2). Although rabbinic Judaism itself represents an apparent successor to the old priestly circles and cultic customs that once ruled among God's chosen people and is certainly a socioreligious reconfiguration that in many ways eclipsed this older, sacerdotal form of life, the rabbinic choice to privilege Leviticus preserves the centrality of the ancient priestly vision. It also sends a clear message for the Church's reflection. As a perennial cornerstone of Jewish identity, Leviticus likewise lays an immovable foundation for Christianity's own order of priestly reconfiguration—or at least it should.[2]

In the middle of this middle book of the Pentateuch, Leviticus 8–10, we encounter one of the most important of several foundational stories about the origins of Israel's priesthood: the account of the first priestly ordination among the Hebrews, which takes place in the wilderness at Sinai. This location is obviously significant. The gift and advent of the priesthood within Israel's national life takes shape within the heart of God's own theophany; priesthood is thus a phenomenon intimately conjoined to the Lord's fiery presence among his people. Indeed, the motif of divine fire, which has been playing variations in the text since Moses' epochal encounter with the burning bush, will be quite central to the entire plotline in these chapters.

The first seven chapters of Leviticus begin as one expects: with long lists of ritual commandments. Chapter 8 suddenly breaks this pattern, inserting a narrative that will progress in three distinct stages: a priestly ordination (chap. 8), the priests' first sacrifices and blessings (chap. 9), and the priests' "original sin" (chap. 10). After this multi-hinged story, the staccato rhetoric of legislation will recommence. The opening of this brief narrative window is framed in meaningful ways on both ends within the macrostructure of Leviticus. It is adequate to apprehend Leviticus 8–10 in its intertextual connections to earlier P traditions, however, notably those preserved in Exodus 29. This passage, which also concerns the ordination of the first priests, is closely related and seems to be dated earlier than the chapters here in view,

2. In all of what follows, I rely heavily upon Jacob Milgrom, *Leviticus 1–16*, AB 3 (New York: Doubleday, 1991). Milgrom's monumental, magisterial three-volume commentary, though controversial on various points, is the undisputed point of reference in the study of Leviticus and Priestly material more broadly. Literature on the Priestly source and its ancient context is immense. For some recent and representative views germane to the material in this present chapter, see, e.g., Avraham Faust, "The World of P: The Material Realm of Priestly Writings," *VT* 69 (2019): 173–218; Jonathan Greer, "The 'Priestly Portion' in the Hebrew Bible: Its Ancient Near Eastern Context and Implications for the Composition of P," *JBL* 138 (2019): 263–84; Nathan Hays, "The Redactional Assertion of the Priestly Role in Leviticus 10–16," *ZAW* 130 (2018): 175–88; and Christophe Nihan and Julia Rhyder, "Aaron's Vestments in Exodus 28 and Priestly Leadership," in *Debating Authority: Concepts of Leadership in the Pentateuch and the Former Prophets*, ed. Katharina Pyschny and Sarah Schulz, BZAW 507 (Berlin: de Gruyter, 2018), 45–67.

broadly serving as a source for the redactor(s) of Leviticus 8–10, though in some ways it might be independent.

The basic structure of the narrative "interruption" contained in Leviticus 8–10 begins with the familiar form of a divine command, followed by Moses' execution of it.

> The LORD spoke to Moses, saying: Take Aaron and his sons with him, the vestments, the anointing oil, the bull of sin offering, the two rams, and the basket of unleavened bread; and assemble the whole congregation at the entrance of the tent of meeting. And Moses did as the LORD commanded him. (Lev. 8:1–4a; cf. Exod. 29:1–4)

This compact opening is a table of contents that will be expanded to cover all the action in chapter 8; yet the narrative unit opened by this summary statement first flashes us back to God's earlier instructions to Moses in Exodus 29. There the Lord had already instructed Moses in great detail what he was supposed to do to consecrate Aaron and his sons; so here, in fact, we finally have the accomplishment of that earlier prescription. The intervening material is not a long and clumsy redactional interlude, moreover. The ordination is delayed until this moment in the story for a plain narrative reason. In order to fulfill the divine prescriptions concerning the consecration of Aaron and his sons, the tabernacle with all its cultic functionality first had to be erected and prepared (Exod. 35–40). The intricate sacrificial procedures likewise needed to be learned (Lev. 1–7). One accordingly apprehends sanctuary, sacrifice, and priesthood as one integral cluster of interacting realities.

In this large mass of material binding the last quarter of Exodus with the first third of Leviticus, we can perceive how the Pentateuch's literary and theological depiction of the beginnings of the priestly ministry has a huge climactic effect, slowly moving over roughly twenty chapters from a divine word of command to its embodied realization. In this regard, it is not incorrect to say that in the vision of the Priestly authors of the Torah, Leviticus 8–9 is in a real sense the great, cumulative *telos*, the end goal of the entire Sinai revelation. It is no coincidence, indeed, that the emergence of the priestly ministry is positioned precisely here in the heart of the middle book of the Torah. For Jacob Milgrom, in fact, the glorious peak at the end of Aaron's inaugural sacrifices in Leviticus 9, when fire bursts forth and consumes the offerings and the glory of the Lord is seen, is nothing other than a second and greater Sinai.

> The importance of the theophany in the newly consecrated Tabernacle cannot be exaggerated. It renders the Tabernacle the equivalent of Mount Sinai. . . . The equivalence of the Tabernacle to Sinai is an essential, indeed indispensable,

axiom of P. The Tabernacle, in effect, becomes a portable Sinai, an assurance of the permanent presence of the deity in Israel's midst.[3]

Of course, the "portable Sinai" realized in the wilderness priesthood, with all its mobile cultic accoutrements, betrays a provisional character; for its "assurance of the permanent presence" of the Lord in Israel's midst has a promissory character and is actually stretched between two distinct Sinai moments: the revelation of glory made to Moses and its reprise at the consecration of the Jerusalem temple (1 Kings 8:10–13; 2 Chron. 7:1–3). In this way, a strong note of eschatological and prophetic tension, pointing to a more perfect and permanent sanctuary, attenuates even the climax carefully orchestrated in Leviticus 8–9. Like Abraham carrying the sacrificial knife and the fire, walking until he reached Mount Moriah, the future site of Solomon's temple (Gen. 22:6; cf. 2 Chron. 3:1), so the tabernacle priesthood of Aaron is created to carry the sacrificial service and the fire of divine glory through the people's experience of exile *bĕmidbar*, "in the desert" (the Hebrew name for the book of Numbers). Yet a more lasting arrangement is already in view. While for the ancient Priestly school the installation of the cult at Moriah/Jerusalem naturally signaled this ultimate arrival, Christians discern a deeper and more definitive fulfillment. Like Abraham, the itinerant priesthood created in the wilderness will also ultimately be called to lay down its knife and recognize the true victim, provided by God, and so be transformed in a new order of sacrificial offering.

Stretched as it is both backward and forward, the mediating position of Leviticus's portable priesthood assumes a recapitulative force. From this viewpoint, an important parallel between the theophanies of Exodus 40:34–38 (glory descending upon the completed tabernacle) and Leviticus 9:22–24 (glory manifested at the inauguration of the cult) becomes quite revealing, for it exposes the full cosmic dimensions here at work. In the theology of the Priestly author, just as the priesthood perfects and completes the cult, so the cult is somehow the *telos* and crown of all creation.

Genesis 1, with its liturgical ordering of the seven days to the sabbath, already gestures in this direction, but Exodus 40 contains a clear echo of the idea. Specifically, in this final chapter of Exodus, a careful parallel has been forged between Moses' execution of the divine plan and those original seven days of creation through the sevenfold repetition of the refrain "just as the LORD had commanded" (Exod. 40:17–38). Behind this intertextual link between creation and the construction of the tabernacle stands the ancient Near Eastern conception of a temple as a kind of microcosm. Leviticus 8–9 contains precisely the same sevenfold repetition, indicating at once that this

---

3. Milgrom, *Leviticus 1–16*, 574.

story is the continuation of the account in Exodus 40 and thereby also a kind of new creation. The seven days of consecration rites only reinforce this notion of a new creation account.[4] Just as the Lord in Genesis first prepared the universal stage and ornamented the world, then accomplished his work with the creation of humankind, so he now, through Moses, creates a new cosmos and adorns it in the tabernacle; then to crown his work he carefully ornaments and creates the priests, a new image of human likeness to God. Later Jewish tradition, reflected in the Dead Sea Scrolls (11QT 15:3–16:4), legislated that the seven-day priestly consecration service was to begin on the first of Nisan: the same day that the tabernacle was consecrated, according to Exodus 40:2, 17, as well as the day on which the universe was created, according to the Talmud (b. Rosh Hash. 10b–11a). A new world begins, embedded within the old creation, through God's creation of the Aaronic priestly service. Starting in the middle of the Torah thus lands us promptly "in the beginning" and at the very center of the Pentateuch's theological vision.

The Elements of Priestly Ordination

Returning to Leviticus 8:1–3, we find squeezed within the five enumerated items in this summary statement a miniature version of the entire course of the following ceremony of consecration. In fact, the ordering of items here has been realigned from the haphazard listing in Exodus 29 to synchronize with the progress of the ritual action about to unfold. (This discrepancy in Exod. 29 between an inventory list and the order of ritual usage is not necessarily a sign of confusion, but corresponds to the same phenomenon in similar Hittite texts.) One may thus take in turn each element mentioned in Leviticus 8:1–3 as a convenient guide through the ordination ceremony itself.

Aaron and His Sons

At the outset, it is well worth highlighting that Aaron and his sons are the first things "taken" (qaḥ). Indeed, they are grammatically treated like objects, ranged in the same syntactic position as the four other items destined here for sacred use: the vestments, oil, sacrificial animals, and unleavened bread. The candidates selected for ordination who will be set apart to be made priests will, in fact, appear throughout this opening part of the narrative very much

4. The weeklong consecration ceremony is echoed in later biblical traditions such as the inauguration of Solomon's altar (2 Chron. 7:9; cf. Ezek. 43:25–26), and it also parallels seven-day temple dedications known from the extrabiblical world, such as that of the Eninnu temple for the god Ningirsu in Lagash (ca. 2090 BC).

like the passive paraphernalia of the sanctuary. A kind of objective holiness, proper to all *sancta*, inheres in these consecrated men.

The *ordinandi* are much more than simple liturgical furniture, of course. In terms of the developing action, the priests here are more like a living extension of the sanctuary itself, the locus where the Lord makes his holy dwelling. Thus, just as the tent of meeting with all its vessels will be smeared with special oil, so Aaron as high priest will be. "Moses took the anointing oil and anointed the tabernacle and all that was in it. . . . [Then] he poured some of the anointing oil on Aaron's head and anointed him, to consecrate him" (Lev. 8:10, 12). In this fusion of the priests and the temple, we discover a living locus of divine presence. There is already a hint here of the christological "temple of his body" (cf. John 2:21), as well as what later appears in the book of Revelation, when John the seer is given a rod and told, "Come and measure the temple of God and the altar and those who worship there" (Rev. 11:1). In this Christian vision, deeply intertwined with the prophecy of Ezekiel (we will have occasion to come back to these themes), the entire worshiping congregation is reckoned together with the temple and the altar as part of the eschatological cultic construction. What begins here with the sacralization of Aaron becomes for all a participation in the character of Christ: not as so many individual temples, but specifically as parts of that one single living temple that is his body.

As an animate locus of worship, the priest who is "taken" perhaps most resembles the sacrificial animal victims themselves (cf. Exod. 29:15–16). Interestingly, in this connection, the verb used in Leviticus 8:6 to describe Moses' fulfillment of God's prescription is not simply a repetition of the verb "to take" but, rather, *wayyaqrēb* in Hebrew or *prosēnenken* in Greek, both terms that often carry the distinct sense of bringing an offering: "and Moses *presented* Aaron and his sons" (AT). The original command in Exodus 28:1 similarly used this same suggestive verb: "You shall present your brother Aaron, with his sons, from among the Israelites, to serve me as priests." Like Aaron and his sons here, the Levites will later simply be "taken," in parallel to the "taking" of their animals, in order to stand as a substitute of all the firstborn of Israel (Num. 3:41). The Levites will further be "presented" in Numbers 8:9–11, and here the cultic connotation becomes quite explicit. After the people impose hands upon the Levites' heads, they are described in openly sacrificial terms as "an elevation offering." This is in order that the Levites "might perform the service/worship of the Lord." All of this echoes the manner in which Abraham is commanded to "take" Isaac (*qaḥ*) and present him as a "burnt [holocaust] offering" in Genesis 22:2.

The simultaneous differentiation and affinity of Aaronide priests and Levites implied in the separate but parallel treatments just evoked is a very

significant and complicated matter. It relates to the establishment of a hierarchical structure within the heart of Israel's temple ministry and is discussed
briefly in excursus 2 at the end of this chapter.

The Vestments (Lev. 8:6–9)

After their selection, the washing and clothing of the priests-to-be is the
first order of business. The various fabrics and weaves used to cover the high
priest correspond to those precious materials and skilled methods of manu-
facture also used to make the veils in the tabernacle. For instance, the blue-
purple, red-purple, and red woolen threads of *rōqēm* embroidery used for
Aaron's sash (Exod. 28:39) are the same fabrics used in the tabernacle's lower
curtains and the same weave employed for the screens at the tabernacle's entrance (Exod. 26:36; 27:16). In fact, the making of the high priest's vestments
suggestively concludes the account relating the components of the tabernacle,
as if these vestments were part of that tabernacle itself (Exod. 39:1–31). The
priest himself thus appears visibly transformed into a living dwelling.

While rich priestly vesture was by no means unique to Israel, in the ancient Near East it was also not unknown for priestly figures to serve in the
sanctuary entirely unclothed. This curiosity is seen, for instance, on multiple
ancient plaques and reliefs depicting ministers officiating in a state of ritual
nudity (e.g., *ANEP* 597, 600, 603, 605, 619). Against this background, God's
explicit commandment that Israel's priests must wear linen undershorts, and
that those who build and ascend an altar of stones (seemingly a private altar)
must not thereby "uncover their nakedness," acquires a much more pointed
cultural resonance (cf. Exod. 28:42; 20:26). An undergarment covering the
loins was not in fact a standard part of ancient dress, and to this extent it
is not irresponsible to suppose that a form of sexual propriety explains this
peculiar priestly girding: a kind of distant forerunner to the Catholic priest's
symbolic cincture (*praecinge me Domine, cingulo puritatis*, "Gird me, O Lord,
with the belt of purity"). In Leviticus 18:6–30 a long list of sexual sins will be
prohibited using the same "uncovering nakedness" formula evoked in Exodus
20, hinting at its moral force. Much later in Ezra, when the priest's marriage
partners will be rigorously regulated, it will become increasingly clear that
the sexual existence of the priest stands subject to special ritual legislation.

The priest's liturgical garb embodies in a certain way the priestly office
itself, mysteriously made visible: a man-shaped ritual space into which successive officeholders will enter. The Talmud says, "When the priests are clothed
in their vestments, their priesthood is upon them; when they are not clothed
in their vestments, their priesthood is not upon them" (*b. Zebaḥ.* 17b). Thus,
Aaron will eventually be stripped of his vestments and they will be put upon
his son Eleazar as a sign of the transfer of the office (Num. 20:25–28); all

subsequent high priests are likewise commanded to don them (Exod. 29:30; see Lev. 21:10). Importantly, this continuity of the transmission of Aaron's vesture/priesthood is prophetically interrupted in the vision of Zechariah 3:1–5, when the high priest Joshua appears accused by Satan and standing in filthy garments: an image of the priesthood and nation's accumulated uncleanness and sin. This Old Testament "Jesus" is then reclothed in new festal apparel, indicative of a regenerated priesthood, linked to a rebuilt temple. We will return to this significant oracle in chapter 4.

If the priestly vestments somehow embody the whole priestly office, two conjoined points of symbolic meaning must also be mentioned. These represent two poles, one human, one divine. First, the ephod, a curious breastplate with twelve stones corresponding to the twelve tribes of Israel, signals that the high priest somehow carries the corporate collectivity of God's people by his office. Second, the headdress and diadem that he wears, which carry the inscription *qōdeš lĕ-YHWH*, "Holy to the LORD," points to the priest's unique place within the divine realm. Both head and members of the whole Christ (*totus Christus*), joined together in one body, are thus typologically signified by the inherent symbolism of the vestments.

The Anointing Oil (Lev. 8:10–12)

After the high priest has been clothed, but before the sons of Aaron are vested, a two-part anointing ritual is prescribed. A special recipe for the precious chrism to be used is provided in Exodus 30:22–25: two parts liquid myrrh, two parts cassia, one part cinnamon and aromatic cane, with olive oil added. In Exodus 29, however, Moses is simply instructed, "You shall take the anointing oil, and pour it on his head and anoint him" (Exod. 29:7). Between the first and second halves of this verse, however, Leviticus 8:10–11 inserts the anointing of the tabernacle, altar, and other implements in the tent. This addition takes care to bind Aaron's unction with that smearing of the *sancta* prescribed in another place (Exod. 40:10–11). Thus, the redactor consciously effects the suggestive parallelism between the high priest and the dwelling already noted.

The anointing of the altar deserves special comment. According to Exodus 40:10, the altar itself shall be "most holy" (*qōdeš qodāšîm*), whereas the other *sancta* are simply "holy" (even if all these tabernacle *sancta* are already "most holy" according to Exod. 30:25–29, so much so that whatever touches them itself also becomes holy). A superlative *summo-sacrality* consequently inheres in the altar, which is *holy of holies* even among the *most holy*. Leviticus ritually translates this eminent holiness of the concrete spot of sacrifice by indicating that the altar was to be sprinkled with the oil seven times over: a rite that evokes the sevenfold sprinkling of blood performed on the Day of

Atonement (Lev. 16:19b). Unlike the annual Yom Kippur, however, this oil rite is a one-time inauguration ritual, meant to unseal the altar and enable it for worthy sacrifice. Though it is admittedly not clear what precisely was repeated during this full week of ceremonies (Exod. 29:35; Lev. 8:33), the sevenfold sprinkling was likely repeated for seven full days, yielding a seven-times-seven measure of holiness: forty-nine sprinklings.

Though Aaron, too, would be doused (not just sprinkled) seven times during the course of the week, as *qōdeš lĕ-YHWH* he is not the holiest object in the tabernacle. The clear subordination of the priest to the supremely holy altar points to the profound and mysterious fact that the priesthood itself must be ultimately cleansed by the power of the very sacrificial service that it is created to offer. This is indicated in the altar's subtle ritual orientation to the Day of Atonement, which hints very discretely at that great forgiveness ceremony's interior connection to this unfolding narrative of the creation of the priesthood—as well as to its imminent fall (cf. Lev. 10:1–7; 16:1).

The precious oil poured upon Aaron's head renders him a "Christ" in the etymological sense of the word. This messianic aura was not lost on later Jewish readers, who quite naturally found in this image of the anointed priest an eschatological agent to place alongside the anointed king (see chap. 5 below). The high priest's anointing is somehow greater than a royal anointing, moreover. Later in the rite, once the first sacrificial blood has been spilled (Lev. 8:21, 30), the sacred chrism mixed with that blood will also be sprinkled upon Aaron to sanctify the priestly vestments. This second anointing also embraces Aaron's two sons and is the only manner in which these auxiliary priests are ever anointed with chrism (cf. Lev. 8:10–13). The same christological head-and-members typology noted in connection with the vestments, a motif echoed in Psalm 133, is thus also suggested here in Leviticus's ritual prescriptions. The extension of the primordial high priesthood of the Aaronic "Christ" is now shared with others—but in a different manner and only after a mighty work at the altar. The generous high priestly unction of the head is thus not simply shared with the whole body in the same way that it is received. It must be mixed with the cleansing and sanctifying power of sacrificial blood before it can be extended to the priestly members.

The Bull and Rams of Sacrifice

Three distinct, progressive types of sacrifice stand between the pure oil of Aaron's anointing and this later christening of his sons (in union with him) with the mixture of chrism and blood. First, a bull is slaughtered as a "sin offering" (Lev. 8:14–17; cf. Exod. 29:35–37). Then two rams are offered: one as a burnt offering (Lev. 8:18–21; cf. Exod. 29:15–18) and one, finally, as the special "ram of ordination" (Lev. 8:22–25; cf. Exod. 29:31–34).

In this context, the giant sin offering is meant to purify and remove unworthiness from the altar (Exod. 29:10–14, 36; Lev. 8:15). It is not offered as an atonement for the priest's own sin (cf. Lev. 4:3). This is striking and profoundly suggestive. Aaron's own titanic sin at Sinai, in forging the golden calf, never complicates his capacity to enter into an elevated priestly service—though the problem of priestly sin will soon be directly faced (cf. Lev. 16:8). Instead, the foundational role of the altar itself as the ultimate sacrificial agent becomes the focus of essential purity and power. To ready the altar for its job, some of the bull's blood is carefully applied to the four horns by Moses', not Aaron's, finger (Lev. 8:15; cf. Exod. 29:12; also 27:2).

The blood of the holocaust/burnt-offering ram is also applied to the altar, but splashed around the sides in a broad gesture, not touched atop the projecting horns with such delicate precision. Unlike the bull, moreover, of which only the choice fatty portions are offered up (the rest of the animal being burned outside the camp [Exod. 29:14]), this ram is burnt whole upon the altar as a "pleasing odor" (Lev. 8:21). The savory smell that reaches heaven signals that the altar now functions as a direct line of communication with God.

At this point, the ordination ram can at last be offered as the climax of the triple rite. This second ram is unique in two regards. First, parallel to daubing the horns of the altar, part of its blood is carefully applied to the extremities of the *ordinandi*: earlobe, thumb, and big toe—once again, head and members (Exod. 29:20; Lev. 8:23–24). This is done before the rest of the blood is then splashed upon the sides of altar. Together, these signs seem to signify the readying of Aaron's hands and feet to complete the sacral work assigned him—handling sacrifices and *sancta* and walking on sacred ground—while his ear is also marked, perhaps to open it to God's word or perhaps to claim him symbolically as God's slave (cf. Deut. 15:17). Strikingly, though, the same triple gesture of daubing blood on the earlobe, thumb, and big toe is also part of the ritual cleansing of a leper in Leviticus 14:1–30. There is an implicit affinity, therefore, between a cleansing and a priestly consecration, which will become explicit in Zechariah 3. The *ordinandi* stand unclean like lepers who must be not only washed but *healed*. The splashing around the altar of the remainder of this blood that has now touched him symbolically suggests that it is the priest's own blood that is somehow being offered as the victim on the altar.

The second unique element in the offering of this second ram is that half of the meat goes to the Lord directly, via the altar, and half is a portion to be consumed by Aaron and his sons. A communion meal between God and man thus seals the sacrificial work of consecration. The power of this gesture is not to be missed. It gains additional force with the actions that immediately follow.

Unleavened Bread (Lev. 8:31)

The unleavened bread is involved only in the final, culminating act of the intricate consecration: the communion meal linked to the ordination ram.

> From the basket of unleavened bread that was before the LORD, he [Moses] took one cake of unleavened bread, one cake of bread with oil, and one wafer, and placed them on the fat and on the right thigh. He placed all these on the palms of Aaron and on the palms of his sons, and raised them as an elevation offering before the LORD. (Lev. 8:26–27)

The placing of these loaves, loaded up with the fatty portions and the prescribed cut of meat, into the hands of Aaron and his sons is the ritual gesture from which comes the actual phrase used to say "ordination" in Hebrew: literally, "filling the hand" (e.g., Lev. 8:33; cf. Exod. 28:41; 29:9, 29; Lev. 16:32; Num. 3:3; Judg. 17:12). The idiom seems to signify a conferral of power ("hand" in Hebrew can also mean power). It is quite revealing what exactly fills up the priestly hands, for this will be the source and store of the priests' power to bless. For seven days, their palms are weighed down, not with silver, as might be hinted at in the story of Micah's dubious priestling in Judges 17, but instead with food: a huge pile of bread and flesh. The passive reception from Moses' hand of these rich sacrificial offerings and emoluments clearly signifies the gift-like character of priestly service and honor. All the priestly rights to this or that part of Israel's offerings participate somehow in this original filling of the priest's hands.

Quite strikingly, Moses no sooner fills the outstretched hands than he immediately takes back what he has given, in order that he might offer it upon the altar (Lev. 8:28). A direct ritual forebear of the *traditio instrumentorum* (handing over of the implements of ordained ministry) still practiced in the Church's ordination rites, this gesture of momentarily holding the bread and meat likens the priests' hands to the altar itself and is explicitly designated as an "elevation offering" (*tĕnûpâ*, traditionally called a "wave offering," indicating a horizontal motion of extending and retracting the arms, but probably in fact a vertical gesture of raising). The "elevation offering" is a common kind of dedication ritual performed in the sanctuary, which functions specifically as a way to transfer something from the domain of the offering to the domain of the deity. Later, as noted, the Levites themselves will be reckoned as an "elevation offering"—dedicated by the people to the Lord as a gift. Here, Aaron and his sons hand back what is being given to them, renouncing in some sense the priestly privilege itself, returning it to the Lord, who first supplied it.

What is surpassingly curious, however, is that the portions of meat that fill the priests' hands include not only what belongs to the priests by right—namely, the right thigh—but also the suet, which belongs to the Lord. Although the reasons why this fat under the skin is reserved for the deity are much less evident than why the blood also belongs to God, suet clearly carried the connotation of "the best" (e.g., Gen. 45:18) and was perhaps considered a delicacy. Elsewhere the suet is always explicitly excluded from the elevation rite (Lev. 7:30; 9:20–21). Milgrom, seldom stumped in arcane ritual prescriptions, comments succinctly about its sudden inclusion in the rite at the end of the ordination: "The solution eludes me."[5] This unique mixture in the hands of the priests of what is already under God's dominion and what must be transferred over to him from the human side (though it also came as God's gift) captures a mysterious and essential element of divine and human cooperation. In the divine work of empowering priests to become sacrificial agents, an element purely and entirely belonging to God must be offered *as though* it were the priest's own. It *is* in fact ritually made the priest's own true possession, in order that he might hand it back over along with what is more properly his. God's own portion must be mingled, blended with the priests' in this way to make of it all a single pleasing odor upon the altar. Unless the perfume that is God's own is entrusted to the priest, his hands will remain empty and without power at the altar.

In addition to the sacrificial flesh, one representative loaf of the three sorts of bread in the basket is included in this climactic dedication rite. Each loaf has a distinct and suggestive eucharistic symbolism. The first, unleavened bread, plainly evokes the Passover and more specifically the seven-day Feast of Unleavened Bread described in Exodus 12. The second, the cake of oil bread, resembles the type of bread that transforms a sacrifice into a "thanksgiving" offering (Lev. 7:12). Finally, the thin, round wafer recalls the grain offering, Israel's preeminent bloodless sacrifice (Lev. 2:1–16). All the ritual power of bread, in its depth of prophetic meaning—power over death, the rendering of thanks, and the offering of a spiritual sacrifice—is thus handed over into the priests' power. Bread offerings, of course, are ultimately the offerings of Israel's poor, the offerings of those who cannot afford to slaughter beasts or even birds. Aquinas sees in the bread—the chosen matter of Christ's own eucharistic sacrifice—the humble poverty of the Lord's human condition. Aaron, who holds in his hands all the offerings of great and small alike, makes them into one single offering, with no distinction. Indeed, in the filled hands of the high priest, all the bewildering varieties of Israel's ritual life are now bound together in a sole offering to God.

Moses burns this symbolic meal of bread and flesh upon the altar and uses the blood therefrom to consecrate and render holy the priestly vestments.

5. Milgrom, *Leviticus 1–16*, 531.

Then Aaron and his sons sit down and feast. They eat the boiled flesh of the ordination ram, together with the bread remaining in the basket. Thereby they communicate with the Lord in a shared human and divine repast—God taking his part on the altar; the priests, as accords with the consumption of holy things, sitting in the forecourt of the tent of meeting. On the seventh day, when this whole vast consecration rite is repeated for the seventh and final time, at the final of these repeated feasts of consummation, the ordination of the priests is perfected. It is fitting in the Septuagint translation that this unique "ram of ordination," which nowhere else appears in the Levitical code, portentously becomes the "ram of perfection" (*teleiōseōs*), the "perfect ram," as Origen keenly observes (*Homilies on Leviticus* 5.2.1).

The Priest-Maker and the Church

In the sacrificial meal just described, which brings to a climax the ordination of Aaron and his sons, a noteworthy provision went unremarked. Moses himself consumes the breast meat of the ram (Lev. 8:29). This is strange, as normally this choice piece is specifically reserved for Aaron and his sons (Lev. 7:31), while the thigh meat is reserved (rather emphatically) for the officiant of the ceremony, which here is obviously Moses (Lev. 7:33). The roles have thus been switched.

This intrusion of Moses into the heart of the communion banquet highlights one last element, in many ways the most important of all, which has not yet been mentioned in the ritual inventory that we have followed: Moses himself, in his own extraordinary role as *high priest–maker*. Although he was a Levite and is called a priest in Psalm 99:6, and a line of priests appears among his descendants (e.g., Jonathan son of Gershom in Judg. 18:30), Moses himself is obviously never ordained, at least in the view of the Pentateuch. (Second Temple traditions will take another view, as we will see in chap. 5.) Still, Moses conducts the priestly ceremonies by which his brother is elevated in status. Later rabbinic voices accept that Moses did serve Israel as high priest during these seven days of Aaron's consecration, though at that time, they say, "the Presence did not come down to dwell in the world. It was [only] when Aaron began to serve as High Priest that, through Aaron's agency, it came down to dwell in the world" (*Pesiq. Rab Kah.* 4.5; cf. Lev. 9:24). Moses' extra-priestly, priestly service is illuminated by the covenant ceremony in Exodus 24:4–8. It is not actually Moses but "young men of Israel" who offer the animals on the altar for sacrifice. His own action in sprinkling the blood is the conventional work of a covenant-maker: a role reserved for chieftains and kings, not priestly agents (e.g., *ANET* 532–33).

If Moses, as the people's patriarch and chieftain, stands outside the priestly institution, yet founds it as the only one who can fulfill this role, his behavior accords with similar ancient cases. Biblical history illustrates many royal figures functioning as priests in various circumstances (e.g., 1 Sam. 13:9–10; 1 Kings 3:4, 15; 12:32–33). Still, a special moment for such extraordinary sacerdotal activity was clearly the inauguration of a cult, Solomon's temple dedication being the preeminent example (1 Kings 8:63–64). Solomon's founding of the cult in Jerusalem included not just the building of the sanctuary and his personal priestlike consecration of its sacrificial altar. The establishment of Zadok, the Aaronide, in the office of the high priesthood, in place of Abiathar, of the line of Eli from the shrine at Nob (1 Kings 2:26–27, 35; but cf. 1 Kings 4:4), is also part of Solomon's actions. In the ancient Near East, we find this same pattern of kings setting up a priesthood consistently repeated. Even if Solomon did not actually ordain Zadok as a priest—this he was by right of lineal descent from Aaron's eldest son, Eleazar—the investiture and, at times, creation of a priesthood regularly belonged to the same person responsible for the dedication of a sanctuary: namely, the king.

The intimate binding of priest and temple, the one ordered to and ordained for the service of the other, is encountered here once again, for the two realities are established in one conjoint operation by one single authority. In the royal ideology of the ancient Near East, of course, it was not simply the king's own personal or charismatic authority that grounded a temple-*cum*-priesthood. It was the patron god (or gods) who, through the king, simply executed the heavenly plan for a divine abode. In this line, a Hittite temple dedication text reads, for example: "Behold this temple we have built for you the deity. . . . It is not we who have built it (but) the gods who have built it" (*KBo* IVl.i.28–30; *ANET* 356). In Israel the same view was held: "Unless the LORD builds the house [i.e., temple], those who build it labor in vain" (Ps. 127:1, "Of Solomon"). In Leviticus 8, it is likewise the Lord himself who, through Moses' agency, divinely establishes the tabernacle priesthood. The sevenfold repetition that Moses acted just "as the LORD commanded" makes this emphatically clear (Lev. 8:4, 9, 13, 17, 21, 29, 36).

Dionysius the Areopagite discerns this divine agency working clearly in Moses, who bases nothing on personal factors but defers entirely to God's command.

> Moses, the consecrator in the hierarchy of the Law, did not confer a clerical consecration on Aaron who was his brother, whom he knew to be a friend of God and worthy of the priesthood, until God himself commanded him to do so, thereby permitting him to bestow, in the name of God who is the source of all consecration, the fullness of a clerical consecration. (*Ecclesiastical Hierarchy* 5.3.5)[6]

6. Translation from Colm Luibheid, *Pseudo-Dionysius: The Complete Works* (New York: Paulist Press, 1987), 241.

Because it is ultimately divine authority that stands behind the creation of a priesthood and a cult of service to the gods, the relationship of priestly to regal authority is more complex than what might appear from what has been said. For kings will also be anointed by priests: Solomon by Zadok, for example (1 Kings 1:39). To appreciate this circular exchange of legitimation, it is essential to appreciate that an ancient Near Eastern king's royal status was itself contingent upon his god-granted, higher-than-high-priestly power of establishing a temple in which that god might dwell, equipped with a full cohort of liturgical servants. A king was not settled upon the throne until he had created such a divine abode and erected a placating divine service in his realm. This alone would hold the surrounding chaos at bay (see excursus 1). In this sense, one is confirmed as king precisely and only insofar as one already possesses that supreme priestly power necessary to erect a temple-*cum*-priesthood.

In view of these reflections it becomes manifest why contemporary portrayals of Jesus as a "layman" whose priestly identity would be an ungrounded fabrication are not only polemically formulated but profoundly confused. It is of immense inherent meaning that, like Moses the priest-maker, Jesus—at least according to his fleshly descent—is not and actually *cannot* be a priest. To found a priesthood, Jesus must stand beyond it in the manner of a king. And as Hebrews says, "It is evident that our Lord was descended from Judah, and in connection with that tribe Moses said nothing about priests" (Heb. 7:14). Jesus is accordingly at this level (and still more than Moses) a royal figure whose own priestly ministry inevitably stands beyond the priesthood that he institutes. Yet, like Moses and all priest-making kings, David included (see excursus 5), Jesus also participates in an extraordinary way in the same sacrificial activities and sanctifying functions by which his new priestly order is erected. As with Solomon, anointed by Zadok, a circular transaction will be exchanged between the Judahite Jesus and the priestly John, as we will later observe more closely. In all the essentials, the model is strikingly upheld. Ultimately (as in the ancient view, so also in the New Covenant), Christ's creative agency in fashioning a new priestly service—an agency at once priestly and royal—is the manifestation and execution of God's own heavenly plan, both perfect and divine.

The *Ekklēsia*

The divine authority of a people's founding hierarch to create a temple-*cum*-priesthood explains another essential aspect of Moses' (and the new Moses') action. He convokes the whole congregation at the entrance to the meeting tent (Lev. 8:3–4). This act is not part of the instruction the Lord gave in Exodus 29, which, as Milgrom argues, may indicate that the redactor of Leviticus 8:3–4 intended to align this scene of Aaron's consecration with Solomon's dedication of the temple in 1 Kings 8:1–2. At the same time, this is not the first time that this extraordinary act of assembling the whole people together has been seen. On the first occasion, in Exodus 35, Moses made an appeal to the whole people for their generous offerings of "gold, silver and bronze; blue, purple, and crimson yarns, and fine linen; goats' hair, tanned rams' skins, and fine leather; acacia wood, oil for the light, spices for the anointing oil and for the fragrant incense, and onyx stones and gems to be set in the ephod and the breastpiece" (Exod. 35:5–9)—the materials, plainly, to enable the realization of divine service. Now, having gathered the people's offerings and constructed the tabernacle and vestments, those who made those earlier offerings are reconvoked.

From a Christian viewpoint, this second convocation at this great and solemn moment carries an inevitable eschatological hint. Reading the Septuagint translation, Cyril of Jerusalem observed that the Greek phrase used in Leviticus 8:3 and 8:4 says, quite literally, to "church the synagogue" (*tēn synagōgēn ekklēsiason, exekklēsiasen tēn synagōgēn*). It is as though now, in the elevation of the people's high priest, Israel ("the synagogue"), formerly gathered for the work of *preparing* exactly this moment, has at last been gathered again and thereby transformed into the Church, by the enacted fulfillment of what she formerly merely prepared. The assembly that had been dispersed is now reassembled around the one who is the clear, prophetic type of Christ. An ecclesiology thus emerges from this creation of hierarchs by the founder of the people. Even rabbinic theology saw a prophetic image of itself as an "academy of elders" in Moses' gathering of elders of the people alongside the priests in Leviticus 9:1 (see *Lev. Rab.* 11.8).

In Leviticus 8:5, Moses addresses the assembly only with the brief words "This is what the LORD has commanded to be done." He then speaks exclusively by his ritual actions. In 9:3–6, however, the congregation reappears and now becomes a key actor in the liturgy.

> "Say to the people of Israel, 'Take a male goat for a sin offering; a calf and a lamb, yearlings without blemish, for a burnt offering; and an ox and a ram for an offering of well-being to sacrifice before the LORD; and a grain offering mixed with oil. For today the LORD will appear to you.'" They brought what Moses commanded to the front of the tent of meeting; and the whole congregation drew near and stood before the LORD. And Moses said, "This is the thing that the LORD commanded you to do, so that the glory of the LORD may appear to you."

This participation in the offering is anything but negligible. As at Mass, the people present the gifts to be offered on the altar. Yet, as at Mass, this is a

Origen and the High Priest

Origen sees in Moses' assembling of the people the lesson that the attendance of the whole congregation is necessary for a correct perception of the high priest's surpassing worth. "For in ordaining a priest, the presence of the people is also required that all may know and be certain that from all the people one is chosen for the priesthood who is more excellent, who is more wise, who is more holy, who is more eminent in every virtue."[a] This is not an obvious description of Aaron, it must be admitted. It better suits the one to whom the Letter to the Hebrews applies the Psalm:

> You have loved righteousness and hated wickedness;
> therefore God, your God, has anointed you
> with the oil of gladness beyond your companions. (Heb. 1:9)

a. Origen, *Homilies on Leviticus* 6.3. Translation from *Origen: Homilies on Leviticus 1–16*, trans. Gary Wayne Barkley, FC (Washington, DC: Catholic University of America Press, 1990), 120.

gesture with no sanctifying power whatsoever in itself. Neither bread and wine nor bulls and goats can command the Lord's favor. The free action of God is required. This is given in the appearance of his glory, at the hand of the priests, which signals at once the confirmation of their office and the acceptance of the people's gift.

The motif of YHWH's theophany to the people in Leviticus 9:6 points directly ahead to 9:23, as we shall presently see. It is also recalled in Numbers 16:19, however, where an important verbal and conceptual echo appears.

> Then Korah assembled the whole congregation against them [i.e., Moses and Aaron] at the entrance of the tent of meeting. And the glory of the LORD appeared to the whole congregation.

The context is the "people's" rebellion against the priestly hierarchy (Num. 16:1–50).

> They assembled against Moses and against Aaron, and said to them, "You have gone too far! All the congregation are holy, every one of them, and the LORD is among them. So why then do you exalt yourselves above the assembly of the LORD?" (Num. 16:3)

The answer to this protest is God's unambiguous theophanic demonstration of support for Moses and Aaron. Korah and his fellow agitators are thereby revealed as helpless protectors of the people against God's dangerous glory, while Moses and Aaron are confirmed in their divine election. Clearly the story is meant to serve as an object lesson.[7]

Korah's rebellion obviously resonates strongly with the Reformation construction of the common priesthood. If the answer that God provides in the form of fire is today deconstructed and simply dismissed as the Priestly authors' self-serving invention, the best that can be said is that the theological commitments that shaped and transmitted the Pentateuch, the very heart of Israel's witness, have through this cynicism been nullified by a particular form of unbelief; for it is clear what the story means to say about the priesthood. The result is a biblical theology of the priesthood that prohibits hearing the priests' own voices, rather than striving (as is proper to a canonical theology) to be polyphonic. This disregard of the old story of Korah may perhaps be considered by some to be an acceptable New Testament view of the matter. Yet Jude 8–11 considers those who "reject authority" to be the direct heirs of Korah, destined to perish as he and his associates did. The early Church saw her leaders implicated in this story and guarded the example to answer envious uprisings against bishops and deacons, which were hardly a new invention in sixteenth-century Europe (e.g., *1 Clem.* 4.12). It is difficult not to take this as a strong canonical rebuff of a certain congregational rejection of priestly status.

The Consuming Fire (Lev. 9)

Aaron's first act after the completion of the ordination rite is to offer up sin offerings to atone for himself and for the people. This is rather striking, since one would have expected that the first order of business in the newly functional cult would be to start in with the twice-daily *tāmîd* offerings, which are the next thing recounted after the instructions for the consecration of priests and sanctuary (Exod. 29:38–42; 30:1–10). Instead, an absolute urgency is placed on the removal of sin.

It is interesting that at precisely this point, but not before, the whole congregation gets involved in the action (Lev. 9:1–7). Obviously, the bull and rams and grain offering for the ordination rite proper had to come from somewhere; but for the Priestly author it is as though they magically materialized out

7. Israel Knohl (*The Sanctuary of Silence: Priestly Torah and the Holiness School* [Minneapolis: Fortress, 1995], 73–85) understands the story to derive from the Holiness School and to be a response to the claim of Israelite kings to perform priestly rites. See excursus 5.

of thin air. The animals for the sin offerings are another matter, however. They come at the cost of the congregation. The message seems to be that the making of priests is God's work alone, quite independent of the people's contribution, while the cleansing from sin implicates the whole congregation quite directly.

This inaugural act of Aaron's priesthood is elaborately recounted; as far as the Priestly author is concerned, it consists in exactly one thing: sacrifices offered on the altar. These are minutely described and the details need not detain us, for the drive of the narrative is clear. At bottom, there are two offerings: one for the priest and one for the people. This will be famously referenced in Hebrews 5:3 and 7:27, and the same two offerings also appear in Leviticus 16 as part of the ritual of Yom Kippur. Although these two rounds of sacrifices are identified as atonement offerings, there is a single expressed purpose for the whole operation: "that the glory of the LORD may appear to you" (Lev. 9:6). The clear impression is that procuring atonement is the first and most essential work of the priesthood. Sin is not removed for its own sake, of course, but only to clear away the obstacle interposed between the people and God's glory. For the entire priestly cult is ultimately ordered to a vision of the Lord's "glory" (*kābôd*).

Theologically, there is a beautiful depth to this precision. Priesthood's purgative action has an illuminative and beatific end. Holy Orders is ordered to the vision of the glory of God. It somehow ignites the light of glory (*lumen gloriae*) within the Church. Historically speaking, this doxological end is not surprising. The god's taking up glorious residence within his temple is always the point of its construction in the first place. Many Mesopotamian temple hymns, for instance, end with a refrain celebrating the enthronement of the deity in the dwelling, feting the processional arrival of the god's cult statue and honorific installment in its place, amid incense and pomp. As Milgrom observes, however, in the Mesopotamian sources "the people behold their deity as his or her images *enter* the temple," whereas "the Israelites behold their god as he *emerges* from the Tabernacle in the form of fire" (Lev. 9:23–24; cf. 1 Chron. 21:26; 2 Chron. 7:1–3).[8]

> Aaron lifted his hands toward the people and blessed them; and he came down after sacrificing the sin offering, the burnt offering, and the offering of well-being. Moses and Aaron entered the tent of meeting, and then came out and blessed the people; and the glory of the LORD appeared to all the people. Fire came out from the LORD and consumed the burnt offering and the fat on the altar; and when all the people saw it, they shouted and fell on their faces. (Lev. 9:22–24)

8. Milgrom, *Leviticus 1–16*, 575.

This fiery surging forth of the Lord from out of his dwelling follows the prior coming forth of Moses and Aaron, who here join together in one shared priestly act of blessing. The hands of the high priest and the hands of the high priest's maker synchronize in one shared gesture, which both releases God's glory and reveals that the people's offering has been accepted. There is a magnificent poetic image here of Augustine's doctrine of Christ as the operative agent in the sacramental ministry, working in synchronized coordination with his priests.

The fire that mysteriously comes forth "from before the LORD" indicates something mysteriously unique about the God of Israel. He is not an inert deity; nor does he hide within his dark, celestial abode. He leaps out from within his dwelling and enters the space of his people to greedily consume the sacrifices that are laid before him, gloriously laying claim to what is his. For "YHWH is a devouring fire and a jealous god" (Deut. 4:24; 9:3). The economic mission of the Son, in both his descending and ascending mediation, is mystically seen in this bursting forth of fire, which takes the explicit form of an acceptable sacrifice for sin.

"I Will Show Myself Holy"

Revelation of YHWH precisely as a consuming fire is the first and most important effect of the newly functional priesthood. The new cultic establishment thus becomes a living instrument by which God's glorious presence can exit the divine dwelling to reach the people. The divine presence proves to be deadly, however. The story of Nadab and Abihu, which follows the theophany directly, makes this immediately and disconcertingly clear.

> Now Aaron's sons, Nadab and Abihu, each took his censer, put fire in it, and laid incense on it; and they offered unholy fire before the LORD, such as he had not commanded them. And fire came out from the presence of the LORD and consumed them, and they died before the LORD. Then Moses said to Aaron, "This is what the LORD meant when he said,
>
> > 'Through those who are near me
> > I will show myself holy,
> > and before all the people
> > I will be glorified.'"
>
> And Aaron was silent. (Lev. 10:1–3)

Milgrom calls this scene the Priestly counterpart to the episode of the golden calf: "Just as the latter followed upon the theophany of God at Sinai, so the former took place in the aftermath of the divine theophany at the tabernacle."[9] Such a comparison reveals a pattern. God's efforts to draw near to his people and have them draw near to him are time and again undone by sin. Gary Anderson accordingly goes one step further and sees the misdeed here as one of multiple biblical images of original sin. His view gains force when we recall the creation imagery so strongly linked with Leviticus 8. It is as though at the very moment that God's entire purpose in creating the world is finally attained, with the theophany in Leviticus 9:24, everything swiftly goes off the rails.[10]

The collocation of "taking" something (i.e., a censer) with the phrase "as he [God] had *not* commanded" contrasts flagrantly with the repeated pattern of Moses' own sevenfold obedient actions (cf. Lev. 8:4, 9, 13, 17, 21, 29, 36). As James Watts says, "The intrusion of the negative particle ["not"] comes like a thunderclap, an aural shock to a listening audience just as YHWH's consuming fire presented a visual shock to the watching Israelites in the story."[11] The double shock is quite real and also quite puzzling. They offered "strange fire" and acted without having been commanded, yet the whole story has the strange character of a "punishment in search of a crime." What precisely was Nadab and Abihu's sin? Was it idolatry, drunkenness, nakedness perhaps? The proposals are numerous, but all equally inconclusive.

In approaching the issue of this deadly disobedience, Anderson helpfully notes that a subtle but important difference distinguishes the obedience of Moses in chapter 8 from that of Aaron in chapter 9.[12] In the ordination rites, as we have seen, Moses follows the special instructions provided in Exodus 29, whereas in offering the sin offerings Aaron is referring back to the legislation on sacrifice provided in Leviticus 1–7. The conclusion that Anderson draws is important and clear. "The period of Mosaic supervision had drawn to a close, and from now on the responsibility will rest on the priest to 'check the manual,' so to speak, as to what comes next."[13] Yet there are limits to what this liturgical manual can provide. Namely, no identification of any rubrical misstep clarifies the tragic case of Nadab and Abihu, such as appears, for instance, in the next story of the ritual error of Eleazar and Ithamar (Lev. 10:17–20), who plainly transgress Leviticus 6:23. It seems, therefore, that in the theology of the Priestly author, who withholds any such similar information

9. Jacob Milgrom, *Leviticus: A Book of Ritual and Ethics* (Minneapolis: Fortress, 2004), 98.
10. See Gary Anderson, "Original Sin: The Fall of Humanity and the Golden Calf," in *Christian Doctrine and the Old Testament: Theology in the Service of Biblical Exegesis* (Grand Rapids: Baker Academic, 2017), 59–73, esp. 65–67.
11. James Watts, *Leviticus 1–10*, HCOT (Leuven: Peeters, 2013), 512–13.
12. Anderson, "Original Sin," 66.
13. Gary Anderson, "'Through Those Who Are Near to Me, I Will Show Myself Holy': Nadab and Abihu and Apophatic Theology," *CBQ* 77 (2015): 1–19 (here 10).

in the case of the two slain sons of Aaron, we are not actually meant to know what Nadab and Abihu did wrong. For to know would imply that it might be mechanically corrected, by simply referring back to the handbook. Priestly ministry is something deeper and more dangerous than mere ritual mechanics, however; and that is precisely the point. Were it not, YHWH could be entirely tamed, approached without fear of his glory or respect for his freedom. In other words, as Anderson concludes: "*However much law a priest may master, every approach to the altar constitutes a potential danger.*"[14] This is the message of the surge of fire that incinerates the two mysteriously errant priests. Despite the gift to his people of a theurgic priesthood, the Lord cannot simply be brought under human control. His holiness will blaze forth and become visible at the cost of those who draw near to him in a manner that is not deemed right—as when Uzzah touched the ark and died on the spot (2 Sam. 6:6–8; 2 Chron. 13:9–11).

On this account, the first encounter with priestly sin (which the Priestly author in no way hides) is not of the sort that we will soon see in the prophets. There is no concrete charge or list of crimes, for the issue actually goes much deeper from the priestly perspective. Priestly sin is presented as the occasion for a manifestation of holiness, for guilty victims will be made unwitting witnesses to God's devouring glory. The story in Leviticus 10:1–3 accordingly takes the form of an earnest warning to priests to respect the dangerous holiness of the Lord. This is clearly a repetition, or rather an anticipation of the very same warning that will be made to Korah and his rebellious clan. (It should have been a double forewarning since Elzaphan, who was charged to help carry away the torched corpses of Nadab and Abihu, was himself head of the Kohathites; cf. Lev. 10:4; Num. 3:30.) Naturally, the priests themselves, who are the most concerned after all, are the first to learn the lesson that divine fire threatens *all* who draw near, the chosen priest no less than the unruly Levite. The message of Numbers 16 read in conjunction with Leviticus 10 is thus not that priestly ministers are holier than their fellows but, rather, that *God is infinitely holier than all*—even the priests! The reservation of certain sacred duties exclusively to the chosen priests is a mechanism in God's economy of salvation, meant to impress upon all that service at the altar is anything but mundane. Rudolf Otto famously defined holiness as *mysterium tremendum et fascinans*, a terrifying and alluring mystery. The accent here is solidly on the *tremendum*.

"Through those who are near me I will show myself holy," says the Lord (Lev. 10:3). As at the burning bush and as again at Sinai, *drawing near* is a properly priestly act of boldness that requires the Lord's explicit permission

14. Anderson, "Apophatic Theology," 18 (emphasis original).

(Exod. 20:18–21; 24:1–3; Num. 16:5–10; 17:13). "Even the priests who approach the Lord must consecrate themselves or the Lord will break out against them" (Exod. 19:22). The care required of the priests is burdened with consequences. "The Lord said to Aaron: 'You and your sons and your

Gregory of Nazianzus and John Chrysostom on Christian Priesthood

In the fourth century, both St. Gregory of Nazianzus and St. John Chrysostom spoke of the weighty responsibility of Christian priesthood:

> I am alarmed by the reproaches of the Pharisees, the conviction of the Scribes. For it is disgraceful for us, who ought to greatly surpass them, as we are bidden, if we desire the kingdom of heaven [cf. Matt. 5:20], to be found more deeply sunk in vice: so that we deserve to be called serpents, a generation of vipers, and blind guides, who strain out a gnat and swallow a camel, or sepulchres foul within, in spite of our external comeliness, or platters outwardly clean, and everything else, which they are, or which is laid to their charge [cf. Matt. 23:13ff.].
>
> With these thoughts I am occupied night and day: they waste my marrow, and feed upon my flesh, and will not allow me to be confident or to look up. They depress my soul, and abase my mind, and fetter my tongue, and make me consider, not the position of a prelate, or the guidance and direction of others, which is far beyond my powers; but how I myself am to escape the wrath to come, and to scrape off from myself somewhat of the rust of vice. A man must himself be cleansed, before cleansing others: himself become wise, that he may make others wise; become light, and then give light: draw near to God, and so bring others near; be hallowed, then hallow them; be possessed of hands to lead others by the hand, of wisdom to give advice.[a]

> A man who loses sheep through the ravages of wolves or the attacks of robbers or through murrain or some other accident, might perhaps meet with a measure of pardon from the owner of the flock. Even if he is called upon to pay compensation, the penalty stops at money. But anyone entrusted with men, the rational flock of Christ, risks a penalty not of money but of his own soul for the loss of the sheep.[b]

a. St. Gregory of Nazianzus, *Oration* 2.70–71, trans. Charles Gordon Browne and James Edward Swallow, *Nicene and Post-Nicene Fathers*, Second Series (New York: Christian Literature Company, 1894), 7:219.

b. St. John Chrysostom, *Six Books on the Priesthood* 2.2, trans. Graham Neville (Crestwood, NY: St. Vladimir's Seminary Press, 1984), 54.

ancestral house with you [i.e., meaning here the non-priestly Levites] shall bear responsibility for offenses connected with the sanctuary, while you and your sons alone [i.e., only the priests] shall bear responsibility for offenses connected with the priesthood'" (Num. 18:1). The whole clerical tribe of priests and Levites together is corporately conceived of as a kind of living fence with the specific job of ensuring that only those who are admitted (called) by God draw near. The Levitical job of temple guard is thus anything but unimportant or merely symbolic. They are not so much guarding the sanctuary's treasures from thieves as they are guarding Israel from the reach of God's consuming fire. The clerical vocation is in this sense to be one who stands in the gap, like a living shield. In just this biblical spirit, the Fathers of the Church were keenly aware of the awful truth that their elevation to the priestly office placed them in a mortally dangerous situation—not that the earth would swallow them alive or that they would be incinerated at the altar, but that a unique and deadly judgment awaited them after their service. Priests shall bear the terrible responsibility for offenses against the Lord's honor and against their own holy dignity as his ministers. In a word, playing priest always means playing with fire: the flaming power of God's glory.

Priest as Nazirite

After Nadab and Abihu's death, the Lord speaks directly to Aaron for the first and only time in Leviticus.

> And the LORD spoke to Aaron: Drink no wine or strong drink, neither you nor your sons, when you enter the tent of meeting, that you may not die; it is a statute forever throughout your generations. You are to distinguish between the holy and the common, and between the unclean and the clean; and you are to teach the people of Israel all the statutes that the LORD has spoken to them through Moses. (Lev. 10:8–11)

The Lord's instruction is a conveniently compact summary of priestly duties, the same duties later denounced in their breach by the prophets. Isaiah's charge about wine-bibbing is quite memorable, for instance: "The priest and the prophet reel with strong drink, they are confused with wine, they stagger with strong drink; they err in vision, they stumble in giving judgment. All tables are covered with filthy vomit; no place is clean" (Isa. 28:7–8). In Leviticus, however, we see these commandments being fulfilled rather than transgressed. Most impressively, teaching the people what is clean and unclean—a complaint in prophetic texts that we shall soon see—is here what will promptly transpire in Leviticus 11–15.

Addressing alcoholic drink at this dramatic moment in this dramatic way appears oddly out of place. It has led some to speculate that this must reveal the cause of Nadab and Abihu's death. More likely, the topic is broached here for other reasons. Clearly, it impresses on Aaron the deadly peril not only of exiting the tent (cf. Lev. 10:7) but also of being in the sanctuary (cf. Lev. 16:2, 13)—as if he required more impressing after the sudden death of his sons. But there is also something more. Moses just instructed Aaron, Eleazar, and Ithamar that they were not to mourn Nadab and Abihu in any way. That task was left to the rest of Israel (Lev. 10:6; cf. 21:10–12). This prohibition, coupled with the injunction on strong drink, effectively treats the priests as being temporary Nazirites during the period of their liturgical service (Num. 6:3–4). For just as they must refrain from all strong drink, no Nazirite may touch a corpse, not even of a close relative (Num. 6:6–7), just as here Aaron and his remaining sons were not to remove the bodies of their sons and brothers, but Mishael and Elzaphan were summoned to do the job.

The assimilation of priest to Nazirite is profoundly important. It gestures at the heightened personal holiness demanded of the priest. It thereby also points toward a union of the "charismatic" and the "official" or "institutional," which are so often and so falsely opposed. A perfecting of this union will be central to the priesthood of Jesus Christ. Here a specific regime of physical abstinence is demanded during the time of the priest's service at the altar. This priestly temperance foreshadows, in a dim Old Testament way, the coming charism of priestly celibacy, which also bears a link to periods of liturgical service. In the Eastern Church today, priests must sexually abstain during the periods of their service, for instance, just as the ancient charism of perpetual chastity, as observed in the Latin Church, is, of course, related to the daily offering of the sacrifice of the Mass. In Israel, too, a perpetual liturgical service was to be ensured. At this level, the priesthood as a corporate undertaking is a fully charismatic, Nazirite enterprise. "You shall not go outside the entrance of the tent of meeting, or you will die; for the anointing oil of the LORD is on you" (Lev. 10:7), Moses just said to Aaron. Avoiding the fate of Nadab and Abihu—that is to say, defeating death—means unbroken priestly service within the tent. "Through their uninterrupted service, the remaining priests exemplify the principle that holiness is more powerful than impurity, that life can conquer death" (see excursus 1).[15]

One final, revealing point of contact between the situation of Aaron and the Nazirites appears in Numbers 6:9–10. Should someone die suddenly— let us say by offering strange fire—catching a Nazirite unawares and causing defilement, a specific rite of cleansing is required and prescribed. It would

---

15. Milgrom, *Leviticus: Ritual and Ethics*, 99.

seem that Aaron perceives himself to stand in precisely this sort of situation. This emerges in the puzzling exchange at the end of Leviticus 10 between Moses and Aaron.

To Moses' displeasure, Aaron consciously determined not to eat the sin/ purification offering within the sanctuary as prescribed, but instead he simply burnt it whole (Lev. 10:16–20). What exactly is at issue? Milgrom explains:

> The priest's immunity stands in stark contrast to the sanctuary's vulnerability.
> . . . The sanctuary is polluted by every physical and moral aberration, even
> those inadvertently committed. But within that same sanctuary the priest is
> impervious to impurity. Once he leaves it his immunity is canceled. . . . Impurity
> pollutes the sanctuary, but it does not pollute the priest as long as he serves
> God in the sanctuary.[16]

The sudden death of Nadab and Abihu, accordingly, pollutes the tabernacle itself, though not the ministering priests. Indeed, were the priests themselves not somehow immune in this way from the deadly stains that they must constantly handle and confront, the entire premise of their priestly action would collapse in debilitating and irreparable fragility. It is, in fact, just this character of personal immunity that differentiates the priest-in-the-sanctuary from the simple Nazirite, who is personally defiled by contact with death. There is an image here of a grace of the sacrament, which is a kind of ineffaceable objective holiness—the condition for an *ex opere operato* ritual cult. Moses' apparent suspicion that Aaron was afraid to touch the polluted sin offerings out of concern for his personal protection is resolved to the former's evident satisfaction. There is something displeasing in the sin offering, in Aaron's view, that must still be resolved. The needed cleansing rite, with its two burnt (not eaten) sin offerings, is about to be revealed (Lev. 16:1–34; cf. 16:27).

The Day of Atonement

After the long instruction on clean and unclean in chapters 11–15, Leviticus 16 is introduced as the direct continuation of the account of Nadab and Abihu. "The LORD spoke to Moses after the death of the two sons of Aaron, when they drew near before the LORD and died" (Lev. 16:1). The rite of Yom Kippur, together with the teaching system of ritual purity, is the Lord's answer to what just happened.

The most striking thing in thus appending the Day of Atonement to the story of Nadab and Abihu is perhaps that it prescribes, in the form of a liturgical manual, a specifically *ritual* response to the problem of sin in the sanctuary.

16. Milgrom, *Leviticus: Ritual and Ethics*, 99.

If the story in Leviticus 10:1–3 is indeed what it appears, however—an apo-phatic warning that priestly ritual has its mysterious limits—the legislation of Yom Kippur, for its part, cannot be what it might otherwise appear: some ultimate liturgical mechanism that will finally bring God's wild holiness under control. This is not one last ceremony to master so as finally to master God. Indeed, the repeated warnings of the deadly character of this most dangerous of all dangerous rites helps keep the example of Nadab and Abihu front and center (Lev. 16:2, 13). For the sake of the nation, the high priest must be ready to risk his life and enter the holy of holies, to face with confidence the divine glory that abides there, surging in a state of violent combustion, agitated by the defiling pollution that has reached it.

After he has completed the rites of atonement, the high priest strips and washes (Lev. 16:23–28). He does this not because he has contracted pollution, for he is immune. On the contrary, it is to wash off the "superholiness" that he has acquired. This is why his supercharged linen garments are left within the sanctuary and not brought outside (16:23). The divesting and bath of the high priest thus function like the veil of Moses (Exod. 34:33–35). There is, nevertheless, a visible increase, not a muting, of his glory in the ritual movement: indeed, one perceives a strong christological typology of humility, "death," and glorification. In Leviticus 16:4, the high priest undertakes his deadly task clothed not in the splendid garments of his full office but in the humbler, white garb common to all the priests. When he emerges, however, he leaves this humble vesture behind and dons his full high priestly regalia. In this way, his ministry on Yom Kippur carries the character of a sort of second ordination, while also being a prophecy of the glorification of the One who humbled himself unto death (Phil. 2:6–11). We will later see this image of the high priest emerging on Yom Kippur, clad in his magnificent vestments, as a biblical high point in the vision of "the sons of Aaron in their splendor" (Sir. 50:13). The moment is, like the acceptable sacrifice itself, another sort of outright theophany.

If the purgative power of Yom Kippur eliminates both the moral pollu-tion (e.g., the sin of disobedience) and the ritual defilement (e.g., through contact with a corpse) that marred the sanctuary in the episode in Leviticus 10:1–3, this is the ultimate priestly triumph. It is the sole means for cleansing the most sensitive of all spots in the land of the most soiling of all Israel's stains: intentional sin. Nevertheless, Yom Kippur in its Old Testament (and ongoing rabbinic) form is celebrated as a day not of victory but of penance and confession. This contrasts with what scholars detect as an earlier, much more joyful New Year's festival, which was eventually submerged beneath an emergency ritual of atonement that came to predominate. The joyful character of this earlier feast is preserved in the proclamation of the Jubilee, the holy year in which all debts are forgiven, bondmen freed, and the land returned to its original owners.[17] This great, liberating event was ordained to happen on Yom Kippur—that is, on the final, tenth day of the New Year's festival (Lev. 25:9). In the definitive work of atonement made by the Church's glorified and heavenly high priest, this ancient, more monarchically oriented expression of amnesty, which belongs originally to an early (eighth century BC?) provenance, before the postexilic period, will reemerge with new moral connotations and take on immense importance, as we shall observe.

Conclusion

The law was given on account of transgressions, St. Paul teaches (Rom. 5:20; Gal. 3:19). In Leviticus we see this apostolic teaching directly confirmed. Law is added to law precisely to address the complicating problem of sin. The Day of Atonement is added on account of the primal priestly transgression of Nadab and Abihu, to be a sort of new law within the law. Similar examples of sin narratives triggering New Torah legislation might be easily added. In Numbers 18, for instance, the Lord adds a great deal of instruction about the priests and Levites, enumerating their various responsibilities and emoluments, in direct response to Korah's rebellion. In Exodus the very election of the Levitical tribe for clerical honor is presented as God's response to their own response to the sin of the golden calf. "Today you have ordained yourselves" (Exod. 32:29; cf. Num. 25:10).

An interior narrative dynamic of human sin and YHWH's statutory response thus helps drive the internal formation of the variegated legal corpus comprising the five books of Moses. Of course, the snowballing accumulation of cultic law is one of the grounding facts of modern pentateuchal study: a Holiness Code atop a P source atop a Covenant (E) Code, and so on. Historically and sociologically, the steady rise of the Aaronic priesthood in the postexilic era was deeply entangled in this swelling work of codification, which was largely the concrete effort of a priestly class to legislate its way through a great moral crisis. The rise of the sacerdotal estate in Israel, that is to say, was bound up very closely with the acute sense of national sin brought on by the exile. It was not only a response to the postmonarchical power vacuum, as a reductionist postmodern power heuristic often imagines. Within this sociohistorical and religious framework, *Aaron's priesthood, as Leviticus presents it, is solidly ordered to the eradication of sin, in full service to the manifestation of God's glory*. Yet this priestly work is itself crippled by

17. See Jacob Milgrom, *Leviticus 23–27*, AB 3B (New York: Doubleday, 2001), 2242–43, 2257–70.

a priestly sin that it cannot eradicate or even quite fathom. By God's intervention, however, a triumphant new sacrifice, a sort of "second ordination," is
introduced that enables a newly purified cult to reassert its renewed and now
greater atoning power and service of divine glory. Typologically, this is the
pattern of the entire biblical story of the priesthood.

SUMMARY OF KEY POINTS

1. The P traditions in the Pentateuch are a much maligned and neglected
   but indispensable deposit of scriptural teaching on the priesthood.
   Without a clear recognition of the theological centrality of Leviticus
   to the whole biblical vision, no balanced canonical appreciation of the
   priesthood will be possible.

2. One of the most significant passages for understanding Leviticus's vision is the narrative sequence found in Leviticus 8–10, which recounts
   the first priestly ordination, the inauguration of Israel's sacrificial cult,
   and the "original" priestly sin. In its wider narrative and redactional
   context, this series of events appears as a genuine climax to the revelation made at Sinai and as a sort of Old Testament "new creation." The
   priesthood is here displayed as having a theophanic purpose—ordered
   to the manifestation of divine glory—while also remaining incomplete
   and stretched prophetically toward an unfulfilled future of still greater
   glory: a more magnificent and permanent temple regime.

3. Five distinct elements comprise the ordination rites, each holding a
   highly expressive symbolic and typological meaning: (1) the *ordinandi*
   themselves are handled as a kind of living sacrifice; (2) the vestments
   are presented as an official ritual space, intimately joined to the tabernacle and greater than any individual officeholder; (3) the oil of
   anointing overtly makes the priest into a "Christ" and links him to
   the specific holiness of the altar; (4) the blood of the bull and rams
   powerfully fuses together the priest and the sacrificial work of the altar;
   (5) the bread offerings recapitulate the acts of the cult with strong
   eucharistic overtones. In the final action of the ordination prior to the
   communion meal, the literal "filling of the hands," it is made clear
   that, in order to empower the priest to become a sacrificial agent, an
   element entirely belonging to God must be offered "as though" it were
   the priest's own—that is, it must ritually be made the priest's own, so
   that he may hand it back over to God, along with what is more truly
   his own.

4. The divine work of creating a priesthood can be accomplished only through the agency of a kind of super-priestly minister. Moses accomplishes this role in conformity to a common ancient Near Eastern royal ideology, by which it belongs to the king to found, on behalf of the god, both the temple and its ministering priesthood.

5. The Church (*ekklēsia*) is in a real way constituted in its corporate identity in connection with the creation of the priesthood-*cum*-cult. This is not done, however, in such a way as to transfer to the congregation an authority equal to or over the priests, as P's story of Korah's rebellion means to teach.

6. The creation of Israel's priesthood coincides directly with the exposure of its immediate and very visible sinful failure. The decision of P not to specify the precise character of the "original sin" of the priests leaves this moral space appropriately capacious. This sin is ultimately meant, however, like the priesthood itself, to reveal the supreme, even savage holiness of God, which overawes every ministerial aspiration to execute a liturgical service. It is not in the first place about the priests' moral status, still less about their legitimacy in exercising their office. The personal holiness of the priest is modeled, rather, in this connection, upon the figure of the Nazirite: a parallel suggestive of the private "charismatic" dimension inhering in the priest's official, public role.

7. The dangerous pollution of the cult contracted through the crime of priestly sin does not have the character of inhibiting priestly action in the sanctuary as such; yet it requires from God the giving of a "New Law" centered upon a new and definitive cleansing, effected through a great sacrifice of atonement.

EXCURSUS 1

Purity and Holiness

"Leviticus is perhaps the Biblical book most remote from modern experience."[1] The best measure of this distance from the modern world is the intricate, not to say bewildering, arcana of the book's purity system, frequently regarded as little more than an aggregate of primitive taboos. More positive estimates are both possible and justified, however.

Social scientists today widely recognize that taboos are not limited to so-called primitive cultures and are not, as a characteristically modern prejudice would have it, the purely negative residue or recrudescence of ignorant superstition. The influential anthropologist and cultural theorist Mary Douglas, for instance, in her enduring classic *Purity and Danger*, worked to show how purity taboos have little in common with fear-driven behaviors and actually serve a vigorously positive purpose in "the central project of religion."[2] Purity taboos are at once instrumental and expressive, functioning creatively as registers of order and as mechanisms of boundary maintenance, while also providing a moral matrix of atonement. At root, the demarcation of pure and impure symbolically articulates a society's recognized zones of danger and thus the landscape of "salvation."

Regarding the Levitical system as the product of one such society, Jacob Milgrom has advanced a positive and highly intelligible, though also controversial, view of biblical purity legislation. For him, this whole code is a

1. Marcel Poorthuis and Joshua Schwartz, "Introduction," in *Purity and Holiness: The Heritage of Leviticus*, ed. Marcel Poorthuis and Joshua Schwartz, Jewish and Christian Perspectives 2 (Leiden: Brill, 2000), 5.

2. Mary Douglas, *Purity and Danger: An Analysis of Concepts of Pollution and Taboo* (New York: Routledge, 2002), 3. The original edition was published in 1966.

coherent symbolic system representing the primordial conflict between the forces of life and death. The great preoccupation with bodily fluids such as semen and menstrual blood, for instance, is explicable by these fluids' constitutive role in the process of passing on life. Their loss thus signals the onset of death and must be carefully controlled as part of the great cosmic struggle. Corpse impurity and other examples fit within the same framework.

Mors et vita duello: death and life are at war. The foundational conflict between the forces of life and death does not leave humanity simply helpless and captive. God intervenes by his law, and the priestly rites of purification work actively in favor of life.

	desecrate, desanctify			*pollute*	
HOLY	⟹	**PURE/COMMON**	⟹		**IMPURE**
qādôš	*ḥillēl, hiqdîš*	*ṭāhôr/ḥōl*		*ṭimmē'*	*ṭāmē'*

	purify			*sanctify*	
IMPURE	⟹	**PURE/COMMON**	⟹		**HOLY**
ṭāmē'	*ṭihar*	*ṭāhôr/ḥōl*		*qiddeš*	*qādôš*
	(ablution, sacrifice)			*(anointment, commandment)*	

Purity itself is actually inert in this system. Like the "common" (the opposite of the "holy"), purity is not contagious. It is the normative state of rest for persons and objects. Holiness and impurity, by contrast, are dynamic and mutually antagonistic states. As such, they are motive energies that evoke directly the battling domains of life and of death. The border between them, like the line of scrimmage in football, is constantly shifting back and forth.

Holiness (*qdš*) is a force that lays claims to a defined group of objects and persons, called *qodāšîm*, which are appropriated and thought of as the personal property of YHWH. The high priest himself, as we have seen, marked out as "Holy to the LORD," bears the divine stamp and belongs, like the tabernacle vessels (God's liturgical set of china), to the vast livery of the Lord. While the process of "sanctification" can be ritually channeled through actions like anointing with oil or even contracted inadvertently by proximity or touch, the ultimate origin of all sanctification is the singular, active holiness of God.[3] It is a dynamic radiation, an effusion of divine energy. Yet unlike similar emanations present in pagan religions, it inheres in no natural forces or objects. Rather, it originates and flows exclusively from the living presence of YHWH.

3. See Baruch J. Schwartz, "Israel's Holiness: The Torah Traditions," in Poorthuis and Schwartz, *Purity and Holiness*, 54.

In the so-called Holiness Code (Lev. 17–26), which represents a certain development within the priestly tradition, a significant new note is added to this quasi-magical dynamism. An ethical obligation on Israel's part becomes prominent as part of the active mechanics: "You shall be holy, for I the LORD your God am holy" (Lev. 19:2). Israel must act in accordance with the Lord's commands in order to somehow "absorb" the radiance of YHWH's holiness. It is as if God were transmitting a radio signal and they must tune in through their behavior.[4]

Impurity is, to prolong the metaphor, a kind of threatening, disruptive static. As a cosmically malign and volatile force, even a physical substance and aerial miasma, it is nevertheless not a living demonic power, it is important to say. This "demythologization" in the biblical picture, in fact, represents a major contrast with the surrounding ancient Near Eastern worldview, at least in Milgrom's view.[5] Impurity, nevertheless, remains in both systems—for Israel as for its neighbors—the axiomatic "implacable foe of holiness wherever it exists; it assaults the sacred realm even from afar."[6]

One of the key armaments in the highly specialized priestly arsenal for beating back and controlling the spread of malefic impurity is the ḥaṭṭāʾt sacrifice, which Milgrom argues should be translated as a "purification of-fering" (rather than as the conventional "sin offering"). This captures the offering's wide significance, which undoes bodily impurities and not only sins. The translation also hints at a standing confusion among scholars, however, both ancient and modern, about where exactly the lines between purity and morality lie.[7] It is an issue that Jesus himself will also address. At the base of the confusion lies, very simply, the Hebrew Bible's use of an overlapping lexicon of defilement to describe both physical/ritual and moral states (cf. Lev. 15:19–24 and 18:24–30). Milgrom's translation, for its part, resonates with a wider trend of scholarly overstatements inclined to reduce all impurity to a ritual matter.

This situation is hinted at in Milgrom's response to the question "Whom or what does the ḥaṭṭāʾt actually purge?" His answer, surprisingly, is the sanctu-ary and its sancta, *not* the offender. Molech worship, discharges of fluid, and corpse impurities are all forbidden, for instance, because they contaminate

---

4. Schwartz, "Israel's Holiness," 57.

5. On the dangers of such value-laden, Israel-pagan comparisons, particularly in Milgrom's work, see Frank H. Gorman, "Pagans and Priests: Critical Reflections on Method," in *Perspectives on Purity and Purification in the Bible*, ed. Naphtali S. Meshel, Jeffrey Stackert, David P. Wright, and Baruch J. Schwartz, LHBOTS 474 (New York: T&T Clark, 2008), 96–110.

6. Jacob Milgrom, "Israel's Sanctuary: The Priestly 'Picture of Dorian Gray,'" *RB* 83 (1976): 393.

7. See, e.g., Jonathan Klawans, *Impurity and Sin in Ancient Judaism* (Oxford: Oxford University Press, 2000).

YHWH's dwelling (cf. Lev. 15:31; 20:3; Num. 19:20). Milgrom rightly sees here that different degrees of misdemeanor somehow penetrate and mar the holy space itself in progressive degrees. The blood of the *ḥaṭṭā't* sacrifice, correspondingly, acts as the "ritual detergent," holding the power to reverse these unwelcome encroachments and stains. Thus, individual inadvertencies reach to the external altar in the forecourt, which they stain and where they must be ritually washed away with blood and so undone (Lev. 4:25, 30; 9:9). Communal inadvertencies push still deeper into the shrine itself, touching the inner altar, where they must likewise be expunged (Lev. 4:5–7, 16–18). Wanton sins, finally, penetrate all the way into the holy of holies, which they defile until the space be washed by the solemn ritual and blood sprinkling of Yom Kippur.

The stepwise advance of polluting impurity, trespassing across the successively graded degrees of divine holiness marked out in the space of the temple, and reaching all the way up to wanton sin and the holy of holies, reveals the specific danger of the system. Israel's impurity might mount so high and reach so far that God's intimate dwelling itself is overrun. Then YHWH in his untouchable holiness can no longer abide in Israel's midst. Milgrom compared the sanctuary in this scenario to the famous *The Picture of Dorian Gray*.

> On the analogy of Oscar Wilde's novel, the priestly writers would claim: sin may not leave its mark on the face of the sinner, but it is certain to mark the face of the sanctuary, and unless it is quickly expunged, God's presence will depart.[8]

This temple-based orientation captures something very important. Still, it also obscures the clear fact that in Leviticus 16:30–33 (cf. 16:19) atonement and cleansing are applied *both* to the sanctuary and to the people. The face of the sinner is, in fact, also marked and must be ritually cleansed and so forgiven. The temple does, all the same, still truly function as the unique *corporate* barometer of Israel's national well-being. Here Milgrom is quite right.

As a measure of corporate standing, the temple is inevitably an ambiguous site of cosmic conflict and flux. On the one hand, it represents an intense locus of holiness, flowing outward like a great solar wind from within the holy of holies, pushing out into the encircling courts and even out into the land beyond, carrying the powerful energy that makes it holy. On the other hand, the sanctuary is a giant moral magnet that attracts all the land's contagion, a defilement that might accumulate and reach such a mass that it will make the system implode like a collapsed star, driving YHWH from its midst—or, rather, compelling him freely to take his leave from sheer disgust at the inordinate pollution.

---

8. Milgrom, "Israel's Sanctuary," 398.

God is not the only one who might grow disgusted. The Qumran community, notably, in a kind of corporate prophetic gesture, decided to enact this divine abandonment of the polluted temple, reckoning it a site of untouchable, foul corruption. From the perspective of the priestly establishment, on the other hand, such an abandonment of the temple would be an unthinkable abdication, consigning not merely the temple but also the land and the people to malign powers. Like the captain of a ship, the priest must stay at the helm even through the most tempestuous storms of corruption. He alone, through his know-how in navigating the ritual system, can steer the people back into calm waters, above all by the propitiation of Yom Kippur. In the sacred geography of the Priestly school there is a single center, a sole landmark of absolute holiness: the temple, which, annually renewed on the Day of Atonement (when Dorian Gray's account returns to zero), abides as a divine oasis, a cosmic garden that hosts YHWH's presence in Israel's midst. The desert, elected by the Essenes at Qumran, is no possible surrogate for the temple but, rather, the dangerous anti-cosmos that stands against it: the formless wilderness into which the goat for Azazel is sent (Lev. 16:10).

It is not hard to see in these violent mortal oppositions how Priestly theology, however unattractive or inaccessible its Levitical ritual wrapping, ultimately participates in the stirring mythological plot of the *Chaoskampf*: the primordial battle of divine order against raging chaos. This affinity should occasion little surprise. The chaos myth is foundational cult theology, vitally concerned with affirming the temple at the very base and center of ancient Near Eastern life and thought. In its briefest form, a god elects a king as his terrestrial agent, a regent whose task is precisely to fight back and tame the tides of cosmic evil and disorder. This king must plant prosperity and peace by establishing his throne and then ultimately by building a temple-*cum*-priesthood, in order to be a home in which the divinity can dwell and be served and exercise his benign and powerful coregency over the realm.

The Priestly overture to the Pentateuch in Genesis 1:1–2:3 is profoundly marked by this myth at once cosmogonic and cultic. In this connection, it is important, first of all, to see that the Priestly creation story, like the priestly cult itself, is not about the final banishment of chaos and evil. It concerns, instead, evil's control—the taming of the churning ocean, which remains a standing threat to be managed and contained. The primordial waters are indeed confined above the sky and in the seas, but they do not disappear. It is like a cosmos-sized junk drawer in perpetual danger of spilling over (e.g., the flood). The poetry of Job 38 captures the scene.

> Or who shut in the sea with doors
>   when it burst out from the womb? . . .

and prescribed bounds for it,
    and set bars and doors,
and said, "Thus far shall you come, and no farther,
    and here shall your proud waves be stopped"? (Job 38:8, 10–11)

Darkness, too, is gathered into one place, called "Night," but not decisively destroyed. The primacy of evening over morning even hints at the primordial character of the chaotic darkness, which constantly floods back and darkens the day. Jon Levenson has helpfully drawn attention in this context to a "false finality" too often attributed to God's work of creation and his status as creator, which is actually a fragile and threatened state of affairs in the Hebrew Bible.[9] The invitation for an eschatological response to this standing fragility should be quite clear. Viewed through the lens of the cultic-cosmogonic theology of the Priestly vision, the Letter to the Hebrews is exactly in tune when it speaks of an Old Testament ritual system forced to offer sacrifices "day after day," without ever accomplishing a final victory over evil (Heb. 7:27).

And yet the Lord is not as helpless as King Canute against the tide, and even the Hebrew Bible encourages a supreme confidence in the final efficacy of the cult. Indeed, no small part of this impression of absolute finality, which Levenson problematizes, comes from Genesis itself, specifically in its P version. The Priestly authors provide a powerful, counter-Babylonian creation account in which, despite clear traces of the old story, the starry heavens and the earth below are made at YHWH's simple word of command—not by a bloody battle against formidable foes, like the gory conflict of Marduk and Tiamat. The mismatched sides and priestly resonance of the biblical narrative of creation are quite clear.

> It describes a process of separation and distinction making in which the dark, ungodly forces are effortlessly overcome by placement in a structure in which they are bounded by new realities created by divine speech alone. This new structure is essentially cultic in character. Its construction is highly reminiscent of the rites of temple building, and even the seven-day sequence shows a probable affinity with the old autumnal and vernal New Year's festivals. More important, in building the new structure that is creation, God functions like an Israelite priest, making distinctions, assigning things to their proper category and assessing their fitness, and hallowing the Sabbath.[10]

"God functions like an Israelite priest." The designation and blessing of the sabbath—like a priest marking out the exact moment when it begins—is

---

9. Jon D. Levenson, *Creation and the Persistence of Evil: The Jewish Drama of Divine Omnipotence* (San Francisco: HarperCollins, 1988).

10. Levenson, *Creation and the Persistence of Evil*, 127.

particularly prophetic, for in Genesis no mention of night ever casts its shadow over this seventh day.

Just as the terrestrial monarch in the ancient Near East embodies the victory over chaos accomplished in union with his tutelary god, so the celestial priest has his priestly incarnations on earth. Thus, not unlike her kings, Israel's hieratic class is engaged in a continual cooperation with and participation in God's own cosmic/cultic work of creation, in whose performative, ordering action they have a principal share. This work is ongoing; yet certain victory is already promised in the power of God's uncontested creative word. An illuminating forecast of the New Covenant priesthood becomes visible in this divine-human cooperation. The priests of the new dispensation will operate in this same sort of intimate union with God's own priestly action, as sharers in the priesthood of the *Logos* incarnate, coworkers with him in his ongoing work of remaking the cosmos a new creation. Christ's priests are agents of God's final victory of life over death, heralding the dawn of the eternal Sabbath.

EXCURSUS 2

Levi, Levites, and the Priesthood

Aaron's election as high priest by God appears as a simple-enough family affair. Such apparent simplicity covers a very tangled reality, however. The constantly developing complexity of Israel's cult, which passed through multiple periods of extraordinary historical change and disruption, inevitably raised questions about the transmission of the priestly office and the apportioning of specialized ministries. The story of the rebellion of Korah in Numbers 16 hints at the intense conflicts that might arise between the Levites and the priests—or, to be more specific, between two closely related Levitical clans, both Kohathites, namely, the Amramites and the Izharites (cf. Exod. 6:14–26; Num. 3:14–38)—about who exactly did what. If the answer given in Numbers is blazingly clear—God has chosen Aaron and his sons alone to perform priestly sacrifice—alternative claims, at times antedating the postexilic priestly establishment behind this text in Numbers, were not so easily resolved (see excursus 4). In any case, the ideal of strict Aaronic descent did not later stop nonconforming claimants from taking the office. The mess and crisis of legitimacy that arose will be taken up in excursus 3. The point here is rather to consider briefly the origins and differentiation of the Levites and priests.

Classically, which is to say since Julius Wellhausen in the late nineteenth century, biblical scholars have explained this complicated history of priests and Levites in conjunction with the centralization of worship, an ideal and event closely associated with the book of Deuteronomy and the religious reforms of King Josiah in the late seventh century BC. For Wellhausen, the Priestly source represents the mature result of this movement of cultic reform. Ezekiel 44:6–16 is a turning point for the clear distinction it introduces between the Zadokites, literally the "sons of Zadok" (i.e., the first high priest to officiate in Solomon's temple and, according to 1 Chron. 6:49–53, tenth in line from Aaron), who are reckoned as "Levitical priests" and have charge of the sanctuary and higher sacrifices, and the *mere* Levites, who are demoted to minor clergy with guard duties and ministry among the laity. Prior to all this, in the circumstance of decentralized worship plainly reflected in the earlier JE traditions, Levites were not imagined as second-class cultic personnel. They were simply the non-Jerusalemite priests who served in the many regional sanctuaries throughout the territories of Israel and Judah.

Today, while Wellhausen's work remains the inevitable point of departure, disagreement exists concerning what might be solidly reconstructed about the early history of the Levites, especially on the basis of texts such as Judges 17–18 and Deuteronomy 33:8–11, traditions that are quite difficult to evaluate with historical confidence. Skepticism about the character and reach of Josiah's reform has also complicated the picture. One key crux is the relation of the "Levitical priests" (e.g., Deut. 17:9, 18; 18:1; 24:8; 27:9) to the "Levites at your gates" (e.g., Deut. 12:12; 14:27; 18:6; 26:13).[1] Arguably, these poor "Levites at your gates" are ultimately themselves displaced, disenfranchised local priests who lost their sanctuaries for any number of reasons, and not only because of an organized, royal reform of the cult: on account of Sennacherib's invasion of the south or the destruction of the Northern Kingdom, for example. Some such patchwork trajectory toward cult centralization need not exclude later, more aristocratically engineered movements, of course. The open recruitment of Levites as temple servants in Ezra 8:16–20, for instance, suggests a very different context for the incorporation of this class of para-priestly actors than a national crisis like an invasion. The Chronicler, who assimilates all non-priestly temple personnel to the group of Levites, gives poignant expression to the established two-class cultic system.

The book of Leviticus itself, ironically enough, makes nearly no mention at all of Levites, referring to their special property rights only in passing (Lev. 25:32–33). In Numbers and Deuteronomy, by contrast, the Levites are very present and active. Although the image of the Levites in these two books is quite different, reflecting divergent Priestly (P) and deuteronomic (D/Dtr) perspectives, Deuteronomy's picture of a primitive pan-Levitical priesthood (e.g., Deut. 18:1–8; cf. Jer. 33:19–22) is not, in fact, entirely detached from an Aaronic point of reference. In Deuteronomy 10:6–9, the election of the tribe for priestly service seems to follow as an implicit consequence of Aaron's death, while in Deuteronomy 33:8–10, on the model of Jacob's blessing of his sons

---

1. See Peter Altmann, "What Do the 'Levites in Your Gates' Have to Do with the 'Levitical Priests'? An Attempt at European–North American Dialogue on the Levites in the Deuteronomic Law Corpus," in *Levites and Priests in Biblical History and Tradition*, ed. Mark Leuchter and Jeremy M. Hutton, AIL 9 (Atlanta: Society of Biblical Literature, 2011), 135–54.

in Genesis 49 (where no mention of Levi's priestly service is made), Moses accords the Levites the Urim and Thummim—that is, priestly status—invoking Levi's loyalty and fidelity to the covenant. This fidelity—which includes the statement that Levi "ignored his kin" (Deut. 33:9)—evidently alludes to the celebrated story in Exodus 32:25–29, when the Levites zealously rally to the Lord and put a violent end to the worship of the golden calf, attaining priestly status in return: "Today you have ordained yourselves for the service of the LORD, each one at the cost of a son or a brother" (Exod. 32:29). While this text is often taken as an anti-Aaronide, pro-Levite polemic, a reading more sympathetic to Aaron can also be defended (see chap. 3 below). The story of Phinehas in Numbers 25 deserves special attention in this connection, for it returns to this motif of gaining priestly status—"my covenant of peace" and a "perpetual priesthood," God says (Num. 25:12–13)—as a specific reward for violent zeal, this time in response to the apostasy of Baal-peor. The story is at the very least a redemption of Aaron's line, if not a retroactive statement that all the Levitical clans, Aaron's included, were involved in Exodus 32. It carefully fuses, in any event, the Exodus etiology of priestly dignity by zeal with a principle of priestly office by pedigree, for Phinehas is already the high priestly heir, as son of Eleazar the son of Aaron. A similar double sanction of holy zeal and physical descent thus accredits both the high priestly line of succession (cf. Exod. 6:16–25) and the wider priestly office held by the whole Levitical tribe.

Ancient Jewish interpreters characteristically concentrated as much upon Levi as upon prominent figures like Phinehas. This focus appears to have been prompted in part by Malachi 2:4–7, which can be read to suggest that God made a personal covenant directly with the patriarch Levi himself (not waiting until Phinehas's show of valor), perhaps via some heavenly ecstasy. Three Second Temple texts—*Jubilees*, the *Testament of Levi*, and the *Aramaic Levi Document*—all record multiple versions of YHWH's choice of Levi as a priest (a textbook case of Second Temple exegetical "overkill").[2] One imaginative version thus recounts an apocalypse or dream/vision in which the sacerdotal office is supernaturally promised to or conferred upon Levi (*Jub.* 32:1; *Test. Levi*; *ALD*). Another tradition mirrors what the Pentateuch already applied to Phinehas and the unnamed Levites in Exodus 32—namely, Levi's violent zeal against the Shechemites was the cause for his priestly elevation (*Jub.* 30:18). The difficulty with this explanation is that Simeon was equally violently zealous. The clever notion of Levi as a "human tithe" helped to

2. On the development of this superfluous multiplicity of Levi traditions, see James Kugel, "Levi's Elevation to the Priesthood in Second Temple Writings," *HTR* 86 (1993): 1–64. See also Robert Kugler, *From Patriarch to Priest: The Levi-Priestly Tradition from "Aramaic Levi" to "Testament of Levi,"* EJL 9 (Atlanta: Scholars Press, 1996).

solve this problem. Jacob, having promised in Genesis 28:22 to offer a tithe of everything that was his, counted his twelve sons, starting backward with Benjamin, and arrived at Levi as the tenth, whom he accordingly consecrated to God as a priest (*Jub.* 32:3; *ALD*; cf. *Tg. Ps.-J.* on Gen. 32:25; *Pirqe R. El.* 37). This seemingly random mode of selection in effect makes the priesthood a fall of the lot—which appropriately keeps the matter in the Lord's hand as a gift. The final and perhaps most interesting tradition is that Levi belonged to a chain of priests reaching all the way back to Adam. In this view, the priestly state was communicated to Levi in a special act of transmission from his grandfather, Isaac, Jacob himself not being a priest (*Jub.* 31:14–16; *Test. Levi* 9:7). *Jubilees* is, in a very particular way, committed to presenting the whole history of the patriarchal age in this manner as a continuous line of priests offering lawful sacrifice since the dawn of creation.

The Bible's many scattered historical memories, along with these later spin-off exegetical fantasies of a priesthood *before* the (Aaronic) priesthood, together constitute a substantial, rich, and very important theological testimony that priestly action and status is something more ancient and deeper than the Mosaic law. For *Jubilees*, of course, creation itself is somehow fully subordinate to the Mosaic-Aaronic order. Adam, Noah, Abraham, and Isaac, all depicted in various ways in the Bible as performing priestly duties, dutifully followed the ritual prescriptions of Leviticus in *Jubilees*' presentation. This theological romance, though the product of a truly brilliant exegetical mind, must be classed with other forms of postexilic erasure of pre-Mosaic difference, however.

For various reasons the Christian vision instinctively discerns resemblances linking priestly existence *before* and *after* Moses, which is to say, in the matter of priests, it often sees a kind of "Mosaic parenthesis" (even if Aaron, in a different context, also presents a potent typological pattern for the true high priest, who supersedes the imperfect priestly order that precedes him; see, e.g., excursus 4). This innate sympathy for pre-Mosaic, regional priestly activity notably includes a very special interest in Melchizedek's royal priesthood. Early Christians also easily identified with the Levites as such. One reason was their landless status, for the Christian people were not a landed ethnos but a universal, priestly people. Another reason was the association of the Levites, as temple singers, with the spiritual sacrifice of praise, a form of worship that outlived the Aaronic dispensation.

Ultimately, however, like the Bible itself in its later and canonical strata, Christians discerned a harmonious coexistence of priests and Levites in a single, multimembered worshiping whole. Indeed, Christians accepted the full hierarchical arrangement as God's ongoing, well-ordered *taxis*—whatever messy historical processes of displaced persons and swollen aristocratic

pretentions might have painfully brought it about. A hugely revealing text
from *1 Clement* communicates this perspective.

> For to the high priest the proper services [*leitourgiai*] have been given, and to
> the priests the proper office has been assigned, and upon the Levites the proper
> ministries [*diakoniai*] have been imposed. The layman is bound by the layman's
> rules. Let each of you, brothers, give thanks to God [*eucharisteitō*] with your
> own group, maintaining a good conscience, not overstepping the designated
> rule of his ministry, but acting with reverence. (*1 Clem.* 40.5–41.1)[3]

The uncomplicated adoption of Israel's neatly ranked hierarchy as a correct
description of the Church's own internal liturgical order is enormously suggestive.[4] Primitive Christians like Clement exercised an easy deference to the
Old Testament regime when the New Testament neither provided an alternative nor abrogated the old model. Three grades of minister—high priest,
priest, and Levite—plus the laity, transferred directly from ancient Israel to
the Church.

3. Michael W. Holmes, ed. and trans., *The Apostolic Fathers: Greek Texts and English Translations*, 3rd ed. (Grand Rapids: Baker Academic, 2007), 99.

4. See the important study of Bryan A. Stewart, *Priests of My People: Levitical Paradigms for Early Christian Ministers*, Patristic Studies 11 (New York: Peter Lang, 2015). Stewart dem-onstrates how the early Church developed the language of Christian ministry under pressure from Old Testament texts, read typologically, leading to a conceptualization of Christian ser-vice in Levitical terms.

3

"Like People, like Priest" (Hosea 4:9)

Priestly Sin and the Prophetic Critique

The most substantial block of negative scriptural views on the priesthood appears in the prophetic corpus. The prophetic books in the Bible are obviously a highly diversified group of texts and traditions, and the canonical collection ranges across many centuries and different historical contexts. The challenges of engaging such materials responsibly are accordingly quite real, but also very different from the obstacles facing a theological encounter with the Priestly traditions. The clear moral immediacy of the prophets lends them an obvious accessibility and power, and it is no surprise that these often highly quotable poetic texts have played a very prominent, often excessive role in shaping biblical views of the priesthood, especially from the Reformation viewpoint.

A balanced and fully canonical Christian hermeneutic must naturally strive to give full voice to this inner-biblical tradition, without amplifying it unduly or being insensitive to the wider context. Alongside the negative critiques, positive prophecies about the priesthood also play an indispensably important role, for instance (see chap. 4). The cultic life of Israel, so powerfully attested in the Torah, represents a social reality and a theological orientation that must be allowed to stand on equal footing with its challenge in the open attacks of the prophets. This invites an important comment, however. Given the fact, long accepted by scholars, that the prophets by and large actually antedate the Pentateuch, it is not surprising if they present a world in which priestly reality looks very different from the highly established and overwhelmingly (but not uniformly) positive picture in the Torah. From a certain perspective it is therefore not, in fact, the prophetic corpus that is responding to the Priestly tradition in Bible, but the reverse. Indeed, we have just seen in the last chapter how Leviticus is quite conscious of the problem of priestly sin. Whether P is given the first or the last word on this problem is a matter of perspective, and the option was taken here to follow the rhetorical solution adopted by the canon. It is important, and consistent with this option, now to air the prophetic critique, expanded and on its own terms, for it brings new force to the issue and will be a key point of reference for Jesus' own ministry and his approach to religious leaders. What is more, the central thrust lies not where it is normally imagined.

The Antagonism Hypothesis

Ancient Israel's prophetic tradition is widely seen as concerned with ethical behavior more than cultic practice. This interest in the ethical goes so far that a violent opposition arises between the two domains, to the full disadvantage of cultic life. A text like Amos 5:21–24 impressively illustrates the intense opposition:

> I hate, I despise your festivals,
>   and I take no delight in your solemn assemblies.
> Even though you offer me your burnt offerings and grain offerings,
>   I will not accept them;
> and the offerings of well-being of your fatted animals
>   I will not look upon.
> Take away from me the noise of your songs;
>   I will not listen to the melody of your harps.
> But let justice roll down like waters,
>   and righteousness like an ever-flowing stream.

As custodians of Israel's cult, the priestly class is obviously implicated in such impassioned pronouncements. A deeply entrenched scholarly consensus has thus long held that a systematic antagonism exists between Israel's morally oriented prophetic voices and her ministering priests, lost in the punctilious performance of their ritual minutiae. This view is so strong that even the plain phenomenon of priests who happened also to be prophets somehow fails to challenge the prevailing account. The ultimate collection, redaction, and canonization of prophetic texts specifically by Priestly circles also somehow fails to register as a foundational objection.

It is only very recently that Old Testament scholars have posed the self-critical question "How, when, and why did the prevailing view of prophet versus priest antagonism—hereafter, the 'antagonism hypothesis'—emerge?"[1] The answer has not been difficult to find. Ziony Zevit points to the "legacy of sixteenth and seventeenth century Reformation thinking that was fascinated with the freedom of the 'word' over against the 'law,'" together with theological judgments bound to "an idealized picture commensurate with what might be acceptable to a nineteenth century Protestant."[2] Broader Enlightenment suspicion of superstitious "priestcraft" in contrast to simple "natural religion" certainly added to the situation. A dubious "psychology of religion" as it developed at the end of the nineteenth century and beginning of the twentieth also contributed to the hardening of the priest-prophet distinction.[3]

The weight of such ideological and dogmatic prejudice has clearly skewed the evidence in a false direction, for the texts themselves do not bear out the perception championed by the antagonism view. A more neutral and nuanced view of the situation accordingly acknowledges that prophetic literature contains negative oracles about sacrifice (e.g., Jer. 6:19–20; Hosea 8:12–13; Amos 4:4–5) and open attacks on priests, but sees that these two tropes have a certain significant independence and never function as revolutionary calls to some alternative, non-cultic form of enlightened ethical religion. In other words, the attacks on sacrificial practice are not of the sort to undermine the priestly profession, nor are criticisms of the priests designed to replace the custom of ritual worship. This is hardly surprising. In the ancient Near East, the offering of a sacrificial cult was an unquestioned premise of correct human behavior before the divine. And just as the highly regulated and sensitive behavior of a priest (or priestess) might be severely castigated in that context, so a god's right to refuse the sacrifices of this or that group for this or that reason is hardly unknown.[4]

Hittite texts, for example, record the gods' raging anger if proper reverence and attention to purity is not shown to them in the matter of cultic offerings.

If some wooden or clay utensils you hold, (and) a pig (or) a dog somehow touches (them), but the kitchen attendant does not dispose of it, so that, that

1. Ziony Zevit, "The Prophet versus Priest Antagonism Hypothesis: Its History and Origin," in *The Priests in the Prophets: The Portrayal of Priests, Prophets and Other Religious Specialists in the Latter Prophets*, ed. Lester L. Grabbe and Alice Ogden Bellis, LHBOTS 408 (Sheffield: Sheffield Academic, 2004), 194.

2. Zevit, "Prophet versus Priest," 194.

3. "Academic psychologists have all but written off psychology of religion because of their low estimation of the quality of its work and its problematic relationship to ongoing developments in psychology" (Zevit, "Prophet versus Priest," 197).

4. See, e.g., Fred Naiden, "Rejected Sacrifice in Greek and Hebrew Religion," *JANER* 6 (2006): 189–223; Naiden, *Smoke Signals for the Gods: Ancient Greek Sacrifice from the Archaic through Roman Periods* (Oxford: Oxford University Press, 2013).

man, from a defiled (vessel) gives the gods to eat; to that one the gods will give excrement (and) urine to eat (and) drink. (*CTH* 264 iii 64–68)[5]

The potty-mouthed (literally, potty in the mouth) parallel to a text such as Malachi is striking.

> [O priests,] you bring what has been taken by violence or is lame or sick, and this you bring as your offering! Shall I accept that from your hand? says the LORD. . . . If you will not listen, if you will not lay it to heart to give glory to my name, . . . I will rebuke your offspring, and spread dung on your faces, the dung of your offerings [literally, "of your feasts"], and I will put you out of my presence. (Mal. 1:13; 2:2–3)

Such extreme displeasure on the part of the divinity at being disrespected by cultic personnel presupposes rather than undermines the functioning of the cult. God wishes sacrifice to be properly offered. This is certainly the assumption that must be borne in mind when the Lord says something ostensibly "anti-cultic" such as "Your burnt offerings are not acceptable, nor are your sacrifices pleasing to me" (Jer. 6:20). Ancient Near Eastern gods were often inscrutable and capricious, and the reply to a god's displeasure in offering was not to cease sacrifice and priestly activity altogether but precisely to determine how to make it pleasing. Abolishing the very institution of sacrifice or suppressing priestly ministrations would have been quite literally unthinkable.

"I Will Not Accept Them"

The God of Israel was as subject to wrath as his divine counterparts in the pagan pantheons around him. At the same time, he was impressively calculable in his anger. Through his covenants with his people, his mood swings could be predicted. One of the keys to rightly understanding the rejection-of-sacrifice motif in the prophets is to situate it precisely within this covenantal framework of reciprocal human-divine relations and exchange. Against this background it can be seen that the Lord's "rejection of sacrifices is a consequence of broken relationships with his people, and is particular to specific historical moments."[6] No prophetic pronouncements suggest the lasting eradication of sacrifice as such (though the covenant itself might hang in the balance).

5. On this passage and these Hittite texts, see Ada Taggar-Cohen, "Covenant Priesthood: Cross-Cultural Legal and Religious Aspects of Biblical and Hittite Priesthood," in *Levites and Priests in Biblical History and Tradition*, ed. Mark Leuchter and Jeremey M. Hutton, AIL 9 (Atlanta: Society of Biblical Literature, 2011), 18.

6. Aaron Glaim, "'I Will Not Accept Them': Sacrifice and Reciprocity in the Prophetic Literature," in *Sacrifice, Cult, and Atonement in Early Judaism and Christianity: Constituents*

Rejection of sacrifice is in truth a prophetic theme employed as a kind of final ominous omen, one last sign before some unique punishment. The failed efficacy of Israel's sacrifice on the eve of national catastrophe, in fact, belongs to a resolutely sacrificial worldview. Had the Lord happily accepted his people's offerings made to him just as an approaching danger was foreseen and then, nevertheless, let his people's enemies overrun them, this would have meant that YHWH was "either capricious or weak, unwilling or unable to help Israel and Judah despite his acceptance of their gifts."[7]

The dynamic nature of ancient sacrifice as a pliable ritual, a transactional event, uniting living subjects, human and divine, and essentially responsive to changing conditions is very important to bear in mind. Both acceptance and rejection are possible outcomes in this mode of reciprocal exchange, as the sacrificial codes themselves advertise (cf. Lev. 22:20, 23). Far too often, however, "sacrifice" is wrongly decontextualized and imagined as some monolithic *principle* of worship, having no relation to historical circumstances and engaged only as a general system. Positive or negative judgments are thus falsely applied to the integral whole as an axiomatic statement about the character of "religion" as such. This contemporary "systemic" view of sacrifice is regularly tempted, moreover, to overplay the embedding of public ritual in economic power structures and social elites. At its extreme, scholars imagine that the prophets protest against sacrifice *as such* on the grounds that wealthy state cults—with their large landholdings, slaves, and coerced contributions, all underwriting a tax-exempt clerical caste—represent a fundamentally exploitative and onerous burden on the poor. That the prophets care dearly for the poor and have harsh words for the rich is not in question. No textual support can be found, however, for this proto-Marxist critique of the social premises of ancient sacrificial activity. Divine law commanded that sacrifice be offered, and that was the final word.[8]

The multiple ruptures and reconciliations that characterize the living relationship between YHWH and his people find reflexes in the variously pleasing or unacceptable character of their sacrifices. The pattern is quite consistent across the key passages in question (e.g., Amos 5:21–27; Hosea 6:4–7; Isa. 1:10–17; Jer. 6:20; 7:21; Mic. 6:6–8).

---

and Critique, ed. Henrietta L. Wiley and Christian A. Eberhart, RBS 85 (Atlanta: SBL Press, 2017), 125. The present section relies heavily on Glaim's analysis.

7. Glaim, "'I Will Not Accept Them,'" 126.

8. Ronald S. Hendel, "Away from Ritual: The Prophetic Critique," in *Social Theory and the Study of Israelite Religion: Essays in Retrospect and Prospect*, ed. Saul M. Olyan, RBS 71 (Atlanta: Society of Biblical Literature, 2012), 59–80. Hendel accepts that sacrifice was accepted *doxa* in Israel, an unquestioned premise and norm, but he contends that it was disrupted and called into question precisely by the radical and nonconformist prophetic voice. This appears to me a misreading of the evidence.

In Amos 5, for instance, cited above, the Lord, using the typical sensorial lexicon of a god's perception of liturgical offerings, says that he will not "smell" the Israelites' feasts, an allusion to the perfumed odor of sacrifices (5:21; cf. Gen. 8:21; 1 Sam. 26:19). Neither will he "look upon" their fattened cattle (Amos 5:22). He is displeased with the sound of their music (5:23), and so forth. The whole cluster of verses comprises a kind of "inverted version of a cultic Gattung, viz. the priestly declaration that the offerings which had been brought forward had been accepted by the deity."[9] The rejection is shocking but situational, as the conditioned "*your* festivals . . . *your* grain offerings . . . *your* fatlings" suggests. The following verse (5:24), normally understood as a call for the practice of social justice in place of worthless sacrificial religion, might, in fact, instead be taken as an announcement of *divine* justice: God's judgment (*mišpāṭ*) and righteous vindication (*ṣĕdāqâ*) will roll down like a torrential flood. Judgment, in any event, is precisely what the immediately preceding verses had predicted. "In all the squares there shall be wailing. . . . Is not the day of the LORD darkness, not light, and gloom with no brightness in it?" (5:16, 20).

The specific denunciation of sacrifices in Amos 5 is in all likelihood localized in the state sanctuary at Bethel, an idolatrous shrine for Baal (cf. 1 Kings 12:29–32; 13:32), repeatedly doomed for destruction by the prophet (Amos 3:14; 4:4–5; 5:4–6; cf. Hosea 10:15). Amos's memorable confrontation with Amaziah, Jeroboam's priest in the royal sanctuary, supplies the limited context in which Amos's harsh oracles must be heard (Amos 7:10–17). Assyrian armies and the pain of exile are the punishment for Israel's sin, which obviously means a total rejection of the Northern Kingdom's cult. It is "a unilateral cancellation of the reciprocal relationship between YHWH and Israel, entailing that divine protection would be withdrawn."[10] No sacrificial action can any longer reverse the judgment. But YHWH himself, the living God, is not thereby erased from history; nor is any word offered about Judah or the Jerusalem temple.

To generalize these and similar prophetic words as timeless reforms embracing all sacrificial activity in all times and places is to fall into a lamentable anachronism and distortion. As Francis Andersen and David Noel Freedman fittingly observe, "The prophets have too often been portrayed as modern free-thinking rationalist monotheists who rejected the cult entirely on the grounds that it was a vestige of primitive conceptions of the deity and worship. There is little doubt that they believed that doing justice and righteousness was more

9. Göran Eidevall, "A Farewell to the Anticultic Prophet: Attitudes towards the Cult in the Book of Amos," in *Priests and Cults in the Book of the Twelve*, ed. Lena-Sofia Tiemeyer, ANEM 14 (Atlanta: SBL Press, 2016), 108.

10. Eidevall, "A Farewell to the Anticultic Prophet," 109.

important than practicing the liturgy. Still, it is difficult to imagine, especially in that setting, that they wished to do away with public worship at the temple or the great festivals, with their multiform sacrifices and public rites."[11] The absolute end of sacrifice is not a biblical idea.

"I Desire Mercy, Not Sacrifice"

The celebrated text of Hosea 6:6, with its opposition of ḥesed and sacrifice, fits admirably within this framework of reciprocal relations.[12] It is not the abstract character of religion but God's concrete dealings with his people that is here at stake. The verse is framed by overt statements of the people's covenant infidelity in 6:4 and 6:7.

> What shall I do with you, O Ephraim?
>   What shall I do with you, O Judah?
> Your love [ḥesed] is like a morning cloud,
>   like the dew that goes away early.
> Therefore I have hewn them by the prophets,
>   I have killed them by the words of my mouth,
>   and my judgment goes forth as the light.
> For I desire steadfast love [ḥesed] and not sacrifice,
>   the knowledge of God [daʿat ʾĕlōhîm] rather than burnt offerings.
> But at Adam [or "like humans"] they transgressed the covenant;
>   there they dealt faithlessly with me. (Hosea 6:4–7)

The fixed covenantal connotations of the key vocabulary in Hosea 6:6 itself must be appreciated. We have here the terms of the agreement between the Lord and his people that have been breached. This covenantal breach is what subjects Israel to a lawsuit (rîb): "There is no faithfulness or loyalty [ḥesed] and no knowledge of God [daʿat ʾĕlōhîm] in the land" (Hosea 4:1). It is an error, moreover, to see in the stipulations of ḥesed and daʿat nothing more than naked ethical values: big, bland words for being good to one's neighbor, as so often supposed. What God desires in Hosea 6:6 is quite specifically to have Israel as his faithful spouse; and this means, in the first place, to have the people's cultic fidelity. In this context, ḥesed and daʿat give direct voice to the Lord's intention to replace the idolatrous Baal cult with his own: "I will take you for my wife forever; I will take you for my wife in righteousness and in

---

11. Francis I. Andersen and David Noel Freedman, *Amos*, AB 24A (New York: Doubleday, 1989), 559.

12. See Paba Nidhani De Andrado, "*Ḥesed* and Sacrifice: The Prophetic Critique in Hosea," *CBQ* 78 (2016): 47–67.

justice, in steadfast love [*běḥesed*], and in mercy. I will take you for my wife in faithfulness; and you shall know [*wěyāda'at*] the Lord" (Hosea 2:19–20).

Before this reconciliation can happen, however, a judgment must come, a judgment that entails the cessation of Israel's unacceptable regime of state-sponsored sacrifice. "The Israelites shall remain many days without king or prince, without sacrifice or pillar, without ephod or teraphim" (Hosea 3:4). At issue again, as in Amos, is the northern monarchy and its promotion of false worship. This concerns the calf cult set up by Jeroboam in the hill country of Ephraim with the calculated intent to oppose the House of David (1 Kings 12:25–33; 2 Chron. 11:13–17).

> They made kings, but not through me;
>   they set up princes, but without my knowledge.
> With their silver and gold they made idols
>   for their own destruction.
> Your calf is rejected, O Samaria.
>   My anger burns against them.
> How long will they be incapable of innocence?
>   For it is from Israel,
> an artisan made it;
>   it is not God.
> The calf of Samaria
>   shall be broken to pieces. (Hosea 8:4–6)

And again:

> And now they keep on sinning
>   and make a cast image for themselves,
> idols of silver made according to their understanding,
>   all of them the work of artisans.
> "Sacrifice to these," they say.
>   People are kissing calves!
> Therefore they shall be *like the morning mist*
>   or like the dew that goes away early,
> like chaff that swirls from the threshing floor
>   or like smoke from a window. (Hosea 13:2–3)

The people with their idolatrous cult shall be made just like their transient *ḥesed*, the prophet proclaims (cf. Hosea 6:4); they shall disappear into exile and vanish like the morning dew.

Yet, after the Northern Kingdom suffers this fate of apparent destruction, with the loss of its apparatus of errant sacrifice, they shall "in the latter days" eventually return and submit to the Davidic kingdom in Judah, predicts

Hosea. "Afterward the Israelites shall return and seek the LORD their God, and David their king; they shall come in awe to the LORD and to his goodness in the latter days" (Hosea 3:5). This "seeking" of the Lord and his goodness, a seeking full of reverential fear, carries a strong liturgical sense, evoking the ambiance of a pilgrimage to the Lord's sanctuary (cf. Hosea 5:6, 15; Ps. 24:6; Zech. 8:22; Mal. 3:1). The sentiment in Hosea 3:5 is accordingly often (but not always) taken to be a late addition. It is certain, in any event, that for the southern redactors of the Book of the Twelve, there is a reference here to the northern tribes' eschatological worship at the Jerusalem temple. Sacrifice, in other words, has not ceased *as such* in the canonized vision of Hosea. One cultic regime (the northern), which lost its way, has vanished, but in God's future it shall be reconciled to the true (in Judah).

Critique of the *Kōhănîm*

Where are the priests in this whole picture? Not as present or singled out as one might think. Tracing the actual uses of the Hebrew word *kōhēn* (priest) within the prophetic corpus is very illuminating in this connection.[13] It reveals that the situation is not at all as obvious as the antagonism hypothesis would suppose. The great majority of uses of the word have no bearing whatsoever on ritual life, and the few instances that do point in a different direction than the lazy consensus suggests.

In Joel 1:13, for instance, the priests and ministers of the altar are invited to wail—not because they have been too invested in their ritual duties but, on the contrary, because these duties are about to be taken from them: "Grain offering and drink offering are withheld from the house of your God." The horrible, threatening tragedy, in other words, is precisely that the sacrificial liturgy of the temple should be halted. In Micah the problem is that the priests are teaching and giving oracles for a price, not that they are somehow caught up in pointless sacrificial liturgies (Mic. 3:11). In Ezekiel 22:26, the problem is the opposite: the priests are now *not* teaching—that is, not rightly teaching. "They have made no distinction between the holy and the common, neither have they taught the difference between the unclean and the clean, and they have disregarded my sabbaths, so that I am profaned among them." Evidently, God wants the supposedly ponderous, nitpicky priestly distinctions between what is clean and unclean to be faithfully upheld and propagated. Here the view of R. R. Hutton seems to be confirmed: "Whenever the prophet criticizes the priest, the complaint is

13. The word appears distributed as follows: Isaiah (3×); Jeremiah (34×); Ezekiel (22×); Hosea (3×); Joel (3×); Amos (once); Zephaniah (once); Haggai (5×); Zechariah (5×); Malachi (once).

not that he is acting just like a priest; rather the objection is that he has *ceased* acting like a priest."[14] Acting like a priest of YHWH, we might hasten to specify. Priests who serve foreign gods are clearly not commended. Thus, Zephaniah 1:4 stands in Hutton's same line. The Lord threatens to "cut off from this place every remnant of Baal and the name of the idolatrous priests." In all of this, priests' holy service at the altar, when executed as YHWH desires it, is nowhere in the slightest manner implicated or condemned.

A helpful catalogue of the various prophets' concrete charges against priests broadly identifies the following major categories of crime: (1) priests' lack of knowledge and their failure to teach (Isa. 56:9–12; Hosea 4:6; Mic. 3:11; Mal. 2:1–9); (2) priests' social injustice (Neh. 5; Isa. 58:3–5; Amos 2:8; Zech. 5:1–4; Mal. 3:5); (3) priests' practice of unorthodox rites (Isa. 57:6–8; 65:3–4; Hosea 4:10–14); (4) priestly intermarriages (Ezra 9–10; Neh. 6; 10; 13; Mal. 2:10–16); (5) priests' cultic neglect (Isa. 61:8; Hosea 4:8; 8:11–13; Mal. 1:6–14); and (6) priests' impurity (Zeph. 3:4; Hag. 2:10–14).[15] It is worth observing that a good number of these sins are not exclusive to the priests, though some plainly concern (and presuppose) their professional domain in a more obvious way. Even in these more direct ritual matters, however, other actors must be recognized. The role of the monarch, for instance, has already been highlighted in Jeroboam's apostasy in the north. The issue of intermarriage is a still more revealing case, since in Ezra this concern is bound up with a construction of the whole people of Israel, not simply the priests, as "the holy seed" (Ezra 9:1–2). It is not simply a matter of ensuring proper priestly pedigrees. The sacralization of all God's people as a "priestly nation" is, in fact, deeply tied together with the whole question of priestly sin.

Jeremiah, who has some of the Bible's strongest language against Israel's sacrifices (Jer. 7:21–26), mentions priests, *kōhănîm*, more than any other prophet, but he never makes any connection between these two ideas. In fact, he never really singles priests out at all, almost always lumping them in with other leaders of the people (e.g., Jer. 2:26; 4:9; 6:13; 8:1, 10; 13:13; 19:1; 23:11; 26:11; 32:32). Very typical is the complaint in Jeremiah 2:8.

> The priests did not say, "Where is the LORD?"
>   Those who handle the law did not know me;
> the rulers transgressed against me;
>   the prophets prophesied by Baal,
>   and went after things that do not profit.

14. R. R. Hutton, *Charisma and Authority in Ancient Israelite Society* (Minneapolis: Fortress, 1994), 161–62 (emphasis original).
15. This analysis is drawn from Lena-Sofia Tiemeyer, *Priestly Rites and Prophetic Rage*, FAT 2/19 (Tübingen: Mohr Siebeck, 2006).

Here the specific sin of the priests concerns a failure to turn people's attention to the Lord through their failure to know him; instruction again seems to be at issue. Nothing is hinted at about any misguided preoccupation with ritual. It is the *prophets*, rather, who are accused of cultic apostasy. In Jeremiah 5:31, it is actually these false prophets themselves who mislead the priests, not vice versa, all to the good pleasure of the people. "The prophets prophesy falsely, and the priests rule as the prophets direct; my people love to have it so."

"Like People, like Priest"

The role of the priests as the people's ritual experts is real but should not be exaggerated, particularly in the preexilic context. "At a minimal level, *kōhănîm* may have been considered absolutely necessary only for the blood manipulations of *ḥaṭṭāʾt* [sin/purity] offerings that could be performed solely on altars with four horns on which sacrificial blood was daubed."[16] If these *sin offerings* represent "the purification/expiation offering par excellence," which had a special power to cleanse individuals from the miasmic stains that accrued from various types of contact, bodily functions, and behaviors, other sorts of liturgical life appear beyond the priestly context. Sacrifices and ritual acts outside the priests' control are clearly attested in the Bible, in any event.

The image of preexilic Israel is particularly marked in this regard. The altar law in Exodus 20:24–26, for instance, presupposes that Israelites are offering holocausts and peace offerings from their herds and flocks, upon altars made of earth, without clergy. In Judges 17, we find the curious tale of an Ephraimite named Micah, who sets up a "house of Elohim," which might mean equally a temple for God or for the gods, furnished with an idol of cast metal, an *ephod*, and *teraphim*. He then installs one of his sons as *kōhēn*, later replacing him with a freelance Levite (17:9–12). When the Danites come and plunder Micah's shrine, they haul away the Levite as well and put him to work in their own cult setting (18:17–31). The *kōhēn* protests, but then accepts the forced promotion from a private house shrine to the service of a whole clan. The ritual ministry of the unattached priestly agent in this strange story is revealed as being desirable but also unnecessary and supremely subservient to cults established and managed by others. Though he is honored and entrusted with his proper domain, the Levite is also quite simply a captive.

It is entirely anachronistic, of course, to appeal to ideals like the independence of the clerical estate over against the secular power. It is, nevertheless, quite useful to be sensitized to this archaic dynamic of priestly subservience to the people—certainly in the time before the "reform" and cult centralization

16. Zevit, "Prophet versus Priest," 200.

associated with Deuteronomy and King Josiah and before the enormous rise in the Aaronic priestly profile during the postexilic (that is, nonmonarchical) period. Bearing this dynamic of humble subservience in mind helps disarm the inflated picture of itself that later postexilic priestly establishment painted. It also, thereby, helps diffuse excessively *sacerdo*-centric readings of Israel's sin.

An illustrative example is Hosea 4:1–10. The passage is a clear case of the famous prophetic *rîb*, a lawsuit with God. Still, like so much in the prophets (especially the preexilic prophets), a great deal here is also very uncertain, beginning with the translation itself. Verse 4:4b, which begins a subunit, is nearly always emended, then rendered as follows: "My *rîb* is with you, O priest." The rest of the oracle follows suit.

> Let no one dispute
>> let no one debate.
>> My contention is with you, priest.
> You will stumble by day
>> and the prophet will stumble with you by night
>> and I will ruin your mother.
> My people are ruined for lack of knowledge.
>> Because you have rejected the knowledge,
>> I will reject you from being priest to me.
> You have forgotten your God's instruction—
>> I will forget your children.
> As they grew proud, so they sinned against me.
>> Their Glory they exchanged for Ignominy.
> The sin-offering of my people they devour
>> and toward their iniquity-offering they lift their throats.
> It shall be: like the people, like the priest.
>> I shall punish each for his conduct,
>> I shall requite each for his deeds.
> They have eaten, but will not be satisfied.
>> They have been promiscuous, but will not increase.[17]
>> (Hosea 4:4–10)

In this translation of Francis Andersen and David Noel Freedman, the priest stands in the dock, with God's accusation squarely laid upon his head. That the priest is explicitly targeted is by no means wrong. He is rejected from his office outright in 4:6. Yet, as Jack Lundbom very rightly says, "The balance between people and priest is delicate and subtle in Hosea's preaching, so much so that it is easily upset by commentators who want the emphasis on one or

---

17. Translation by Francis I. Andersen and David Noel Freedman, *Hosea*, AB 24 (New York: Doubleday, 1980), 342.

the other."[18] The oracle that begins in Hosea 5:1 is an excellent indication of the balanced audience of the prophet: "Hear this, O priests! Give heed, O house of Israel! Listen, O house of the king!"

Critical to striking the correct balance in the present text is the elusive sense of Hosea 4:4b, which in the Masoretic Text (basically followed by the Septuagint) is not in fact a direct address to the priest but actually reads "Your people are like the contentions of a priest" or perhaps "Your people are like those who contend with a priest." The first option seems more likely, although the Vulgate understands the latter. In the light of 4:4a, being contentious, of course, whether it be priest or people, is not a good idea when it is God who is prosecuting, as he declares in 4:1. It is the *people*, at all events, who are the announced subject of the wrangling.

Thematically this more accurate rendering of Hosea 4:4b pairs strikingly well with the ending verse of the unit—especially in Hebrew, where there is much phonetic similarity between the two verses: "Therefore it shall be: like the people, like the priest" (4:9a). The broken-up bicolon thus functions as a sort of *inclusio*, both framing and illuminating the whole oracle in 4:4b–9a. The result is that, through the comparison between the people and the priest broached at the beginning, and the strong rebuke of the priest in the middle verses, the fate of the people is climactically declared. If they behave like the priests in striving against God, they will be judged like the priests, who are rejected. "Before Yahweh both people and priests are guilty. Modern scholarship has missed this point entirely by placing all the blame on the priest," Lundbom says.[19]

Sharing the Blame

A large part of the problem has certainly been the conventional assumption that the priestly cult *as such* comes under heavy fire in these verses. The situation is not so simple, however. What Andersen and Freedman translate above as "sin-offering" and "iniquity-offering" (and the graphic gulping down of sacrificial portions by lifting up the gorge) over-translates and need not be understood in this technical ritual sense. The *ḥaṭṭā't* offering of Leviticus 4 is, in fact, very unlikely to be in view, as most scholars agree. The notion of literally *eating sin*, nevertheless, suggests for nearly all commentators the priests' greedy appetite for sacrificial perquisites—that is, the portions of the sacrificial animals that came by right to the priests. The sin of the sons of Eli

---

18. Jack Lundbom, "Contentious Priests and Contentious People in Hosea IV 1–10," *VT* 36 (1986): 52.

19. Lundbom, "Contentious Priests and Contentious People," 68.

at Shiloh in 1 Samuel 2:12–17 presents the obvious analogy. It is revealing to observe the conclusions that are drawn. One evangelical author comments, "Instead of teaching the people the nature of righteousness and motivating them to seek it, the priests are prospering via the OT equivalent of selling indulgences."[20] Another, in the same vein, declares that in Hosea 4:8 "exactly as in 6:6 the sacrifices, *which are against God's will*, are set in antithesis to the priests' real duty—characterized in a positive sense in 4:6 as 'knowledge of God' and 'teaching of your God.'"[21] The antagonism hypothesis stands in plain view.

It is very important to be careful here. The larger context of Hosea is critical for appreciating the full resonance of the ritual language of this oracle. In that larger context of the prophet's preaching, a clear battle with the Baal cult is at stake. "I will punish her for the festival days of the Baals, when she offered incense to them" (Hosea 2:13); "On that day, says the LORD, you will call me, 'My husband,' and no longer will you call me, 'My Baal'" (2:16; cf. 2:8). It is in this frame of reference, and within the grand metaphor of ritual adultery that structures the book, that the curious mention of "your mother" and "your children" becomes intelligible. It is not, as scholars like Andersen and Freedman suppose, used in reference to a priestly dynasty, like that of Eli at Shiloh. The reference to mother and child belongs to the cultic contest with Baal, as is quite clear from Hosea 2.

"I will destroy your mother" (4:5).	"Plead with your mother, plead—for she is not my wife and I am not her husband" (2:1).
"I also will forget your children" (4:6).	"Upon her children also I will have no pity, because they are the children of whoredom. For their mother has played the whore; she who conceived them has acted shamefully" (2:4).

From the very first verses of the book, we read as a governing motif that "the land commits great whoredom by forsaking the LORD" (Hosea 1:2). It seems probable that in this connection "your mother," destined for doom, is in fact a reference to the mother-goddess, Asherah, who figures in the Canaanite cult against which Hosea was fighting. Asherah was the consort of El or Baal, and much scholarly speculation exists about a famous inscription that suggestively speaks of "YHWH and his Asherah." This would provide a perfect example of the idolatrous syncretism openly repudiated in 2:1: "She is not

20. Douglas Stuart, *Hosea–Jonah*, WBC 31 (Waco: Word, 1987), 79.
21. Hans Walter Wolff, *Hosea*, Hermeneia (Philadelphia: Fortress, 1974), 81 (emphasis added). Cf. the similar judgment of A. A. MacIntosh, *Hosea*, ICC (Edinburgh: T&T Clark, 1997), 145.

my wife and I am not her husband!" The "children" born of this illicit union are likened to Hosea's children had by Gomer, who receive symbolic names like *Lo-ammi*, "Not my people"—a direct reversal of the Lord's covenant/marriage formula: "For you are not my people and I am not your God" (1:9).

Whore language fills the whole book—but it is never linked in any special way to the priests (Hosea 2:2, 5; 3:3; 4:10, 12–15; 5:3–4; 9:1). So, when the punishment for whoredom comes at the end of our oracle in Hosea 4:10, after foretelling the ruin of this mother and children, it is difficult to suppose that the third-person plural subject of the verb refers to no one but the priests: "They shall play the whore, but not multiply" (4:10). The whoring behavior is the misdeed of all, priest and people: priest as embodiment of the people, and people as the "employer" of the priest.

> *My people* consult a piece of wood . . .
> a spirit of whoredom has led them astray,
>   and they have played the whore, forsaking their God.
> They sacrifice on the tops of the mountains,
>   and make offerings upon the hills. (Hosea 4:12–13)

The "spirit of whoredom," perhaps some form of a sacred marriage cult, or at the very least a fertility rite by which the whole community is prostituting itself on the high places to Baal, leads the Lord now solemnly to promise to make them *infertile* (cf. Hosea 2:9). They have been promiscuous but will not increase (cf. 4:10). This ending of their fruitfulness comes in direct answer to the fact that "the more they increased, the more they sinned against me" (4:7). That is to say, the more Israel was blessed, the more it attributed its great blessings to the false gods: "Israel is a luxuriant vine that yields its fruit. The more his fruit increased the more altars he built" (10:1). The end of this false "fruitfulness" of Israel's growing unfaithfulness accordingly entails the end of their false sacrifice: "The LORD will break down their altars, and destroy their pillars" (10:2).

Once we read the oracle of Hosea 4:4–10 in the light of this broader ritual context of promiscuous sacrificing and setting up of sacred pillars, eating "the sin of my people" in 4:8 takes on a different color altogether, much more concrete. The Lord's people's "sin" is manifest: it is their cultic alliance with Baal—a dalliance sealed in the eating of raisin cakes, which were part of the fertility rite, associated with Asherah as the maternal fertility goddess (cf. Jer. 7:18). "The LORD said to me again, 'Go love a woman who has a lover and is an adulteress, just as the LORD loves the people of Israel, though they turn to other gods and love raisin cakes'" (Hosea 3:1). Consuming these cakes of cultic adultery leads to a prophecy of the temporary termination of Israel's sacrificial life in Hosea 3 (vv. 3–4), a hint at the priest's rejection from his office in Hosea 4. "They shall eat, but not be satisfied" (4:10a) is the warning for those who consume this sin, clarified by the synonymous parallel in the next stich: "They shall play the whore, but not multiply" (4:10b). So much for the priests peddling indulgences. The scene is much more like St. Paul's condemnation of participation at the communion table of demons (1 Cor. 10:21; see the discussion in chap. 6 below). The critique is to this degree much more severe than a simple castigation of priestly greed. It is a complete national betrayal of the sacrificial system as such, which is why the whole corrupt nexus of infidelity stands in peril. The "iniquity offering," for its part, which has a nice clerical ring, but which, as Andersen and Freedman admit, actually has "no direct warrant . . . in the ritual literature" whatsoever, might be translated instead like this: "They will bear their guilt to the point of death," or, "They set their heart on iniquity," or even, to be more literal still, "They [the people] set his [the priest's] heart on their iniquity."[22]

The Priestly Sins

With these adjustments in place, it is possible finally to get a better handle on what exactly the priest's guilt really implies. The priest's specific sin is described as a delict against correct instruction, forgetfulness of "the law [tôrâ] of your God," a common and important priestly infraction seen several times already (cf. Isa. 56:9–12; Jer. 2:8; Mic. 3:11; Mal. 2:1–9). It is worth noting that Hosea is aware of the Lord's written Torah (Hosea 8:12); the priest seems to be imagined as responsible for the mastery and implementation of some divine code, although scholars agree that the five canonical books of the Torah postdate an early prophet like Hosea. Certain formative traditions were doubtlessly already in place, however; very possibly what is "written" (by God's finger?) is the Decalogue, a covenant digest, for in Hosea 4:2 the list of transgressions echoes Exodus 20 quite closely.

> The LORD has an indictment against the inhabitants of the land.
> There is no faithfulness or loyalty,
>   and no knowledge of God in the land.
> Swearing, lying, and murder,
>   and stealing and adultery break out;
>   bloodshed follows bloodshed. (Hosea 4:1–2)

The sins here generally belong to the second, social table of the Decalogue: lying, murder, stealing, adultery. In Hosea 6:9, a group of priests is directly

22. Andersen and Freedman, Hosea, 358–59.

accused of murder, though it is hard to know what this stylized charge might actually mean—perhaps guilt for the (tacit?) condoning of violence but also, perhaps, outright violence. Complicity in the "bloodshed" denounced at the opening of the *rîb* thus figures as part of the priest's transgression.

At the same time, the first table of the Decalogue is hardly absent from Hosea's vision. The mention of written Torah in Hosea 8:12 is reckoned as a "strange thing" (*zār*) by the people. This presents an interesting echo of the "strange fire" (*'ēš zārâ*) offered by Nadab and Abihu (Lev. 10:1), since an account of the people's rejected sacrifice follows directly in Hosea 8:13. Sacrifice on the high places and with temple prostitutes (Hosea 4:13–14; cf. Deut. 13:2; 32:16) is obviously no less prohibited or serious than the social sins. The framing of lying, murder, and stealing in Hosea 4:2 between swearing and adultery is notable in this connection. The metaphoric, cultic freight of adultery in Hosea hardly needs restatement; later in the book, swearing carries the distinct meaning of forging a cultic bond with Baal.

The "swearing" of covenant oaths is, in point of fact, the reason for the contentious lawsuits (*rîb*) that represent the whole context of Hosea 4.

> With empty oaths they make covenants;
> so litigation springs up like poisonous weeds. (Hosea 10:4)

In Hosea 8:1, trespassing against Torah is made parallel to breaking the covenant. Since the category of covenant controls the whole marital/adultery metaphor of the book while providing the legal framework for the lawsuit, it is in this connection that the priest's transgression should be plotted. His grave sin, as a covenant offense, has at once both moral and ritual dimensions, not simply the former.

The simultaneously moral and ritual character of the priest's failure in instruction is easily missed, not only on account of the normal understanding of the supposed prophetic critique of the cult, but also because Hosea's language is subtle and multilayered. The prophet speaks twice about "knowledge" (*da'at*) in charging the priest. This, of course, is sexually charged discourse, for to "know" someone in the Bible is to be intimate on the level of a married couple. More than this, for Hosea it is the precise formulation of God's promise to restore his marriage covenant with unfaithful Israel: "I will take you for my wife in faithfulness; and you shall know [*wĕyāda'at*] the LORD" (Hosea 2:20). Thus, when the priest himself is rejected for having rejected "knowledge," it is not a way of saying that he has neglected to provide lessons on the respectable citizen's non-cultic, strictly ethical good behavior. Quite the contrary—it means that he has rejected the right cult; that is, he has forgotten the covenant relationship with the true God. The misbegotten children, born of this false union, are not "children of the living God" (1:10).

The Golden Calf

Idol worship in Israel always points to the archetypal apostasy, and Hosea 4:7, at the very center of the passage, makes direct allusion to the episode of the golden calf.[23] Here formative pentateuchal traditions prior to the Pentateuch are again influential in the prophet.

> As they grew proud, so they sinned against me.
>   Their Glory they exchanged for Ignominy. (Hosea 4:7 [trans.
>   Andersen and Freedman])

This allusion is clearly evoked with the language of "exchange," a biblical trope that made its way as far as St. Paul (e.g., Rom. 1:23). Psalm 106 is the locus classicus.

> They made a calf at Horeb
>   and worshiped a cast image.
> They exchanged the glory of God
>   for the image of an ox that eats grass. (Ps. 106:19–20)

It is striking that this tradition of the golden calf, so tightly connected to Aaron (who does not cut such a fine figure in the Exodus version), should so regularly and bluntly be charged against the people. Psalm 106, in fact, mentions Aaron only in order to say, "They were jealous of Moses in the camp and of Aaron, the holy one of the LORD" (Ps. 106:16). In Jeremiah 2:11, we hear again the same motif:

> Has a nation changed its gods,
>   even though they are no gods?
> But my people have changed their glory
>   for something that does not profit.

Nehemiah 9 follows the same pattern of seeing the blame not with the priest but with the people. The latter even ostentatiously avoids mentioning Aaron as the speaker of the infamous words "These are your gods, O Israel!" (Exod. 32:4). "Even when they had cast an image of a calf for themselves and [*they*] said [!], 'This is your God who brought you up out of Egypt,' and had committed great blasphemies, you in your great mercies did not forsake them in the wilderness" (Neh. 9:18–19). The tradition of exculpating Aaron and blaming the people continues up to the point that, in Pseudo-Philo's *Liber Antiquitatum Biblicarum*, Aaron even puts up a protest:

---

23. The story of Baal-peor is also recalled in characterizing Israel's past: "Like grapes in the wilderness, I found Israel. . . . But they came to Baal-peor, and consecrated themselves to a thing of shame, and became detestable like the thing they loved" (Hosea 9:10).

They gathered together to Aaron, saying, "Make gods for us whom we may serve, as the other nations have, because that Moses through whom wonders were done before our eyes has been taken away from us." And Aaron said to them, "Be patient. For Moses will come, and he will bring judgment near to us and will illumine the Law for us and will explain from his own mouth the Law of God and set up rules for our race." And while he was speaking, they did not heed him. (*L.A.B.* 12:2–3)[24]

Josephus takes a more discrete route of exculpation and simply avoids all mention of the golden calf whatsoever. Only in Deuteronomy 9:20 is God's anger against Aaron ever mentioned.

What has puzzled scholars about the original story in Exodus 32 is how such a negative image of the high priest could be tolerated in a Priestly Pentateuch. Often it is taken as a Levite polemic against the Aaronides. This makes sense insofar as the Levites appear as zealous defenders of God's honor, while Aaron's role is more ambiguous to say the least. Moses' call to rally around him and the Lord is answered by all the Levites, however (cf. Exod. 32:26), which technically would include Aaron and his sons.

James Watts has taken a more compelling approach, which harmonizes well with the trajectory of Aaron's reception just outlined. On the one hand, Watts notes that Aaron's prestige and that of the priests in the Second Temple period was not such as to be plausibly harmed by certain frank admissions of fault. On the other hand, he sees that the postexilic period was also a time when the sins of preexilic Israel were quite openly confronted. He concludes that a different strategy and polemic is at work.

> Exodus 32 can be read, then, not as an anti-Aaronide polemic but rather as a pro-Aaronide apologia for the priests' complicity in preexilic heterodoxy. In the Second Temple period, when priests led the people to internalize the guilt of their ancestors, the story admits their role in preexilic calf cults. But it lays the principal blame for going astray not on the kings, as the Deuteronomistic History does, much less on the priests, but rather on the people. In other words, the message from Aaronide priests to people is: "Like you, we did wrong, but we were only doing what you wanted!"[25]

The priests are rarely given a voice in answering the prophets' charges, but perhaps the story of the golden calf represents such an occasion.[26] Or perhaps,

---

24. Translation by D. J. Harrington in *OTP* 2:320.

25. James W. Watts, "Aaron and the Golden Calf in the Rhetoric of the Pentateuch," *JBL* 130 (2011): 429.

26. See Tiemeyer, *Prophetic Rage*, 88–112. An alternative candidate for a priestly version of the golden calf tradition might appear in the anti-Levite polemic of the Zadokite redactional

if the literal translation suggested above for Hosea 4:8 is correct, the priests and prophets were at least agreed in this: "They [the people] set his [the priest's] heart on their iniquity."

In the end, for Andersen and Freedman, speaking of Hosea, "there is a difference in the way the priest and people are treated. . . . Theirs are the sins of ignorance and omission, his of deliberation and initiation. They are more to be pitied and he is more to be scorned."[27] This gives the priest as he appears in the prophet far too much credit. "The people are, in Hosea's perspective, the main character in the cult."[28] The priest's failure to cultivate the proper covenantal knowledge of God among the people is ultimately reckoned by Hosea not as a deliberate stratagem but as a *forgetfulness* of the Lord's Torah, a sluggish lack of mindfulness, which is less sinister and plotting yet in a way is more awful than apostasy by design. God has ceased to be a thought in the priest's mind.

The priest has forgotten. But his dangerous amnesia parallels directly Hosea's other use of the verb: "*Israel* has forgotten his Maker" (Hosea 8:14).

> When I fed them, they were satisfied;
>> they were satisfied, and their heart was proud;
>> therefore they forgot me. (Hosea 13:6)

Priests and people together abandon all thought of the Lord and blithely go with the surrounding flow of the Canaanite cult. Prosperity dulls their memory (cf. Deut. 32:15–18). Both are to be equally pitied and scorned.

Conclusion

Joseph de Maistre's celebrated dictum "Every nation has the leaders it deserves" applies also, in its own way, to the social body that bears the priestly order. Priests are, after all, inevitably drawn from the people to whom they belong, however much they may become a class apart. Priests bear the moral makeup of their time and place and also the tragic flaw of their human nature. Through the prophets the priests are harshly condemned, but as part of a larger lump judgment. Priests, king, and people: all fall short and exchange the glory of God for something that does not profit.

This situation exposes an important theological problem for the priest's basic role as mediator. How shall a man drawn from this *massa damnata*,

---

strand in Ezek. 44. See Jon Levenson, *Theology of the Program of Restoration of Ezekiel 40–48*, HSM 10 (Missoula, MT: Scholars Press, 1976), 134–35.

27. Andersen and Freedman, *Hosea*, 350.

28. Jutta Krispenz, "Idolatry, Apostasy, Prostitution: Hosea's Struggle against the Cult," in Tiemeyer, *Priests and Cults in the Book of the Twelve*, 16.

enmeshed in networks of social sin and congenital perversion, be anything other than unfit for his duties of reciprocal divine-human exchange? The priest's ultimate crime, in a sense, is the crime of being human. That at least is his protest, when forced to justify himself. A more impressive justification—in the strong Pauline sense of the word—will obviously be required if the priestly ministers elected by God are to accomplish his will.

God's intervention in the inevitable moral decay of an all-too-human priesthood becomes all the more urgent when we observe that, among the charges brought forward, the principal failing proper to the priest and the one accusation that finally sticks is the priest's failure in instruction. "The lips of a priest should guard knowledge, and people should seek instruction from his mouth" (Mal. 2:7). Failure to foster the cult-based knowledge that alone will make Israel fruitful is a failure specifically in divine-human mediation,

Cyril of Alexandria on the Knowledge of God

The "knowledge of God" that is better than holocausts and sacrifices (Hosea 6:6) is, says Cyril of Alexandria, the perfect knowledge of the Father that we discover in Christ.

> There is no doubting the fact that he brought the mind of those approaching him to knowledge of the one who is truly God, for he had set himself for us as an image of the one who begot him, saying to his true disciple, namely, Philip, "Do you not believe that I am in the Father and the Father is in me? Whoever has seen me has seen the Father. The Father and I are one" [John 14:10, 9; 10:30]. If, on the other hand, you were to say also that he means the Son is the *mercy* of the Father, better than *sacrifice* and *holocausts*, your interpretation would be correct, for thus he has been called by divinely inspired Scripture; the God and Father said of him to us, "My righteousness approaches rapidly, and my mercy has been revealed" [Isa. 51:5; 56:1]. The prophetic authors said to him, "Show us your mercy, O Lord, and grant us your salvation, O Lord" [Ps. 85:7]; Christ is truly *mercy* from the Father, his purpose being to remove sins, to forgive faults, to justify by faith, to save the lost and make them proof against death. What excellent gifts, in fact, has he not given us? Therefore, *knowledge of God* is better than *sacrifices and holocausts* when achieved in Christ; it is through him and in him that we have come to know the Father, and are enriched with justification by faith.[a]

a. St. Cyril of Alexandria, *Commentary on the Twelve Prophets*, vol. 1, trans. Robert C. Hill, FC 115 (Washington, DC: Catholic University of America Press, 2007), 142.

which will only be overcome when a superior knowledge descends unsullied from on high.

The purpose of stressing the common human nature of priestly sin is not to minimize the horror of priestly guilt in the slightest. It merits and receives the sharpest form of divine judgment: a blistering, complete rejection. Still, this priestly guilt must be viewed within its proper context. The enduring value of the cult is a basic part of this context, even the premise of much of the prophetic critique. The conjoint horror of a supposed "nation of priests" whoring collectively after false gods is also part and parcel of the problem of wicked priests. While this raises a chicken-and-egg problem about the ultimate source of the ills, it also moderates too one-sided a construction of "the sons of Aaron in their splendor" (Sir. 50:13), as though even the priests' sins were superhuman. The prophetic corpus, with its broadside indictments, thus helpfully serves to hold in balance P's lofty vision of priestly status, in which a man is elevated in some real sense above his kin. The priests' sins are, from the prophets' perspective, also the sins of the people's leaders. The sins are aggravated and amplified by the influence and responsibility of position yet also, through the corporate personality of such position, inevitably by acts undertaken in the public's name. This is as true for the king as for the priest.

On this note of solidarity, finally, the priests not only shared in the guilt as the people's leaders, but they also shared and led the people in repentance: the těšûbâ called for by the prophets. The pronounced priestly elements that structure the emergent tradition of penitential prayer in the Second Temple period are worth highlighting in this connection, for it is a tradition of prayer consciously modeled on the spiritual sacrifice of a contrite heart, itself the fruit of the prophetic critique (see excursus 5). Far from undermining the cult, this communion in the misery of sin instead animated the sacrificial life of the people and infused it with a new depth through heartfelt prayer. Ezra's paradigmatic confession of sin, for instance, which he offers with ritual gestures of lament at the house of God and in union with the evening sacrifice, relies on key priestly categories throughout (Ezra 9:5–15).[29] In a similar and still more impressive way, the Day of Atonement provided the nation with a primordial template for the composition of its penitential prayers. Through the ritual formulary "We have committed iniquity, we have transgressed, we have sinned," which was modeled on Leviticus 16:21, the high priest's gesture of laying his hands on the scapegoat's head and confessing Israel's sins became a liturgy in

29. See Karl William Weyde, "Ezra's Penitential Prayer: Priestly Vocabulary and Concepts in Ezra 9," in *Houses Full of All Good Things: Essays in Memory of Timo Veijola*, ed. Juha Pakkala and Martti Nissinen, PFES 95 (Göttingen: Vandenhoeck & Ruprecht, 2008), 238–50.

which the entire people could personally share through a new and deeper mode of union.[30]

SUMMARY OF KEY POINTS

1. The corpus of prophetic writings, much more expressive and accessible than the P material in the Pentateuch, includes a group of negative oracles that has long exercised a disproportionately influential role in biblical reflection on the priesthood, especially in the Reformation context. As a corpus largely composed prior to the Pentateuch, the P school actually constitutes a response to the prophetic charges, at least historically speaking.

2. A common heuristic lens for reading these negative prophetic texts has been the so-called antagonism hypothesis. This hypothesis insists upon an exaggerated, false dichotomy between ethics and cult, imagining revolutionary calls to alter the fundamental structure of religious behavior in a purely interior reformulation. Such an unhistorical and decontextualized strategy of interpretation owes more to modern Protestant and Enlightenment conceptions than to the actual character of the scriptural texts.

3. Ancient sacrifice was a transactional event, with both acceptance and rejection by the deity as possible outcomes. Seen in their proper context, biblical oracles forcefully challenging Israel's cult must accordingly be situated within a concrete, covenantal framework of reciprocal divine-human exchange. Texts such as Amos 5 and Hosea 6, for instance, belong to the concrete case of the Northern Kingdom's engagement in prohibited calf worship and idolatrous cultic behavior. Such texts are framed with the revealing terminology of a covenant lawsuit and are not meditations on the abstract character of religion. The final Judean redaction of these prophetic texts preserves and promotes hope in a future cultic life centered in Jerusalem and pleasing to YHWH (e.g., Hosea 3:5). This aligns the negative prophetic critique with the positive oracles that must also be considered to gain a balanced picture (cf. chap. 4 below).

4. Direct prophetic critique of the kōhănîm is relatively rare and never configured as an attack on the priests simply for being priests; rather,

---

30. See Richard J. Bautch, "The Formulary of Atonement (Lev 16:21) in Penitential Prayers of the Second Temple Period," in *The Day of Atonement: Its Interpretations in Early Jewish and Christian Traditions*, ed. Thomas Hieke and Tobias Nicklas, TBN 15 (Leiden: Brill, 2012), 33–48.

it is directed toward priests not functioning as priests properly should. Moreover, many of the stereotypical, grievous priestly sins are shared with other leaders of the people.

5. The general subservience and lowly status of the priests relative to the people in the preexilic context must not be conflated with a later, postexilic priestly preeminence. Retrojection of an excessive textual preoccupation with the priests in the early prophets is thus an interpretative error to be avoided. The example of Hosea 4:1–10 is a strong illustration of how the guilt of priests and people in fact comingles in the context of a corporate national idolatry ("whoredom"). The episode of the golden calf is arguably a later priestly expression of this precise perspective of shared guilt for the sins that ultimately brought on the punishment of the exile—with the rise of the priestly regime as an answer for, not the cause of, the problem.

6. Within a more nuanced and historically informed picture, the characteristic priestly sin of not promoting "knowledge" of YHWH can and should be recognized to have both ethical and cultic resonance.

EXCURSUS 3

The Corruption of Priests and Temple

As seen clearly in the two books of the Maccabees, the second century BC was a moment of intense trial and religious crisis in Judea. The temple itself was subjected to the gross indignities of pagan defilement. During the tumultuous period from about 175 to 150 BC, Antiochus IV and his successors repeatedly sold the Jewish high priesthood to the highest bidder, rather than honoring the traditional principle of hereditary succession. In fact, according to 2 Maccabees 11:3, Lysias, the local Seleucid governor, intended to establish an annual sale of the office, abolishing altogether the ancient Jewish custom of a dynastic appointment for life, in order to remake the office into a steady stream of imperial income. Something like this revolving-door high priesthood did eventually appear in the Roman era, when, after the Hasmonean moment, Herod the Great began naming and deposing high priests with alarming caprice.

According to the evidence of Nehemiah 12 (supported by papyri from Elephantine in Egypt), a succession of six high priests, all standing in direct lineal descent—Jeshua, Joiakim, Eliashib, Joiada, Johannan (Jonathan), and Jaddua (12:10–11)—carried the Jerusalem cult through the postexilic Persian period over a course of some two hundred years.[1] This Jeshua, first in the line, is the one who appears in the prophecy of Zechariah 3:8 (see chap. 4 below). To follow the reporting of Josephus, somewhere around the 320s BC, at the

---

1. The definitive study on the topic of the high priestly succession is James C. VanderKam's *From Joshua to Caiaphas: High Priests after the Exile* (Minneapolis: Fortress, 2004).

beginning of the Hellenistic age, Jaddua's successor became Onias I, Jaddua's son, who was in turn followed by Simon, Onias's heir. With a couple of small, lateral hiccups, the line continued in proper dynastic succession from father to son, through Onias II, Simon I's son, to Simon II, Onias II's son (and the great hero of Ben Sira), and finally to Onias III, son of Simon II. Onias III was in office as the great crisis hit.

While attempting to counter a seditious plot, Onias was betrayed when his brother Jeshua (who revealingly took the Greek name Jason) "obtained the high priesthood by corruption" (2 Macc. 4:7), offering the Seleucid powers a huge bribe of hundreds of talents of silver and promising to implement a radical Hellenizing program—and eventually pay still more. Jason ruled only briefly (175–172 BC) and was followed by Menelaus (172–162 BC), who was the brother-in-law of Jason and perhaps a priest (though there are reasons to doubt this), but not himself of the Oniad family in any case. Having no valid claim, the usurper Menelaus simply bought the office outright, with the support of the wealthy but non-priestly Tobiad family (2 Macc. 4:24–25). When the Seleucids grew dissatisfied with Menelaus, they had him killed and determined to change the high priestly family yet again, installing Alcimus, who carried the religious disorder to new heights, among other things attempting to destroy the wall of the inner court of the temple, called "the work of the prophets" (1 Macc. 9:54). The suggestion that Alcimus was a former high priest, who had willfully defiled himself (2 Macc. 14:3–7), is not a good interpretation of the Greek and should probably be read instead in light of the alternate version in 1 Maccabees 7:5, which says that he aspired to the office but not that he held it. Not only was Alcimus therefore no legitimate Oniad, but the wall he tore down seems to be that wall of division derived from Ezekiel's vision separating the Zadokite and non-Zadokite priests (see excursus 6).[2]

The whole messy affair is obviously an ugly story of simony and a sort of Jewish investiture contest: sad species of clerical corruption and political interference familiar enough to those who know a bit of Church history. To those who know a bit of the history of the ancient Near East as well, such sale of priestly offices will be even less surprising. In Egypt and Babylonia, for instance, farming out priestly positions to wealthy nobles was a common practice dating back to at least the sixth century BC.[3] Later in Rome, Julius

---

2. So L. Dequeker, "1 Chronicles xxiv and the Royal Priesthood of the Hasmoneans," in *Crises and Perspectives: Studies in Ancient Near Eastern Polytheism, Biblical Theology, Palestinian Archaeology and Intertestamental Literature*, ed. A. S. van der Woude, Oudtestamentische Studiën 24 (Leiden: Brill, 1986), 102.

3. See, e.g., Andrew Monson, "The Jewish High Priesthood for Sale: Farming Out Temples in the Hellenistic East," *JJS* 67 (2016): 15–35. It is interesting to note that Egyptology, not only biblical studies, has felt the deep influence of Enlightenment prejudice against the priesthood,

Caesar was no innovator when he used lavish bribes to gain the (elected) title of *pontifex maximus*. The complicating factor in the Maccabean context, of course, was the strict Jewish dynastic system. One must therefore imagine, in addition to the religious outrage occasioned by all the sacrilege involved, the supplementary fervor of a French royalist, who must watch a Napoleon III sit on the throne that belongs by divine right to the Bourbon heir.

When the Hasmoneans, accordingly, appeared on the scene as strongmen and savior figures, they purified the temple and provided relief from the foreign meddling, yet they also arrogated to themselves and their family a dubious claim upon the high priesthood—and ultimately an utterly outrageous claim on the royal title as well. Although an effort was made to find (or produce) a Zadokite lineage, as a strategy of legitimation the house of Mattathias attached themselves to the figure of Phinehas (1 Macc. 2:23–26), more on account of his violent zeal for the Lord than his impeccable genealogical credentials as Aaron's grandson.[4]

Onias III, rightful heir unjustly deposed, outlived his brother Jason, but was ultimately murdered near Antioch in 170 BC. It is likely impossible to ever settle the mystery, but it is nevertheless suggestive and has been proposed (however improbably) that the mysterious "Teacher of Righteousness" who founded the community at Qumran was actually Onias III's surviving son, true scion of the legitimate Oniad house.[5] Whoever he was—some would see here a kind of office—this Teacher of Righteousness stands opposed to the one the Scrolls call "The Wicked Priest."[6] This shadowy villain is also cloaked in mystery. Perhaps he was Hyrcanus II. Alexander Jannaeus, Aristobulus II, and Jonathan the high priest have also all been proposed, with many votes going to the latter. One sees the common denominator clearly enough: all are Hasmonean claimants to the Aaronic high priesthood. The so-called Groningen hypothesis holds that, under the successive uses of the title "Wicked Priest" in *Pesher Habakkuk*, a series of six different priests is actually intended. This notion of a cipher for all the high priests remains controversial, but it does at

---

which is often portrayed excessively as "a power hungry, underhanded, political force." See "the attempt to stop the lingering influence of this discourse" in Samuel Jackson, "The 'Wicked Priest' in Egyptology and Amarna Studies: A Reconsideration," *Antiguo Oriente* 6 (2008): 185–211.

4. The patriarch of the Hasmonean line, Mattathias, was a priest from the house of Jehoiarib, who appears first in the list of priestly courses in 1 Chron. 24 but is absent from all earlier genealogical lists. Dequeker ("Royal Priesthood," 103) takes this as a sign that "the Hasmonean origin of the list in 1 Chron. seems certain."

5. See Paul Rainbow, "The Last Oniad and the Teacher of Righteousness," *JJS* 48 (1997): 30–52.

6. See, e.g., Reinhard G. Kratz, "The Teacher of Righteousness and His Enemies," in *Is There a Text in This Cave? Studies in the Textuality of the Dead Sea Scrolls in Honour of George J. Brooke*, ed. Ariel Feldman, Maria Cioata, and Charlotte Hempel, STDJ 119 (Leiden: Brill, 2017), 515–32.

least correctly capture the sentiment that the whole lot of these Hasmonean usurpers was pontificating without warrant and any one of them might well be meant. The Groningen theory also represents a growing challenge to historicist readings of the data. Thus, one might understand "the 'Wicked Priest' as a stereotype of the Jerusalem priesthood" at large.[7]

Whatever its proper referent, the sobriquet "the Wicked Priest"—in Hebrew, *hā-kōhēn hā-rāšā'*—is itself a nasty pun on the title *hā-kōhēn hā-rō'š*, "the head priest." The various grievances lodged against this priestly pretender are couched as interpretations of passages from the prophet Habakkuk. The following example illustrates the intensity of ill feeling.

> *Moreover, wealth betrays a haughty man, and he is unseemly, who opens his soul wide like Sheol; and like death he cannot be sated. And all the nations are gathered about him, and all the peoples are assembled to him. Do not all of them raise a taunt against him and interpreters of riddles about him, who say: "Woe to the one who multiples what is not his own! How long will he weigh himself down with debt?"*
>
> Its interpretation concerns the Wicked Priest, who was called by the true name at the beginning of his standing, but when he ruled in Israel, his heart became large, and he abandoned God, and betrayed the statutes for the sake of wealth. And he stole and amassed the wealth of the men of violence who had rebelled against God, and he took the wealth of peoples to add to himself guilty iniquity. And the abominable ways he pursued with every sort of unclean impurity. (1QpHab col. 8, lines 4–13)[8]

Arrogance and financial misconduct fit the profile of the priests of the period. The military campaigns and violent seizures by the Hasmonean leaders are likewise in view. Purity concerns also arise here as part of the overall picture. It is important to remember that impurity might entail not only ritual but also moral defilement—a problem that is clear enough from the Wicked Priest's "heaping of sinful iniquity upon himself." Ritual matters are surely also implied, however, and this refers not simply to the priest's (or priests') individual behavior but to a deeper point of tension—for the Essene community's interpretation of purity legislation conflicted with that adopted by the temple (cf. 4QMMT). The highly sensitive issue of proper priestly instruction, which is so stressed in the prophetic corpus (cf. Mal. 2:1–9), here becomes very concrete. The grave charge of being a false teacher thus further compounds the negative construction of the Wicked Priest—while also putting

---

7. Kratz, "Teacher of Righteousness," 530.

8. Translation from James H. Charlesworth, ed., *The Dead Sea Scrolls: Hebrew, Aramaic, and Greek Texts with English Translations*, vol. 6B, *Pesharim, Other Commentaries, and Related Documents* (Tübingen: Mohr Siebeck, 2002), 175.

the *Teacher* of Righteousness in his proper priestly and sapiential light. He is the one who fits the ideal of the pious sacerdotal scribe described by Ben Sira. Particularly telling in gauging the absolute wickedness of the Wicked Priest is his famous pursuit of the Teacher of Righteousness on the Day of Atonement, Yom Kippur.[9] This extraordinary suggestion of an active campaign of antagonism has been traditionally understood to refer to some sort of actual raid on the community's site at Qumran. At the very least, it signals that, in addition to the other mounting objections, the temple establishment was observing a festal calendar that did not accord with that approved by the movement at Qumran—for no high priest should be out warring on that holiest of all holy days.

The breakaway movement in the Judean desert was not alone in perceiving the rampant corruption on the Temple Mount, even if their response took a particularly extreme and separatist form. Rabbinic tradition records some very direct (though comically exaggerated) memories about the extent of priestly corruption.

> Therefore it is said: "Behold I give him [Phinehas] my covenant of peace" (Num. 25:12): this teaches us that from him arose eighteen high priests during the time of the First Temple; but during the time of the Second Temple, there arose from him eighty priests. Because they sold it [the priesthood] for money, their years were cut short. It happened that one sent with his son two measures of silver, filled with silver, and with silver measuring instruments. Then it happened that one sent with his son two measures of gold, filled with gold, and with gold measuring instruments. It was then said: "The foal trumped the candelabrum." (*Sifre Numbers* 131; cf. *Lev. Rab.* 21.9; *y. Yoma* 1.1; *b. Yoma* 9a)[10]

The obscene simoniacal bidding wars are here comically but sadly portrayed and linked with Phinehas the Hasmonean hero. Another tradition records a series of priestly profanations of the sanctuary, culminating in the perennially derisible figure of the fat priest.

> Our Rabbis taught: The Temple court cried out four cries.
> The first: "Depart from here, sons of Eli!"—for they defiled the sanctuary of God. And it cried out again: "Depart from here Issachar of the village of Barkai!"—for he honored himself and profaned sacred things.
> And the court cried out again: "'Lift up your heads, oh gates,' (Ps. 24:7) and let enter Ishmael ben Phiabi, the disciple of Phinehas, so he may serve as high priest."

9. See 1QpHab col. 11, lines 3–8.
10. Translation from Jonathan Klawans, *Purity, Sacrifice, and the Temple: Symbolism and Supersessionism in the Study of Ancient Judaism* (Oxford: Oxford University Press, 2006), 178–79.

And the court cried out again: "'Lift up your heads, oh gates,' (Ps. 24:7) and let enter Yohanan ben Narbai, the disciple of Pinkai, and he will fill his stomach with sacred offerings." It was said of Yohanan ben Narbai that he would eat three hundred calves, and drink three hundred barrels of wine, and eat forty *seahs* of birds for dessert. They said that all the days of Yohanan ben Narbai there were never any sacrificial leftovers in the temple. (*b. Pesaḥ.* 57a; cf. *t. Menaḥ.* 13:18–22)[11]

Faced with the same objective reality of a corrupt priesthood and compromised temple establishment, the difference between the proto-rabbinic response of mixed horror and humor, with continued fidelity to the institution, and the Essene answer of blistering venom, open schism, and the effort to be perfectly pure resembles in a way the difference between the two paths taken in sixteenth-century Europe. One group, seeing the issues, worked within the system; the other walked out to claim the higher moral ground. The proto-rabbinic (Pharisaic) reaction, vulnerable perhaps to the accusation of enabling, nevertheless enjoys a certain Catholic appeal. The note of satire is particularly noteworthy. As Eamon Duffy has remarked, in the late Middle Ages bemoaning the state of ecclesial affairs while lampooning fat and unchaste monks was perfectly normal among Catholic reformers—what was new with the Reformation was freely letting them marry and enjoy the table like Luther. This particular indulgence has no resemblance with the ascetic project at Qumran, of course. Indeed, what is quite different (and where the analogy fails) is that in ancient Judea both sides were agreed not only on the need for priestly holiness but on the God-given nature of the priestly cult. This was the very premise of the dispute—and at a basic level the sectarian Essenes obviously had right on their side in protesting vehemently against the malfeasance of priestly usurpers.

11. Klawans, *Purity, Sacrifice, and the Temple*, 181.

EXCURSUS 4

The Priesthood of Eli
and Sons at Shiloh

At the conclusion of his searing temple sermon, the prophet Jeremiah, speaking for a very displeased God, challenges the Judahites' complacent confidence in the inviolability of the Jerusalem cult:

> Go now to my place that was in Shiloh, where I made my name dwell at first, and see what I did to it for the wickedness of my people Israel. And now, because you have done all these things, says the LORD, and when I spoke to you persistently, you did not listen, and when I called you, you did not answer, therefore I will do to the house that is called by my name, in which you trust, and to the place that I gave to you and to your ancestors, just what I did to Shiloh. (Jer. 7:12–14)

The threat, or rather the promise, to repeat in Jerusalem the destruction formerly done to the northern shrine of Shiloh during the eighth-century Assyrian invasion is clearly meant to rattle Jeremiah's audience. While scholars wonder whether an invitation is made here to go and physically visit still-visible temple ruins, for readers of the wider Bible a trip to Shiloh is an easy textual journey.

The oracle of the anonymous "man of God" who appears in 1 Samuel 2:27–36 to announce the fate of Eli's priestly line presents the decisive word of ruin. In narrative form, it is the most open of prophetic rejections of priestly service. In substance, it is one of the characteristic speeches tied to the hand and interests of the Deuteronomistic redactor.

> Thus the LORD has said, "I revealed myself to the family of your ancestor in Egypt when they were slaves to the house of Pharaoh. I chose him out of all

the tribes of Israel to be my priest, to go up to my altar, to offer incense, to wear an ephod before me; and I gave to the family of your ancestor all my offerings by fire from the people of Israel. Why then look with greedy eye at my sacrifices and my offerings that I commanded, and honor your sons more than me by fattening yourselves on the choicest parts of every offering of my people Israel?" Therefore the LORD the God of Israel declares: "I promised that your family and the family of your ancestor should go in and out before me forever"; but now the LORD declares: "Far be it from me; for those who honor me I will honor, and those who despise me shall be treated with contempt. See, a time is coming when I will cut off your strength and the strength of your ancestor's family, so that no one in your family will live to old age. Then in distress you will look with greedy eye on all the prosperity that shall be bestowed upon Israel; and no one in your family shall ever live to old age. The only one of you whom I shall not cut off from my altar shall be spared to weep out his eyes and grieve his heart; all the members of your household shall die by the sword. The fate of your two sons, Hophni and Phinehas, shall be the sign to you—both of them shall die on the same day. I will raise up for myself a faithful priest [*kōhēn ne'ĕmān*], who shall do according to what is in my heart and in my mind. I will build him a sure house [*bayit ne'ĕmān*], and he shall go in and out before my anointed one forever. Everyone who is left in your family shall come to implore him for a piece of silver or a loaf of bread, and shall say, Please put me in one of the priest's places, that I may eat a morsel of bread." (1 Sam. 2:27–36)

The momentous prophecy here of a "faithful priest" who will replace the corrupt house of Eli is explicitly said to be fulfilled in 1 Kings 2:27, when King Solomon finally sends away Abiathar, the last of Eli's line, from the Jerusalem court, making way for the appointment of Zadok as chief priest. Frank Moore Cross detects behind this the rivalry of two ancient priestly houses, both Levite and both Amramite—namely, the Aaronide and Mushite (i.e., Mosaic) lines.[1] An Elide claim on Mosaic priestly descent could indeed be alluded to in the man of God's mention of an ancestor elected as priest in Egypt—though this might alternatively hint at the patriarch Levi himself, a tradition with other echoes (cf. Deut. 33:8). The clan of *mûšî* is named in the archaic fragment in Numbers 26:58 listing the Levitical groups (cf. 1 Chron. 23:14). The phenomenon of a very ancient Mushite priesthood would be paralleled, in any case, by the priestly family of Jonathan son of Gershom, son of Moses at the temple in Dan (Judg. 18:30).

---

1. See Frank Moore Cross, *Canaanite Myth and Hebrew Epic: Essays in the History of the Religion of Israel* (Cambridge, MA: Harvard University Press, 1973), 197–98. According to 1 Chron. 24:3, Ahimelech, Abiathar's father, is himself a descendant of Ithamar, the son of Aaron. In the context of the Chronicler's larger project, however, this is plausibly taken as a retroactive effort to clean up postexilic genealogical confusion and give all priestly figures a proper Aaronide pedigree.

The Mosaic character of the worship at Shiloh is certainly clear. In the first place, the ark is said to rest at Shiloh (1 Sam. 3:3; 4:3–5), which ties the site directly with the wilderness cult. Direct mention of the "tent of meeting" in 1 Samuel 2:22 additionally suggests that the wilderness tabernacle itself served as a tent shrine at Shiloh. Scholars have doubted the accuracy of this claim, supposing it to be a late, postexilic attempt to link the sins of Hophni and Phinehas to the flagrant crimes recounted in Numbers 25, which took place "in the sight of Moses and in the sight of the whole congregation of the Israelites, while they were weeping at the entrance of the tent of meeting" (Num. 25:6). This intertextual link is undoubtedly real, for like the Israelite man who lay with the Midianite woman—evidently inside the tabernacle itself (!) (Num. 25:8)—Hophni and Phinehas "lay with the women who served at the entrance to the Tent of Meeting" (1 Sam. 2:22).[2] As Moses' own Midianite wife hovers uncomfortably in the background of the original Phinehas story,[3] however, the conclusion to draw is simply that 1 Samuel 2, like Numbers 25, is an exaltation of the Aaronides over their fraternal Mushite rivals (cf. Num. 12). In other words, the heavy-handed polemic in 1 Samuel against the sins of Eli's sons and their looming dynastic annihilation has been carefully keyed to Solomon's change of priestly lines when he consecrated the Jerusalem temple.[4] This double transition is manifest in the promise that the Lord will "build him a sure [faithful] house" for the faithful priest (1 Sam. 2:35), a clear parallel to the same promise made to David in 2 Samuel 7. As in that royal application, there is here a double dynastic and architectural sense to the word "house," for the new line of Zadokite priests will serve, not like Eli in a tent, but in a solid sanctuary: a clear image of cultic perpetuity.[5]

What we see is supersessionism in the Old Testament mode: the replacement of one cult system, with its sanctuary and conjoined priesthood, by another definitive and lasting institution. Note how intimately allied the two priesthoods are, however—born of the same parents, with the more ancient

2. The original sense of Num. 25:8 might have implied that Cozbi was in fact the priestess of a local tent-shrine and was killed there, though the common understanding was established very early, as is already supported by the LXX. See S. C. Reif, "What Enraged Phineas? A Study of Numbers 25:8," *JBL* 90 (1971): 200–206.

3. David P. Pettit ("Expiating Apostasy: Baal Peor, Moses, and Intermarriage with a Midianite Woman," *JSOT* 41 [2018]: 468) argues that "the Baal Peor incident of Num. 25.1–18, with the intermarriage of Zimri and Cozbi, both confronts Moses for his failure to oversee the people and implicates his own marriage with a Midianite."

4. Augustine (*City of God* 17.5) is correct in all his typological reasoning about the passage but is mistaken on this point of detail, believing Eli to be of the Aaronic line.

5. The text of 1 Samuel possibly suggests a permanent temple building as the place where the ark was kept, described as the Lord's "house" and *hêkāl* (1 Sam. 1:9, 24; 3:3, 15). After three archeological missions at Shiloh and a fourth ongoing, material evidence of the cultic center has not yet been found. See Scott Stripling, "The Israelite Tabernacle at Shiloh," *Bible and Spade* 29 (2016): 89–94.

Mosaic cult destined to disappear and be replaced by a new, ascendant priestly order. Note further that the person of the prophet (i.e., Samuel) is not the ultimate replacement of the corrupt line of priests. One priesthood, represented as the perennial establishment, simply supplants another, tied to the transient wilderness order. In all this, the pattern of Christian supersessionism is prophetically anticipated point for point.

It would be quite wrong, of course, to limit the entire story to a tale of Zadok's house's increase and Eli's decrease. There is a very lively moral question at stake that goes much deeper than genealogy and is the overt interest of the text—for the "sons of Eli were scoundrels; they had no regard for the LORD or for the duties of the priests to the people" (1 Sam. 2:12). Fattening themselves like proto-versions of Yohanan ben Narbai and unchaste as a monk in Chaucer, the Elides' greed and contempt for the people and for their sacrificial duties earn their priestly house a proleptic place of dishonor already in Hannah's song of reversal: "Those who were full have hired themselves out for bread" (1 Sam. 2:5). Having stuffed themselves, they will beg for a morsel, the man of God repeats.

The faithful priest who arises is accordingly not celebrated for his Aaronide lineage. Rather, he is worthy inasmuch as he shall act according to the heart of the Lord (1 Sam. 2:35). The Deuteronomistic redactor has embedded a key theme and prepared a very suggestive echo with this phrase about God's heart, for several chapters later, when Saul is informed that he will lose his office, just as Eli here is dethroned (cf. 1 Sam. 1:9; 2:8; 4:13), his replacement as king is announced in just these terms.

> Samuel said to Saul, "You have done foolishly; you have not kept the commandment of the LORD your God, which he commanded you. The LORD would have established your kingdom over Israel forever, but now your kingdom will not continue; the LORD has sought out a man after his own heart; and the LORD has appointed him to be ruler over his people, because you have not kept what the LORD commanded you." (1 Sam. 13:13–15)

At Saul's second offense of the same sort of cultic disobedience, the principle is made perfectly clear.

> And Samuel said,
>
> > "Has the LORD as great delight in burnt offerings and sacrifices,
> >   as in obedience to the voice of the LORD?
> > Surely, to obey is better than sacrifice,
> >   and to heed than the fat of rams.
> > For rebellion is no less a sin than divination,
> >   and stubbornness is like iniquity and idolatry.

> Because you have rejected the word of the LORD,
> he has also rejected you from being king." (1 Sam. 15:22–23)

It somehow requires a prophet, a Samuel or a man of God, to ensure a realignment of the cult with God's commandments. Faced with prophetic censure, the fall of Saul and of Eli's house have in common, despite the offering of ritual worship, their failure to obey according to the heart of YHWH. Eli himself has nothing to do with kings, of course. The rise of the faithful priest, by contrast, signals the advent of a new priestly and monarchical order, for the new priest "shall go in and out before my anointed one [literally, "my Messiah," "my Christ"] forever" (1 Sam. 2:35). This reveals, as a prophetic counterpoint to the punishment of a disobedient regime, the coming union of royal and priestly power, bound morally as one in acting according to God's heart. In the mind of the Deuteronomist, the verse not only points to Zadok's service of King Solomon but also hints at the fact that Abiathar, last in the line of Eli, fatally did not support Solomon's claim to the throne but belonged rather to the party of Adonijah (1 Kings 1:19–25).

For Christian readers, a different Son of David comes to mind, recognized as the rightful Christ/Anointed. Jeremiah's threats that "inviolable" Jerusalem would be made like Shiloh were truer than he knew—though he rightly foresaw that God would give Israel "pastors after my own heart," inaugurating a new era of worship without the ark (Jer. 3:15–16). The rejection of Eli is accordingly the type of a further fulfillment: a new priesthood beyond the whole Mosaic (and not only Mushite) order. As Augustine says:

Who that now views these things with a believing eye does not see that they are fulfilled? Since, indeed, no tabernacle, no temple, no altar, no sacrifice, and therefore no priest either, has remained to the Jews, to whom it was commanded in the law of God that he should be ordained of the seed of Aaron; which is also mentioned here by the prophet, when he says, "Thus says the Lord God of Israel, I said your house and your father's house shall walk before me forever: but now the Lord says, That be far from me; for them that honor me will I honor, and he that despises me shall be despised." . . . The death of this man's [Eli's] sons signified the death not of the men, but of the priesthood itself of the sons of Aaron. But what follows pertains to that Priest whom Samuel typified by succeeding this one. Therefore the things which follow are said of Christ Jesus, the true Priest of the New Testament: And I will raise me up a faithful Priest that shall do according to all that is in mine heart and in my soul; and I will build Him a sure house. (*City of God* 17.5)[6]

---

6. Translation from Philip Schaff, ed., *The Nicene and Post-Nicene Fathers*, First Series (Edinburgh: T&T Clark, 1993), 2:344.

4

"I Will Clothe You with Festal Apparel" (Zech. 3:4)

The Promise of a New Priesthood

The divine word communicated to the prophets was never a merciless word. Terrible and real as the judgment for sin was, hope for Israel is ever integral to the prophetic message. This is as true of the prophetic vision of the guilty priesthood as it is of the whole guilty people. An example like Ezekiel's extended tongue-lashing of the "shepherds of Israel"—"You eat the fat, you clothe yourselves with the wool, you slaughter the fatlings; but you do not feed the sheep" (Ezek. 34:3)—is, accordingly, not his final statement on the matter. The prophet also foretells the Lord's intention to intervene and set things right, as only the Lord himself can: "I myself will be the shepherd of my sheep" (34:15).

Respecting this fundamental prophetic pattern of problem-followed-by-promise always brings the Old Testament to its characteristic point of "resolved tension." The answer to the problem is given but not yet implemented. In the matter of the priesthood this means overcoming national and priestly sin through the increasing eschatological expectation of a cleansed clergy, centered upon a new high priest. In postexilic Israel such expectation became quite pronounced.

An evident movement in this climate of growing Jewish expectation is the increasingly tight fusion of this high priestly agent with the messianic Davidic heir. A new mode of royal priesthood thus appears, ultimately reinforced by the Hasmonean model of governance. In this context, notably in Ben Sira, the high priestly persona emerges as an epiphany of enormous cosmic dimensions: a theophany of divine Wisdom and cosmic *ordo*. The realized eschatology of this sapiential vision remains subtly aware of its own inadequacy, however. Thus, the canonical witness retains its essentially expectant, prophetic orientation. Indeed, the early Christian decision to order the books of the Bible so as to give the prophetic witness the final Old Testament word reveals a hermeneutic that, on this point of the priesthood at least, ultimately amplifies the voice that the Jewish canon gives to the Writings.

Joshua the High Priest and the New Temple

One of the most extraordinary and evocative of all the biblical oracles of the renewed priesthood appears in Zechariah 3. The prophecy concerns Joshua the high priest.

> Then he showed me the high priest Joshua standing before the angel of the LORD, and Satan standing at his right hand to accuse him. And the LORD said to Satan, "The LORD rebuke you, O Satan! The LORD who has chosen Jerusalem rebuke you! Is not this man a brand plucked from the fire?" Now Joshua was dressed with filthy clothes as he stood before the angel. The angel said to those who were standing before him, "Take off his filthy clothes." And to him he said, "See, I have taken your guilt away from you, and I will clothe you with festal apparel." And I said, "Let them put a clean turban on his head." So they put a clean turban on his head and clothed him with the apparel; and the angel of the LORD was standing by.
>
> Then the angel of the LORD assured Joshua, saying "Thus says the LORD of hosts: If you will walk in my ways and keep my requirements, then you shall rule my house and have charge of my courts, and I will give you the right of access among those who are standing here. Now listen, Joshua, high priest, you and your colleagues who sit before you! For they are an omen of things to come: I am going to bring my servant the Branch. For on the stone that I have set before Joshua, on a single stone with seven facets, I will engrave its inscription, says the LORD of hosts, and I will remove the guilt of this land in a single day. On that day, says the LORD of hosts, you shall invite each other to come under your vine and fig tree." (Zech. 3:1–10)

As in the book of Joshua, the Septuagint of Zechariah naturally speaks here of "*Jesus* the high priest"—an inspired precision as portentous, from the

Christian point of view, as any prophetic clairvoyance might ever claim to be. The context of Zechariah's prophetic ministry (i.e., Zech. 1–8) is the Persian period. More specifically, it occurs between February 15, 519, and December 7, 518 BC (cf. Zech. 1:7; 7:1). The "Joshua" immediately in view is accordingly that first of Israel's high priests after the exile, the son of Jehozadak, mentioned several times in the Bible (Hag. 1:1, 12, 14; 2:2, 4; Ezra 2:2; 3:2; Neh. 12:10–11; cf. excursus 3).[1] Together with the two prophets, Haggai and Zechariah himself, Joshua was one of the key religious leaders of the returned exiles who worked to rebuild the temple in Jerusalem, following Cyrus's decree in 538 BC (2 Chron. 36:22; Ezra 1:1).

On account of the Babylonian deportation and destruction, Jehozadak, Joshua's father, never served in his priestly office (cf. 1 Chron. 6:15). Jehozadak belonged to a world that had disappeared. As the scion of the legitimate Zadokite line, he is thus the priestly pendant and parallel to Zerubbabel, the dethroned Davidic heir. Both embodied the destitute fate of their destitute people. It was the fate of Jehozadak's *son*, Joshua, however, to return from Babylonia in the company of Zerubbabel and others (Ezra 2:2; 3:2; cf. Neh. 7:7) to reestablish the cult and community in Judea, now called "Yehud" in the Persian satrapy of *Abar Nahar* ("Beyond the River"). The returned exiles first set up the altar and began offering again the morning and evening sacrifices, soon making the holocaust offerings as well. This ritual service was the most urgent matter, before any work on the ruined temple was begun (Ezra 3:3, 6). Rebuilding the ruined sanctuary was the objective, however, even at the level of Cyrus's court, so timber was brought and Levites engaged to help oversee the construction (Ezra 3:7–8).

The moving liturgical celebration that accompanied the eventual laying of the foundations is easily imagined and poignantly described in Ezra 3:10–13. The emotion of joy mixed with the pangs of old trauma was overwhelming: "The people shouted so loudly that the sound was heard far away" (Ezra 3:13). The effort to bring to completion the good work thus begun unfortunately proved to be enormously difficult, however. Haggai chronicles the struggles that were involved, though Zerubbabel, more than Joshua, gets special attention from this prophet, who closes his book with the promise to make this son of David like a chosen signet ring (cf. Hag. 2:20–23).

Zechariah's greater interest in Joshua is shown by his implication in three separate oracles: here in 3:1–10 (Joshua's reclothing); in 4:6–14 (the two olive branches—namely, Zerubbabel and Joshua); and in 6:9–15 (Joshua's crown-

---

1. On Joshua and his historical context, see above all James C. VanderKam, *From Joshua to Caiaphas: High Priests after the Exile* (Minneapolis: Fortress, 2004), 1–42. On the interpretation of Zech. 3, see Carol Meyers and Eric Meyers, *Haggai, Zechariah 1–8*, AB 25B (New York: Doubleday, 1987). The following paragraphs owe much to both of these works.

ing). A basic concern across these oracles is the desire to correctly define his priestly office, especially in its relationship to the Davidic power. It is notable, in this regard, that the preexilic (First Temple) dominance of the monarchs over the priests was not and could not be repeated in the Second Temple context—the Judean monarchy being for the whole period suppressed and Zerubbabel being a deputed governor, not a king. Joshua and his high priesthood accordingly represent the first dawn of an entirely new ordering of God's people, on the far side of the ravages of national sin.

Reversing the *Rîb*

The scene presented in Zechariah 3:1–10 sets us within a courtroom. Joshua himself is the defendant, and Satan is the prosecutor, while the angel of the Lord plays the role of defense attorney. The Lord himself is, of course, the judge. Though we are familiar from the book of Job with Satan's habit of pressing charges—his name in Hebrew actually means "the Accuser"—in Zechariah we do not hear any of his accusatory speech. Instead, we join the trial after Satan's accusations are already made. With the hefty prophetic critique of the priesthood just behind us, however, it is not too difficult to summon up the sorts of priestly sins he might have rehearsed in his discourse. Indeed, in the immediate wake of the exile, the people's and the priesthood's impurity and guilt had just reached high tide.

What is immediately striking in this setup is that the action begins (or, rather, we join the action) with a frontal rebuke of the Accuser's accusation. We are suddenly not just in a courtroom but in a court of appeal. "The LORD rebuke you, O Satan! The LORD who has chosen Jerusalem rebuke you! Is not this man a brand plucked from the fire?" (Zech. 3:2). The postexilic prophetic court scene is thus revealed to be a sort of reversal of the classic preexilic prophetic *rîb*, built upon the old divine council motif. "Revealed" is not too strong a word, for the figure of Satan, who makes no appearance in the more ancient strata of Israel's Scriptures, historically comes out of hiding right around this moment—and his presence puts everything in quite a new light. The dynamic here is not at all unlike the famous case of the parallel passages of David's plague. In 2 Samuel 24:1, God incites David to sin, while in 1 Chronicles 21:1, Satan is said to have been the true and proximate inciting actor. In Zechariah 3, which forms a visionary sequel to and subversion of the old *rîb* genre, we can imagine the same variety of theodicy at work. The nasty role in pushing the prosecution against God's elect is no longer attributed to YHWH himself, as it was in a book like Hosea. It is now possible to perceive the Evil One instead actively at work trying to bring an end to God's plans for Joshua and the high priesthood. Satan, who will later try to sift Simon like wheat, already has long had it in for the priests of God's people. But just as the Lord suddenly intervenes to halt the advance of the deadly plague in 1 Chronicles 21, saying to the destroyer, "Enough, stay your hand" (1 Chron. 21:15)—that is, "Thus far shall you come, and no farther" (Job 38:11; cf. excursus 1)—so the Lord's rebuke also sets a boundary to Satan's mischief here.

The critical substance of Satan's charge—whatever its particulars—can be divined from the shape of the rebuke (cf. Jude 9). The charge concerns, quite simply, an effort to undermine the Lord's election. But Satan somehow goes too far and contradicts the fact that the Almighty, who has chosen Jerusalem as his holy city, has been pleased to snatch a priest from the flames of its destruction. Indeed, what good would a chosen temple city be without a ministering priesthood? God's powerful, intervening hand must not be missed here. How easy, indeed, it would have been for Nebuzaradan simply to kill the young Joshua, together with his father, and snuff out the high priestly line altogether, as the Babylonian captain had without scruple executed Seraiah, the chief priest and Joshua's grandfather, and Zephaniah, the so-called second priest (2 Kings 25:18; cf. Jer. 52:24). While the very fact of Joshua's deportation to Babylon may, ironically, form part of Satan's charge—the high priestly heir is defiled from his sojourn and upbringing in an unclean, idolatrous land (cf. Hosea 9:3–4; Amos 7:17)—this narrow escape was no historical happenchance but a salvific act of rescue and part of a divine design to restore Jerusalem and its cultic dwelling. God's providential toppling of the Babylonian power and the rise of Persia obviously contributed mightily to the dramatic reversal that suddenly found Joshua, the descendant of Aaron, alive and offering sacrifice in the burnt-out shell of the Lord's own temple. This man has been mercifully saved from the fire of blazing judgment, by which the Lord shows himself holy (cf. Lev. 10:3)—in order, with his fellows, to be a "sign" (Zech. 3:8).

"Take Off His Filthy Clothes"

Joshua's condition of utter filthiness carries many connotations. It suggests the haggard appearance of one who has had a close call with national sin, as he certainly has. It also hints at ritual and perhaps even moral pollution, though the Hebrew word $\d{s}ô'îm$ is not a technical term of impurity. The removal of the dirty clothes is, nevertheless, presented directly as a removal of "your guilt" in Zechariah 3:4. Although "your" is here singular, what is most likely evoked by this image is the entire cultic situation of Jerusalem itself—high priest, priests, and people together—defiled and profaned seemingly beyond all repair: a collective fatality of its own collective guilt.[2]

2. See Lena-Sofia Tiemeyer, "The Guilty Priesthood (Zech 3)," in *The Book of Zechariah and Its Influence*, ed. Christopher Tuckett (Aldershot: Ashgate, 2003), 1–20.

A purification of the entire community of returned exiles is envisioned as necessary (and coming soon) in Ezekiel 36:22–29, soiled as many of them evidently were from having joined in the idolatry of the nations among which they had been scattered. Priests, too, no doubt lost faith in YHWH and transferred their worship to the by-all-appearances victorious gods of Babylon (cf. Isa. 36:18–20). Perhaps Joshua himself is stained by this very sin. Marriage to foreign women was no less a problem faced by the returning exiles, however, including the priests (Ezra 2:59–63). The sons of Joshua are even mentioned by name in this connection (Ezra 9:2; 10:18–19). The Targum on Zechariah 3:3 thus, unsurprisingly, links the filthy garments with this particular sin, though the chronological gap between the oracle in Zechariah, somewhere around 520 BC, and the events of Ezra 9–10, near 450 BC, makes this a problematic background.

The ongoing problems of the community replanted in Yehud (as opposed to during the time of exile itself) are an issue all their own, of course, and this sets in well before the problems recounted in Ezra. Thus, one further dimension to bear in mind in considering the image of filth and the strength of the Accuser's full case against restoring the cult and priesthood for the people is the continued guilt of the nation, even immediately after the return. In Haggai 2:10–14, the prophet says directly that they are a contagion of death, spreading impurity to everything they touch.

> On the twenty-fourth day of the ninth month, in the second year of Darius, the word of the LORD came by the prophet Haggai, saying: Thus says the LORD of hosts: Ask the priests for a ruling: If one carries consecrated meat in the fold of one's garment, and with the fold touches bread, or stew, or wine, or oil, or any kind of food, does it become holy? The priests answered, "No." Then Haggai said, "If one who is unclean by contact with a dead body touches any of these, does it become unclean?" The priests answered, "Yes, it becomes unclean." Haggai then said, So is it with this people, and with this nation [hā-gôy] before me, says the LORD; and so with every work of their hands; and what they offer there is unclean.

Scholars have suggested that, in harmony with Haggai's general message, the Judahites' failure zealously to finish the work they had begun in rebuilding the temple or, perhaps, their failure properly to rededicate the altar in accordance with the rituals prescribed in Ezekiel 43:18–27 explains the impurity in Haggai 2:14.[3] Ultimately, it seems likely that Haggai sees the people here as impure—even using for them the slur gôy, a pagan nation—because of a

---

3. See, e.g., David L. Petersen, *Haggai and Zechariah 1–8*, OTL (Philadelphia: Westminster, 1984), 84–85.

lack of clean sacrifices and clean priests. This reading hangs to some extent on grammatical details obscured by the normal translation (reflected above): "*What* they offer there is unclean," which supplies more than the Hebrew says and faces several problems, even if it is not in the end so misleading. Literally, it should probably read, "Whoever draws near there, he is unclean/defiled," as the Septuagint understands the verse, or else perhaps, "The place where they make their offerings is unclean."[4] The "there" or "place" in question is, of course, the altar or temple at large. Either reading thus confronts us with Milgrom's portrait of "Dorian Gray" (cf. excursus 1): both sinners and sanctuary are in desperate need of cleansing. This makes the situation worse than what is faced by any normal Yom Kippur. Having lost the standing battle against sin and pollution and having been completely overrun, the priests now defile whatever they touch. What offering can they thus make to purge the defiled sanctuary? The nation, become like a pagan thing, requires a new creation: a new consecration.

"I Will Clothe You with Festal Apparel"

Joshua's change of garments from filthy to festal apparel signals the wiping away of all guilt. "See, I have taken your guilt away from you, and I will clothe you with festal apparel" (Zech. 3:4). In Isaiah 61:10–62:5, Israel's postexilic restoration is captured in a similar image: she is no longer called "Forsaken," but dressed as a bride and adorned with a crown. Such ritual redressing is a powerful image of complete renewal and cleansing that persists to the present day in Christian baptism (cf. Gal. 3:27). In the ancient Israelite context there were also liturgical echoes to this gesture, and two distinct rites were associated with the ceremonial reclothing of the high priest: his ordination (Lev. 8) and his ministry on the Day of Atonement (Lev. 16).

Scholars commonly observe that Joshua is already high priest, concluding that an ordination cannot, therefore, here be in view. This is correct enough, insofar as Joshua is already the rightful heir and regularly recognized as high priest by both Haggai and Zechariah. Perhaps, then, something like a "vetting" ceremony, a kind of civil recognition process modeled on contemporary Persian court protocols, stands in part behind the scene.[5] It is worth observing that the title "high priest" is conspicuously withheld from Joshua by Ezra and Nehemiah, however. This points to something significant. Even as the true son of Aaron, Joshua, like any of his predecessors, would have required a proper

---

4. See the discussion of Lena-Sofia Tiemeyer, *Priestly Rites and Prophetic Rage*, FAT 2/19 (Tübingen: Mohr Siebeck, 2006), 233–36.

5. So Jason M. Silverman, "Vetting the Priest in Zechariah 3: The Satan between Divine and Achaemenid Administrations," *JHebS* 14 (2014): 1–27.

ritual elevation in order to assume his office. The problem of when and how this should have occurred must accordingly be faced. With the (not yet rebuilt) temple itself standing in a state of complete, defiled impurity and a high priest required to cleanse it by the rites of Yom Kippur, a serious conundrum appears. It is a tight theological circle of considerable interest: the temple needs the high priest, and the high priest needs the temple. Fallen Israel—like fallen humankind—cannot pull itself up by its liturgical bootstraps.

The problem addressed in Zechariah 3 is thus something like the crowning of an emperor. Who has the authority to confer his right upon him, he who stands above the rest? If a pope (not infrequently strong-armed into the job) was the conventional solution to this problem in medieval Europe, a similar appeal to a higher power seems to be at work in the prophetic investiture of Joshua. The Persian administration is no more able to confer, of itself, a priestly power on this son of Aaron than Cyrus can function in reestablishing the cult without YHWH's higher intervention. Zechariah thus sees in his vision nothing less than a divine coronation. Like the dreams and visions of Levi, in which the patriarch receives his priesthood directly from God (cf. excursus 2), a supernatural accreditation is here offered through the prophet's clear communication of Joshua's election.

In the vision of Zechariah 3:5, a "clean turban" (*ṣānîp ṭāhôr*) is placed on the Aaronide's head. The ritual purity expressed here is technical and intended. The singling out of the turban alone among all the vestments is also noteworthy and points ahead to the closely related passage in 6:9–14.

> The word of the LORD came to me: Collect silver and gold from the exiles—from Heldai, Tobijah, and Jedaiah—who have arrived from Babylon; and go the same day to the house of Josiah son of Zephaniah. Take the silver and gold and make a crown [plural *'ăṭārôt* MT; *stephanous* LXX], and set it on the head of the high priest Joshua son of Jehozadak; say to him: Thus says the LORD of hosts: Here is a man whose name is Branch: for he shall branch out in his place, and he shall build the temple of the LORD. It is he that shall build the temple of the LORD; he shall bear royal honor, and shall sit upon his throne and rule. There shall be a priest by his throne, with peaceful understanding between the two of them. And the crown shall be in the care of Heldai, Tobijah, Jedaiah, and Josiah son of Zephaniah, as a memorial in the temple of the LORD. (Zech. 6:9–14)

Again Joshua is crowned—but here the deed is not confined to the prophet's ecstatic vision but transpires in real life, in one of the prophet's famous symbolic actions, with named individuals joining in the fabrication of a real golden crown, which is really set on Joshua's head in the house of Josiah. The elaborate gesture nevertheless preserves its symbolic character, not unlike the anointing of Jesus at Bethany.

It is pedantic and misleading to object that there is no hint of ordination in Zechariah's oracles and actions. It is nonetheless true that the thrust of these traditions is distinct. As much as it serves to repair his impaired high priestly status, the election of Joshua that Zechariah reveals cannot be imagined as a simple evocation of the model of consecration in Leviticus 8–9. In this new context new expedients are required, and the designation and ritual dressing of Joshua has its main concern elsewhere. The prophet means to reveal the high priest's divinely established, coequal place in collaboration with the "Branch." The "peaceful understanding" announced as reigning between this one, who bears the royal honor, and the "priest by his throne" recalls the "faithful priest" of 1 Samuel 2, destined to serve in union with the coming messiah (see excursus 4). The oracle in Zechariah 4:10–14 actually speaks of the "two anointed ones" (literally, "sons of oil"), meaning Zerubbabel and Joshua: the beginning of a double messianism that will become very strong at Qumran and leaves marks on the New Testament itself (see chap. 5 below). The *new priest*, on the far side of sin, cannot be imagined in his office apart from the Branch.

The Day of Atonement

If Joshua's reclothing expresses a kind of priestly elevation touched with new regal dressing, the reclothing in Leviticus 16 is also in play. As on the day of his ordination, the ritual dressing and washing of the high priest were an essential part of the rites of Yom Kippur. In various ways, in fact, "for the high priest the Day of Atonement functions as a yearly ritual confirmation of his high priesthood."[6] The key that clinches the allusion to this feast in Zechariah 3, however, is the Lord's added statement in 3:9 that "I will remove the guilt of this land in a single day." As Lena-Sofia Tiemeyer observes, "The only such day known in the Hebrew Bible is the annual Day of Atonement."[7] Thus, while relevant cultic terms such as *ḥaṭṭāʾt* and *kippēr* do not appear in the passage, many scholars nevertheless accept an association of this oracle with Yom Kippur.

In this connection, a subtle nuance in the Hebrew once again arises, suggesting the possibility of quite an interesting modification in the translation. The verb rendered above as "remove" (i.e., "I will remove the guilt in one day") is more likely to be intransitive in the form that it takes in this verse, thus carrying the sense of "to depart." The resulting translation would be "I will depart with the guilt of the land in a single day" (Zech. 3:9). If this

---

6. Deborah Rooke, "The Day of Atonement as a Ritual of Validation for the High Priest," in *Temple and Worship in Biblical Israel*, ed. John Day (New York: T&T Clark, 2007), 345.

7. Tiemeyer, *Prophetic Rage*, 249.

grammatical interpretation is correct, "it appears that the clause is intended to present YHWH as in some sense taking on the role of the 'scapegoat.'"[8] Such a role would be surprising to say the least, and the philological and interpretative ice here is admittedly thin. Still, as Daniel Stökl Ben Ezra explains, "While frequently, the scapegoat is linked to evil figures, the notion of a (positive) figure functioning as scapegoat appears also in other Jewish texts."[9] A fascinating yet typically fragmentary text from Qumran (4Q521), for instance, with a number of interesting links to the *Testament of Levi* (cf. excursus 2), significantly portrays a priestly figure who shall "make atonement for all the sons of his generation and be *sent out* to all his people." This is a reference, in Stökl Ben Ezra's view, to the sequence of rites in Leviticus 16:20–22—namely, atonement followed by the sending out of the goat.

An allusion in Zechariah 3 to God himself acting as the scapegoat would, of course, be enormously suggestive. It would mean that the Lord himself somehow enters the ritual action and would plainly evoke the true high priest's bearing away the burden of sin. Christian texts are, indeed, quite familiar with this positive, christological interpretation of atonement by the "sending out" (*šlḥ*) of the "cursed" Christ (e.g., Gal. 3:13; 4:4–5).[10] The christologically redolent but pre-Christian portrayal of the Suffering Servant in Isaiah 53:4–6, moreover, as the one physically bearing (*nāśā'*) "the iniquity of us all," so that his life becomes an atonement for sin, literally a "guilt offering" (*'āšām*, Isa. 53:10; cf. Lev. 5:19), clearly plays upon a strikingly similar set of images and ideas. The abusive mistreatment of the Servant further recalls the ritual abuse of the scapegoat (e.g., spitting), which was evidently an ancient Jewish tradition as attested in multiple places (*m. Yoma* 4.2; 6.4, 6; *Tg. Yer. I* on Lev. 16:22; Philo, *On Planting* 14.61; *1 En.* 10:4–5). The same tradition of ritual abuse is further attested in *The Epistle of Barnabas* 7.5–11, which makes the christological application.[11]

> Pay attention to what he commanded: "Take two goats, fine and well-matched, and offer them, and let the priest take one for a whole burnt offering for sins."

8. Max Rogland, "Verb Transitivity and Ancient Hebrew מוש in Zechariah 3:9," *VT* 62 (2013): 498.

9. Daniel Stökl Ben Ezra, "Fasting with Jews, Thinking with Scapegoats: Some Remarks on Yom Kippur in Early Judaism and Christianity, in Particular 4Q541, *Barnabas* 7, Matthew 27, and Acts 27," in *The Day of Atonement: Its Interpretations in Early Jewish and Christian Traditions*, ed. Thomas Hieke and Tobias Nicklas, TBN 15 (Leiden: Brill, 2012), 178.

10. A very illuminating interpretation of Paul's Jesus-as-curse language in Galatians in the light of scapegoat imagery is offered by Daniel T. Schwartz, "Two Pauline Allusions to the Redemptive Mechanism of the Crucifixion," *JBL* 102 (1983): 259–83. The key is in Gal. 4:4, where the rare verb *exapostellō* is used (cf. Lev. 16:21–22 LXX).

11. See Hans Moscicke, "Jesus as Goat of the Day of Atonement in Recent Synoptic Gospels Research," *CBR* 17 (2018): 59–85.

But what shall they do with the other one? "The other one," he says, "is cursed."
Notice how the type of Jesus [*ho typos tou Iēsou*] is revealed! "And all of you
shall spit upon it and jab it, and tie scarlet wool around its head, and then let
it be driven out into the wilderness." . . . What is the meaning of this? Note
well: "the one is for the altar, and the other is cursed," and note that the one
cursed is crowned. For they will see him on that day, wearing a long scarlet robe
about his body, and they will say, "Is this not the one whom we once crucified,
insulting and piercing and spitting on him?" (*Barn.* 7.6–9)[12]

While it is not clear how precisely the Day of Atonement was celebrated at
the time of Joshua and Zechariah, there are reasons to take note of these
traditions.

First of all, the postexilic configuration of Yom Kippur should be seen in
the light of the Mesopotamian Akitu festival, an elaborate New Year liturgy
(like Yom Kippur itself) that featured the ritual humiliation of the Babylonian
king, including the stripping of his crown and royal insignia, his physical
abuse, and his offering a lengthy confession of guilt. At the end of this, the
king was, of course, recrowned. In chapter 2, mention was made of the way
the high priest, on the day of Yom Kippur, humbled himself by donning the
simple linen garb shared by all his brother priests, removing the vestments
distinguishing him in his office. Only after this act of debasement and after
carrying out all the deadly rites was he reclothed in all his glory. In view of
the expanded, king-like prestige accorded the postexilic Jewish high priest,
his own divesting and confession of sins over the scapegoat might have easily
taken on aspects of the impressive ritual that Israel would have experienced
in Babylon.

Sending off a goat to Azazel was itself, for its part, understood as handing
it over to some archdemon; in the expanding demonology of the postexilic
period (also a result of the experience of Israel in Babylon), Azazel became a
rebel angel in heaven (*1 En.* 10:4–8). As Satan himself, in the same atmosphere,
acquired a similar demonic persona, Joshua's unnarrated confrontation with
this demon in Zechariah 3 might have very easily taken on considerable imaginative color. Imagining the poorly clad high priest as somehow handed over
to demonic accusations and abuse would fit the situation and the scene in
Zechariah 3 rather well.[13]

One signal that the high priest had a recognized ritual share in somehow
"bearing" the people's sins is the pendant fastened to the turban of his cos-

---

12. Michael W. Holmes, ed. and trans., *The Apostolic Fathers: Greek Texts and English
Translations*, 3rd ed. (Grand Rapids: Baker Academic, 2007), 403.
13. On the evocative power of mentioning Satan in this context, see Lester Grabbe, "The
Scapegoat Tradition: A Study in Early Jewish Interpretation," *JSJ* 18 (1987): 152–67 (esp. 157,
166).

tume. Its simultaneous guilt-bearing and favor-finding function is already evident from its description in Exodus:

> It shall be on Aaron's forehead, and Aaron shall take on himself any guilt incurred in the holy offering that the Israelites consecrate as their sacred donations; it shall always be on his forehead, in order that they may find favor before the LORD. (Exod. 28:38)

The turban was the only distinguishing element of high priestly apparel that the high priest wore into the holy of holies and during all the prescribed rites. It alone, therefore—symbol of the head of the mystical body—participates in the rites of humiliation and confession, as well as in the subsequent "glorification" of being reclothed. Joshua's headdress is, interestingly, the only part of his vesture that Zechariah specifically mentions (Zech. 3:5). If, as some scholars think, the mysterious "stone" upon which the Lord will engrave an inscription (Zech. 3:9) is in fact a reference to this ornament, inscribed as it was with the words "Holy to the LORD," we would have a very compact and expressive symbol of the high priest's special two-sided role.[14] In his dirty garments he bears the guilt and in his cleansed vestments he finds favor.

Prophetic Priests

Joshua is not the only priest who appears in Zechariah's vision. Attention must also be drawn to the wider circle of priestly "colleagues" who sit before the high priest in Zechariah 3:8 and are called "men of *môpēt*"—that is, "men of omen." Joshua is clearly envisioned not as a solitary pontiff but as the presiding member of a priestly college, who together animate the nation's worship. This is a point of prime importance for establishing the continuity of an eschatological priestly class that collaborates with the true Jesus, our high priest. The high priest does not minister alone.

The specific "portent" or "omen" connected to the men of this priestly college is difficult to interpret, but Carol and Eric Meyers offer a very alluring explanation.

> Whereas in the preexilic period the prophets loomed as the ultimate recourse in the seeking of God's purposes, the emerging status of the Torah literature as the community rule in the post-exilic period gave to the guardians and promulgators of that literature, namely the priests, the function of communicators of divine will that had previously rested with the prophets. . . . Zechariah's utilization

14. Tiemeyer, "Guilty Priesthood," 9–10.

of the phrase "men of portent" thus reflects the process of priestly absorption
of a function previously associated chiefly with the prophets.[15]

In other words, far from foretelling the end of the *priesthood*, prophecy foresees instead its own eclipse! For most scholars, the second half of Zechariah
(chaps. 9–14) already represents a move in this fateful direction of the dissolu-
tion of classical prophecy into apocalyptic.[16] By the time the Hellenistic age
arrives, the "cessation of prophecy" has the appearance of an acknowledged
fact (cf. Dan. 3:38 LXX; Ps. 74:8; 1 Macc. 4:46; 9:27; 14:41; 1QS 9, 11; 4Q175,
5; *b. Sanh.* 11a; *t. Soṭah* 13.2).

Exaggerated scholarly estimates of this situation have not been helpful,
it must be said.[17] In Julius Wellhausen's (d)evolutionary reconstruction of
ancient Israel, for instance, "the Babylonian Exile completed the triumph of
the law" and marked the death of "the old freedom" and "religious spirit"
of true prophecy. "We may call Jeremiah the last of the prophets," he says,
for "those after him were prophets in name only."[18] If this reflects a typically
problematic distaste for all "priestcraft" as such, the recognition of a major
socioreligious caesura is not misguided. Without a monarchy, how could classical prophecy, which functions in conjunction with the royal court, possibly
retain its original form? Differing perspectives on what counts as prophecy
obviously shape our perception of prophecy's cessation or continuation in
the postexilic era. At a minimum, however, one can affirm an epochal change
in the character of the prophetic charism as it functioned within Israel. The
long arc traced from pre- to postexilic prophecy within the Book of the Twelve
Minor Prophets is itself adequate to measure something of this movement
and transformation.[19]

15. Meyers and Meyers, *Zechariah 1–8*, 200.

16. The classic articulation of this theory is Paul D. Hanson's *The Dawn of Apocalyptic: The
Historical and Sociological Roots of Jewish Apocalyptic Eschatology* (Philadelphia: Fortress,
1984). See also Eric Meyers, "Messianism in First and Second Zechariah and the 'End' of Biblical Prophecy," in *"Go to the Land I Will Show You": Studies in Honor of Dwight W. Young*,
ed. Joseph E. Coleson and Victor H. Matthews (Winona Lake, IN: Eisenbrauns, 1996), 127–42.

17. See Benjamin Sommer, "Did Prophecy Cease? Evaluating a Reevaluation," *JBL* 115
(1996): 31–47.

18. Julius Wellhausen, *Prolegomena to the History of Israel* (Atlanta: Scholars Press, 1994),
402–3.

19. See Edgar Conrad, "The End of Prophecy and the Appearance of Angels/Messengers
in the Book of the Twelve," *JSOT* 73 (1997): 67, 75:

> The Twelve as a collage pictures the rise and fall of a prophetic past and the reinstitution
> of an angelic/messenger presence. Prophecy in the Twelve is valued as a past institution
> that is coming to an end. . . . Although the design of the Book of the Twelve indicates that
> the former individuals from Hosea through Zephaniah were prophets, . . . by the end of
> the Zechariah section of the Book, prophecy itself is seen to have no future. . . . By the
> end of the Book of the Twelve, prophets have dropped from the scene. One encounters

In the new order Zechariah foresees, the priests will be the "men of the omen," the source of the divine instruction that the prophets fault the earlier priests for failing to give. This role of the priest-scribe as a neo-prophetic (i.e., neo-Mosaic) personage, the prime dispenser of divine communications, is seen clearly in the figure of Ezra, who in the manner of a new Moses reads the Torah to all the people (Neh. 8:1–3). Ezra's overt casting as a priestly neo-Moses fits within a broader scheme closely linked to Deuteronomy 18. The *raising up* of the "faithful priest" in 1 Samuel 2:35 is of foundational importance in this regard for the way it reinterprets in an explicitly priestly direction the *raising up* of a "prophet like Moses" announced in Deuteronomy 18:15. In depicting Samuel, the Deuteronomist further plays with a *"priest* like Moses" twist on Deuteronomy 18:15.[20] Similarly, in Ezra 2:63 and Nehemiah 7:65—in direct contrast to the decision in 1 Maccabees 4:46 and a self-serving Hasmonean reading of Deuteronomy 18:15—unresolved halakic disputes are allowed to stand until *a priest* bearing the Urim and Thummim should "arise." The most important and overt priestly appropriation of Deuteronomy 18:15 appears in *Testament of Levi* 18, a text of great interest that will be considered in the following chapter. The Gospels will build directly upon this whole tradition.

We thus meet once more, under another, now quite expressive angle, a fusion of charismatic and official functions, observed in chapter 2 in the Nazirite affinities of priestly service. Against such a background we can better understand the remark about Caiaphas in John's Gospel: "He did not say this on his own, but being high priest that year he prophesied" (John 11:51).

The Old Testament Canon as a Union of Priests and Prophets

Zechariah's next-door neighbor in the canon is the book of Malachi. As the final prophet at the very end of the Book of the Twelve, a collection that is itself placed (in both the Greek and Hebrew canonical order) after all the books of the Major Prophets, the final words of Malachi embody in a special way the canonical cessation of the prophetic word. It is of deep significance in this light that we find in the final words of this final book of the final prophetic collection an editorial appendix expressing both the centrality of the Mosaic law, with all its careful prescriptions for the Levitical and priestly regime, and prophecy's own prophecy of its ultimate, eschatological return.

---

only the LORD's messenger, *mal'ākî*, "my messenger." The days of the prophets are over; and the only prophets mentioned are those from the past, Moses . . . and Elijah.

20. See Mark Leuchter, "Samuel: A Prophet or a Priest like Moses?," in *Israelite Prophecy and the Deuteronomistic History: Portrait, Reality, and the Formation of a History*, ed. Mignon R. Jacobs and Raymond F. Person Jr., AIL 14 (Atlanta: Society of Biblical Literature, 2013), 147–68.

> Remember the teaching of my servant Moses, the statutes and ordinances that
> I commanded him at Horeb for all Israel. Lo, I will send you the prophet Elijah
> before the great and terrible day of the LORD comes. (Mal. 4:4–5; 3:22–23 MT)

Moses, the original and archetypal prophet, the unique mediator of God's
Word, has here entirely assumed the shape of a lawgiver issuing statutes and
ordinances, like Ezra. This reflects the historical moment when the five books
of Moses were also finding their final canonical form. Prophecy also still has
a place and a mission, however. Brevard Childs offers a very important comment on this conjunction of motifs.

> The theological relation between the law and the prophets is strikingly illus-
> trated by Malachi. The prophet utters a condemnation of the priestly cul-
> tic worship which is as penetrating and critical as any of the eighth-century
> prophets. Yet the final appeal to the normative role of the Mosaic law serves
> not to restrict, nor soften the prophet's proclamation, but rather to reaffirm
> the ground of Israel's existence testified to in the entire Old Testament. The
> canonical form of Malachi bears witness to Israel's conviction that the law and
> the prophets were not in opposition to each other, but constituted an essential
> unity within the divine purpose.[21]

Israel indeed ultimately discerned an "essential unity" between the institutional priesthood and the prophetic critique, as Childs so rightly observes.
This fact must not be misread, however, for such unity was a kind of self-
evident fact, not the harmonistic surmounting of a modern Protestant problem. Malachi's vision of the peaceful, proto-canonical coexistence of priest
and prophet is, in other words, hardly meant as an answer to Wellhausen's
strong value judgments in favor of prophecy over the priesthood.

　To avoid misconstruing the moment of canonical synthesis, we are encour-
aged to rethink Malachi's pairing of Elijah and Moses in light of the fusing
of prophetic and priestly identities that we have seen. Indeed, the return of
Elijah must be reconsidered in light of the priestly interpretations of Deuteronomy 18:15 surveyed above. The two, in fact, intersect. Ben Sira, who already
knows the Twelve in the form of a collected canonical whole (Sir. 49:10),
refers directly to Elijah's return at the end of Malachi, a rare, rather muted
but revealing glimpse of this wisdom book's eschatological expectations:
"At the appointed time, as it is written, you [Elijah] are destined to calm the
wrath of God" (48:10). For Ben Sira, moreover, Elijah majestically "arises"
(qûm, anestē, Sir. 48:1; cf. 47:1): yet another identification with the Mosaic
prophet, and another reason to wonder whether we might not confront here

21. Brevard Childs, *Introduction to the Old Testament as Scripture* (Philadelphia: Fortress,
1979), 497.

an Elijah as the Moses-like prophet carrying out an eschatological priestly service. Ben Sira's Elijah is, indeed, suggestively described as burning with "zeal" (48:23–24): the signal mark of Phinehas, whose own zeal won him an enduring priestly covenant (45:23).

Elijah and the Ideal Levite

Somewhere between the blended redaction and reception histories of Malachi, between the creation of a canon and the history of that canon's own internal self-interpretation on the part of Israel's scribes, Elijah the prophet came to be awaited specifically as the great high priest of the messianic era. This transformation is perhaps surprising, but a well-attested Jewish expectation.[22] Recent research, above all a fine study by Lotta Valve, has shown that this notion is much earlier than often recognized and has a prehistory reaching deep into the Second Temple period.[23] Sirach betrays early evidence of the notion, but the text of Malachi stands at the center of the story.

The book of Malachi is the earliest written source concerning Levi that has been preserved. The prophecy itself is a scribal production, likely stemming from a Levitical circle. The Targum fancifully identifies the "Malachi" in the book's superscription by the clause "whose name was Ezra the scribe," a suggestion that fits well with certain concerns shared by both the prophet and the priest/scribe—endogamy, for example (Ezra 9:1–2; 10:10–24). For modern scholars, by contrast, the prophetic personage identified as "Malachi" and named as author of the book in Malachi 1:1 is retroactively drawn from the mysterious figure called "my messenger" in 3:1. Like the author of the book, this messenger in 3:1–4 is also often considered part of the priestly establishment.[24] We face priest-prophets on all sides.

The account of the sending of the messenger is a very famous text, thanks to both Handel and the Gospels.

See, I am sending my messenger [mal'ākî] to prepare the way before me, and the Lord whom you seek will suddenly come to his temple. The messenger of

22. On this tradition, see Robert Hayward, "Phinehas—the Same Is Elijah: The Origins of a Rabbinic Tradition," *JJS* 29 (1978): 22–34; and Alexander Zeron, "The Martyrdom of Phineas-Elijah," *JBL* 98 (1979): 99–100.

23. Lotta Valve, *Early Modes of Exegesis: Ideal Figures in Malachi as a Test Case* (Åbo: Åbo Akademis, 2014).

24. See Julia M. O'Brien, *Priest and Levite in Malachi* (Atlanta: Scholars Press, 1990), 143–48. See also B. Malchow, "The Messenger of the Covenant in Mal. 3:1," *JBL* 103 (1984): 252–55; and Rex Mason, "The Prophets of the Restoration," in *Israel's Prophetic Tradition: Essays in Honour of Peter R. Ackroyd*, ed. Richard Coggins, Anthony Phillips, and Michael Knibb (Cambridge: Cambridge University Press, 1982), 149–50.

the covenant in whom you delight—indeed, he is coming, says the LORD of
hosts. But who can endure the day of his coming, and who can stand when
he appears?

For he is like a refiner's fire and like fullers' soap; he will sit as a refiner and
purifier of silver, and he will purify the descendants of Levi and refine them
like gold and silver, until they present offerings to the LORD in righteousness.
Then the offering of Judah and Jerusalem will be pleasing to the LORD as in
the days of old and as in former years. (Mal. 3:1–4)

Evident here is an example of what one scholar calls "the sudden appearance of *mal'ākîm* [i.e., messengers] in the Persian section of the Book of
the Twelve [i.e., Haggai-Zechariah-Malachi]."[25] Great interest naturally
arises concerning the identity of this particular *mal'ākî* figure here at the
end of the collection of the Minor Prophets.[26] It is important, however, not
to overlook the action in searching for the agent. As in Zechariah 3:1–10,
but using a different image, Malachi is concerned with the purification
of *the temple priesthood*—not only the high priest but *the whole tribe of
Levi*. The final goal of the purification is very plainly stated: the righteous
offering of pleasing sacrifice. This is not a non-cultic, purely "spiritual"
priesthood.

One additional, noteworthy "messenger" appears within the book, in the
description of the ideal Levite/priest in Malachi 2:4–7.

Know, then, that I have sent this command to you, that my covenant with Levi
may hold, says the LORD of hosts. My covenant with him was a covenant of life
and well-being, which I gave him; this called for reverence, and he revered me
and stood in awe of my name. True instruction was in his mouth, and no wrong
was found on his lips. He walked with me in integrity and uprightness, and he
turned many from iniquity. For the lips of a priest should guard knowledge,
and people should seek instruction from his mouth, for he is the messenger of
the LORD of hosts.

The heavy emphasis laid here both upon the word "covenant" and upon the
ideal of priestly instruction is striking. It contrasts directly with the actual
state of affairs revealed in the following verse.

But you have turned aside from the way; you have caused many to stumble by
your instruction; you have corrupted the covenant of Levi, says the LORD of
hosts. (Mal. 2:8)

25. Conrad, "End of Prophecy," 69.
26. The echo in Mal. 3:1 of Exod. 23:20 is strong (especially in the Greek), as all the commentators note: "Behold, I send an angel/messenger [*mal'āk*, MT; *ton angelon mou*, LXX]
before you to guard your way."

The "corruption" of the covenant made with Levi, on account of the priests' bad example and bad instruction, makes all the more compelling the coming of the "messenger of the covenant" in Malachi 3:1. An eschatological rescue operation is underway to ensure that the covenant with Levi might endure (Mal. 2:4; cf. Exod. 40:15; Num. 25:13; Jer. 33:17–18, 20–22). A fabulous wordplay in Malachi 3:2 underscores this interest. The messenger of the covenant will wash the sons of Levi with *bōrît*, "soap"—a word that in the Hebrew text has the same form as the word for "covenant," *běrît*. If we wonder what *běrît* is here at stake, the specific description of the "covenant with Levi" in 2:4 as a covenant of life and well-being (*šālôm*) echoes the formula in Numbers 25:12 quite directly: "I hereby grant him [Phinehas] my covenant of peace [*běrîtî šālôm*]."

This echo is not empty. Evidence of an emergent canon-consciousness is visible here; and there are, in fact, significant hints of interaction between Malachi and the Phinehas tradition in Numbers 25.[27] In addition to the link with the "covenant of peace" (Num. 25:12; cf. Sir. 45:24), we may note Levi's turning many away from sin, mentioned in Malachi 2:6. If the Levi figure in Malachi 2 is read as the patriarch himself—as ancient readers seem to have presumed—the Shechem episode in Genesis 34 presents itself as the only possible narrative referent. This violent episode was understood in certain later Second Temple traditions to have merited Levi his priesthood (see excursus 2); it was specifically viewed as preventing the sin of intermarriage between the Israelites and their pagan neighbors, a misdeed closely connected to cultic "adultery" as already seen in the case of Hosea in the preceding chapter. The continuation of Malachi's oracle in Malachi 2:8–16 points to a keen contextual interest in exactly this issue and pursues an open polemic against intermarriage. In this light, the corrupting of the "covenant of Levi" in Malachi 2:8 would concern the same issue addressed in Nehemiah 13:29, which speaks of the "defilement of the priesthood and the covenant of the priesthood and the Levites."[28] Nehemiah spoke of such defilement because of the sin of intermarriage, and he found guilty even one of the sons of Jehoiada, son of the high priest Eliashib and Joshua's great-grandson (Neh. 13:28; cf. 13:23–29; Ezra 9:1–2; 10:10–24). Ezra, for his part, knows of seventeen priest violators (Ezra 10:18–22).

In view of this nexus of covenant marriage motifs, the connection of Malachi to the covenant made with Phinehas is easily seen. Like his forefather Levi, Phinehas, who speared the Israelite coupling with a Midianite woman,

---

27. In what follows, I closely follow Valve, *Ideal Figures in Malachi*, 63–89.

28. On this important issue in Second Temple context, see Martha Himmelfarb, "Levi, Phineas, and the Problem of Intermarriage at the Time of the Maccabean Revolt," *JSQ* 6 (1999): 1–24.

was recognized as a zealot not simply against idolatry but specifically against intermarriage, idolatry's precursor and symptom. More positively stated, Phinehas's zeal acts in favor of absolute fidelity to the Lord. To maintain the covenant uncorrupted meant observing proper sexual purity and absolute fidelity to YHWH. In this light, Malachi's messenger of the covenant, the ideal Levite, who will purify the sons of Levi, has the essentially Ezra-like task of sifting through Israel's priestly company, case by case, picking out the holy remnant. From this purified priestly college, the covenant of peace with Levi will be rebooted, and the continuity of the restoration with the old order will be ensured.

Where is Elijah in all of this? By sheer proximity and similarity of description, the "messenger of the LORD of hosts" in Malachi 2 was easily identified with the "messenger of the covenant" in Malachi 3. For a number of reasons, not least proximity once again, the latter figure was understood from the context to be equal to Elijah, whose coming is described in a similar way. Once Elijah was thereby linked through Malachi 3 to the ideal Levite in Malachi 2, the dynamic interior to that earlier chapter equated him with the priestly personage of Phinehas, the high priest. Wherever precisely Ben Sira/Sirach stands in this process of inner-biblical reading, the overt identification of Elijah with Phinehas is complete at the latest by Pseudo-Philo's *Liber Antiquitatum Biblicarum* (48:1) in the first century AD.[29] This is of great importance, for, as we will see in chapter 5, the Gospels presuppose exactly this priestly background of the prophet Elijah.

The Return of Glory to God's Temple

The zealous arrival of Elijah/Phinehas like fire into the midst of God's temple should sound a familiar note. It recalls the fire of God's glory that blazed in the desert, fell upon Solomon's altar, and then departed from the temple in Ezekiel's vision. In the pitiful conditions of postexilic Israel, the barely rebuilt temple and its haggard, impure priestly staff fell shamefully short of the glorious visions of the rebuilt city. The great, overriding expectation and longing in Israel was for a return of the divine *kābôd*. In this context Elijah arises again, "a prophet like fire" (Sir. 48:1), and "like a refiner's fire" he enters the temple.

Malachi's messenger's arrival follows closely upon the closing vision of Zechariah 14, which is a depiction of Jerusalem's final restoration. The temple, the Lord's dwelling, here stands at the center of a giant universal pilgrimage festival, while the waters that flow out of this eschatological city

---

29. In contemporary scholarship, "Ben Sira" commonly refers to the Hebrew form of the book and "Sirach" to the Greek version.

(Zech. 14:8) recall Ezekiel's temple vision (see excursus 6)—as does the return of God's majestic glory from the east (14:4–6). Ezekiel, of course, had orchestrated a reversal of the Lord's departure from the temple, as witnessed at the river Chebar, through a replay of the glorious descent of divine *kābôd* in Exodus 40:34–38. This pentateuchal high point, we have seen, has its pendant and ultimate climax in the cultic glory of the priestly ordination rites in Leviticus 8–9. Not unlike Leviticus's relation to Exodus, Malachi thus brings Zechariah and indeed the vision of the whole prophetic corpus to its final priestly consummation.

The Old Testament thus displays an express interest in glorified temple worship as the culminating form of its prophetic expectation. Malachi adds a final, distinctly priestly note to this vision of eschatological glory in a purified temple (a priestly orientation reinforced by Zechariah, as well). So, unless we are prepared to imagine an eschatological temple without a priesthood— which is certainly not what the Old Testament had in mind (but which will be an honest question posed by our two following New Testament chapters)—we are left with a prophetic vision awaiting an eschatological high priest, one destined to purify the priests and revive the covenant of Levi.

The Catholic canon goes one step further, of course, for it includes the slightly later, so-called deuterocanonical books. Accordingly, the Catholic Bible both responds to the "post-prophetic" apocalyptic movement and attains a kind of balanced, canonical symmetry reprising the Pentateuch's hefty priestly interest in a striking new way otherwise lacking from the Protestant Scriptures. A very brief look at the book of the priest-scribe Jesus ben Sira will make this clear and provide a fitting way to terminate our necessarily selective survey of the Old Testament theology of the priesthood. Like Malachi, but in a very different fashion, the remarkable book of Ben Sira presents an impressive "canonical" synthesis and reformulation of Israel's sacred traditions.

"His Glorious Robe"

Like the prophets, Ben Sira manifests a deep interest in ethics, and spiritual sacrifice is an idea present in his doctrine (cf. chap. 3 above). He is thus a critic of cultic abuse from this characteristically prophetic point of view (e.g., Sir. 34:21–35:16). Missing, however, are other sharp and negative views of the Jerusalem priesthood, especially their marriage practices, as these views developed at Qumran and in extrabiblical apocalyptic texts like *1 Enoch* and *Aramaic Levi*.[30] In the *Book of the Watchers* (*1 En.* 12–16), for instance, the

---

30. See Benjamin G. Wright III, "Ben Sira and the *Book of the Watchers* on the Legitimate Priesthood," in *Intertextual Studies in Ben Sira and Tobit*, ed. Jeremy Corley and Vincent Skemp,

fallen Watchers, who descend to earth and have relations with the daughters of men, are priestly angels fallen from the heavenly temple who represent the Jerusalem priests who have entered into illicit unions contrary to legislation like that of Leviticus 21. What we find, instead, in Ben Sira is a robust affirmation of the temple establishment. This is all the more impressive when we take account of the manifest corruption plaguing the priestly office at the time of the Oniads, when Ben Sira was written (see excursus 3). As a theological point of orientation, therefore, in the bewildering jungle of late, "intertestamental" Judaism (here obviously a Protestant category), it would be hard to underestimate the importance of Ben Sira's serene canonical pointer to the priesthood. The authoritative tradition did not opt to follow the apocalyptic road of radical rejection.

Ben Sira's intense interest in the sacrificial liturgy of the temple and in other priestly themes, like priestly legitimacy and the high priestly office, is unmistakable.[31] His many contacts with the P traditions are particularly noteworthy. In 45:8–13 Aaron's "splendid vestments" are elaborately and accurately described; in 45:14 and 16 mention is made of the atoning sacrifices; in 45:15 Moses' consecration of Aaron with holy oil is evoked; the rebellion of Korah is recalled in 45:18–19 (cf. chap. 2 above).

Nowhere is this priestly sympathy so evident as in chapters 44–50, however, in the section called the "Praise of the Fathers." Certain scholars convincingly contend that, at a time when Israel lacked a king and had not had one for several centuries, the vision promoted in Sirach 44–50 is that the high priest himself is the legitimate leader of the people and that the nation, in fact, requires no king. Kingly qualities are accordingly attributed to priestly figures, while royal figures take on a priestly color. Thus, David's role as custodian of the sanctuary and liturgy is celebrated in a way already familiar, for instance, from Chronicles (see excursus 5). The compact voice of Ben Sira is, nonetheless, distinct.

> He placed singers before the altar,
>> to make sweet melody with their voices.
> He gave beauty to the festivals,
>> and arranged their times throughout the year,
> while they praised God's holy name,
>> and the sanctuary resounded from early morning. (Sir. 47:9–10)

The long eulogy of Aaron in Sirach 45:6–22 and the attention paid to Phinehas in 45:23–24 demonstrate Ben Sira's positive perspective on the priesthood and

---

CBQMS 38 (Washington, DC: Catholic Biblical Association of America, 2005), 241–54. Scholars commonly postulate that the bitter views toward the priestly establishment that come to expression in such materials stem ultimately from disenfranchised priestly and Levitical circles that were marginalized by the reigning Zadokite regime.

31. See Saul M. Olyan, "Ben Sira's Relationship to the Priesthood," *HTR* 80 (1987): 261–86.

reveal his acceptance of an exclusive "covenant of friendship/peace," a seemingly pan-Aaronide priesthood, entrusted to Aaron and all his descendants.

Ben Sira's fusion of priest and king was not yet possible at the time of Zechariah, whose diarchic messianism still makes a clear distinction between the "two sons of oil."[32] Ben Sira's perspective, which is advanced in the later Greek translation, thus represents an important final stage and addition to the earlier fusion of priest and prophet. Revealing in the context is the transfer of motifs connected with the eternal covenant and mercy promised to David to Phinehas, who is likewise granted mercy and an eternal covenant. Of subtle but special significance in this new composite, royal rendering of the priest is also his intimate connection to wisdom. The construction of the priest as a scribe/sage and interpreter of Torah has deep roots in Deuteronomy and the Deuteronomic reform, of course. Notably, in this context, the king was to devote himself to study of the Torah like a scribe:

> When he has taken the throne of his kingdom, he shall have a copy of this law written for him in the presence of the Levitical priests. It shall remain with him and he shall read in it all the days of his life, so that he may learn to fear the LORD his God, diligently observing all the words of this law and these statutes. (Deut. 17:18–19)

Now this activity becomes the proper preoccupation of Aaron and his sons, who are also (like Moses) "to teach Jacob the testimonies, and to enlighten Israel with his [God's] law" (Sir. 45:17).

The acme of Ben Sira's theology of the priesthood appears in the paean to the high priest Simon ben Onias in Sirach 50.[33] The magnificent passage, probably depicting Simon II, "the Just" (219–199 BC), is the climax of the book and merits a full citation. After a brief account of Simon's accomplishments for the physical welfare of Jerusalem (50:1–4), the encomium continues with a long poetic description of the glorious sight of Simon ministering liturgically in the temple (50:1–21).

> The leader of his brothers and the pride of his people
> was the high priest, Simon son of Onias,

---

32. On the subtle messianism of Ben Sira, see Jeremy Corley, "Seeds of Messianism in Hebrew Ben Sira and Greek Sirach," in *The Septuagint and Messianism*, ed. Michael Knibb, BETL 195 (Leuven: Leuven University Press, 2006), 301–12. Corley envisions a mild form of diarchic messianism, which entertains "some kind of future hope for the Davidic dynasty, alongside the priestly leader" (303). Note the evocation of both Zerubbabel and Joshua in Sir. 49:11–12.

33. On this text, see Otto Mulder, *Simon the High Priest in Sirach 50: An Exegetical Study of the Significance of Simon the High Priest as Climax to the Praise of the Fathers in Ben Sira's Concept of the History of Israel*, JSJSup 78 (Leiden: Brill, 2003).

who in his life repaired the house,
    and in his time fortified the temple.
He laid the foundations for the high double walls,
    the high retaining walls for the temple enclosure.
In his days a water cistern was dug,
    a reservoir like the sea in circumference.
He considered how to save his people from ruin,
    and fortified the city against siege.
How glorious he was, surrounded by the people,
    as he came out of the house of the curtain.
Like the morning star among the clouds,
    like the full moon at the festal season;
like the sun shining on the temple of the Most High,
    like the rainbow gleaming in splendid clouds;
like roses in the days of first fruits,
    like lilies by a spring of water,
    like a green shoot on Lebanon on a summer day;
like fire and incense in the censer,
    like a vessel of hammered gold
    studded with all kinds of precious stones;
like an olive tree laden with fruit,
    and like a cypress towering in the clouds.
When he put on his glorious robe
    and clothed himself in perfect splendor,
when he went up to the holy altar,
    he made the court of the sanctuary glorious.

When he received the portions from the hands of the priests,
    as he stood by the hearth of the altar
with a garland of brothers around him,
    he was like a young cedar on Lebanon
    surrounded by the trunks of palm trees.
All the sons of Aaron in their splendor
    held the Lord's offering in their hands
    before the whole congregation of Israel.
Finishing the service at the altars,
    and arranging the offering to the Most High, the Almighty,
he held out his hand for the cup
    and poured a drink offering of the blood of the grape;
he poured it out at the foot of the altar,
    a pleasing odor to the Most High, the king of all.
Then the sons of Aaron shouted;
    they blew their trumpets of hammered metal;
they sounded a mighty fanfare
    as a reminder before the Most High.

> Then all the people together quickly
>   fell to the ground on their faces
> to worship their Lord,
>   the Almighty, God Most High.
>
> Then the singers praised him with their voices
>   in sweet and full-toned melody.
> And the people of the Lord Most High offered
>   their prayers before the Merciful One,
> until the order of worship of the Lord was ended,
>   and they completed his ritual.
> Then Simon came down and raised his hands
>   over the whole congregation of Israelites,
> to pronounce the blessing of the Lord with his lips,
>   and to glory in his name;
> and they bowed down in worship a second time,
>   to receive the blessing from the Most High. (Sir. 50:1–21)

This beautiful description is generally taken to depict the high priest's ministry on Yom Kippur.[34] The image of liturgical glory is expansive, however, and the highest work of sacrificial atonement serves as a kind of cultic *pars pro toto*. The donning of Simon's "glorious robe" similarly captures in compact fashion the mood and meaning of the poem, making explicit reference back to the elaborate detailing of Aaron's vestments and "glorious robe" in Sirach 45:7–13. "Before him such beautiful things did not exist. No outsider ever put them on, but only his sons" (45:13). As one of Aaron's sons, invested with Aaron's vestments, discharging the sacred rites of Yom Kippur, Simon's forcible continuity with Aaron's priestly office makes Sirach 50 a kind of Hellenistic rendition of Leviticus 8–10.

Three things can be briefly highlighted about Sirach 50. First, Simon is not an isolated priestly figure but is presented as the "leader of his brothers" (50:1), a collegial motif we have encountered multiple times (also possibly a Davidic motif; cf. Ps. 151 in 11Q5). These assisting priests form "a garland of brothers around him," so that, preeminent among them, "he was like a young cedar on Lebanon, surrounded by the trunks of palm trees" (50:12). The liturgical function of these brother priests further engages the laypeople in one vast, collective hymn of worshipful praise (50:16–19). It is an integrated vision of the hierarchically ordered and unified ecclesial cult.

Second, while the offering of sacrifice is emphatically a corporate action (Sir. 50:12–13), Simon's construction works are a signal deed somehow credited to him alone. Royal and priestly functions have fused here yet again in this image of the patron of the holy city. The high priest's corporate personality

---

34. A minority view (i.e., Rosh Hashanah) is taken by Mulder, *Simon the High Priest*.

thus comes to the fore; but so, too, does a certain messianic and prophetic perspective in what might otherwise seem curiously mundane. In particular, although an eschatological perspective is generally missing from Ben Sira, it is important not to miss the enormously charged significance, even for this book, of rebuilding Jerusalem, its temple, and its walls. Rebuilding Jerusalem was a messianic deed, as Zechariah already saw.[35] What Simon has done in rebuilding the city remains, in fact, an incomplete work: only the image of a still-fervent expectation. In Sirach 36:18–21, Ben Sira thus prays:

> Have pity on the city of your sanctuary,
>   Jerusalem, the place of your dwelling.
> Fill Zion with your majesty,
>   and your temple with your glory.
> Bear witness to those whom you created in the beginning,
>   and fulfill the prophecies spoken in your name.
> Reward those who wait for you
>   and let your prophets be found trustworthy. (Sir. 36:18–21; cf. 48:25)

Despite the appearance of attained perfection, Ben Sira's high priest's job is not yet done.

Simon's perfected appearance has its proper place, of course, for finally and most importantly the high priest is presented as a radiant epiphany of divine glory. His blessing *is* quite simply the blessing of the Most High (Sir. 50:20). He is likened to the rainbow, sign of the Lord's own *kābôd* (50:7; cf. Ezek. 1:26–27). His priestly vestments clothe him in "perfect splendor." Most impressive of all, though, is the way Simon's likeness has been systematically coordinated with the depiction of Wisdom, the Lord's Torah, in Sirach 24.

Sirach 24	Sirach 50
24:10: "In the holy tent I ministered before him"	50:5: Simon comes out of the sanctuary, from behind the veil
24:12: "I took root in an honored people"	50:8c: "like a green shoot"
24:13a: "I grew tall like a cedar in Lebanon"	50:12c: "like a young cedar on Lebanon"
24:13b: "like a cypress on the heights of Hermon"	50:10b: "like a cypress"
24:14: "like rosebushes in Jericho"	50:8a: "like roses in the days of first fruits"
24:14: "like a fair olive tree in the field"	50:10a: "like an olive tree laden with fruit"
24:14: "like a plane tree beside water"	50:8b: "like lilies beside a spring of water"
24:15: "like galbanum, onycha, and stacte, and like the odor of incense in the tent"	50:9: "like fire and incense in the censer"

35. See, e.g., Nathan C. Johnson, "The Messianic Temple Builder in the Dead Sea Scrolls, Midrash Rabbah, and Targum Jonathan," *AncJud* 8 (2020): 199–232.

We must not miss the import of this theopoetic assimilation. Just as ancient Near Eastern royal ideology understood the temple-building monarch
as the instantiation upon earth of divine order, so now a similar cosmic role
as the ultimate agent of peace, prosperity, and order in creation descends
upon the ministering high priest. The high priest has become the actual,
earthly embodiment of personified Wisdom: a living Torah ministering in the
tent/temple. Theological space is opened here for what Philo of Alexandria
would similarly understand as the cosmic high priesthood of the *Logos*. The
christological implications are obviously immense.

Ben Sira's perception of a well-ordered cosmos, permeated by divine wisdom, functions as the fundamental "substrate" uniting the eclectic book's
widely diverse interests.[36] The specific, privileged place of Israel's cult and
priesthood within this vast cosmic vision of a harmonious *ordo* reveals that
praise of God is the proper role of humanity, and particularly of the Jewish
people. In orchestrating this praise in a preeminent way and leading the great
chorus of praising voices, the high priest stands atop the hierarchical cosmos
as a figure uniquely entrusted with maintaining and advancing universal order.
The high priest himself somehow embodies creation: he is like the sun and
the stars and the plants of the earth, Ben Sira poetically says. This harmonizes perfectly with the symbolism that the priestly vestments had over time
acquired. As Josephus tells us:

> The high-priest's tunic . . . signifies the earth, being of linen, and its blue the
> arch of heaven. . . . His upper garment, too, denotes universal nature, which it
> pleased God to make of four elements; being further interwoven with gold in
> token, I imagine, of the all-pervading sunlight. . . . By the girdle wherewith he
> encompassed it he signified the ocean, which holds the whole in its embrace.
> Sun and moon are indicated by the two sardonyxes wherewith he pinned
> the high priest's robes. As for the twelve stones, whether one would prefer
> to read in them the months or the constellations of like number, which the
> Greeks call the circle of the zodiac, he will not mistake the lawgiver's inten-
> tion. Furthermore, the headdress appears to me to symbolize heaven, being
> blue; else it would not have borne upon it the name of God. (*Ant.* 3.184–86
> [LCL])

Ben Sira's microcosmic high priest and living image of cosmic Wisdom thus
bridges the space between earth and heaven, creation and creation's source.
Yet this universal agent is planted solidly within Israel, like Wisdom in Sirach
24. Election functions here as a kind of expression of the cosmos's inherent
hierarchical order. Here, more than anywhere else in the Scriptures, we find

36. This is the thesis argued in A. Jordan Schmidt, *Wisdom, Cosmos, and Cultus in the Book
of Sirach*, DCLS 42 (Berlin: de Gruyter, 2019).

adequate resources to elaborate a truly comprehensive theology of hierarchical priesthood precisely as *holy order*.

Significantly, the Hebrew version of Ben Sira's praise of Simon concludes with a short prayer that Simon and his family will minister in perpetuity as the rightful heirs of the "covenant with Phinehas" (Sir. 50:21–24). This mention of Simon's family and the eternal covenant with Phinehas is missing from the Greek (and Syriac) version.[37]

Sirach 50:24 (LXX)	Ben Sira 50:24 (MsB; Heb.)
May he entrust with us his mercy, and in our days let him redeem us. (NETS)	May he entrust with Simon his mercy, and may he keep for him Phinehas' covenant so that he does not cut off [the office of the high priest] from him and his seed as long as heaven is above the earth [*kîmê šāmāîm*].

Most scholars have taken the Greek translation to reflect a later, updated edition, which, somehow disenchanted, no longer entertains the same hope for the Oniad cause after the treacherous murder of Onias III and the family's loss of priestly office and flight into Egyptian exile (see excursus 3). It is also possible, however, that the Hebrew prayer actually represents not the earlier but the later form.[38] As such, it would express rather an anguished hope for the return of the true priestly line of Phinehas, similar to Jeremiah's hope for a return of the Davidic line despite the monarchy's seeming dead end in exile (e.g., Jer. 33:14–26). A direct echo, in fact, links the Hebrew of Sirach 50:24 with the words about David in Psalm 89:29: "I will establish his line ["seed"] forever, and his throne *as long as the heavens endure* [*kîmê šāmāîm*]." The so-called Land of Onias (Leontopolis) in Egypt ultimately became the site of a rival Jewish temple and cult, where the house of Onias installed itself and settled upon a parallel ritual existence. It was not a solution theologically prepared to put Jerusalem's claims ahead of the family. The problem of holding true temple and true priesthood together finally reaches a point of critical stress: a regression back to Egypt and to the itinerancy of the wilderness priesthood. The Old Testament story thus ends very much where it started.

37. The two divergent texts are each very ancient and were evidently both already in existence before the end of the second century BC. (The grandfather Ben Sira wrote around 190–180 BC, and the grandson translated the book into Greek before 116 BC.) Such conflicting manuscript traditions are hardly an isolated case in this unique book. The wild textual pluriformity of Ben Sira/Sirach poses a serious challenge, in fact, for a canonical reading, if that hermeneutic is envisioned as a strictly synchronic enterprise, insensitive to the dynamic historical movement interior to the biblical tradition itself.

38. So argues Anssi Voitila, "The End of the High Priestly Family of Simon and the Conclusion of the Book of Ben Sira," *BN* 179 (2018): 69–84.

The polyphonic canonical text of Ben Sira/Sirach, in whichever direction the two traditions are taken, brings to poignant expression a problematized attachment to the Oniad cause. In the midst of intense commitment to the cultic priesthood, the realities of clerical corruption and an experience of sacerdotal exile intrude, landing the institution in a mortal crisis. The situation, which from at least one perspective looks downright hopeless, can in the end be remedied only by an act of covenantal fidelity, revealing the Lord's merciful aid.

Conclusion

Canonically considered, the Old Testament witness winds down in an intricate fashion. Yet the priestly character of Israel's hope is unmistakably clear. The prophetic corpus ultimately sounds out unambiguously in this pro-priestly direction, notwithstanding the critiques of the priesthood that the prophets also bring. The vision of a gloriously rebuilt temple and city is particularly important as the consummate and foundational form of Israel's prophetic hope. The eschatological Jerusalem as a cultic city is the presupposition that corresponds to the ministry of a cleansed priestly clan gathered around a unique priestly leader. Various figures emerge here with a messianic color: eschatological messengers and priests, Joshua, Elijah, and a Moses-like priest-prophet.

The Writings, as sampled here, reinforce this prophetic vision, even if a kind of "realized eschatology" makes the priestly picture attain a new theophanic perfection in the person of Simon. The similarity of Ben Sira's idealized vision of the priest-king to the messianic idealizations characteristic of Chronicles is particularly noteworthy (see excursus 5). Nevertheless, notes of enduring dissatisfaction and expectant hope penetrate this late Second Temple discourse of perfect liturgical order in the form of a prayer (sometimes even a cry) for the intervention of God's mercy. The typological hermeneutic that is invited by these idealized scriptural images thus stands interiorly open to a christological fulfillment.

At the end of our Old Testament survey, finally, the high priestly vestments emerge as an important scriptural idiom, expressing the character of priestly glory. From Aaron's elaborate, temple-like wardrobe, to Joshua's soiled and supernaturally cleansed apparel, to Simon's epiphanic robe—sign of the cosmic status and covenantal continuity of the priesthood—the special priestly garments represent a red (or, rather, a purplish) thread tying together the Pentateuch, Prophets, and Writings. As the Mosaic covenant's most treasured *sacramental*, the priestly vestments express and embody both the theophanic nature and the expectant prophetic orientation of the old dispensation's priestly order. We accordingly find here a line that will lead us directly to Jesus, the new Moses, and his New Covenant's sacraments of grace.

SUMMARY OF KEY POINTS

1. The prophetic corpus in the Bible was shaped by its redactors to give final priority to the hopeful promise of renewal. It is therefore a misconstrual of the prophets' rhetoric to intone the negative oracles about the cult without attending still more to the counterbalancing vision of a cleansed priesthood and a new high priest. This form of a "resolved tension" by means of prophetic promise, characteristic of the Old Testament material, ultimately points beyond itself to the actual accomplishment of the prophesied future.

2. The postexilic oracle of Joshua the high priest in Zechariah 3 reverses the older prophetic *rîb* motif, presenting a vindication and cleansing of the priesthood under the symbolic image of a changing of the high priestly vestments. The role of this newly purified high priest is inseparable from the restorative work of the royal-messianic "Branch." It climaxes in decisively removing all collective guilt, as on the day of Yom Kippur.

3. In Zechariah's prophetic vision the purified high priest appears within the context of a wider priestly college: he is not represented alone as an isolated priestly agent. These priestly "men of good omen" hint at a gradual fusing of prophetic and priestly charisms, which corresponds to an emergent priestly reading of Deuteronomy 18 that will prove very important (see chap. 5).

4. As the last book in the collection of the Twelve, Malachi is of particular importance for understanding the canonical rhetoric of the prophetic corpus. It is quite significant in this connection that the book asserts at its close an expression of complete harmony between the Mosaic law and the prophetic tradition—that is, between the "institutional priesthood" and the prophetic critique.

5. Beginning with the closing text of Malachi and its evocation of the figures of Elijah and Moses, an apocalyptic priestly-prophetic identity appears, which will become increasingly influential in later Second Temple traditions leading up to the New Testament period. The interpretative merger of Malachi's ideal Levite and the messenger of the covenant is of considerable significance in preparing this advancing development.

6. The return of divine glory to Israel's cult envisioned by the positive prophetic tradition finds an echo and amplification in the late postexilic

sapiential vision of Ben Sira. Here the priestly vestments again possess a central symbolic value. Although an explicit apocalyptic paradigm is wanting, Ben Sira's cosmological perspective depicts the high priest as an epiphanic embodiment of divine, ordering Wisdom. In that sense, such "realized eschatology" corresponds to a kind of visible fulfillment of the prophetic promise. The fusion of priest and king also at work in Ben Sira's vision represents a final step in the parallel prophetic trajectory that begins with Zechariah's oracles of the "two sons of oil." Through this material the Catholic canon accordingly includes a late reprise of the Pentateuch's theophanic priestly tradition that effectively absorbs and advances important prophetic perspectives in a sort of historical/ incarnational vision.

EXCURSUS 5

David's Royal Priesthood

Unlike the Christian canon, which follows the Septuagint order, the Hebrew Bible ends not with the prophets but with history—and not with the Greek history of the Maccabees but with the two books of Chronicles. This has its own justification in the character of Chronicles as a vast retrospect and rereading of the whole of Israel's history. The first word of 1 Chronicles 1:1 is "Adam," and the final verses in 2 Chronicles 36:22–23 recount Cyrus's decree granting permission for the rebuilding of the temple, marking the end of the exile and reckoned by the Chronicler himself to be the fulfillment of Jeremiah's prophecy of the seventy years.[1] Ending on such a promising note, none of the disillusionment and struggle that soon confronted the returning exiles enters in to cloud the story. In this sense, Chronicles is a sort of narrative counterpart to the glorious, idealistic prophecies of Trito-Isaiah (Isa. 56–66), even if written later, at the end of the Persian or perhaps even at the beginning of the Hellenistic era. The continuation of the Chronicler's work in Ezra and Nehemiah, by contrast, has more contacts with the honest and earthly realism of the twelve Minor Prophets (i.e., Hosea–Malachi). If not prophecy, then, Chronicles nevertheless represents history written in an eschatological and, given the story's strong monarchical focus, a distinctly messianic key.

Characteristic of the Chronicler's triumphant vision is a particularly robust expression of the special Hebrew spin on ancient Near Eastern royal ideology. That is to say, the monarch's share in divine kingship, especially in the case

1. Envisioning sacred history as essentially ordered to the fulfillment of this specific prophecy of Jeremiah will continue to shape Second Temple thought, though in an eschatological rather than historical mode.

of Israel's two greatest kings, Solomon and David, asserts itself in the deep intertwining of temple and throne. A strikingly priestly picture of royal rule is the result, centered on the Jerusalem temple as the locus of YHWH's supreme theophanic power. The military force that the Chronicler sees somehow concentrated in Israel's liturgical action is a particularly revealing expression of this powerful fusion of cult and kingdom (e.g., 2 Chron. 13:3–13).[2]

The highlighting of this sacral monarchy is not to deny a clear division of roles, which the kings in particular might trespass: the leper king, Uzziah, is the proof (2 Chron. 26:16–21). Not only is Uzziah struck down for daring to burn incense like a priest (recall Korah and company), but an unclean leprous spot pointedly appears on his *forehead*: precisely the place where the high priest bears the divine name.[3] Still, the clean diarchy so strongly intoned in Zechariah gives way in this new configuration to a different vision of office.

> The Second Temple owed its construction in part to the efforts of the Davidide Zerubbabel and the high priest Jeshua [= Joshua], but the edifice was authorized and supported by a succession of Achaemenid kings (2 Chron. 36:22–23; Ezra 1:1–4, 7–11; 5:13–16; 6:1–12; 7:11–24, 27–28; 8:36; 9:9; Neh. 2:8–9, 18; 5:14; 11:23; 13:6). The author reclaims the Temple and its cultus for the Davidides. The priests and Levites are not autonomous, but function as part of a national administration. Even in demarcating the respective duties of Levites and priests, the Chronicler's royalism shines through. . . . The sacerdocy takes its orders from David. The Chronicler's king, much like the Mesopotamian kings . . . is in command.[4]

The Davidic king's rivaling of Persian potentates has the end effect of engulfing the entire temple and priesthood as a part of the state apparatus. It is entirely consonant with this that David himself, at the end of his life, as part of his final preparatory arrangements for Solomon's later work of temple construction, not only stockpiles building materials but also offers elaborate instructions about the precise priestly and Levitical duties (1 Chron. 23:1–27:34). The consistent attention to the priestly (re)appointments at key cultic moments is also noteworthy, especially in comparison with the parallel material in Kings, where attention to cultic reform never includes this element

---

2. Great emphasis is laid on this fused vision in Scott Hahn's evocatively titled *The Kingdom of God as Liturgical Empire: A Theological Commentary on 1–2 Chronicles* (Grand Rapids: Baker Academic, 2012).

3. The story of Korah is arguably aimed by the Holiness School against the same lay claims of the kings to enjoy full priestly rights. See Israel Knohl, "Melchizedek: A Model for the Union of Kingship and Priesthood in the Hebrew Bible, *11QMelchizedek*, and the Epistle to the Hebrews," in *Text, Thought, and Practice in Qumran and Early Christianity*, ed. Ruth Clements and Daniel Schwartz, STDJ 84 (Leiden: Brill, 2009), 255–66.

4. Gary Knoppers, *1 Chronicles 10–29*, AB 12A (New York: Doubleday, 2004), 633.

of interest. Josiah's restoration, for instance, carefully attends to putting all the temple personnel in the right positions: "The priests stood in their place, and the Levites in their divisions according to the king's command. . . . The singers, the descendants of Asaph, were in their place according to the command of David. . . . The gatekeepers were at each gate" (2 Chron. 35:10, 15).

This energetic, idealist institutional orientation obviously shapes the depiction of the clerical class itself, which becomes a direct extension of the divine kingship and thereby acquires an unprecedented air of stability, legitimacy, and good order. The challenge confronting a balanced theological hermeneutic (i.e., respecting the inner-biblical *analogia fidei* of part to part) lies in determining how to respect the Chronicler's retrojected and idealized vision of an impeccably well-organized cultic regime for the synthetic vision it is, without allowing its imperialistic perspective to erase all the dissonant voices. Chronicles is a late (perhaps very late, i.e., mid-third century BC), neatly ironed-out version of the history of the (preexilic) monarchy, deeply colored by the postexilic priesthood. As the single largest monument of intrabiblical rereading within the Old Testament canon, its particular intrabiblical contribution is most poignantly found in establishing authoritative trajectories and typological forms.

David is cast by 1 Chronicles in a distinctly Moses-like way. He is revealed both as the true interpreter of the law and as a kind of Moses redivivus. It is David, for instance, who, after the death of Uzzah, explains in 1 Chronicles 15:2 (to the priests and Levites, who should have known) that only the Levites may touch the ark. It is David who, like Moses, is given a heavenly "pattern" (*tabnît*) for the sanctuary and all its worship (1 Chron. 22, 28). Like Moses he organizes the craftsmen and materials. This depiction, of course, hearkens directly back to the hoary tradition of the ancient Near Eastern king as the supreme patron of a temple and its priesthood. A famous diorite statue in the Louvre, for instance, dating from 2100 BC, shows the neo-Sumerian Gudea, ruler of Lagash, holding on his lap a tablet with a stylus and the inscribed plan of a temple. Two associated, inscribed cylinders describe how Gudea received divine instructions in a dream in which the plan of a temple, written with a stylus on a lapis lazuli tablet, was given to him to have built in honor of Ningirsu. David's own careful preparations are a kind of divine inspiration, yet his unfulfilled desire for the construction of YHWH's temple leaves his kingship conspicuously incomplete by the ancient measure—not unlike Moses' failure to enter into the promised land. As Moses' work was left to Joshua to complete, so the son of David was heir to a project of greater priestly and royal glory than his father.

The shedding of blood, though seemingly supported by God, ultimately prohibits David from building the temple. Whether this posed a temporal, ritual, or ethical impediment (or perhaps all three) is not clear. In any case, the capture of Jebusite Jerusalem—already called the "city of David" in 1 Chronicles 11:5—is David's first reported act as king in Chronicles' version (1 Chron. 11:4–9); and this prompt securing of the cult site of the future temple is not random but is obviously essential to his whole royal agenda. One sees here with clarity the way that David's battles and his founding of the cult intertwine all though the narrative of 1 Chronicles 11–20. Indeed, the two most significant aspects of David's career for the Chronicler are his actions in war and his cultic patronage. He is, in an admirable phrase, "the warrior-poet of Israel."[5]

The *poet* part of this title also deserves attention. With its waxing canon consciousness and liturgical orientation, it should occasion little surprise that Chronicles manifests a special interest in David as author of the Psalms—that is, David as liturgist and master of ritual psalmody (e.g., 2 Chron. 23:18; 29:30; cf. Neh. 12:24, 36, 45–46).[6] This aligns the king naturally with the Levitical order of singers and again comes to expression in connection with David's Zion-centered royal agenda. In the narrative in 1 Chronicles 15–16, which recounts David's transfer of the ark to Jerusalem after subduing the Philistine foe (14:16–17), long parts of three canonical psalms are embedded in the action, as Asaph and his kinsmen sing at David's direction (Pss. 105:1–15; 96:1–13; and 106:1, 47–48; 1 Chron. 15:16–24; 16:4–36). Ultimately, "the psalms were, for the Chronicler, Temple hymns, even before there was a Temple."[7] In fact, though prose prayers are quite common in 1–2 Chronicles, psalmody is strikingly reserved to public rites concerning the ark or the temple. Thus Solomon, later, will cite Psalm 132:8–10 during the dedication of the temple in 2 Chronicles 6:41–42 (cf. 1 Kings 8). The reason for this careful placement of the psalms, says Adele Berlin, is "not only that psalms were part of the Temple worship in the Chronicler's time, but, more importantly, that in the Chronicler's view, the Levitical hymnology was divinely ordained, whereas the personal prayers of kings and other individuals were not."[8]

The Psalter as an authoritative order of public worship thus comes into view as a liturgical tradition supportive of, yet very distinct from, the sacrificial protocols of the priests recorded in P. In Roman religion, it was characteristic

---

5. See Bradley C. Gregory, "The Warrior-Poet of Israel: The Significance of David's Battles in Chronicles and Ben Sira," in *Rewriting Biblical History: Essays on Chronicles and Ben Sira in Honor of Pancratius C. Beentjes*, ed. Jeremy Corley and Harm van Grol, DCLS 7 (Berlin: de Gruyter, 2011), 79–93.

6. See Adele Berlin, "Psalms in the Book of Chronicles," in *Shai le-Sara Japhet: Studies in the Bible, Its Exegesis and Its Language*, ed. Moshe Ben-Asher et al. (Jerusalem: Bialik Institute, 2007), 21*–36*.

7. Berlin, "Psalms in the Book of Chronicles," 26*.

8. Berlin, "Psalms in the Book of Chronicles," 29*.

that liturgical rites were most frequently performed without accompany-
ing words, but in Israel the situation was different. Many psalms are clearly
meant to function in conjunction with acts of ritual sacrifice (e.g., Pss. 4:5;
20:3; 27:6; 54:6; 66:15; 107:22; 116:17; 141:2), giving voice to the mute actions
at the altar. A strikingly ethical note, relativizing the rites, also finds clear
expression, however (e.g., Pss. 40:6; 50:8, 14, 23; 51:16, 19).

> Sacrifice and offering you do not desire,
> > but you have given me an open ear.
> Burnt offering and sin offering
> > you have not required.
> Then I said, "Here I am;
> > in the scroll of the book it is written of me.
> I delight to do your will, O my God;
> > you law is within my heart." (Ps. 40:6–8)

The living accompaniment of such song as the complement of ritual worship
within "the great congregation" (*en ekklēsia megalē*, 39:9–10 LXX), as two
parts of one grand temple liturgy, is perhaps the strongest evidence of the
ultimately peaceful coexistence of the prophetic and priestly perspectives.

Chronicles' part in the postexilic construction of David as the divinely
inspired authority behind the Psalter, accepted as Israel's national hymnal,
helped confer a prophetic character on the psalms that was not limited to their
ethical interests. Through the singing of the Psalms, the temple liturgy itself
became invested with a messianic forward thrust, as the people continually
prayed for a king that they no longer had. With the attribution of the Psalms
to David, an ever more idealized picture of him and of his messianic heir
inevitably took root.

From the theological perspective and in view of the basic framework of
New Testament messianism, the Chronicler's depiction of the Davidic king as
both creator and curator of Israel's holy orders, and of David's participation
in crafting the nation's corpus of liturgical prayer, puts Jesus' institution of
the priesthood in its clearest typological light. It is as son of David and not by
another title that Jesus will claim his own priestly dignity. Likening himself to
the Davidic priest-king celebrated in Psalm 110, a coronation psalm, and on
the archaic model of the Jebusite Melchizedek (Gen. 14:17–24), Jesus takes
his place as supreme head of the people. Like David, who calls him Lord,
Jesus will "defend his priestly authority by claiming succession to the order
of Melchizedek."[9]

---

9. Tomoo Ishida, *The Royal Dynasties in Ancient Israel: A Study on the Formation and
Development of Royal-Dynastic Ideology*, BZAW 142 (New York: de Gruyter, 1977), 140.

Similar to Chronicles, Psalm 110—which scholars have great difficulty in dating—accredits the Davidide king as both a military and a cultic leader. While it may appear odd that the Melchizedek-priest of verse 4 is suddenly shattering kings and crushing heads in verses 5–6, this conjunction harmonizes with what we find in Chronicles and fits perfectly with the iconography of royal propaganda found in ancient Egypt, Mesopotamia, and Syro-Palestine, where the mixed depiction of kings' priestly roles with violent warrior motifs is perfectly common.[10] The rhetorical goal is certainly to display the monarch maintaining order and stability through his cultic and military actions (i.e., *Chaoskampf*). In Genesis 14, of course, Melchizedek blesses Abraham after his victory over the four kings, so the military and liturgical are also native to the Melchizedek tradition.

In 11QMelchizedek, a text from Qumran attesting to a waxing theological fascination with Melchizedek at the time of Jesus, the priest-king of (Jeru-) Salem appears as the end-time agent who at once acts as "judge," executing vengeance on God's enemies and defeating the hand of Belial, and who also forgives sins by proclaiming the eschatological Jubilee. The text of Isaiah 61:2 is cited and gives prophetic voice to Melchizedek's two-sided role. He is "to proclaim the year of the LORD's favor, and the day of vengeance of our God." The echo of this text in Luke 4, during Jesus' sermon in Nazareth, plots Jesus in the place of the eschatological Melchizedek. Like him, Jesus proclaims a Jubilee amnesty, the "year of favor." Yet, instead of continuing Isaiah's prophecy with the note of violent vengeance, the Lord breaks off the passage and discloses a coming mission to the Gentile nations (Luke 4:25–30). Thus, while Jesus decisively defeats Belial like a warrior-king (e.g., Luke 4:1–12, 33–37), his hands will not be bloodied as David's were. They will be bloodied instead by his own suffering on the cross, as he offers his own "Melchizedek's offering" of bread and wine. In this way, the son and Lord of David is the new Solomon, the true man of peace: the Davidide destined to build the eschatological temple.

---

10. See Richard Anthony Purcell, "The King as Priest? Royal Imagery in Psalm 110 and Ancient Near Eastern Iconography," *JBL* 139 (2020): 275–300.

EXCURSUS 6

Transfiguration of the Temple and the Future of Theophany

There can be no new priesthood without a new temple. These two things belong inextricably together. This is nowhere as clear as in the most ample biblical vision of the integrally renewed cult, fully and forever purified of past abuses, which appears in the final chapters of Ezekiel (40–48). An incredibly detailed account of the temple, intentionally evocative of the *tabnît*, the pattern of the tabernacle seen on Sinai by Moses, is shown to Ezekiel, whom God suggestively sets atop "a very high mountain" (Ezek. 40:2). Cubit by cubit, all the courts are carefully measured out in what is seemingly the earliest layer of the tradition: the meticulous blueprint of a transfigured, idealized temple (Ezek. 40–42). Two additional, intermingled thematic strata in the following chapters then supplement this temple vision with ritual regulations organized around the leading personnel—that is, a "prince" (*nāśîʾ*) layer and a Zadokite redactional strand.

In contrast to Chronicles, the Davidic king, who seems to be behind the figure of the more modest "prince," is not the great animating agent of liturgical life in Ezekiel's vision. This prince is a privileged and devoted lay participant who readily joins in the cult as a central player, if unambiguously on the side of the people (Ezek. 44:3; 45:16, 22; 46:2, 9–10).[1] The high priest, who strik-

---

1. See Jon Levenson, *Theology of the Program of Restoration of Ezekiel 40–48*, HSM 10 (Missoula, MT: Scholars Press, 1976), 55–108. "Ezek 40–48 hoped not for a restoration of the monarchy, but for a restoration of the monarch, who is now redefined according to his deepest and truest function as the servant of God, one devoted to the divine service, to liturgy" (143).

ingly never even appears in Ezekiel, is also not the radiant ritual figurehead, as would quite reasonably be expected. Zadok has admittedly emerged as the suddenly very visible patriarch of the priestly caste (more on that below).[2] Nevertheless, it is the priestly college, the *sons* of Zadok, the whole sacerdotal clan of legitimate *kōhănîm*, that occupies the place of priestly focus. This is a highly revealing aspect of the prophet's essentially theocratic vision.

There is, in fact, "a democratization of the high-priesthood among all legitimate priests" at work in Ezekiel 40–48.[3] Laws otherwise restricted to the high priest in the P legislation in Ezekiel apply now to all priests—the obligation to marry a virgin, for instance (Ezek. 44:22; Lev. 21:14; cf. 21:7).[4] Architecturally, the same leveling tendency finds expression in the startling *tôrat habbāyit*, the law of the temple, which declares that the whole territory on top of the mountain and all around, on every side, enjoys the same sanctity as the holy of holies (Ezek. 43:12). Every priest is now like the high priest on the great day of Yom Kippur. This explains Ezekiel's legislation on the priestly garments, which are no longer to be wool but only white linen, and which are to be changed and left in the sanctuary upon entering the outer courts, "so that they may not communicate holiness to the people with their vestments" (cf. Ezek. 44:18–19)—all in close imitation of the high priest on the Day of Atonement (Lev. 16:4, 23).

This remarkable sharing of the high priest's own surpassing holiness with an exclusive sacerdotal college—for the so-called democratization is emphatically *not* extended to all the people or even to all the Levites in Ezekiel's vision—is a prophetic image of the sharing of Christ's unique grace of priestly headship with a well-defined, intra-ecclesial priestly group. Ezekiel's carefully stratified vision accordingly represents, from the perspective of a theology of the Christian Bible, a rather powerful prophetic argument against a theology of an undifferentiated, nonhierarchical, end-time elect "nation of priests."

---

2. In 1 Chron. 27:17 Zadok is called "prince" (*nāgîd, śar*) of Aaron's family, though he does not stand at the head of a branch of the family to whom the priesthood is exclusively entrusted (cf. 1 Chron. 5:27–41; 6:34–38). Along with other signs, this is likely to be evidence that the Zadok traditions in Ezekiel represent a redactional layer later than Chronicles, which does not yet know this new idea about Zadok. The quite late and rather limited interest in Zadok, concentrated largely at Qumran (1QS) and in Ben Sira (51:12i), would concur with this judgment. See Nathan MacDonald, *Priestly Rule: Polemic and Biblical Interpretation in Ezekiel 44*, BZAW 476 (Berlin: de Gruyter, 2015), 114–39.

3. Levenson, *Program of Restoration*, 141–44 (here 141).

4. The absence of the high priest in Ezek. 40–48 has been used by some to argue that this material is older than the P traditions in Leviticus, dating from before the rise of the high priest. A major difficulty with this view is that if texts like Lev. 21 rely on Ezek. 44 and develop it (rather than the reverse), Ezekiel's emphatic distinction between (Zadokite) priests and Levites has for some reason been entirely ignored. A clear view of the redactional strata in Ezek. 40–48 is very important for interpreting this material. See MacDonald, *Priestly Rule*.

Ezekiel's carefully controlled extension of high priestly status significantly takes the specific form of a New Torah. The material in Ezekiel 40–48 is noteworthy, in fact, as the only corpus of Old Testament legislation that is not revealed through the mouth of Moses. Similar to the Mosaic Torah, of course, Ezekiel's temple code is preoccupied with characteristic priestly concerns— for example, the sanctuary and its furnishings, cultic offices, and the system of sacrificial offerings. The apportionment of the land to each tribe, which concludes the vision in Ezekiel 48, similarly evokes the structure of the Pentateuch. In this context, the special portion reserved for the priests is said to be at once both the temple and YHWH himself (Ezek. 44:28; 45:4; 48:8–14). The interchangeability of these two, God and the temple, within the space of a couple verses is deeply suggestive. It hints at the unbreakable bond being renewed between these two, and it points already to Revelation 21:22, where the temple of the new Jerusalem is replaced by the Lord God Almighty and the Lamb. Ultimately, in this light and as in the Mosaic Torah, Ezekiel's revelation on the mountain ultimately prepares for the intimate dwelling of God's *kābôd* in the new sanctuary and among the people (Exod. 40:34–38; Ezek. 43:1–9).

While Ezekiel thus has obvious contacts with the Torah and Priestly school, and notably with the Holiness Code—contacts still in search of a concise and accurate, widely accepted description—important differences also emerge in the way divine theophany is conceived. The complete absence of the ark, the lampstand, and the table of showbread is particularly notable in Ezekiel's temple vision. A post-Mosaic order, of the sort prophesied by Jeremiah and typologically signaled by the fall of Shiloh (Jer. 3:16; 7:12; see excursus 4), is here being visually depicted. The cultic character of God's *kābôd* remains constant; but several distinctive features characterize the prophet's vision, above all the permanently residing, anthropomorphic glory of the Lord.

> With P, we are dealing with an all-consuming, fiery brightness, which must be shielded by a cloud in order to be bearable; with Ezekiel, [the divine glory] is something involving a human form. . . . While for P the [glory] sets down at will in the "tent of the meeting," for Ezekiel, the Jerusalem temple is [the glory's] actual domicile.[5]

The overall dynamic leads Stephen Cook to speak of "the God that the Temple blueprint creates" as "Ezekiel's God Incarnate."[6] Cook even goes so far as to invoke the model of "a hypostatic union for the divine glory in Ezekiel,"

5. Stephen L. Cook, "Ezekiel's God Incarnate! The God That the Temple Blueprint Creates," in *The God Ezekiel Creates*, ed. Paul M. Joyce and Dalit Rom-Shiloni, LHBOTS 607 (London: Bloomsbury, 2015), 134, 139.
6. Cook, "Ezekiel's God Incarnate!" See also, more generally, Cook, *Ezekiel 38–48*, AYB 22B (New Haven: Yale University Press, 2018).

underlining the way God's presence is at once physically bound to the single site of the temple in the humanlike form of the divine glory and yet also locally free, by the divine Spirit, which ranges across the entire earth and enters the hearts of the people (e.g., Ezek. 36:27; 37:14).[7] A christological and a pneumatological pole thus become evident in Ezekiel's theology.

On the christological end, an interesting interplay exists in Ezekiel between the beautiful, carefully proportioned, and tightly controlled "classical body" of the new temple, laid out with all its well-defined courts in Ezekiel 40–48, and the "grotesque" image of the old temple in chapters 8–11, which is shown to the prophet with a revealing "hole" in the wall (8:7–8), through which the images of "creeping things, and loathsome animals" seem to penetrate and defile it (8:10). The abomination of idolatrous worship and the entrance of foreigners into the inner courts are the issues driving this prophetic symbol (cf. 44:8–9). When the glory of the Lord thus departs in disgust from the punctured temple in 9:3, pollution rushes in like a flood to fill the void and an immediate command is given to "defile the house and fill the courts with the slain," literally with the pierced or the profane (9:7): "pierced bodies for a pierced Temple."[8]

The new temple that appears in Ezekiel 40–42, by contrast, fits with other postexilic visions of Jerusalem rebuilt in shining, celestial splendor (e.g., Isa. 54:11–12; Tob. 13:16), though much debate exists whether Ezekiel presents a utopian vision or a plan for the community to enact. Either way, the new temple ultimately prepares for the final and lasting return of the departed glory of the Lord (Ezek. 43:1–5). The permanent shutting of the doors in 44:2 is a definitive sign that no more pollution will ever flood in (cf. Mal. 1:10), and by the same token that God's presence will no more depart from this chosen dwelling. What does "depart," however, is the river of the waters of life (Ezek. 47:1–12). The pierced temple now transfigured manifests its glorified wounds, like Christ pouring out the Spirit (John 7:37–39; 19:33).

The pneumatological waters that flow from the temple-body heal and vivify and bless the whole land, making it habitable and fit to be distributed as an inheritance (Ezek. 48).[9] Flowing to the east, the water must pass by one key landmark in the renewed temple landscape, which stands in the way of the water's eastward flow. While sanctuary furniture like the golden lampstand

7. Cook, "Ezekiel's God Incarnate!," 141–43.

8. Jacqueline E. Lapsley, "Body Piercings: The Priestly Body and the 'Body' of the Temple in Ezekiel," *HBAI* 1 (2012): 241.

9. Ezekiel's image recalls Zech. 13:1, where "a fountain shall be opened for the house of David and the inhabitants of Jerusalem" that washes the land clean of all impurity and sin. This fountain is lexically and thematically linked to the "spirit of compassion and supplication" that the Lord similarly pours out "on the house of David and inhabitants of Jerusalem," when they look on the one whom they have pierced (12:10).

and table have all disappeared, as was already noted, the one great feature that remains is what Ezekiel calls "the mountain of God"—that is, the ziggurat-shaped or perhaps ramp-like altar described in Ezekiel 43:13–15, the seven-day consecration of which is recounted in detail (43:18–27). The place is like a mini-Sinai, the new temple's theophanic center, which the priests mount by stairs and from which a pillar of smoke ascends. The waters that mysteriously well up, as in Genesis 2:6, and the determined eastward direction, as in Genesis 2:8, also make this "mountain of God" surmounting Mount Zion into a mini-Eden, nourishing a garden of trees (Ezek. 47:12). The altar is thus the pinnacle's pinnacle and the source of all cultic blessing. Ezekiel's effective melding of the holy of holies with the whole temple complex has the end result that the inner sanctum is replaced in some sense by the altar outside. Indeed, the square, 20 × 20 cubit shape of the altar, placed at the exact center of the square, 500 × 500 cubit temple court complex, certainly shows its importance and evokes the 20 × 20 cubit dimensions of Solomon's holy of holies. The book of Revelation's appropriation of this vision will finally disclose the eschatological altar/dwelling, from which the living water of paradise flows, as being also the "throne of God and of the Lamb" (Rev. 22:1–3): the cross on which Christ is sacrificed and proclaimed as king. This is the center of the living, temple-less sanctuary.

It is highly revealing that this outside altar in Ezekiel is still used for all sorts of sacrifice, including sin and guilt offerings (Ezek. 40:39; 42:13; 44:29; 45:8, 17–25; 46:20). The complete eradication of human sin is obviously not a part of Ezekiel's vision, idealized as it may be. And yet, as already hinted, "there is no counterpart [in Ezekiel] to the ceremony of Yom Kippur in P, in which only Aaron may go behind the veil in the sanctuary."[10] Despite the supreme importance for Ezekiel of zealously preserving the integrity of the temple's spatial distinctions and all the distinct categories of cult personnel, no attention is given to this most important distinction of all in the old Priestly vision. It is as though the purging of the sanctuary and its priests, accomplished annually on Yom Kippur, has now somehow been finally and forever accomplished—just as the Letter to the Hebrews will in its turn repeatedly claim to be exactly the case (Heb. 7:27; 9:12, 26; 10:10). At the same time, the ongoing use of the all-important altar signals an ongoing sacrificial cult. A new priest-*cum*-temple regime has been erected that is no longer threatened by the moral catastrophe symbolized by YHWH's abandonment, God having now bound himself with a new permanency to his temple-body. Still, this priestly regime continues its daily business of beating back the tide of daily transgressions—like the Church of God in every age.

10. Levenson, *Program of Restoration*, 143.

Although Yom Kippur plays no ongoing role in Ezekiel's purified temple, the Day of Atonement is not without relevance to the whole vision. The date notice offered in Ezekiel 40:1 places the prophet's vision specifically on the tenth day of the month at the beginning of the year, in the twenty-fifth year of the Judeans' exile. Debate exists whether this envisions a civil or cultic calendar. If it is the former, however, this would be the day of Yom Kippur. The reference to the twenty-fifth year is taken by most scholars, in either case, to hint at the midway point in the Jubilee cycle—halfway, that is, to the proclamation of the Jubilee on Yom Kippur in the fiftieth year (Lev. 25:9–10; cf. Ezek. 46:17). In this way, Ezekiel sees his vision of a permanently cleansed temple along with its cleansed priesthood as a reality not yet attained, yet pointing ahead to a coming day of final atonement that is already approaching. It is by this great Jubilee that the land shall finally be returned to its exiled owners, as stipulated in Leviticus 25 and foretold in Ezekiel 48. The whole arc of Ezekiel 40–48 is thus ordered directly to the proclamation of the final Jubilee.

The special inheritance and perquisites of the priests, who have no landed portion, are broached already in Ezekiel 44 (cf. Num. 18; Ezek. 48:8–12), by contrast, before the distribution of the land to the other tribes at the end of the book. It is as though the unique priestly share in the coming Jubilee (like that of the prince) must be resolved first and in anticipation, before Israel at large can partake in the blessing. The priests' good lot of the Lord as their inheritance is *already* a taste of the *not yet* in the present age.

If the eschatological return of the exiles to the land inevitably means first driving out the Gog and Magog of the foreign nations (Ezek. 38–39), Ezekiel 44 sees a similar dynamic at work in the sons of Zadok claiming the Lord's own house as their inalienable home (cf. Ezek. 45:4). From this vantage point, a critical text for the whole logic of Ezekiel 40–48 is Ezekiel 44:8–9.

> You have appointed foreigners to act for you in keeping my charge in my sanctuary.
> Thus says the Lord GOD: No foreigner, uncircumcised in heart and flesh, of all the foreigners who are among the people of Israel, shall enter my sanctuary.

An inner-biblical tête-à-tête between Ezekiel 44 and Isaiah 56, which expresses a much more inclusive perspective, is usually seen to be at work here. Isaiah 66:21 goes so far as to say that God will choose foreigners "as priests and as Levites" (or perhaps as "Levitical priests"?). Ezekiel, in any case, stands, like Ezra, on the side of a strictly guarded priestly caste. The sons of Zadok alone among the descendants of Levi are permitted to approach the Lord to minister to him as priests (Ezek. 40:46; 44:9–15).

Efforts to unravel the genealogical polemic and social dynamics at work in the Zadokite layers of the tradition in Ezekiel 40–48 inevitably remain a

speculative house of cards. Still, Ezekiel's valorization of a mysterious Aaronide, David's chief priest in Jerusalem and the high priest of Solomon, who
putatively stood in the line of Phinehas, is typologically potent. Theologically enticing, too, is the "Jebusite hypothesis," which accepts that Zadok's
impeccable Aaronide genealogies in 1 Chronicles are a late invention and
that Zadok was in historical fact the priest-king of Jebusite Jerusalem, who
was set in place over the cult there by David when he took the city.[11] Fragile
as it is, this remains the best explanation of the earliest data, and it places
Zadok squarely in the priestly line of Melchizedek and the liturgical memory
cultivated in Genesis 14 and Psalm 110. Against this view, Jon Levenson raises
in objection the important question, "Could those who revered the memory
of Melchizedek, the Jebusite priest-king of Salem, have also been zealous
guardians of YHWHistic purity over against all foreigners?"[12] It does, prima
facie, seem incongruous.

In answer, following Nathan MacDonald's recent work, the "historical
Zadok" should be distinguished from the constructed figure in Ezekiel. Ezekiel's "sons of Zadok," in other words, ought to be approached not as a
potent and polemicizing branch of the exilic-era Aaronide family but as a late
creation of inner-biblical interpretation, directly influenced by the scriptural
history of David's reign. Accordingly, equipped with a whitewashed Aaronide
pedigree and identified as the "faithful priest" of 1 Samuel 2, Zadok, in truth
a sort of "second Melchizedek," ironically became the implicit victim of his
own remarkably successful inner-biblical career. He is a foreigner baptized as
the bulwark against all foreign encroachments. Said in another way, the Bible's
latter-day Melchizedek, the Davidic priest of the eschatological temple, was
progressively fused with and submerged beneath all Israel's reigning priestly
icons and ideology, whence he was waiting to reemerge in his original colors
in the gospel.

11. See the clear and judicious presentation of Aelred Cody, *A History of the Old Testament Priesthood*, AnB 35 (Rome: Pontifical Biblical Institute, 1969), 89–93.
12. Levenson, *Program of Restoration*, 139.

PART 3

"THE ORDER OF MELCHIZEDEK"

5

"Feed My Sheep" (John 21:17)

The Inauguration of New Covenant Ordo

Pivotal to the premise of a sacramental, New Covenant priesthood is obviously our handling of the Gospel data. If Jesus himself cannot convincingly be fit into our priestly picture, both as a priest and as a priest-maker, our priestly picture is biblically and hence theologically void. Both Synoptic and Johannine materials must naturally be brought into consideration here, and, while a book like this can never offer any exhaustive presentation, the current chapter will draw upon both of these broad evangelical traditions to advance a straightforward line of argumentation. First, using the Synoptics, I will describe Jesus' own priestly identity as it is articulated through a cluster of Second Temple Jewish idioms. Then, using John, I will expose the transmission of this priestly dignity, along with a transition from the earlier idiom into a characteristically Christian, pastoral register. At the center of this will stand Jesus' reconfiguration of hierarchical authority (*exousia*) as self-sacrificial service (*diakonia*). Though the assertions at each step are bold and though we must move at an appropriate pace, the stability of the structure will hold exegetical weight.[1]

---

1. For a more complete and fully annotated version of the argument for Jesus' identity as eschatological high priest and Jesus' identification with Ps. 110, see chaps. 13–14 of Anthony Giambrone, *A Quest for the Historical Christ: Scientia Christi and the Modern Study of Jesus* (Washington, DC: Catholic University of America Press, 2022).

Jesus as Eschatological High Priest

Eschatological expectation in Second Temple Judaism of so-called "chief agent" figures—in effect, expectation of *messiahs* minus the name—is famously variegated. It is possible, nonetheless, to note certain fundamental patterns that incontestably shaped the context in which Jesus lived and the Gospels were written. The expectation of an eschatological high priest is one of these stable points of reference, diversified as its expressions demonstrably are. With the prophecies of Zechariah and Malachi, the preceding chapter has already discussed two of the most important biblical bases for the growth of priestly expectations in the subsequent Jewish context. It is sufficient here to evoke a single extrabiblical text, already mentioned in the last chapter in passing, in order to observe the concrete shape this priestly expectation had taken around the time of Jesus.

The "New Priest"

The extensive description of the "new priest" in *Testament of Levi* 18:1–14 is a most impressive witness to the developed Second Temple expectation of an eschatological, priestly chief agent. The *Testaments of the Twelve Patriarchs* represents a more mainstream tradition of Judaism than the sectarian perspectives unique to Qumran, but it is also a complicated and controverted corpus. Recent scholarship has, nevertheless, strongly defended this material's significance as a witness to pre-Christian—and, notably, Hasmonean—Judaism, despite some later Christian editing of the texts (editing that now appears more restrained and isolable than has often been supposed).[2]

The text of the *Testament of Levi* itself, one of the twelve individual *Testaments*, though not transmitted in a pristine and untouched form, preserves a substantial Jewish core. This is clear from the positive and perduring value placed upon the temple cult (e.g., *Test. Levi* 9:5–7), but above all from *Testament of Levi*'s open relation to a range of parallel Levi traditions, attested in unambiguously pre-Christian literature of the Second Temple period, especially in the so-called *Aramaic Levi Document* (cf. *Test. Levi* 8–9, 11–14; also *Jub.* 30:1–32:9).[3] The unmistakable elevation of Levi common to all

---

2. See, e.g., Robert Kugler, "The *Testaments of the Twelve Patriarchs*: A Not-So-Ambiguous Witness to Early Jewish Interpretative Practices," in *A Companion to Biblical Interpretation in Early Judaism*, ed. Matthias Henze (Grand Rapids: Eerdmans, 2012), 337–60; and David A. deSilva, "The *Testaments of the Twelve Patriarchs* as Witnesses to Pre-Christian Judaism: A Re-Assessment," *JSP* 23 (2013): 21–68.

3. On the interrelation of these diverse Second Temple Levi traditions, see James Kugel, "Levi's Elevation to the Priesthood in Second Temple Writings," *HTR* 86 (1993): 1–64; and Robert Kugler, *From Patriarch to Priest: The Levi-Priestly Tradition from "Aramaic Levi" to "Testament of Levi,"* EJL 9 (Atlanta: Scholars Press, 1996).

these traditions is thus impossible simply to explain away as a Christian innovation.[4] The *Testaments'* Levi motifs present the framework of a genuine Jewish expectation.

The *Testaments* are not prophetic or apocalyptic literature in the proper sense, but the whole text is replete with eschatological and messianic prognostications. In this connection, important as "the new priest" of *Testament of Levi* 18 is to the document's overall vision, he is not the only chief agent in the *Testaments'* eschatology. He appears, instead, within a kind of "two-messiahs" framework. Such diarchic messianism—the expectation of an Aaronic and Davidic messiah—though often (rightly) associated with Qumran, is an idea with clear biblical roots. This key scriptural background has already been seen. The "faithful priest" in 1 Samuel 2:35 is closely paired with the Davidic messiah, for instance. Zechariah's sustained interest in Joshua and Zerubbabel, called the two "sons of oil" in Zechariah 4:6–14, certainly contributed still more to the later typology of two anointed eschatological figures (cf. 4Q254).

So, while it remains difficult to sort out the tangled witness of the *Testaments* with absolute clarity, one may in any case affirm that "some of the *Testaments* articulate an expectation of two messianic figures, a priestly one emerging from the line of Levi and a kingly one coming from the line of Judah, a messianic view also well attested among the Dead Sea Scrolls."[5] Multiple indications seem to suggest, moreover, that the priestly Levitical agent stands over the Judean royal figure (e.g., *Test. Jud.* 21:1–4). The roles of the two agents, nevertheless, display a complementary relation, and at times the two figures even appear to be fused as one (e.g., *Test. Levi* 2:11; *Test. Dan* 5:4; *Test. Gad* 8:1; *Test. Jos.* 19:7). Remarkable, in this regard, is the elevation of Levi as "king" (e.g., *Test. Reub.* 6:11–12): a dynamic that accords quite well with other Hasmonean currents we have already seen.

The end-times appearance of the *Testaments'* new priest not only belongs within this recognizable Second Temple two-messiahs pattern but also fits within a familiar eschatological narrative framework. Specifically, reliant upon Daniel's seventy-weeks prophecy (*Test. Levi* 17:1–11), a degenerative series of "Jubilees" appears: seven ages of an increasingly debased priesthood, culminating in priests who are "adulterers, money lovers, arrogant, lawless, voluptuaries, pederasts, those who practice bestiality" (*Test. Levi* 17:11). The list of delicts resonates with clerical misconduct of every age (though the bestiality is a little shocking, even by the standards of the most shameful papal court). Precisely at this point—a nadir of priestly sinfulness—the saving figure of this "new priest" finally appears.

4. See deSilva, "*Testaments,*" 50.
5. DeSilva, "*Testaments,*" 36.

And after vengeance on them will have come upon them from the Lord, the priesthood will fail. Then *the Lord will raise up a new priest*, to whom all the words of the Lord will be revealed; and he will execute a judgment of truth upon the earth in course of time. And his star will arise in heaven, as a king, lighting up the light of knowledge as by the sun of the day; and he will be magnified in the world until his assumption. He will shine as the sun on the earth and will remove all darkness from under heaven, and there will be peace on the earth. The heavens will exult in his days and the earth will be glad and the clouds will rejoice, and the knowledge of the Lord will be poured out on the earth like the waters of the sea and the angels of the glory of the presence of the Lord will rejoice in him.[6] (*Test. Levi* 18:1–5)

A priest-king shall arise, heralding a new era of light, as the old priestly order fails in a show of divine judgment.

The prophecy sounds remarkably suited to the Christian perspective— and it certainly is. At the level of the narrative grammar, however, it must be observed, in further confirmation of the thoroughly Jewish character of this tradition, that an obvious logic links the Danielic/Jubilee storyline laid out in *Testament of Levi* 17 with the resolution that comes with the arrival of the priestly agent in the denouement of *Testament of Levi* 18. Specifically, the new priest arrives to bring an end to priestly corruption. Like Ben Sira's Simon he shines gloriously like the sun in the heavens, thus marking the end of the darkness. The resemblance of *Testament of Levi*'s essential plotline to the pattern of priestly degeneration and rescue by an end-time priestly agent directly recalls Malachi with his saving messenger figure, as presented in the preceding chapter. Indeed, in harmony with the ideal Levite in Malachi 2, the *Testaments*' new priest is amply depicted as a literal fountain of instruction (cf. *Test. Levi* 18:9). The Jewish matrix of expectation is still thicker, however. We have here a very open affinity with the specific eschatological vision of 11QMelchizedek, one of the most famous of the Dead Sea Scrolls, in which the eschatological priest-king Melchizedek also appears in a Danielic framework at the critical culmination of a downward spiral of Jubilees. In this light, it is not without interest when *Testament of Levi* 18:12 records of the new priest that "Beliar will be bound by him." This is exactly what was also expected of Melchizedek in 11QMelchizedek: "He will deliver all the captives from the power of Belial" (II,13 25; cf. CD 4:17–18; *Test. Levi* 14:5–8). In sum: the block of traditions in *Testament of Levi* 17–18 can hardly be construed as representing anything other than this same, dense Second Temple pattern of thought.

---

6. Translation from Harm Hollander and Marinus de Jonge, eds., *The Testaments of the Twelve Patriarchs: A Commentary*, SVTP 8 (Leiden: Brill, 1985), 177.

Within this common Second Temple eschatological-priest matrix, additional details in *Testament of Levi* 18 are likewise traceable to a Jewish milieu. Most importantly, the pregnant expression "raise up" applied to the new priest paints him in the recognizable colors of the awaited "prophet like Moses," whom the Lord had promised to "raise up" in Deuteronomy 18:15. The idea in *Testament of Levi* 18 is transmitted, as we have seen, by way of the anonymous *man of God*'s prophecy of the "faithful priest" whom the Lord will also "raise up" in 1 Samuel 2:35.[7]

> I will raise up for myself a faithful priest, who shall do according to what is in my heart and in my mind. I will build him a sure house, and he shall go in and out before my anointed one forever.

We have already explored the original context of this passage, which foretells the appearance in Solomon's court of a new, non-Elide dynasty—namely, Zadok and his high priestly line. The prophecy of an idealized priestly agent clearly fueled later, additional speculations and expectations, however. Thus, what one scholar takes to be a smoking-gun indication of intrusive Christian theology in the description of the new priest in *Testament of Levi* 18—namely, the eternity of the reign of the new priest, understood as Jesus and modeled on Psalm 110—is, in fact, a feature lifted directly from this prophecy in 1 Samuel.[8] "He shall go in and out before my anointed one *forever*." Whether a connection between the "faithful/new" priest's unending priesthood and Psalm 110:4's "priest forever according to the order of Melchizedek" was one that had already been made in the pre-Christian Jewish context may remain an open and intriguing question. The strong linkage just noted between the priestly visions of *Testament of Levi* 18 and 11QMelchizedek makes the possibility plausible and enticing. The priest-king identity of both the new priest and Melchizedek reinforces the suspicion of a connection.

I would offer one final observation regarding Second Temple views of Melchizedek's priesthood, which ties off the Jewish expectation of an eschatological priest in a pretty bow. In 11QMelchizedek the priest-king is entrusted specifically with making a momentous proclamation of forgiveness of sins. He is accordingly cast as a *messenger* figure (see lines 17, 19), identified with the "messenger" character who stars in Isaiah 61. The eschatological Melchizedek

---

7. The importance of Deut. 18:15, read through 1 Sam. 2:35, must be stressed as the controlling allusion in *Test. Levi* 18:2, without denying the allusion to Balaam's oracle (Num. 24:17) in the following line. The suggestion of Kugler (*Testaments of the Twelve Patriarchs*, 52) that the entire passage should be read as "resting squarely on Balaam's oracle" unfortunately misses this critical intertextual dynamic.

8. Marinus de Jonge, *Jewish Eschatology, Early Christian Christology and the Testaments of the Twelve Patriarchs: Collected Essays* (Leiden: Brill, 1990), 202.

is thus within easy reach of that other end-time priest identified (albeit with a different Hebrew word) as God's messenger in Malachi 2–3: the eschatological Levite who stands at the base, not only of so much pre-Christian expectation, but also of the Gospels' perspective, as we shall presently see. Jesus' own foundational role as the messenger/proclaimer of the kingdom of God—another enacted exegesis of Isaiah 61 (see Luke 4; 7)—thus stands in perfect alignment with the priestly protagonist envisioned by the Dead Sea Scrolls. Both figures announce comfort, peace, and the good news that "your God reigns."

The Transfiguration

With this broad Jewish expectation of the coming of an eschatological priest firmly in view, we turn now to Jesus, specifically identified in Hebrews 2:17 as a "faithful high priest"—a citation of 1 Samuel 2:35—and identified three times in Hebrews 5–6 as the priest like Melchizedek in Psalm 110 (Heb. 5:6, 10; 6:20). The basis for such christological claims is well grounded in the Gospels. Although it has failed to grab the attention of modern biblical scholars, all three Synoptic Gospels present Jesus very forcefully as the fulfillment of Jewish priestly expectations. The strongest revelation of this occurs in Jesus' transfiguration.

Just as Moses took the original priestly triad, Aaron, Nadab, and Abihu, with him up to the top of Mount Sinai, where they saw the God of Israel (though apparently only his feet; see Exod. 24:1–11), so Jesus "takes" a new triad, Peter, James, and John, and leads them up a high mountain, where they behold his brilliant transformation in glory.

> Six days later, Jesus took with him Peter and James and John, and led them up a high mountain apart, by themselves. And he was transfigured before them, and his clothes became dazzling white, such as no one on earth could bleach them. And there appeared to them Elijah with Moses, who were talking with Jesus. Then Peter said to Jesus, "Rabbi, it is good for us to be here; let us make three dwellings, one for you, one for Moses, and one for Elijah." He did not know what to say, for they were terrified. Then a cloud overshadowed them, and from the cloud there came a voice, "This is my Son, the Beloved; listen to him!" Suddenly when they looked around, they saw no one with them any more, but only Jesus. (Mark 9:2–8)

At the Jordan the Father expresses his good pleasure in Jesus (Mark 1:11). At the transfiguration the message is different. The Father's command to the disciples to "listen" to Jesus identifies Jesus as "the prophet like Moses" whom the Lord promises to "raise up" and to whom the people must "listen" (Deut. 18:15). It is notable that in Deuteronomy 18 this figure is given in response to the people's fear of the theophany at Horeb, when they shuddered for fear at hearing the voice of God and seeing the great fire (cf. Deut. 5:23–31). The fit with the transfiguration is perfect. The disciples "were terrified" (Mark 9:6) at the blaze of glory on Mount Tabor and the divine voice from heaven. The theophany then vanishes and leaves Jesus alone, empowered to speak in the Lord's own name (cf. Deut. 18:18).

Through this whole narrated allusion to Deuteronomy 18:15, the Father's voice from heaven offers a hint that readers of this book will by now recognize. Jesus is identified as the awaited new priest: the priest-prophet "raised up" like Moses. The identification is invested with an impressive symbolic force, as we shall see.

Moses and Elijah

By plotting Jesus' transfiguration in the personal presence of Moses and Elijah, the Gospels plant us squarely in the final verses of Malachi, where both of these portentous figures appear. The disciples' well-placed question likewise drops us in the busy world of Second Temple scribal interpretations: "Why do the scribes say that Elijah must come first?" (Mark 9:11).

The priestly credentials of Elijah have already been explored (see chap. 4). This is not a late rabbinic association, as we have seen.[9] Elijah's pairing on Tabor with Moses reinforces this priestly understanding. As commentators observe, the appearance of these two together with Jesus not only is a reference to Malachi but is also indebted to the similar traditions connected to these two figures' mysterious ends. Specifically, the story of Elijah's assumption into heaven (2 Kings 2:1–9) was mirrored by a similar tale surrounding Moses. As the end of Deuteronomy said that no one knows the place where Moses was buried (Deut. 34:6), the legend developed that, like Elijah, he had also been carried into heaven.[10] "Arising" or being "raised up" like Moses in the manner of Deuteronomy 18:15 takes on a new meaning in this connection: it now evokes the idea of going up into heaven.

The legend of Moses' assumption is crucial for understanding Jesus' transfiguration, for it introduces a new priestly dynamic. The *Assumption of Moses*, an apocryphal text preserved in Latin but originally written in Hebrew and dating from the first or second century BC, unfortunately does

9. The "Interpreter of the Law" awaited at Qumran (e.g., CD 7:18–19) is possibly already a reference to the view of Elijah as the messianic priest (cf. 4Q558; 4Q521). See John C. Poirier, "The Endtime Return of Elijah and Moses at Qumran," *DSD* 10 (2003): 221–42.

10. On the origins of this tradition, see Ryan Stokes, "Not over Moses' Dead Body: Jude 9, 22–24 and the Assumption of Moses in Their Early Jewish Context," *JSNT* 40 (2017): 195–98.

not preserve the critical narration of Moses' actual assumption.[11] One extant verse does refer to Moses' heavenly existence, however, and this is described in a highly significant manner.

> Then will be filled the hands of the messenger [*implebuntur manus nuntii*], who is in the highest place appointed [*in summo constitutus*]. (*As. Mos.* 10:2)[12]

The phrase "filling the hands" should sound familiar. It is the technical Hebrew idiom for the ordination of a priest. Moses himself, in another place, is also called *magnus nuntius*, the great messenger, and like a priest he is shown interceding day and night, placating the Lord on Israel's behalf (*As. Mos.* 11:7; cf. 12:6).[13] The language of a *nuntius* is worthy of note, for arguably the Latin covers a Hebrew reference to the Levitical messenger of Malachi. As the preeminent covenant-maker in the Scriptures, who, indeed, better than Moses to be Malachi's mysterious "messenger of the covenant" (Mal. 3:1)? Along with Elijah, Moses' cameo at the end of Malachi 3 puts him—he was an actual Levite, after all—in a contextually advantageous position to be exegetically identified as the priestly *nuntius*. This identification becomes all the more compelling when we consider the messenger's Torah instruction in Malachi 2: "True instruction was in his mouth . . . and people should seek instruction from his mouth, for he is the messenger of the LORD of hosts" (Mal. 2:6–7); "Remember the teaching of my servant Moses" (Mal. 4:4; 3:22 MT).

If the ascended Elijah's *descent* from heaven carries priestly connotations in Second Temple sources, Moses' *ascent* on high seems to carry the same association. Specifically, the phrase "in the highest place" (*in summo*) in *Assumption of Moses* 10:2 pictures Moses' entering into heaven's sanctum, where, having his hands filled, he becomes a priest. The idea appears to be modeled upon Moses' ascent of the holy mountain of Sinai and his entrance into the cloud and YHWH's living presence; in the suggestive phrase of Exodus 19:3, "Moses went up to God" (*'ālâ 'el-hā'ĕlōhîm*). In the Dead Sea Scrolls, we find the same idea in a text that calls Moses "God's anointed one"—literally, "his messiah" (4Q377 ii 5). The title is nowhere else conferred upon Moses, but in this case it directly evokes his priesthood, for his entrance into the cloud is described as a "sanctification" or "consecration," evidently envisioned as a kind of ordination (cf. Exod. 28:41; 29:33).

11. See Johannes Tromp, *The Assumption of Moses: A Critical Edition with Commentary*, SVTP 10 (Leiden: Brill, 1993).
12. Translation by J. Priest in *OTP* 1:932.
13. See Jan Willem van Henten, "Moses as Heavenly Messenger in Assumptio Mosis 10:2 and Qumran Passages," *JJS* 54 (2003): 216–27.

Moses the man of God, was with God in the cloud. And the cloud covered him because . . . when he was sanctified [*bhqdśô*], and like a messenger [*wkml'k*] he would speak from his mouth. (4Q377 ii 10–11)[14]

Once again, we find an allusion to Malachi's messenger. The phrase "from his mouth" also indicates that we are dealing with a Mosaic reading of Malachi's figure, for in Malachi 2:7 Torah/instruction comes "from his mouth."

Moses' entrance into the cloud is not an isolated motif lacking a wider scriptural background.[15] The cloud of incense that enveloped the high priest when he entered the holy of holies, a smokescreen guarding his life from the mortally dangerous vision of God (Lev. 16:13), would have also been very easily connected to the cloud that descended upon Sinai, which was portrayed like a giant tabernacle—or, rather, vice versa: the tabernacle was envisioned as a mini-Sinai.[16]

It seems profoundly unlikely that the cloud that appears at Jesus' transfiguration upon the mountain could have failed to evoke Moses' ascension into the mysteries of God (Exod. 24:15). The miracle transpires in Moses' presence, while the Lord designates Jesus/Joshua as Moses' successor. Read in the light of Moses' twinned terrestrial and otherworldly ascensions into the sanctifying mysteries of God's presence, Jesus' own entrance into the cloud atop the high mountain takes on the striking shape of a priestly ordination via celestial journey: the foretaste of a more definitive celestial priestly initiation in his coming assumption/resurrection/exaltation. Jesus is the prophet-priest like Moses, from whose mouth comes authoritative divine instruction, to which the disciples must *listen*. Like Moses' "ascension" up Sinai, Jesus' ascent up the mountain into the divine presence is an earthbound heavenly journey—and an image of that more perfect priestly entrance into the holy of holies that the Letter to the Hebrews will locate after his death.

"His Clothes Became Dazzling White"

The controlling image of Jesus' epiphany upon the mountain, the miraculous change of the appearance of Jesus' clothes (also his face in Matthew and Luke), is rarely analyzed by scholars. Although an allusion to Moses'

14. Translation by J. VanderKam and M. Brady in *The Dead Sea Scrolls Reader*, part 3, *Parabiblical Texts*, ed. Donald W. Parry and Emanuel Tov (Leiden: Brill, 2005), 599.

15. Similar to 4Q377, Ps. 99:6–7 links Moses' priesthood closely with Moses' speech to God in the cloud. Paul, too, arguably knows the notion of Moses being mystically *sanctified* by his entrance into the cloud (cf. 1 Cor. 10:2).

16. "The equivalence of the Tabernacle to Sinai is an essential, indeed indispensable, axiom of P. The Tabernacle, in effect, becomes a portable Sinai, an assurance of the permanent presence of the deity in Israel's midst" (Jacob Milgrom, *Leviticus 1–16*, AB 3 [New York: Doubleday, 1991], 574).

veil is often passingly suggested, the evidence actually points in a different direction.

The gleaming garments of Jesus have their clearest parallel in traditions about the radiant glory of the high priestly vestments. We have already seen the sustained attention paid to these vestments in texts like Ben Sira. The Dead Sea Scrolls and other Second Temple traditions were similarly captivated by the luminous power of these priestly clothes (e.g., L.A.B. 26:9; 4QpIsaᵈ). In the thirteenth of the *Songs of the Sabbath Sacrifice*, for example, the high priest, by virtue of his vestments, manifests "the appearance of splendor and the likeness of the spirit of glory" (4Q405 23 ii 9), an allusion to the theophany in Ezekiel 1:28 ("the appearance of the likeness of the glory of the LORD"). The origins of this tradition of vibrant, epiphanic priestly vesture reach back to the Pentateuch, of course, and Exodus 28:2, which commands, "You shall make sacred vestments for the glorious adornment of your brother Aaron." The wearing of the glorious divine name upon the high priest's forehead also fueled this whole tradition (cf. 1QSb 4:28).

Later rabbinic traditions of Adam's "garments of glory" (e.g., *Gen. Rab.* 12.6; 20.12; *Pirqe R. El.* 14)—a prelapsarian vesture of light—are sometimes brought into discussion of the transfiguration.[17] This motif should be seen as an extension of the older tradition of luminous priestly vesture, however. In Ezekiel 28:13–14, for instance, the primal man is elaborately adorned with a garment studded with precious jewels, reminiscent of the ephod, and set upon "the holy mountain of God," where an "anointed" cherub stands by him. This configuration is reminiscent of Adam's primal priesthood, which became a major motif in Second Temple sources. The "garments of glory" motif, in fact, seems to be derived from exactly this anachronistic fantasy. Specifically, ritual clothing woven of light was a solution offered to the problem created by conceiving Eden as a sanctuary with Adam as its priestly minister, for priests were specifically prohibited from exposing their nakedness (Exod. 20:26; 28:41–42). The concern is evident in *Jubilees* 3:27–31, for instance, where Adam's behavior in covering his shame is interpreted to be a special privilege, not granted to any of the animals, being rather an expression of the first man's careful observance of his priestly dignity as one who offers a pleasing sacrifice.[18] The priestly character of Adam's light-imbued garments fits within this same conception.

17. See the discussion in Joel Marcus, *Mark 9–16*, AB 27 (New York: Doubleday, 2000), 1112–15.

18. See Jessi Orpana, "Awareness of Nudity in Jubilees 3: Adam Portrayed as a Priest in the Garden," in *Crossing Imaginary Boundaries: The Dead Sea Scrolls in the Context of Second Temple Judaism*, ed. Mika S. Pajunen and Hanna Tervanotko, PFES 108 (Helsinki: Finnish Exegetical Society, 2015), 241–58.

Possibly the most direct parallel to Jesus' own donning of radiant clothes appears in an unambiguously priestly scene: the redressing/ordination of Enoch in 2 Enoch 22:8–9.

> The LORD said to Michael, "Take Enoch, and extract him from the earthly clothing. And anoint him with the delightful oil, and put him into the clothes of glory." And Michael extracted me from my clothes. He anointed me with the delightful oil; and the appearance of that oil is greater than the greatest light, its ointment is like sweet dew, and its fragrance like myrrh; and its shining is like the sun.[19]

With his heavenly "clothes of glory" and the "delightful" oil of anointing, Enoch is raised to a priestly dignity. While the text and tradition are difficult to date precisely, it is of special interest that Enoch's priestly "ordination" transpires in the form of a journey into the heavenly sanctuary, such as we just saw in the *Assumption of Moses*. The emerging convention of an otherworldly elevation to the priesthood evokes one prominent strain of what James Kugel describes as typical Second Temple exegetical "overkill" in explaining Levi's reception of priestly status: the tradition, namely, that the patriarch Levi himself was ordained by means of a celestial vision/voyage, where he was initiated into the angelic cult of heaven (cf. *ALD*; *Jub.* 31:2; *Test. Levi* 2–5; 8).[20] Levi sees a high mountain and then: "behold the heavens were opened" (*Test. Levi* 2:5–6; see also *Test. Levi* 5:1; 18:6; cf. 4QTestLevi[a] II 13–17).

The traditions of Levi's ordination vision/voyage also display an active interest in the priestly vestments.

> And I saw seven men in white clothing, saying to me:
>> Arise, put on the robe of the priesthood
>> and the crown of righteousness
>> and the breastplate of understanding
>> and the garment of truth
>> and the plate of faith
>> and the turban of (giving) a sign
>> and the ephod of prophecy.
> And each of them carried these things and put them on me, and said:
>> From now on become a priest of the Lord, you and your seed, forever.
> And the first anointed with holy oil. . . .
> The third clothed me with a linen vestment like an ephod.
> The fourth put round me a girdle like (a) purple (robe). . . .

19. Translation by F. I. Andersen in *OTP* 1:139.
20. Kugel, "Levi's Elevation," 7–13, 27–30.

The sixth put a crown on my head.

The seventh put on me a diadem of the priesthood. And they filled my
    hands with incense that I might serve as priest to the Lord. (*Test.
    Levi* 8:1–10)[21]

Like Aaron in Leviticus 8–9, Levi's *hands are filled* and he is dressed in special
(here white) vestments. Light imagery is also prominent in describing Levi's
transformation into the glory of a priest: "You will light up a bright light of
knowledge in Jacob, and you will be as the sun to all the seed of Israel" (*Test.
Levi* 4:2); "He will shine as the sun on the earth and will remove all darkness
from under heaven" (*Test. Levi* 18:4).[22]

It is impossible to say whether a less fragmentary vision of Second Temple
traditions of Moses' ascension might attest to a similar interest in his own
glorious vesture. It begins to look likely. What is clear, in any case, is that a
metamorphosis/glorification/apotheosis somehow outfitting the mortal flesh
of Moses for his sojourn in the heavenly place is also known to authors like
Philo (e.g., *Mos.* 2.288) and that this idea bears close contacts with Enochian
vestment tradition.[23] In the symbolic universe of Second Temple Judaism, vestments were more than vestments: they represented a mysterious bodily bearing of the Lord's *kābôd*. A heavenly priesthood from this perspective obliged
some such manner of transfiguration in glory. How else might one worthily
enter the holy of holies in heaven? The pattern is repeatedly confirmed. The
Apocalypse of Abraham provides yet another example.[24]

Zechariah's prophecy of the reclothing of Joshua the high priest provides
a scriptural base for this developing view (Zech. 3:1–10). The eschatologically
renewed and newly glorified priestly order is symbolized and defined by its
new order of priestly vesture. No longer wearing old and soiled vestments, a
new Joshua/Jesus appears in new "clean garments": an image of the transformation and purification of the priestly establishment.

It is useful to recall here once again the particular company that Jesus
keeps when he dons his bright white vestments, for this recalls another model
of ordination that also shapes the Levi tradition. Kugel calls this the "chain

21. Translation from Hollander and de Jonge, *Testaments*, 149.

22. Whether it represents another case of "overkill" or not, Levi's vestments are not the only
symbol of his new status. Like Moses the messenger (*nuntius*) in *As. Mos.* 10:2, Levi's hands are
filled in expression of consecration; and like the use of the weighty word "anointed one/messiah"
for Moses in 4Q377, Levi (like Enoch) is anointed with a holy unction as priest (cf. *ALD* 6).

23. See Stokes, "Assumption of Moses," 196.

24. In the *Apocalypse of Abraham*, as in many Jewish pseudepigraphical narratives, the
hero's access to the sacred realm coincides with his metamorphosis as a celebrant of the heavenly
liturgy. This translation, hinted at symbolically via the change in Abraham's garments, was
often taken to mark the transition from the earthly to the celestial. Here, as in the Yom Kippur
ordinance, the changes affecting the celebrant's wardrobe are the climax of the transformation.

of priests" motif—namely, elevation to sacerdotal rank through personal transmission, in Levi's case from an ancient line of priests, reaching through Abraham and Noah all the way back to Adam.[25] Not only were instructions about ritual matters passed on through these intergenerational meetings, but the priestly garments were likewise handed down. "And his [Levi's] father put priestly clothes on him and filled his hands" (*Jub.* 32:4; cf. *ALD* 9).[26] Such hand-to-hand transmission of the high priestly garments is scripturally grounded in Numbers 20:26–28, where the vestments are ceremonially removed from Aaron and transferred to his son Eleazar (cf. Exod. 29:29). Here in Numbers, the stripping of Aaron and clothing of his heir is carried out by Moses. This highlights Moses' prominent place in the Pentateuch as the Lord's designated *high priest–maker*, a role we have already seen (cf. Exod. 29; Lev. 8–9). In view of the sacerdotal character of Moses and Elijah, and Jesus' clear status through Deuteronomy 18:15 as a designated successor, the very Elijah-like motif of transmitting garments stands well within imaginative reach of the transfiguration's symbolic universe. It is likely that Jesus here is somehow inheriting from Moses and Elijah a kind of approbation as the one prophetically foretold. Jesus is personally invested with their priestly authority over the old and the new cult, respectively.

Mark's understated way of describing Jesus' transfigured clothing may appear at first rather mundane, with its appeal to the lowly trade of a cloth-carder. Jesus' clothes became "dazzling white, such as no one [fuller] on earth could bleach them" (Mark 9:3). Mark humbly evokes the otherworldly through an absolute contrast with the worldly and well known. We may ask, however, whether in this precise language we ought not hear an allusion to the strange "fullers' soap" (*bōrît mĕkabbĕsîm*) that is like a "refiner's fire" for purifying the corrupted priesthood (Mal. 3:2). Jesus stands revealed as a priest, an ideal Levite, purer than the Old Covenant (*bĕrit*) could imagine. Although hues of crimson and blue were threaded into the earthly vestments of Aaron and his sons when they appeared "in their splendor" (Sir. 50:13), pure linen garments were the priestly garb in Ezekiel's vision of the eschatological temple (Ezek. 44:15–18), as described in excursus 6. This simple white vestment, extended to the entire priesthood of the eschatological temple, was the assigned garment of the high priest for his ministry on the day of Yom Kippur. More: in *1 Enoch* 14:20, in the holy of holies of the heavenly temple, God himself is depicted as wearing the same simple white linen garment of

---

25. Kugel, "Levi's Elevation," 17–24.

26. See Kugel, "Levi's Elevation," 49. The case of Jacob is special, as he was not himself considered a priest; Levi thus (also) received the priestly dignity from his grandfather, Isaac, who was imagined as a priest. The text in *Jub.* 32:4 binds the handing over of the garments specifically with the "Jacob counts backward" motif.

the high priest.[27] Jesus on Mount Tabor is dressed in the manner of the living Lord: depicted as high priest ministering in the true dwelling in the innermost sanctuary on high!

Building Booths

This brings us finally to the Feast of Booths. Peter's confused attempt to erect booths is short-circuited on the mountain. This must not be misunderstood, however, for the reference to the Feast of Sukkoth is fitting and reinforces a priestly reading. The feast is calendrically hinged to the celebration of Yom Kippur and the ritual reclothing of the high priest. Indeed, Sukkoth comes five days after the Day of Atonement, making rather suggestive the otherwise free-floating chronological allusion in Mark 9:2, "six days later."

The internal linkage of Booths to the Day of Atonement becomes evident in the pronounced associations of this major pilgrimage feast. As the immediate festal pendant to the high priest's annual cleansing of the cultic machine, Sukkoth embodied the inauguration of the newly purified cult. In Ezra 3:4, on the Feast of Booths, the returned exiles, led by Joshua and his fellow priests, inaugurate the altar, relaying its foundation and offering the first sacrifices since the time of their deportation (cf. Neh. 8:14–17). Following the Maccabean crisis, the purification/rededication of the temple became associated with the Feast of Sukkoth, which thus gained a keen importance for the new Hasmonean order (e.g., 2 Macc. 1:18; 10:6). Especially in the Hasmonean and Herodian periods, the festival accordingly became the day on which the acclamations of kings were made and high priests formally assumed their office: another interesting blending of royal and sacerdotal dignity (e.g., Josephus, *Ant.* 15.50–52; *J.W.* 1.437). In 1 Maccabees 10:21, we thus learn that "Jonathan *put on the sacred vestments* in the seventh month of the one hundred sixtieth year, *at the festival of booths*." Both the technical expression employed here for a high priestly ordination—putting on the sacred vestments—and the festal time of its occurrence at the Festival of Booths are a perfect fit for the transfiguration.

Graphically, of course, at the center of the Feast of Booths stands the symbolic action of constructing a building. All the Jews flock to the holy city and build little shacks. It is still quite a sight in Jerusalem down to this day. In Jesus' day, it was an eschatological rebuilding of the temple that was expected. When Peter suggests interrupting Jesus' journey to Jerusalem, he fails to understand that the Anointed One's definitive work of booth building, by which the prophetic vision of Zechariah 14:16–21 will be fulfilled (i.e., a universal, end-time pilgrimage of all nations to Jerusalem for the Feast of Booths), will come only

---

27. On the high priestly allusions in this passage in *1 Enoch*, see Martha Himmelfarb, *Ascent to Heaven in Jewish and Christian Apocalypses* (New York: Oxford University Press, 1993), 18.

at the consummation of Jesus' final pilgrimage. Jesus' own symbolic cleansing of the Jerusalem temple and his offering of the true atoning sacrifice are what will enable the pagans to be joined like mini-temples to the one great temple, revealed as a "house of prayer for all nations" (Mark 11:17).

In a word, Peter, who "rebuked" Jesus for his prophecy of suffering, in thinking now of booths, does not understand the temple of Jesus' body. The second-century *Apocalypse of Peter* intuitively captures the theological dynamic quite well.

> And I [Peter] said to him, "My Lord, do you wish that I make here three tabernacles, one for you, one for Moses, and one for Elijah?" And he said to me in wrath, "Satan makes war against you and has veiled your understanding, and the good things of this world conquer you. Your eyes must be opened and your ears unstopped that . . . [it is] a tabernacle, which the hand of man has not made but which my heavenly Father has made for me and for the elect." And we saw it full of joy.[28]

The glorified body of Jesus on Tabor reveals the "pattern" (*tabnît*), like that seen by Moses in the cloud atop Sinai: the blueprints for building the true tabernacle of God's presence.

Jesus' solemn announcement in Caesarea Philippi—precisely six (inclusive) days before his metamorphosis—that, like a "Davidic temple builder" (with Eliakim's priestly vesture in the background), he was laying a new *foundation stone*, is closely followed by Jesus' investiture in glorious garments at the Feast of Booths: a conjunction that implies a portentous statement.[29] This one, confessed by Peter as the Messiah, is the priest-prophet like Moses, the messenger of the covenant like Elijah. He is *Joshua*, the true high priest, whose garments are cleansed that he may enter Jerusalem, purify the cult, and rebuild the (true) temple.

Jesus' Institution of the Priesthood

The Synoptic Gospels know any number of motifs that might be explored as communications of Jesus' priestly status to a chosen band. The Father's

28. Translation from Wilhelm Schneemelcher, ed., *New Testament Apocrypha*, vol. 2, *Writings Relating to the Apostles; Apocalypses and Related Subjects* (Louisville: Westminster John Knox, 1992), 635 (Akhmim 21; Ethiopic 16). In the Akhmim version (17–20), Peter is shown men in "shining raiment of angels," identified as "your high priests."

29. See Michael Barber, "Jesus as the Living Temple Builder and Peter's Priestly Role in Matt 16:16–19," *JBL* 132 (2013): 935–53 (esp. 944–45). On the living temple motifs at work in Matt. 16, see Tom Holmén, "Caught in the Act: Jesus Starts the New Temple—A Continuum Study of Jesus as the Founder of the *Ecclesia*," in *The Identity of Jesus: Nordic Voices*, ed. Samuel Byrskog, Tom Holmén, and Matti Kankaanniemi, WUNT 2/373 (Tübingen: Mohr Siebeck, 2014), 181–231.

command "Listen to him" in testimony of his Son's faithful priesthood (Mark 9:7; cf. Deut. 18:15) informs, for instance, Jesus' words to the specially commissioned Seventy (or Seventy-Two): "Whoever listens to you listens to me" (Luke 10:16). Jesus' sending out of these "laborers for the harvest" comes with a commission to preach the kingdom of God and with a grant of authority "over all the power of the enemy" (Luke 10:1–20). The bearing of such eschatological *exousia*, authority in word and deed, modeled on and moored to the divine authority of Jesus, the eternal Son, is the essential priestly substance we seek. The Great Commission of the Eleven to teach and baptize is another solemn articulation of Jesus' sharing of priestly power that could very profitably be expounded, notably for the way it incorporates sacramental ritual into the authoritative preaching mission (Matt. 28:16–20).

The Gospel of John has its own characteristic interests and manner of speaking. One of these interests is the transmission of Jesus' authority. This theme finds a related but different, stronger, more explicit, and more symbolic expression in the Fourth Gospel than it has in the Synoptics. To see how it functions we must first consider briefly Jesus' priesthood in John, then the scene of his commissioning of Peter.

Jesus' High Priesthood in John

One of the famous omissions in the Fourth Gospel is an account of Jesus' transfiguration. Raymond Brown, however, was keen to observe of John 1:14 that "there is much to recommend the suggestion that 14c–d is an echo of the Transfiguration."[30] In Jesus, God's glory has *tabernacled* and built its booth among us. If John's prologue indeed contains an allusion to the transfiguration scene, so central to the Synoptic Gospels, his presentation of Jesus' priesthood has also shifted in major ways. The symbolism of Jesus' vesture has, nevertheless, found expression in John's famous attention to Jesus' seamless garment (John 19:23–34), which has long elicited exegetical speculation, including the claims of an allusion to the high priest's vestments. Indeed, as described by Josephus, the high priest's outermost sacred tunic "is not composed of two pieces to be stitched at the shoulders and at the sides: it is one long, woven cloth with a slit for the neck, parted not crosswise but lengthwise from the breast to a point in the middle of the back" (*Ant.* 3.161 [LCL]).

The connection of Jesus' garment to Josephus's account is intriguing, even if apart from a larger Johannine construction of Jesus as the new high priest

---

30. Raymond Brown, *The Gospel according to John I–XII*, AB 29 (New York: Doubleday, 1966), 34.

it is difficult to insist upon a priestly connection.[31] This larger construction, if subtle, is not lacking, however.[32] At the center of John's vision stands a series of artfully understated but forceful contrasts between Jesus, identified as the Good Shepherd, and Caiaphas, high priest "for that year." To discern these hints, by which Jesus at once submits to and replaces Caiaphas, one must be well accustomed to discerning John's amazingly delicate manner of making his point.

A magnificent example is the subtle Johannine double meaning that appears in the repeated statement that the disciple whom Jesus loved "was known [gnōstos] to the high priest" (John 18:15–16). On account of being so known, this beloved disciple and companion of Peter finds entrance into the high priest's court. The Greek word for this court is aulē, which is strikingly the same word used several times for the "sheepfold" of the Good Shepherd in John 10. Peter, by contrast, stands outside at the "gate" (thyra)—another clear verbal link to the discourse in chapter 10 ("I am the thyra of the sheep," 10:7, 9). That Peter, through the ministry of the disciple known to the high priest, ultimately enters precisely through the gate puts him in the position not only of being one of the sheep but also of being the shepherd. "The one who enters by the gate is the shepherd of the sheep. The gatekeeper opens the gate for him" (10:2–3). This will be expanded at length in John 21, as we shall presently see. In John 10, of course, Jesus had insisted on the mutual knowledge of the sheep and the shepherd: "I know [ginōskō] my own and my own know [ginōskousi] me" (10:14). The overtone of the phrase in John 18:15–16 is that the disciple loved by Jesus is known to and beloved of the one who is himself now identified as being the true high priest, presiding over the true sheepfold/aulē.

The word "true" is chosen here with intent, for it is one of the key Johannine categories for describing the redirection of Israel's life initiated by the Word made flesh. In the context of the famous, so-called high priestly prayer in John 17, just before Jesus' confrontation with Caiaphas in John 18, this concept of truth takes on particular force. Most importantly, Jesus prays: "Sanctify [hagiason] them in [the] truth; your word is truth. . . . For their sakes I sanctify [hagiazō] myself, so that they also may be sanctified [hēgiasmenoi] in truth" (17:17, 19). An allusion to the priestly language of the Pentateuch is widely recognized in this hagiazein (sanctify/consecrate) motif, though

---

31. Ignace de La Potterie (The Hour of Jesus: The Passion and the Resurrection of Jesus according to John [New York: Alba House, 1989], 99) rejects Jesus' high priesthood on the basis of the seamless garment. See also Elizabeth Pemberton, "The Seamless Garment: A Note on John 19:23–24," ABR 54 (2006): 50–55. Pemberton understands the detail to indicate that Jesus was unconcerned with ritual purity.

32. See especially John Paul Heil, "Jesus as the Unique High Priest in the Gospel of John," CBQ 57 (1995): 729–45.

one must equally recognize that the cultic notion of consecration, as here deployed, has been drawn into a "radically reconstructive reading" of the Levitical traditions.[33] "True worshipers" and "worship in spirit and truth," rather than a simple continuation of the temple cult in Jerusalem (or on Gerizim), is what the prayer and passion of Jesus advances (4:23).

That in John's vision Caiaphas, in contrast to Jesus, is something less than the ultimate priest and Good Shepherd of the people becomes clear in a number of ways. Three times the officeholder is identified specifically as high priest *for that year* (John 11:49, 51; 18:13). This implies, on the one hand, the limited character of Caiaphas's service, which gestures implicitly toward a more lasting priesthood. But, on the other hand, the phrase more directly hints at Caiaphas's principal duty, for in Leviticus 16:34 it is stipulated that once a year, on Yom Kippur, atonement shall be made for all the people. The word used in the Septuagint of Leviticus is *eniautou*, the same used for Caiaphas's season of service in the Gospel, as if to underscore that Caiaphas's one great priestly deed shall be to offer the one great sacrifice for sins: the offering of the Lamb who is also the *Logos*. That Caiaphas's entire priestly ministry is intimately bound to the atonement offering of Jesus is plain from the words that Caiaphas himself speaks: "He did not say this on his own [*aph' heautou*], but being high priest that year he prophesied that Jesus was about to die for the nation, and not for the nation only, but to gather into one the dispersed children of God" (John 11:51–52). If Caiaphas presides over Jesus' death, as the principal action and exercise of his own priesthood, in a more eminent way this high priestly offering is the work of Jesus himself. The laying down of his life is a free self-offering, not a sacrifice forced upon him (10:18). In this sense, the *Logos*-Lamb assumes for himself the high priestly role.

Two things are to be noted in the statement of Caiaphas about Jesus' sacrifice. First, the "dispersed" children of God are described with the classic vocabulary of scattered sheep (cf. Jer. 10:21; 23:1–2; Zech. 11:16; 13:7), while Caiaphas's purpose is formulated as an intention that the people and the whole nation might not be "destroyed" by Rome (*apolētai*, John 11:50). This interest, though political and worldly, directly echoes the Good Shepherd's similar concern to protect the flock against the thief who comes only "to steal and kill and destroy [*apolese*]" (10:10). Jesus' promise as Good Shepherd is, indeed, to give eternal life to the sheep, so that "they will never be destroyed/perish [*apolōntai*]" (10:28), while his boast in the so-called high priestly prayer in 17:12 is that he did not lose or *let perish* a single one of those entrusted to him, except the "son of destruction." If this purpose is the same, the contrast between Caiaphas's manner of holding at bay the danger of death and the

---

33. See Harold Attridge, "How Priestly Is the 'High Priestly Prayer' of John 17?," *CBQ* 75 (2013): 1–14.

destruction of the flock is entirely different than the manner of Jesus, the true shepherd. When John says that Caiaphas "did not say this on his own" or "of himself," for instance, we have another double meaning. Caiaphas speaks by a prophetic inspiration proper to his office. He also speaks, however, *about* someone else, for this shepherd of the people will not lay down *his own life* to save the flock. He will sacrifice instead an innocent lamb. Caiaphas is thus exposed as being precisely like the wicked shepherds in Ezekiel 34: he slaughters the sheep and never seeks out the lost. In fact, in striking the shepherd, Caiaphas actively scatters the sheep (cf. Matt. 26:31; Zech. 13:7). Jesus, by contrast, lays down his own life to rescue the others from death. "Jesus answered, 'I told you that I am he [*egō eimi*]. So if you are looking for me, let these men go.' This was to fulfill the word that he had spoken, 'I did not lose a single one of those whom you gave me'" (John 18:8–9). In this way, the *aph' heautou* of Caiaphas in 11:51 stands in telling contrast with Jesus' own double *ap' emautou* in the previous chapter: "I lay down my life in order to take it up again. No one takes it from me [*ap' emautou*], but I lay it down of my own accord [*ap' emautou*]" (10:17–18).

Jesus' healing of the mutilated ear of the high priest's servant (*doulos*) as he formally hands himself over illustrates this free decision and is a particularly interesting indication of the priestly character of the passion, for beyond the charitable deed toward Malchus, the healing hints at the proper ritual execution of Jesus' free sacrifice. The "servant of the high priest" was, it seems, not a lowly domestic slave but the *segan hakohanim*, a high-ranking official mentioned in the Mishnah (e.g., *m. Yoma* 3.9; 4.1) who served as the high priest's deputy and chief assistant: the "general of the temple," as he is called in Luke 22:4 (cf. Josephus, *J.W.* 6.5.3). It was this official's highest duty to be the understudy of the high priest, ritually ready to step in to complete the rites of Yom Kippur should the need arise (cf. *b. Soṭah* 42a). A physical blemish such as having his ear cut would have explicitly disqualified him from this eminent liturgical role (cf. Lev. 21:16–23; Josephus, *Ant.* 14.13.10). Jesus' healing deed thus ensures, on the one hand, the symbolic integrity of the sacrificial action that now formally commences. On the other hand, the gesture is part of an ongoing pedagogical project of Jesus vis-à-vis his own understudy and vicar. Peter must learn to be a shepherd, not after the model of Caiaphas, the wicked shepherd, who sends out his deputy with violent intent, armed and leading a band with swords and clubs, determined to take rather than to give life. Rather, Peter must learn to sheath his sword and "follow" the example of the one who freely lays down his own life, binding up the wounded (e.g., Malchus) like the divine shepherd prophesied in Ezekiel 34:16.

When in John 18:19–24 Jesus at last stands formally on trial before Annas, also called the high priest—perhaps as a kind of emeritus title or perhaps carrying the more general sense simply of "chief priest" (cf. 11:47)—a final forceful contrast is made. Jesus says he has always spoken openly to the world, teaching publicly where all the Jews gather. "I have said nothing in secret" (18:20). In other words, the sheep hear and know the shepherd's voice (10:3–5, 16). Caiaphas and Annas, by contrast, plot in secret councils and act in nocturnal meetings. Jesus' answer to the soldier's question "Is that how you answer [speak to] the high priest?" thus entails another Johannine double meaning. "If I have spoken rightly, why do you strike me?" means not only "If I have answered your question well" but also "If I have done well in thus always speaking and acting in the open"—in damning contrast to the manner of these high priests. For his refusal to offer more testimony than this and to participate in the high priests' illicit, secretive trial, Jesus is bound and condemned.

More could be added to this rich picture, but the main outlines are sufficiently clear. For John, Jesus is at once the innocent Lamb and the Good Shepherd. He at once presides over the *aulē* and offers the great atonement sacrifice. Caiaphas is an anti-image of these same high priestly spheres; he is thus cast in the role of Ezekiel's wicked shepherds. The presentation is not nearly so bitter, but one might think of John's Caiaphas a bit like the Wicked Priest, the *hā-kōhēn hā-rāšā'* at Qumran (1QpHab; 4QPs^a; cf. excursus 3). The Good Shepherd, on the other hand, corresponds in a way to the Scrolls' Teacher of Righteousness and is John's positive priestly pendant to Caiaphas's bad example as a priest and leader of the people—the fulfillment of God's promise in Ezekiel 34 to himself replace the wicked shepherds.

Within this context the garments of Jesus thus take on a more convincingly sacral hue. Scholars' attention to John's resonant use of the word *anōthen* in describing the garment's fabrication is also helpful in this connection, for it enables Jesus' clothing to appear as a thing of divine origin, coming like Jesus himself "from above." In John 13, Jesus' garments are the symbol of his earthly life, laid down and picked up again. That the seamless garment though handed over remains untorn recalls from this angle Jesus' own body, which similarly remains unbroken on the cross in fulfillment of scriptural prophecy (John 19:33–36). In both Matthew and Mark, of course, the veil of the temple is torn from top (*anōthen*) to bottom, while in Luke it is torn down the middle (Matt. 27:51; Mark 15:38; Luke 23:45). Should we acknowledge John's knowledge of this Synoptic tradition—and there are many reasons to do so—an implied allusion contrasting Jesus' vestment/body to the torn temple veil becomes very attractive. The pentateuchal linkage of the priestly vesture and the temple/tabernacle textiles would make the symbolic connection quite strong. The end effect would be to position Jesus' temple-body, streaming with living water, as the successor to the temple served by Caiaphas and all of Israel's high priests. It is a symbolic system quite different from the Synoptic evocation of Jesus' high priestly vestments, yet a powerful christological extension of the same theme.

Shepherds after the Lord's Own Heart

Shepherds as Potentates, Priests, and Predators

Ultimately, in place of the vestments, which rest on the margin, the Good Shepherd clearly stands at the center of John's symbolism of priestly office. As a central, even controlling image, the shepherd motif is unusually evocative. It has deep cultural roots, and it is useful to gain some measure of this background.

Shepherd-kings are as ancient as civilization itself. In Sumer the king's royal crown was a stylized shepherd's hat, and ancient reliefs depict these kings holding sheep in their arms. In seal impressions dating from around 3300–3100 BC, the shepherd-kings of Uruk, dressed in priestly garb and standing at the head of a group of priests, are depicted ritually feeding the sacred flocks of the goddess Inanna. The royal regalia of the Egyptian pharaoh included a ritualized shepherd's crook and flail, expressive symbols inherited from predynastic times. Sennacherib's Neo-Assyrian royal protocol, with its typical titular usage, lauded him as "great king, strong king, king of Assyria, unrivaled king, pious shepherd who reveres the gods, guardian of truth who loves justice" (Bellino Cylinder); "king of the four corners, the wise shepherd, favorite of the gods" (Hexagonal Prism); and so on. In Israel, the Hebrew word *nāgîd*, which is based on an Old Akkadian root and usage and literally means "shepherd," came through a natural transformation to be, first, an attribute of the title of a ruler and later a synonym of the title itself. The Zion theology of Psalm 23 plays directly upon this shepherd-king motif. The Old Greek translation of Psalm 2:9, followed closely by the Aramaic Targum, declares to the Davidic king, "You shall shepherd [*poimaneis*] them with a rod of iron." In Psalm 70:70–72 David is taken from the sheepfold to shepherd the people (cf. 11Q5). In the Dead Sea Scrolls he is explicitly called the "shepherd-prince" (4Q504). *Psalms of Solomon* 17 develops the motif at length in the manner of a messianic type. And on and on. In short, the shepherd-king theme was for millennia an extraordinarily resilient metaphor: a ubiquitous piece of ancient Near Eastern royal propaganda impregnating the cultures and courts of ancient Mesopotamian, Egyptian, and Canaanite rulers, including the Davidic house.

The accent of the shepherd image falls squarely upon the ruler's royal status, and this is terribly important. It is an error to lose from view the strong priestly connotations, however. The image derives from a situation in which these two identities were in fact fused. If the kings of Uruk were depicted as priests tending a flock of sacred sheep, this was not a sentimental pastoral picture or simple allegory of a leader. It was a real responsibility of the king/ priest to feed the gods and goddesses, like Inanna; this meant raising actual livestock on actual farms, then slaughtering the living animals on actual altars in the gods' temples. More will be said about such sacred plantations in the following chapter. The point here is that, as chief sacrificial agents, priests were responsible for organizing and coordinating vast farming enterprises and were thus, to varying degrees, in the real business of being shepherds, while the king stood atop this vast hierarchical and hieratic, pastoral pyramid as highest custodian of the god's dwelling and the chief shepherd/high priest. Even those involved in the more rustic aspects of herding were obliged to make all sorts of regular animal sacrifices, tithes of offspring, wool offerings, and so forth, as we know from ancient inscriptions (e.g., *IPriene* 362), so that a regular commerce and contact existed between pastoral producers and the priests in local temples and shrines. Such sacrificial slaughter of the flock obviously projects an image rather different from the Gospels' self-sacrificing Good Shepherd. Yet such a historical background is essential to understand and acknowledge, for it puts the gospel in correct perspective and guards us against a sentimental misconstrual. A politically innocent, pastoral idyll is not the tone of this image. Shepherd discourse of this nature communicated a highly legible message of hierarchical/hieratic, monarchical power. It entailed an allusion to the ancient (less industrial, more agriculturally ordered) version of the "military-industrial complex."

Ezekiel 34 already began to deconstruct the exploitative character of this system in exposing the people's shepherds as predators rather than pastors. "Prophesy against the shepherds of Israel. . . . You eat the fat, you clothe yourselves with the wool, you slaughter the fatlings; but you do not feed the sheep" (Ezek. 34:2–3). The plural "shepherds" might target several or all of Israel's kings considered together (cf. Jer. 23:1); or, more likely, it might embrace a wider circle of ruling officials—thus indicting the priestly establishment as well, priests belonging integrally to the whole state apparatus, of course. At a later postexilic moment, the focus begins to shift, however, so that the Zadokite hierocracy has been discerned as the main group behind the mercenary "shepherds" of the "flock doomed to slaughter" condemned in Zechariah 11:4–17. "Those who buy them kill them and go unpunished; and those who sell them say, 'Blessed be the LORD, for I have become rich'; and their own shepherds have no pity on them" (Zech. 11:5–6). Clearly, as the high priests of Israel increasingly filled the royal vacuum—and became rich indeed—the transfer of the shepherd metaphor from king to priest would have been entirely natural. Priests' very visible role in concretely slaughtering the fatlings and eating the fat would have made the metaphoric application all the easier.

Inaugurating a New Pastoral Ordo

Jesus' discourse in John 10 activates all these deep cultural echoes. Through its interaction with this dense symbolic background, the gospel image gains considerable power as Jesus announces a reversal of the ancient world's hierarchical/hieratic power structure. The role of the absolute ancient Near Eastern monarch, blurred with the postexilic Israelite high priest, is at once appropriated and redefined in the tradition of Ezekiel 34, Zechariah 11, and the prophesied Davidic messiah.[34] The subversive message of John 10's disconcertingly *good* shepherd is obviously impractical from the perspective of *Realpolitik*. From this perspective, John 10 is justly compared to the Synoptic saying about servant lordship:

> The kings of the Gentiles lord it over them; and those in authority over them are called benefactors. But not so with you; rather the greatest among you must become like the youngest, and the leader like one who serves [*ho diakonōn*]. For who is greater, the one who is at the table or the one who serves [*ho diakonōn*]? Is it not the one at the table? But I am among you as one who serves [*ho diakonōn*]. (Luke 22:25–27)

It is worth observing several things about this statement, presented in its Lukan form. First, Jesus establishes here a new hierarchical form: a new, evangelical definition of the one who is greater. It is the *institution*, we may say, of a new *ordo*. Luke's highly suggestive redactional embedding of the logion within the eucharistic context of Jesus' Last Supper (immediately after the institution narrative, no less) indicates the importance of this specific "transvaluation of values" via christological *diakonia* for the enduring character of the central act of the Christian cult. Something constitutive of "do this in remembrance of me" is here being enacted. The concept of *diakonia*/service, incidentally, means not only works of mercy and waiting on tables (cf. Acts 6) but also specifically "cult" or "worship" in Hebrew (*'ăbōdâ*)—just as we can still speak of a church "service," for instance. Finally, the *diakonia* character of the Church's cult entails not simply Jesus' own kenotic act of becoming the least and the one who serves. A shared conformity to this archetypal *service* modeled by Jesus is envisioned, for the saying is addressed to Jesus' apostles in

---

34. On the Davidic shepherd-king motif, see Joel Willitts, *Matthew's Messianic Shepherd-King: In Search of "The Lost Sheep of the House of Israel,"* BZNW 147 (Berlin: de Gruyter, 2007).

the plural. The apostles are to embody Jesus' example as part of their liturgical remembrance (*anamnesis*) of this Church-and-cult defining moment. We are dealing in this command of *diakonia* with one of the most foundational elements of the essence of the *apostolicity* of the Church.

The obvious comparison in John to this text of Luke 22:25–27 is the scene of the foot washing in John 13. "I have set you an example" (John 13:15). While humble service is clearly central to the scene, the driving power of Jesus' intense love, which inspires the extremities of his humble service, is a still more important part of the Johannine message.[35] "Having loved his own who were in the world, he loved them to the end"; "I give you a new commandment, that you love one another. Just as I have loved you, you also should love one another" (13:1, 34). The extravagance of Jesus' deed becomes the manner by which the apostles are promised to receive a "share with me [*meros met' emou*]" (13:8). This *meros* is a special share in the whole paschal mystery and the fruits of Jesus' self-emptying love. Theologically speaking, the communication of this love from Christ to his apostles in a ritual dynamic of formal/exemplary causality is a profound source for contemplating the special grace and the sacramental sign of Holy Orders.

Within John's narrative, Jesus' "laying down" and "taking up" of his garments in John 13 is a recognized symbol of his self-sacrifice and a direct echo of the same language used in the Good Shepherd discourse (John 10:11, 15, 17–18). This linguistic connection helps confirm that the replication of the master's model, given on the vigil of his passion, is best expressed through the idiom of the shepherd. Accordingly, what is of particular interest for us at this point is the reflex that the Good Shepherd image in John 10 triggers in the Gospel's epilogue in John 21. In the Johannine vision, a commissioning ceremony and solemn handing over (*traditio*) of Jesus' pastoral authority is the final evangelical event that must be narrated. Peter, of course, is the one specially chosen to manifest and reembody Jesus' paschal service as the Good Shepherd.

Purifying Peter's Heart by Philia

Peter's election finds many expressions in the Gospels. As mentioned, his special destiny to play the role of shepherd in John 21 was already foreshadowed in John 10: "The one who enters by the gate is the shepherd of the sheep. The gatekeeper opens the gate for him" (John 10:2–3). After finding entry through the gate in chapter 18, Peter's three denials of Jesus promptly follow. This betrayal and the bitter sorrow created by Peter's sin accordingly

35. See Jan van der Watt, "The Meaning of Jesus Washing the Feet of His Disciples (John 13)," *Neotestamentica* 51 (2017): 25–39.

stand in the very forefront of his (re)constitution as a living icon of the Good Shepherd. Note that it is not the beloved disciple, who stood faithfully by the cross, who is selected by Jesus for this shepherd's role. It would be impossible to find a better proof of Scripture's frontal reckoning with the weakness and sin of the Church's leaders.

The charcoal fire on Tiberias's shore is a graphic, narrative link to Peter's denials in the high priest's *aulē*, as is the threefold question "Do you love me?"

> When they had finished breakfast, Jesus said to Simon Peter, "Simon son of John, do you love me more than these?" He said to him, "Yes, Lord; you know that I love you." Jesus said to him, "Feed my lambs." A second time he said to him, "Simon son of John, do you love me?" He said to him, "Yes, Lord; you know that I love you." Jesus said to him, "Tend my sheep." He said to him the third time, "Simon son of John, do you love me?" Peter felt hurt because he said to him the third time, "Do you love me?" And he said to him, "Lord, you know everything; you know that I love you." Jesus said to him, "Feed my sheep. Very truly, I tell you, when you were younger, you used to fasten your own belt and to go wherever you wished. But when you grow old, you will stretch out your hands, and someone else will fasten a belt around you and take you where you do not wish to go." (He said this to indicate the kind of death by which he would glorify God.) After this he said to him, "Follow me." (John 21:15–19)

There is a famous philological twist to this exchange in the variable Greek word choice in Jesus' repeated questions. Contrary to a tradition of bad sermons, however, with just enough New Testament Greek to do some damage, Jesus' interview of Peter is not a humiliating demonstration of the latter's failure in love. Peter is not challenged beyond his power to ascend from mere *philia* to *agapē*. Quite the reverse! The climactic sequence, on my reading, goes more like this.

> *Question*: "Simon, Son of John, do you love me [*agapas me*] more than these?" This might mean either "Do you love me more than these others love me?" or "Do you love me more than you love these others?"
>
> *Answer*: "Yes, Lord, I am your friend [*phileō*]," meaning "I love you most of all." This handles either question. "Yes, Lord, I love you more than they do and more than I love the others. You are more; you are my friend."
>
> *Commission*: "Good, then *feed my lambs*. Give pasture to the lambs who already belong to my flock." Is it fanciful to discern in this feeding motif a eucharistic allusion? Possibly. But possibly not. From the earliest days the early Christians understood the feeding and drinking imagery in the pastoral words of Psalm 23 as a eucharistic allusion. The only question is how early such a pastoral allegory might have been established. At the

very least, one may say that the Fourth Gospel's pronounced interest in feeding on Jesus' flesh and being refreshed in him as in living waters invites a sacramental reading of Peter's charge to provide pasture for the sheep. The feeding of the multitude, with its simultaneous pastoral and eucharistic overtones, is very strong evidence that the connection between these ideas was already present in the evangelist's mind and the most primitive gospel tradition. We also note that Jesus' questions to Peter come directly after the action of breaking the bread after breakfast. So: "If you love me with a special love, preside at my eucharistic banquet."

Question: "Peter, do you love me [*agapas me*]?" That is, "Peter, did you hear yourself just now? Are you aware that you changed the verb? Did you perhaps mean to say that you *agapē* me?"

Answer: "*Phileō*! I said it and I mean it. You are my friend!"

Commission: "Good, then *tend my sheep* [*poimaine ta probata mou*]." Tending the sheep recalls Ezekiel's image of binding up the wounded and seeking the lost, bringing and holding the scattered together. This is a harder chore than feeding the lambs. One thinks of the healing at the Sheep Gate (*epi tē probatikē*), where the invalids, the lame and blind and paralyzed, gather by the waters (John 5:2). Our attention is turned as well to those "other sheep" (*alla probata*) that also belong to Jesus, yet not to this fold (10:16). A universal mission is thus implied in this word. So: "If you insist that you are indeed my friend, bind up the wounded, seek out the lost, gather God's scattered children, bringing them in by the gate, so that there may be one flock and one shepherd."

Question: A third time Jesus asks, "Peter, are you my friend?" Which is to say, "With this unsubtle reminder of your three denials, let's be finally sure that you are clear what this pasturing and tending actually obliges."

Answer: Peter is troubled that he asks a third time. "You know [*oidas* = *savoir, saber*] all things, you experience [*ginōskeis* = *connaitre, conocer*] that I love with the full love of friendship."

Commission: "Very good, then *follow me*."

What is this full promise of Peter's committed friendship, which has its seal not simply in a pastoral charge but in *following* Jesus? *Philia* is hardly a failure in John's Gospel; it is, in fact, the greatest love. "No one has greater love than this, to lay down one's life for one's friends" (John 15:13). The gravity of the friendship that Peter has promised sends him straight back to chapter 10: "The good shepherd lays down his life for the sheep" (10:11).

This is the master's final instruction. True love of him, real friendship with him, *following* Christ and imitating him as a shepherd, means dying for love of those he knows and loves to the end.

In this intimate commissioning scene, which becomes a prophecy of Peter's own cross, we have, I propose, an image of Peter's priestly ordination. Jesus openly shares with Peter his identity as the self-sacrificing Good Shepherd. Jesus returns to the Father but will not leave his own as orphans. He ensures the continued care of the sheep of his pasture. The supreme monarch, the Davidic messiah, and the heavenly high priest communicates to his Church an enduring service of *diakonia* and a plenary pastoral *potestas*. Could stronger scriptural evidence be imagined for the simple but far-reaching claim that Christ's authority as head is not restricted to a purely spiritual force somehow exercised immediately from heaven, but continues through real, chosen human agents on earth? If Jesus is "ordained" by a cosmic journey, Peter's priesthood comes through a chain of transmission and a transformation of the "ordination by zeal" motif. He who violently unsheathed his sword in the garden in a zealous, Phinehas-like moment is now remade through the excellence of his self-sacrificing Christlike *philia*. The flock remains Christ's own, but Peter is elevated to office at Jesus' own hands, through a threefold purgation of his sin, in an exchange of trust and love—and, let us not miss it, through the prophetic image of a vestition (John 21:18–19). Peter will stretch out his hands to put on the wooden shirt of a cross, girt about with a rope fastening him in place where he would rather not be.[36] In this way Peter slips into Jesus' own purified high priestly vestments, sharing in the glorification of the one raised up and honored by the worldly dishonor of the stripping-off of the old priesthood's seamless garment.

Conclusion

Jesus appeared in Israel as the eschatological high priest, rightful heir to supreme headship of the chosen people's cult. His ministry of righteous Torah instruction (e.g., Matt. 5) and the proclamation of a Jubilee of forgiveness (e.g., Luke 4) resonate directly with Malachi's ideal Levite and the heavenly Melchizedek of the Essenes. Consumed with Phinehas-like zeal in his cleansing of the temple, Christ laid public claim to a priestly role as custodian of the sacred precinct. As Good Shepherd he unites in his person all sacral and

---

36. On the "ample literary and artistic evidence for the use of ropes rather than nails to secure the condemned to the cross," see, e.g., Joseph Zias and Eliezer Sekeles, "The Crucified Man from Giv'at ha-Mivtar: A Reappraisal," *IEJ* 35 (1985): 22–27; and John C. Robinson, "Crucifixion in the Roman World: The Use of Nails at the Time of Christ," *Studia Antiqua* 2 (2002): 25–59.

royal *potestas*—possessing indeed "all authority [*exousia*] in heaven and on earth" (Matt. 28:18).

Jesus' authority, however, is a kenotic *diakonia* that inverts the world's tyrannical hierarchies of domination. And Jesus communicates this new form of *exousia* and gospel *ordo* of service to certain chosen successors. In a way, Christ's institution of the priesthood is as simple as that. A holy reordering of society is erected within the Church, an order that knows only the honor of taking "the last place," like the One who serves at the eucharistic table.

All the Twelve, like the wider college of the Seventy-Two, receive a share, a special *meros*, in Jesus' mission. In the end, however, if we desire to have a solid New Testament doctrine of ecclesial office, it is impossible to get around the person of Peter. His centrality and leadership position are uncontested. Jesus entrusts the sheep of his flock into Peter's hands; and yet, despite having transferred the flock, he remained the Head and the flock remained his own ("my sheep"!), as St. Augustine says. Is it responsible to pull out a pastoral principle from this exceptional commission?

Efforts to limit the significance of Peter's pastoral charge are a recognized heritage of the Reformation. Recent Protestant scholarship has shown itself ready to give more attention to Peter's extraordinary importance, however.[37] On the other hand, an apologetic Catholic approach that insists on seeing the legitimation of the papacy in every Petrine wink and nod is not convincing or helpful. So, was Peter, important as he is and was, an isolated case—the first and last of his kind? As Aquinas already saw long ago, this would be a very short-sighted view and not sit at all well with Jesus' promise that his Church would endure till the end of the world (*SCG* 4.76). On another level, it would also be surpassingly strange to insist that Peter was somehow the Church's exclusive earthly shepherd, since this would demand a willful ignorance of the robust pastoral discourse that immediately took root in the primitive Church as a designation for all her leaders (see excursus 8). The Petrine tradition itself sought to share this special dignity as shepherd with a presbyteral-pastoral college united under the one *archipoimenos*, the chief shepherd who is Christ (1 Pet. 5:1–3). It is, accordingly, much better to recognize Peter, especially in the commissioning scene of John 21, as the personal face of pastoral minis-try in the Church. The communal allegories and constructions of apostolic authority that so often control modern exegesis of the Fourth Gospel can here be profitably put to service. Peter is not simply Peter: he is a personified

---

37. See Helen Bond and Larry Hurtado, eds., *Peter in Early Christianity* (Grand Rapids: Eerd-mans, 2015), especially Hurtado, "The Apostle Peter in Protestant Scholarship: Cullmann, Hen-gel, and Bockmuehl," 1–15, and Markus Bockmuehl, "Scripture's Pope Meets von Balthasar's Peter," 321–40. See also Bockmuehl, *The Remembered Peter in Ancient Reception and Modern Debate*, WUNT 262 (Tübingen: Mohr Siebeck, 2010).

instance of an entire ecclesial sphere. No one has recognized this with greater theological sensitivity and success than Hans Urs von Balthasar in *The Office of Peter and the Structure of the Church*.[38] Balthasar's treatment also gives the best reply to Yves Congar's warning of a degenerate "hierarchiology" (a theology of the Church's structure, without reference to her inner life), for it stresses almost to a fault the personal union of office and love so manifest in both Christ and Peter.[39]

As noted in chapter 1, Karl Rahner objected that Peter's commission undermines the scriptural argument for Christ's institution of a sacramental priestly office, since the Petrine office itself is not sacramental.[40] In response we may now reply: Rahner sees only popes where we, more foundationally, also see priests. In establishing Peter as the shepherd of the flock, Jesus' institution of a new hierarchical *ordo* in his Church expresses and fully presumes Peter's intimate, embodied share in Christ's own priestly *potestas*. There is, in fact, something oddly ultramontane and subtly but deeply distorted in Rahner's hypostasizing a kind of papal quintessence, some nonsacerdotal Petrine status. Must such a high priesthood not inevitably become a purely juridical or honorific role, like secular imperial power, separated from the sanctifying power that comes from a privileged personal union with Christ's atoning sacrifice?[41]

Luther, in his polemical treatise *The Babylonian Captivity of the Church*, perceived with perfect intuitive clarity that without the sacrament of Orders the papacy itself as an institution must simply collapse: "Unless I am mistaken, if this fictitious sacrament should ever fall, the papacy itself will hardly survive."[42] Luther's own immense frustration with a priestly caste that refused to reform itself helps explain his strategic desire to raze the social bastions, create a classless society of all the baptized, and so give to secular leaders

---

38. Hans Urs von Balthasar, *The Office of Peter and the Structure of the Church* (San Francisco: Ignatius, 1985).

39. "The fact that this transfer of ministry [from Christ to Peter] cannot possibly be the institution of a mere 'office' becomes quite clear when we consider, first, that Christ's ministerial authority (the 'high priesthood') consisted of his privilege and ability to give his life for his sheep, and second, that as a condition for the transfer of the ministry of the Good Shepherd to Peter, greater love (demanded three times) is required, and furthermore the promise that this union of ministry and love is (analogously) feasible is guaranteed by the prophecy of Peter's crucifixion" (Balthasar, *Office of Peter*, 16).

40. See Karl Rahner, *The Church and the Sacraments* (New York: Herder & Herder, 1963), 42.

41. "The attempt to soften it [Peter's preeminent position] into an 'honorary primacy' is totally alien within the context of a Church that knows no other honor than that of the 'last place,' of service rendered without thanks. This interpretation derives from the ideology of the Byzantine empire" (Balthasar, *Office of Peter*, 110).

42. Quoted in the very useful article by B. A. Gerrish, "Priesthood and Ministry in the Theology of Luther," *Church History* 34 (1965): 404–22 (here 406).

the power to reform by force what the supposedly "spiritual" leaders were leaving undone. Whether the caesaropapism of such radical unmaking of the Church's inverted hierarchical structure did more in the long run than create new problems (and reinscribe old ones) by letting the kings of the nations "lord it over" every last one of their subjects, now in good conscience and in the name of God, is a fair question. Admittedly, Luther's invitation to the emperor (who declined the offer) and local princes (who were more disposed to respond) to assume for themselves, on purely secular grounds, what the pope and bishops were claiming by right of priestly ordination was meant to be a grant of power to be used in Christian service. The dismantling of a formal, institutional refusal of worldly authority was not an obvious step in the direction of assuring Christlike *diakonia* in the Church, however. On the other hand, the papocaesarism of a clerical college swollen with landed estates and worldly *exousia* was also an obstacle—in fact, *the very same obstacle*—to the true Petrine pastoral model of laying down one's life: "Peter began to say to him, 'Look, we have left everything and followed you'" (Mark 10:28).

In the end, the Church's monarchic rule under Christ the Good Shepherd cannot be imagined in a worldly way, for it is an authority based upon the supreme anti-authoritarian, cultic act of the Lamb laying down his life for his friends. If Peter's commission to don the vestments of Christ's cross is thus a symbolic wearing of Christ's own pallium as the Good Shepherd, an "honor" that is shared by all the Church's commissioned pastors (though it be "shame" in the eyes of the world), this must entail a share in Christ's unique *diakonia* of priestly power—unless the "great shepherd of the sheep" himself is not at the same time a "great high priest" (Heb. 13:20; see excursus 10).

── SUMMARY OF KEY POINTS ─────────────────────

1. The Synoptic Gospels bring Jesus' priestly identity to forceful expression through a cluster of traditional Second Temple idioms. John, by contrast, begins a powerful transformation of the presentation of Jesus' priestly identity into a more distinctively early Christian—that is, pastoral—register. At the center of both of these movements stands Jesus' own reconfiguration of hierarchical authority (*exousia*) in the form of self-sacrificial service (*diakonia*).

2. Second Temple Jewish expectation of a priestly chief agent developed scriptural oracles (e.g., Deut. 18:15; 1 Sam. 2:35; Zech. 3; Mal. 2–3) into a form of focused hope centered upon the coming of a new priest. While various articulations of this expectation exist, the *Testament of Levi*

brings it to remarkably clear expression. At the same time, a somewhat blurry royal-priestly, two-messiah framework surrounds this vision, both in the wider context of the *Testaments* literature and at Qumran.

3. The Synoptic account of Jesus' transfiguration is best interpreted against the background of this Jewish expectation of the Lord's raising up of the new eschatological priest. Multiple considerations in the Gospel scene push in this direction, most notably the use of Deuteronomy 18:15, the motif of the heavenly journey, the presence of Moses and Elijah, and the image of the glorious, cleansed garments. In the dialogue with Jesus' disciples following the event, further support is given for accepting some form of diarchic priest-king messianism as the proper background for this epiphany of Jesus' priestly glory.

4. The transferal of Jesus' *exousia* as eschatological high priest to chosen collaborators takes multiple forms but comes to most sustained expression in the Gospel of John. While links exist in John to the symbol of the high priestly vestment, the image of the Good Shepherd here takes on clear prominence and serves to articulate the transfer of authority from Jesus to Peter. John's choice of the Good Shepherd motif is not lacking deep Old Testament roots—and vital to its adoption is Jesus' reorientation of a classical image of hierarchical power around a pronounced emphasis upon self-sacrifice and humble service.

5. The important scene of Jesus conferring this self-sacrificial shepherding authority upon Peter places Peter's profession of love front and center. This focus on a love conformed to Jesus' own love works as a response to Peter's tragic sin and necessary action of cleansing for his pastoral ministry.

EXCURSUS 7

Israel's Last Prophet

The bad blood and finally mortal friction between Jesus and the religious leaders of his day represents an important starting point for any New Testament approach to the Old Testament priesthood. It is very easy to misapprehend the significance of this confrontation, however. A dichotomous either-or construction that celebrates Jesus as the anti-institutional martyr-hero is a common but flawed reading. Adjusting this view requires, among other things, attending more closely to the actual evidence.

The identification of Jesus as a prophet by many of his contemporaries certainly owes much to his violent attacks on the religious authorities and practices of his day. Like the Old Testament prophets, Jesus made impassioned protests that took form both in words and through symbolic action. Given its evident affinities to the earlier biblical tradition, it is no great surprise that Jesus' critique has, like biblical prophecy more broadly, been drawn into the problematic antagonism hypothesis contested above in chapter 3. As in the case of biblical prophecy more broadly, it is needful to take a more balanced view here.

In the Gospel tradition, the sharpest and most concentrated "prophetic critique" issuing from Jesus' mouth appears in the seven woes of Matthew 23, paralleled in Luke 11. This material targets not the *priests* but the scribes and Pharisees (in Luke, also the lawyers). This fact recalls the supposed obsession with priests already exposed as an illusion in the context of the prophetic corpus. By all appearances, until the passion, the temple priesthood did not loom large in Jesus' or the evangelists' field of vision. When it does appear before the passion, moreover, there is no sign of ill will. Jesus' sending of the cleansed leper to the priests to make the offering prescribed by Moses (Mark

1:44; Matt. 8:4; Luke 5:14) is, for instance, rightly invoked as revealing a very traditional acceptance of the cultic regime that Leviticus and the Torah had established (Lev. 13:49; cf. 14:4; also Matt. 17:24–27).

Jesus' focused attack on the Pharisees—a mutual affair, it seems—is worth a moment's reflection in this connection, for it actually points to a shared priestly affinity and orientation, not a basic rejection of cultic worship. It was the Pharisees' specific effort, after all, to impose their own halakic system of law—their particular, applied understanding of the Mosaic Torah—upon the temple and all the people. Thus, they represented a concerted attempt at appropriating the vast heritage and hegemony of Israel's Priestly school. The attempt was successful; the Pharisees appear to have had sufficient social leverage at one point to have required an oath on the part of the high priest before the ritual of Yom Kippur that he would follow their (rather than the Sadducees') interpretation of the rites (*m. Yoma* 1.5). Multiple disputes about matters of cultic comportment caused friction not only with the priestly party of the Sadducees but also with the Essenes at Qumran, who shared Sadducean perspectives on a number of points and who, like Jesus, vehemently opposed certain aspects of the Pharisees' vision. In other words, a dispute with the Pharisees was inevitably a dispute about the law, which itself implied a priestlike (although post-Priestly) engagement in questions about such matters as clean and unclean. The contested halakic space in which Jesus and the Pharisees and other Jews of the period wrestled was thus a ritual arena, inviting Malachi's ideal Levite (or the Essene Teacher of Righteousness, or halakic Elijah) to come, enter the fray, and teach rightly. As essentially a lay movement (though some priests were variously associated), largely preoccupied with extending clerical holiness to nonclerics, the Pharisaic program challenged traditional categories and understandings of priestly difference, blurring various conventional lines. So, while it is true that Jesus (like the Essenes) had his own program of extending the reach of God's reign, he was nevertheless supremely impatient with the Pharisees' failure to make obvious distinctions between what was truly holy and what was profane.

The reasoning that Jesus levels against his Pharisee opponents in his woe on the matter of oaths is quite revealing as an example. Excessively interested in secondary matters like money and gifts, the Pharisees, he says, have failed to appreciate the much greater holiness of the sanctuary and the altar.

> Woe to you, blind guides, who say, "Whoever swears by the sanctuary is bound by nothing, but whoever swears by the gold of the sanctuary is bound by the oath." You blind fools! For which is greater, the gold or the sanctuary that has made the gold sacred? And you say, "Whoever swears by the altar is bound by nothing, but whoever swears by the gift that is on the altar is bound by the oath." How blind you are! For which is greater, the gift or the altar that makes

the gift sacred? So whoever swears by the altar, swears by it and by everything
on it; and whoever swears by the sanctuary, swears by it and by the one who
dwells in it; and whoever swears by heaven, swears by the throne of God and
by the one who is seated upon it. (Matt. 23:16–22)

God dwells enthroned in the sanctuary, Jesus says. No hint here of any rejection of the temple, priests, or cultic behavior. Quite the contrary! As in
Matthew 5:23–24, where similar language appears, it is simply assumed that
gifts are being (and *should be*) brought to the altar. If, in Matthew 5, reconciliation with one's brother stands as a precondition for offering an acceptable
gift, and ethics is thus bound inextricably to cultic service (as in the classical
prophets and in the Holiness Code), certain scholars' labored efforts to insist
that Matthew 5 "does not presuppose a priest functioning as an intermedi-
ary" and that, moreover, "one need not postulate the intervention of such a
priest" are an unconvincing attempt to exclude what is not mentioned because it is self-evident and beside the point.[1] In Matthew 23, it would be no
less strange and strained to imagine that the same language of "gifts" and
"the altar" somehow implies a priestless temple, run by laypeople, robots,
or clerical phantoms.

In the following verses in Matthew 23, Jesus acknowledges that on at least
one revealing point the Pharisaic halakah is correct (in contrast to the errors
implied in Matt. 23:16–22).

Woe to you, scribes and Pharisees, hypocrites! For you tithe mint, dill, and
cumin, and have neglected the weightier matters of the law: justice and mercy
and faith. It is these you ought to have practiced without neglecting the others.
You blind guides! You strain out a gnat but swallow a camel! (Matt. 23:23–24)

It is proper to pay tithes, Jesus allows, as multiple texts in the Torah show
(Lev. 27:30–33; Num. 18:21–32; Deut. 14:22–29), even if mint, dill, and cumin
are the Pharisees' own specifications (cf. *m. Demai* 2.1; *m. Ma'as.* 4.5). These
tithes were the perquisites of the Levites to be paid at the temple, which indicates that where Jesus and his opponents are agreed is—it is not a small
point—precisely on the material support of the priestly cult. The key principle of Jesus' critique is not the rejection of ritual worship. It is not even
the rejection of a minor prescription but, rather, the identification of justice,
mercy, and faith as "weightier" matters of Torah. These moral laws should
have been observed "without neglecting" the tiniest ritual prescriptions, just
as gifts should be brought to the altar after reconciliation has been made.

1. Hans Dieter Betz, *The Sermon on the Mount: A Commentary on the Sermon on the
Mount, Including the Sermon on the Plain (Matthew 5:3–7:27 and Luke 6:20–49)*, Hermeneia
(Minneapolis: Fortress, 1995), 222.

The *both-and* of morality-and-cult in Jesus' prophetic critique could hardly be more apparent.

A note quite characteristic of the Matthean Jesus is plainly at work in these traditions. "Do not think that I have come to abolish the law or the prophets; I have come not to abolish but to fulfill. For truly I tell you, until heaven and earth pass away, not one letter, not one stroke of a letter, will pass from the law until all is accomplished" (Matt. 5:17–18). This reverence for both Moses and the prophets helps put Jesus' citation of Hosea 6:6 in Matthew 12 in correct perspective, for it concerns his manner of reading the Law and the Prophets. His view of sacrifice should not fall victim to the overblown conclusions of the antagonism hypothesis.

> At that time Jesus went through the grainfields on the sabbath; his disciples were hungry, and they began to pluck heads of grain and to eat. When the Pharisees saw it, they said to him, "Look, your disciples are doing what is not lawful to do on the sabbath." He said to them, "Have you not read what David did when he and his companions were hungry? He entered the house of God and ate the bread of the Presence, which it was not lawful for him or his companions to eat, but only for the priests. Or have you not read in the law that on the sabbath the priests in the temple break the sabbath and yet are guiltless? I tell you, something greater than the temple is here. But if you had known what this means, 'I desire mercy [*eleos*] and not sacrifice,' you would not have condemned the guiltless. For the Son of Man is lord of the sabbath." (Matt. 12:1–8)

Again Jesus stands opposed to the Pharisees on a question of law, though on this occasion he is not the aggressor but the accused. Instead of an angry prophet, his persona as a teacher and scholar of the law here comes to the fore. The particular point of interpretation concerns the observance of *pe'ah*—namely, the injunction to leave a portion of the field unharvested for the benefit of the poor (Lev. 19:9–10; 23:22; Deut. 24:19–22; cf. *m. Pe'ah*). The question is whether the observance of sabbath overrides this prescription intended to help the hungry.[2]

The implicit comparison of Jesus and his followers to priests in the temple pushes the logic in multiple directions.[3] For Irenaeus (*Against Heresies* 4.8.3) it was an indication of the priestly dignity of the disciples. This cannot be discounted. In any case, Jesus' reply clearly lands in favor of charity as the ranking obligation—an excellent instance where we see applied what he called the "weightier" matters of justice and mercy at work.

---

2. On this halakic background to this controversy in the Synoptics, see Maurice Casey, *Aramaic Sources of Mark's Gospel*, SNTSMS 102 (Cambridge: Cambridge University Press, 1998).

3. See the eight possible interpretations listed in W. D. Davies and Dale Allison, *The Gospel according to Matthew*, vol. 2, *VIII–XVIII*, ICC (Edinburgh: T&T Clark, 1991), 310–11.

This position can be lexically demonstrated. Through linguistic changes affecting the Hebrew word *ḥesed* during the course of the Second Temple period, the text of Hosea 6:6 had, in fact, taken on a new sense by the first century. In Jesus' day it had come to mean "I desire *almsgiving*, not sacrifice." The justice and mercy ignored by the Pharisees in Matthew 23:23 could also hide the two related Hebrew ideas of *ṣĕdāqâ* and *ḥesed*, both meaning charity. Heard in this way and in the context of this precise debate, the prophet Hosea helps to interpret correctly the law of Moses. The text is here understood as saying, "I desire charity *more than* (not instead of) sacrifice." This efficiently scores the point, since the sacrificial service itself, which continues uninterrupted by the priests, even on the sabbath as Jesus notes, clearly trumps sabbath observance. Note, therefore, that the whole argument for the superiority of charity requires the cultic action of the priests in the temple in order to function. There is no rejection of cultic worship in this passage.[4]

In Matthew 12:6, Jesus' startling statement "Something greater [*meizon*] than the temple is here" might thus be taken to mean "Charity/mercy is greater than the temple." This is different from the christological sense that is often accepted (cf. Matt. 12:41–42; Luke 11:31), but it suits the neuter (not masculine) form that is used here (i.e., *meizon* = *to eleos*) and would effectively buttress Jesus' argument and render it admirably clear. It would also echo the "great is *x*" rhetoric attested in rabbinic literature, found in controversies of ranking conflicting rules, as in Matthew 12: "Great is circumcision! It supersedes the stringent sabbath" (*b. Ned.* 31b); "Great is charity! for it hastens the redemption!" (*b. B. Bat.* 10a). In the end, Jesus' ranking of love above the temple is not a rejection of the cult as such, any more than the rabbis rejected the sabbath simply because circumcision took precedence.

Jesus' saying at the end of Mark's version of this same scene (Mark 2:27) is useful for grasping Jesus' vision—namely, "The sabbath was made for humankind, and not humankind for the sabbath." This forceful teaching puts the deepest origins of cultic observance in a new light. In effect, Jesus attacks a very ancient, very tenacious, anthropomorphic perspective. Unlike an ancient Mesopotamian worldview, in which the human race was created to serve as the liturgical slaves of the gods in order to assure the gods' own rest and leisure, Jesus says, "Quite the reverse! Cultic rest is a gift *from* God *for* men." God is not in need of rest; he is working until now, as Jesus says in the context of another controversy over the sabbath (John 5). If this is so, and cultic service is God's gift to men, Jesus' meaning can hardly be that this divine gift should be taken away or neglected. His point is rather that ritual

4. The argument is structurally parallel to the argument of Raba in *b. Shabb.* 132b that if the eighth day falls on a sabbath, the child shall nevertheless be circumcised.

observances like the sabbath, understood in the proper light, will cease to be a burden on humanity and become a source of divine benefaction.

It is at the level of this divine benevolence that Matthew's Christology becomes engaged. Matthew concentrates on the final part of the saying in Mark 2:28: "The Son of Man is lord even of the sabbath." Implicit here is an extraordinary claim on Jesus' part to be the one whose authority determines what the sabbath is for and how to observe it correctly. This claim comes in the immediate wake of Jesus' similarly lordly promise to provide "rest" for those who are "heavy burdened" (*pephortismenoi*) and who will carry his light burden (*phortion elaphron*) and easy yoke (Matt. 11:28–30): a plain reversal of the old Babylonian heavy-burdened-slaves-of-the-gods theology. A direct echo and inverse of Jesus' own promise also comes in Matthew 23:4, when Jesus attacks the Pharisees for teaching as God's law just the opposite of what Jesus offers: "They tie up heavy burdens [*phortia barea*], hard to bear, and lay them on the shoulders of others; but they themselves are unwilling to lift a finger to move them." Jesus' yoke is thus understood to be the call of Wisdom, the gift of the Lord's easy Torah, contrasted with the Oral Torah of his Pharisee foes. The *rest* that he offers reveals Jesus as lord of the sabbath—as God's gift to men, he defines what sacred service is.

Since Jesus is Lord of the law, his Torah requires a righteousness, *sĕdāqâ*, a charity, that surpasses that of the Pharisees' legal regime. Charity is the supreme principle of the correct observance of the law, to which all things are subordinated. In Jesus' formulation, love is the greatest commandment, on which all the other laws depend, and this love commandment has a double form: love of God and love of neighbor (Matt. 22:36–40). If there is a tendency at times to neglect the implicit cultic character of the first half of this two-pronged formulation, it is illuminating to read it in view of *Testament of Issachar* 5:2–3.

> Love the Lord and your neighbor;
> be compassionate toward poverty and sickness.
> Bend your back in farming,
> perform the tasks of the soil in every kind of agriculture,
> offering gifts gratefully to the Lord. (*Test. Iss.* 5:2–3)[5]

The insertion on farming, which has firstfruits in mind, should not distract from the clear chiasm that structures the thought: (a) love the Lord; (b) love your neighbor; (b') give alms; (a') make offerings. In other words, the double love commandment implies a dual affirmation; it upholds both vertical sacrifice and horizontal works of mercy.

---

5. Translation by H. C. Kee in *OTP* 1:803–4.

Having said all this and identified Jesus' halakic hermeneutic of *ḥesed* as a principle for putting the Law and the Prophets in proper order, it remains to address, albeit briefly, Jesus' controversial confrontation with the cult itself, when he drove out those buying and selling and overturned the tables in the temple. As a symbolic action, in the full tradition of the Old Testament prophets, the deed is open to a broad range of interpretations, as the history of scholarship shows. The most basic question dividing recent scholars has been whether it is best to view the incident as announcing the temple's coming destruction (which Jesus clearly prophesied) or whether it signals, instead, a "cleansing" of corrupt practices, as has been more traditionally understood.[6] It is not false irenicism to decide that "it is wrong to oppose the two interpretations," for "protestation against abuses and symbolic expression of judgement belonged together."[7] Of course, such a perspective reveals that Jesus had a much more complicated view of the temple than has been seen before this defining moment in the Gospels.

Although it is often read in an exclusively negative light, the complexity of Jesus' view of the temple is evident even from the isolated act of driving out the merchants. For the two prophetic texts that Jesus cites draw on two different sorts of tradition and accordingly point in two divergent directions. The verse lifted from Jeremiah's famous temple sermon (Jer. 7:11) is redolent with preexilic doom. The language of "robbers" (*lēstai*) might even point directly to the rebel Jewish Zealots, who occupied the temple just before its fall to the Romans in AD 66–70. On the other hand, the citation of Isaiah 56:7 envisions a glorious eschatological renewal characteristic of the postexilic Trito-Isaiah. Still more interesting in view of the sabbath material discussed above, Isaiah 56:1–8 is one of the most densely packed sabbath passages in the entire Hebrew Bible, mentioning sabbath observance three times (vv. 2, 4, 6) and sabbath profanation twice (vv. 2, 6). Ultimately, in this oracle, the eschatological temple is imagined as a "house of prayer," reserved for those, including the pagans, who observe the sabbath correctly.

> And the foreigners who join themselves to the LORD,
>   to minister to him, to love the name of the LORD,
>   and to be his servants,
> all who keep the sabbath, and do not profane it,
>   and hold fast my covenant—

---

6. E. P. Sanders, *Jesus and Judaism* (Philadelphia: Fortress, 1985), 61–76. See also Craig A. Evans, "Jesus' Action in the Temple: Cleansing or Portent of Destruction?," *CBQ* 51 (1989): 237–70.

7. W. D. Davies and Dale Allison, *The Gospel according to Matthew*, vol. 3, *XIX–XXVIII*, ICC (Edinburgh: T&T Clark, 1991), 136.

> these I will bring to my holy mountain,
>> and make them joyful in my house of prayer;
> their burnt offerings and their sacrifices
>> will be accepted on my altar;
> for my house shall be called a house of prayer
>> for all peoples.
> Thus says the Lord GOD,
>> who gathers the outcasts of Israel,
> I will gather others to them
>> besides those already gathered. (Isa. 56:6–8)

By banishing the signs of servile work and invoking Isaiah's image of a "house of prayer," Jesus presents the temple as a giant synagogue on a giant sabbath. In cleansing the temple, the lord of the sabbath thus imposes a "rest" upon the house of God. He does this as if to invite the realization of Isaiah's radical vision: a liturgical community and even a priesthood opened up to the pagan nations (cf. Isa. 66:21; Mark 11:17). Jesus' allusion to this text from Isaiah thus serves as a very important point of interpretative leverage in understanding Ezekiel's vision of the end-time temple. The eschatological "sons of Zadok" are those who "keep my sabbaths holy" (Ezek. 44:24)—that is, the priests in Jesus' eschatological temple will be those who prolong his unique sabbath ministry, laying primacy on works of mercy, expressed through acts of forgiveness and healing.

In the temple, Jesus shows his priestly credentials by enforcing sabbath rest with a Phinehas-like zeal: "Zeal for your house will consume me" (John 2:17; cf. Ps. 69:9). Thus Jesus, who in other settings seems strangely tolerant of forbidden work, in the temple shows the fierce limits of this indulgence. He also shows how he understands the intersection of sacred space and sacred time (an ancient link, as the ancient Near Eastern heptadic temple-building traditions show; see chap. 2). Jesus clears a space within the temple defined by a new sort of festal time, beyond the time marked by calendars and seasons. In effect, he creates a sabbath. On the one hand, Christ's symbolic deed is a clear allusion to the eschatological Feast of Booths, a celebration open to all the nations where the prophet foretells, "There shall no longer be traders in the house of the LORD of hosts on that day" (Zech. 14:21). At the same time, given his unseasonal cursing of the fig tree, one begins to sense how Jesus' behavior is synchronized with a higher liturgy beyond time: the eternal "today" that the Letter to the Hebrews connects with true sabbath rest (Heb. 4:4–11).

The form of the sabbath rest imposed by Jesus on Israel's cult is best apprehended through the identification of his own death with the fate of the temple: a link symbolically revealed in the tearing of the temple veil at the precise moment of Jesus' death. This identification is, in fact, the critical difference that separates Jesus' prophecy of the temple's destruction from the many contemporaneous Jewish parallels.[8] Many Jews of the period foresaw the sanctuary's bitter end, though most also saw it somehow gloriously remade. Only Jesus foresaw this corporate fate as being bound up with his own death and resurrection. The prophecy of *rebuilding* the temple after three days, which appears in the trial scene in Mark 14:48 (cf. Acts 6:14) and is put in Jesus' own mouth in John 2:19, holds the deepest truth revealed in his symbolic action. The temple will be destroyed and the curtain torn. Like the sons of Eli, the Levites and offspring of Aaron will finally be put out of God's presence and the Jerusalem cult will be ended and made desolate like Shiloh. Yet one prophetic supersession here simply replaces another. As the northern cult ceded place to Jerusalem's temple, so Zion now gives way to the temple of Jesus' body.[9]

The sentence of destruction on the Levitical order happens, as prophesied, because of priestly sin (cf. Mal. 2:1–3). The priests—even the high priest himself—have definitively rejected teaching. How? They have rejected it in solemn session in rejecting the Christ, who sat day after day teaching in the temple (Matt. 26:55). "I have spoken openly to the world; I have always taught in synagogues and in the temple, where all the Jews come together" (John 18:20). The momentous meeting of Jesus with the Jewish high priest, where the fate of both is decided, presents us not with raving anti-institutional accusations but with Jesus' calm prophecy that he is the coming eschatological Melchizedek foretold in Psalm 110.[10] Jesus' extreme restraint, his startling reserve and respect when interrogated by Israel's holders of priestly office, must indeed be reckoned against any exaggerated hypothesis of antagonism. "'Is that how you answer the high priest?' Jesus answered, 'If I have spoken wrongly, testify to the wrong. But if I have spoken rightly, why do you strike me?'" (John 18:22–23). The Lord seems considerably more agitated by the Pharisees than by the heirs of Aaron.

This does not imply that there is no cult critique on Jesus' part. But this critique stands in harmony with the view of Israel's earlier prophets. Scholars are accordingly not wrong when they see in Jesus' momentary interruption of the machinery of ritual worship and in his depiction of the temple as a "house of prayer" a statement of theological distance from the bloody *work* of the priestly service. But neither are they entirely right when they absolutize this (or the torn temple veil) into a simple death of the temple cult, with no

8. On this, see Anthony Giambrone, *A Quest for the Historical Christ: Scientia Christi and the Modern Study of Jesus* (Washington, DC: Catholic University of America Press, 2021), chap. 15.

9. See Giambrone, *A Quest for the Historical Christ*, chap. 10.

10. See Giambrone, *A Quest for the Historical Christ*, chap. 14.

return. The paradigm is rather a death and transfiguration. For unless Jesus'
use of Isaiah 56:7 stands in open conflict with Isaiah's own prophetic vision,
the ongoing relevance of *sacrifice* to Jesus' conception of the eschatologically
resurrected temple cannot be wished away (for "their burnt offerings and their
sacrifices will be accepted," Isaiah says).

The deep discontinuity in the character of the new cult, nevertheless,
emerges from the extreme importance placed by Isaiah on correctly observing the sabbath. This form of cult, observance of the sabbath, was specifically
linked to an unbloody, worldwide synagogue worship—though attuned to the
bloody worship of the one temple—and it was increasingly important in the
Second Temple period. This is the prophetic precursor of the new vision of
cultic sacrifice. Pleasing offerings will not cease in the rebuilt temple, defined
by the eschatological community's right honoring of the sabbath. This correct
end-time observance is quite simply the new observance of the Lord's Day
adopted by believers: unbloody participation in the death of the Lord until
he comes (1 Cor. 11:26).

EXCURSUS 8

The Language of Pastoral Order

The messy range of vocabulary used in the New Testament to speak about early Christian leaders does not make it simple to get an orderly picture. Reading surveys of the topic can consequently be a disheartening business. Part of the issue is plainly due to regional and authorial diversity; part is the inevitable confusion linked with forging a lexicon to name an emergent reality, in this case a mysterious eschatological reality with ancient roots, yet energized by divine newness. Gradual consolidation of a stable vocabulary obviously eventually occurred, though the process was still underway in various contexts well into the third century and beyond. Clearly, the primitive situation reflected in the New Testament texts demands extraordinary flexibility and caution if the hierarchical structures of the earliest Church are to be studied both in a historically and a theologically responsible way.

With those caveats in place, not everything is absolute chaos. A solid foundation emerges with unambiguous clarity: the absolute primacy of Jesus Christ as the supreme hierarch in the Church. He is the unique high priest (Heb. 3:1; 4:14; 5:5, 10; 6:20; 7:26–27; 8:1; 9:11). He is the "one mediator between God and humankind" (1 Tim. 2:5). He is even called in a preeminent way an "apostle" (Heb. 3:1), the great cosmic messenger and go-between. Jesus is the "great shepherd of the sheep" (Heb. 13:20) and the "shepherd and guardian of your souls" (1 Pet. 2:25): in a word, the "good shepherd" par excellence (John 10). He is the sole "foundation" upon which the building rises (1 Cor. 3:11) and the key or cornerstone that gives the entire Church its solidity and its shape (Eph. 2:20; cf. Mark 12:10; Matt. 21:42; Luke 20:17). He is head of the body that is the Church (Eph. 1:22; 5:23; Col. 1:18).

It is significant that many of these varied terms applied to Jesus' unique place in the cult, in the congregation, and in the spiritual temple are extended and applied also to early Church leaders. Indeed, though the word *hiereus*, "priest," is not used in describing Christian ministers in the New Testament (as discussed below in chap. 6), the wider and highly expressive titles of Christ's special ecclesial status do directly redound to her leaders. "There will be one flock, one shepherd" (John 10:16), Jesus says with no room for error; nevertheless, others are also very openly called "pastors"—literally, "shepherds"—and not without direct precedent from Jesus himself (John 21). Some are also qualified as "apostles," openly patterned on the Son's own sending by the Father: "As the Father has sent me, so I send you" (John 20:21; cf. 13:20). Others may even be reckoned (again, even by Jesus himself!) as the foundation stones of the edifice of the Church (Matt. 16:18; Eph. 2:20; Rev. 21:14). A sharing in Jesus' exclusive role of ecclesial headship is evidently possible for those to whom it is somehow given. It is a theological canard to argue that some form of privileged participation in Jesus' unique high priesthood is, in principle, an incommunicable grace within the body of Christ.

Within the scope of its diverse headship language, pastoral terminology holds an honored position in the New Testament constellation. As a favored image in the discourse of the Gospels, it reflects not simply Jesus' agrarian outlook but, more significantly, his Davidic and thus messianic self-understanding (cf. Mark 6:34; Matt. 2:6; 26:31). The prominence of shepherd imagery in establishing the contours of ecclesial office was already examined in the key passage of John 21 and the commissioning of Peter. An additional revealing passage for its concentration of relevant terms, including some new ones, appears at the end of 1 Peter.

> Now as an elder myself [*sympresbyteros*] and a witness [*martys*] of the sufferings of Christ, as well as one who shares [*koinōnos*] in the glory to be revealed, I exhort the elders [*presbyterous*] among you to tend the flock [*poimanate to poimnion*] of God that is in your charge, exercising the oversight [*episkopountes*], not under compulsion but willingly, as God would have you do it—not for sordid gain but eagerly. Do not lord it over those in your charge, but be examples to the flock. And when the chief shepherd [*archipoimenos*] appears, you will win the crown of glory that never fades away. (1 Pet. 5:1–4)

If the language of shepherding appears to inexperienced modern readers like a rustic or idyllic image, untouched by institutional or hierarchical social distinctions, the elevated title *archipoimēn*, "chief shepherd," applied here to Christ, is quite revealing. Tending flocks in the ancient world was serious business and, in fact, a highly stratified affair. Many ancient papyrus contracts, for instance, expose the existence of an extensive hierarchy of herdsmen, from the *archipoimēn* at the apex, through ordinary shepherds (*poimenes*), who were part owners, to the hireling (*nomeus*) with no financial share in the flock, all the way down to the simple boys who cared for the lambs. Here in 1 Peter 5, the simple form, *poimēn*, should be supplied for the presbyters, who tend the flock together with Peter, although the noun is not directly used, only the verb and its object ("to tend the flock"). As willing pastors, they are decidedly not hirelings (*nomeis*) interested only in "sordid gain," as Peter insists in verse 2. An allusion back to Jesus' Good Shepherd discourse (or the tradition behind it) should be noted in this side-glance at the figure of the "hireling" (*misthōtos*, John 10:12). The implicit lesson of laying down one's life is similarly heard in the unmistakable phrase "not lording it over" in verse 3, which for its part directly recalls Christ's teaching about servant leadership addressed to the Twelve in Mark 10:42. In adopting the pastoral metaphor to describe its leaders, the early Church not only followed the lead given by Jesus himself as recorded in the Gospels but also discovered both an ethical program and a ready-made taxonomy for putting itself in proper order.

Peter's repetition here of Jesus' own teaching in telling the presbyters that they should tend the flock according to the rule of self-sacrifice and service is a moment of supreme ecclesiological importance. Through the subtle but manifest allusions back to Peter's own commissioning by Jesus, a principle of the transmission of authority is attested in the Church that continues the parting act of Christ as *archipoimēn*. The flock shall never be left without shepherds. Scholars, of course, debate whether this letter derives from the apostle Peter himself or whether it only channels Peter's voice. Theologically the point is immaterial at this juncture. The early Church either preserved or constructed a memory and belief that what was handed by Christ to Peter was in its turn also handed on by Peter himself. This is not a narrow act of papal succession, moreover, but a living *traditio* of Petrine pastoral office shared with a wider circle of authority, as the prepositional prefix *sym-* (with, co-) in *sympresbyteros* makes emphatic.

The Church's college of shepherds plainly remain fully subordinate to Christ, the *chief shepherd*, yet they are just as plainly coworkers with him in the continuing task of tending *his* sheep ("the flock *of God* in your midst"). Indeed, it is not impossible that the prefix *sym-* carries a hint of this vertical dimension, to the extent that *presbyteros* and *poimēn* are taken as equal. It is clear in any event that the elders are employed as coshepherds, engaged together in Jesus' own work. "The locusts have no king, yet all of them march in rank," says Proverbs 30:27; but flocks are not self-guiding entities. In the same way, there can be no chief shepherd or subshepherds without sheep. Implicit in the governing metaphor used here for Church leaders is thus a rigorous and qualitative (may we say ontological?) distinction between the people and their leaders. It is not articulated in the language of laity and priests; yet the pastoral idiom, with its unmistakable and pronounced ancient royal connotations, is much stronger and more challenging (for both sides) than any ancient priestly titles, if we are honest. In view of the Christian concept of the people as a living temple, the traditional priest-temple semantic nexus (*hiereus-hiera*) has been replotted on the living matrix of shepherd-sheep.

Those who share in the care of Christ's flock are explicitly identified in 1 Peter 5 as *presbyteroi*, "elders." What is noteworthy here is that this group has the job of "exercising oversight" (*episkopountes*). This fits within a larger New Testament pattern treating *episkopoi*, "overseers/bishops," as synonymous with elders. In Titus 1:5–7, for instance, Titus is told to appoint presbyters in every town; then the qualities of an *episkopos* are promptly listed. In Acts 20, again, Paul summons the presbyters of the church of Ephesus to come and meet him; then he addresses them as *episkopoi* called "to shepherd the Church of God" (Acts 20:17, 28).

While the double naming of the structure of local ecclesial authority indicates a fundamental identity between *episkopoi* and *presbyteroi*, each term obviously conveys its own unique semantic content. The Christian position of "overseer/bishop," for instance, has a suggestive analogue in the *mebaqqer* at Qumran (CD; 1QS; 11QTemple), as multiple scholars have observed.[1] The *mebaqqer* was a community leader, a Levitical (rather than Aaronite) priest, whose official title was built on the Hebrew root *b-q-r*, prominently used in Ezekiel 34:11–12 and translated by the Greek root *episkep-* in the LXX.

> Thus says the Lord GOD: I myself will search for my sheep, and will seek them out [*ûbîqqartî, episkepsomai*]. As shepherds seek out [*kěbaqqārat*] their flocks when they are among their scattered sheep, so I will seek out [*'ăbaqqēr*] my sheep.

In view of his position as the community's pastoral "seeker," a note of compassionate care was closely associated with the *mebaqqer* figure. "He shall love them [i.e., the members of the community] as a father loves his children, and shall carry them in all their distress like a shepherd his sheep" (CD 13:9).[2] The concrete aggregate of administrative duties committed to the seeker—instruction of and care for members, management of community property, mediation as a go-between and community extern—bears a real resemblance to the work of the early Christian *episkopos*, and, as one scholar says, "a Qumran background for the term would readily account for

1. See, e.g., B. E. Thiering, "*Mebaqqer* and *Episkopos* in the Light of the Temple Scroll," *JBL* 100 (1981): 59–74.
2. Geza Vermes, *The Complete Dead Sea Scrolls in English*, rev. ed. (London: Penguin, 2004), 144.

the bishops' becoming priests" insofar as "at Qumran they were subordinate priests, who could take the place of an Aaronite priest for most duties."[3] This is not the place to plumb all the delicate relations between the primitive Christian community and the Essenes, but the various parallels and contrasts are clearly positioned to illuminate the cultic identity of Christian pastors.

According to an influential stream of scholarship, reaching back at least to Rudolf Sohm in the nineteenth century and later advanced by Hans von Campenhausen and others, the fusion of the titles "elders" and "overseers" reflects a deeper fusion of divergent primitive models of ecclesial organization: one Pauline, charismatic and free, marked by the fluid roles of *episkopoi* and *diakonoi* (Phil. 1:1); and one Jewish-Christian, structured on the old synagogue office of the "elders." It was from this mongrel agglutination of organizational models that "degenerate" early Catholicism with its tripartite, institutional system of ranked offices—bishop, priest, and deacon—was born. The strong (pro-Pauline, anti-Jewish/Catholic) Protestant value judgment implicit here is not the inevitable conclusion, and one might take a more san- guine view of the way Jewish structures and the Gentile mission clashed and merged. Yet the (Hegelian) dialectical analysis itself is also open to question. An alternative, fully Jewish background was just proposed for the *episkopos*, for instance. Another model also contends that *episkopos* and *presbyteroi* do not stem from essentially divergent (not to say incompatible) ecclesial contexts but are both at home in the same patriarchal, domestic matrix, where "overseer" tends toward the singular role of a *paterfamilias* (cf. 1 Tim. 3:4–5)—recall the fatherly note of compassion of the *mebaqqer*—while the collective "elders" signals a plural, collegial notion, better located at the level of extended familial/tribal organization.[4]

In this vision, the configuration of Church leadership is tethered to the natural, interior formation of a family/tribe/people. The household codes of the Pastoral Letters help support this organic social and conceptual plotting of ecclesial office. It is in this social and conceptual matrix where the explicit no- tion of Christ as spouse of the Church is also encountered: "For the husband is the head of the wife just as Christ is the head of the church" (Eph. 5:23). A whole world of theological reflection upon capital grace—that is, Christ's grace as head of the Church—opens up through this particular evocative nexus, by which the model of ecclesial headship is shifted from shepherd of the sheep and replotted as bridegroom and bride. Although a new sort of par- ity, and indeed an intimate unity, is introduced by this model (Eph. 5:28–32), we should not import modern democratic notions to the social model being

3. Thiering, "*Mebaqqer* and *Episkopos*," 72.
4. So, e.g., R. Alastair Campbell, *The Elders: Seniority within Earliest Christianity*, Studies of the New Testament and Its World (Edinburgh: T&T Clark, 1994).

presented (cf. 1 Pet. 3:7). The mystery of the Church is ordered like an ancient family in which the father, the husband, and the elders were understood to bear an uncontested right to rule—which is obviously something other than a license for tyrannical abuse, as Ephesians makes clear.

On a different theological order, but still working within the same patriarchal context, Ignatius of Antioch depicts the monarchical bishop specifically as an image of God the Father. At work here is a Christology of the transparence

Heavenly Hierarchies

Already at Qumran we find the earthly community presented as mirroring the host of heaven. God has established the holy ones—that is, the angels—"so that for him they can be priests [of the inner sanctum in the temple of his kingship,] the servants of the Presence in . . . his glorious sanctuary."[a] Early in Christianity, the degrees of Holy Orders were seen as reflective of the heavenly hierarchy. Clement of Alexandria (d. ca. 215) writes, "According to my opinion, the grades here in the Church, of bishops, presbyters, deacons, are imitations of the angelic glory."[b] This perception comes to fullest fruition in the writings of Dionysius the Areopagite:

> The sacred institution and source of perfection established our most pious hierarchy. [God the Father] modeled it on the hierarchies of heaven, and clothed these immaterial hierarchies in numerous material figures and forms so that, in a way appropriate to our nature, we might be uplifted from these most venerable images to interpretations and assimilations which are simple and inexpressible.[c]

> Our own [earthly] hierarchy is blessedly and harmoniously divided into orders in accordance with divine revelation and therefore deploys the same sequence as the hierarchies of heaven. It carefully preserves in its own human way the characteristics which enable it to be like God and conform to him.[d]

a. 4Q400 frag. 1 col. I. Translation from *The Dead Sea Scrolls Study Edition*, ed. Florentino García Martínez and Eibert J. C. Tigchelaar, 2 vols. (Grand Rapids: Eerdmans, 1997–98), 2:809.

b. Clement of Alexandria, *Stromata* 6.13.107. Translation from *Ante-Nicene Fathers*, 10 vols. (Buffalo: Christian Literature Publishing Company, 1885), 2:505.

c. Dionysius, *The Celestial Hierarchy* 1 (121 C). Translation from Colm Luibheid and Paul Rorem, *Pseudo-Dionysius: The Complete Works*, Classics of Western Spirituality (New York: Paulist Press, 1987), 146.

d. Dionysius, *The Ecclesiastical Hierarchy* 6 (536D–537A). Translation from Luibheid and Rorem, *Pseudo-Dionysius*, 248.

of the Son, as well as the notion of a double hierarchy, one celestial and one earthly, similar to what is found in the *Hodayot* at Qumran and later made explicit in Dionysius the Areopagite. The Church itself, in its ordered ranks, functions here as a kind of echo of the eternal in time: a revealed mirror image of the hidden life of God.

The good pastoral order promoted in the New Testament's household codes works specifically to resist and dissolve a whole range of personal and relational disorders. Hierarchy counters chaos, like the good government of God on high. Accordingly, the linkage of pastoral and presbyteral/episcopal service, evident in 1 Peter 5, stands opposed to the damaging work of "savage wolves" in Acts 20:28–29 (cf. Matt. 10:16; John 10:12), who represent a sort of anti-hierarchy constantly at work and requiring the vigilant, full-time ministry of "oversight." In 2 and 3 John, the "Presbyter" similarly finds himself countered by the "deceivers" and "antichrists" and those like Diotrephes, "who likes to put himself first, but does not acknowledge our authority" (3 John 9). If these "wolves" and "antichrists" thus represent a principle of communal division, especially on the order of false doctrine, the principle of unity is invested in the person of the pastor, modeled on the Good Shepherd. A mere hired hand, by contrast, "sees the wolf coming and leaves the sheep and runs away—and the wolf snatches them and scatters them" (John 10:12).

Short as they are, 2 and 3 John are profoundly revealing texts of Scripture. We see at once the gendered, male-female construct of ecclesial headship—the "Presbyter" writes to the "Elect Lady"—alongside the pronounced authority of a singular leader, *Ho Presbyteros*, totally identified with his position. Here, interestingly, we do not encounter this elder figure in his collegial dimension. We meet instead an individual, almost numinous figure, surrounded by an aura of reverence, a special bearer of Tradition, a living well of supernatural memory, due the same unique reverence paid to all elders in the ancient world—and due still more. While it is common and well justified, therefore, to identify the first clear language of the so-called *monepiskopos* in the letters of Ignatius, the canonical letters of John offer the striking example of a *monopresbyteros*. In view of the fluidity of the relevant language, this ought to be taken much more seriously as a primitive model on par with Ignatius's later (but hardly late) witness to "early Catholic" organization.

The paternal style of the Elder in John's epistles is very clear from his characteristic manner of addressing believers: "my children" (3 John 4); "my little children" (1 John 2:1; cf. 2:12, 28; 3:7, 18; 4:4; 5:21); and sometimes "her [Lady Church's] children" (2 John 1, 4, 13). This note of fatherly solicitude and position of patriarchal authority does not erase a simultaneous collegial sense, however. The Elder thus hopes to have ever more "co-workers with the truth" (3 John 8).

In the Johannine context, ecclesial unity, so important in the face of all forms of division, ultimately participates in the supreme unity of the Son with the Father (John 17:21). It is, therefore, not difficult to discern the prophetic/pastoral origins of a monepiscopal/monopresbyteral model. It is the ecclesial reflection of a christological truth, as the Church is the echo of Christ: "There will be one flock, one shepherd" (John 10:16; cf. Ezek. 34:23–24). It is precisely this intensely Christocentric ecclesiology of John that stamps the early "monarchical" exercise of ecclesial headship in a way that does not displace Christ in his unique monarchical role of priestly headship. Personally effaced and even nameless, the Beloved Disciple and the Elder render Christ himself present in his singular love for the sheep. The laying down of the pastor's life, on the model of the Master, is an example that Christ gives to the Twelve and to Peter, not to be admired but to be embodied, incarnated, and followed. In this way the Son's epiphany of the Father's unifying love can through them and in them, each as an *alter Christus*, be repeated and spread through the world (John 13:15; 21:18–19). Pastoral language for John is intimately, inextricably bound to the saving sacrifice of the Lamb.

6

"A Spiritual Temple, a Holy Priesthood" (1 Pet. 2:5)

Priestly Sacrifice and the New Law

The radical newness of Christ's New Law must not be underestimated. Obviously, the gospel must not be viewed in isolation or complete discontinuity with what went before in the old dispensation. Still, in fulfillment of his promise, in Christ God has done something thoroughly *new* (Isa. 43:19; cf. 65:17–25; Acts 13:41; Rev. 21:1).

In this spirit, although scholars have the habit of speaking of the New Testament as literature of Second Temple Judaism, rightly stressing the many important organic links with the Judaism of this era, it would in many ways be more accurate, both historically and theologically speaking, to perceive instead the dawn of *post-temple* Judaism. The most visible revolution of early Christian praxis was its radical character as a religion with no temple cult (soon to animate much Roman misunderstanding and persecution). Admittedly, the New Testament itself still belongs to a twilight moment of transition, bridging Judaism's loss of the temple and rooted in the time just before it. Nevertheless, even in the New Testament, Christian faith entails a clear pattern of worship no longer engaged in the offering of bloody animal sacrifice and no longer fundamentally attached to any particular sanctuary.

"Our slaughter of tame animals for sacrifices . . . is common to us, and to all other men," wrote Flavius Josephus, the Jewish historian, in his apologetic work *Against Apion*.[1] The common ancient assumption that animals were to be ritually slaughtered and offered to the gods—an assumption shared by Israel's law and presupposed by Israel's prophets—was radically challenged and interrupted by the early Church. It is undoubtedly this circumstance and the special sacrificial theology that arose to describe both Jesus' unique self-offering on the cross and its new form of cultic memorialization in the Eucharist that must contextualize the widely advertised, and almost equally widely misinterpreted, failure of New Testament sources to use the Greek word *hiereus* as a technical term for the Christian community's leaders.

If the English word "priest" carries sacrificial connotations that are a cause of discomfort for many Protestant Christians, it is rather significant to recall that this problem word "priest" is etymologically derived directly from the New Testament term *presbyteros*. Theologically, this is exactly what we should expect. The sacrificial color of the concept has thus not come from some lexical sleight of hand on the part of a Church, eschewing the doctrinal lead of New Testament authors and introducing a problematic pagan word. The sacrificial color comes, very simply, from the ecclesial creation of a new core concept, crafted to describe a reality proper to the Christian cult. The Christian presbyter/priest plays a presiding role in the community's worship, from which sacrificial meaning was never excluded, although radically redefined. This redefinition essentially sees sacrifice within the new context of Christ's mystical body, viewed as a *hieratic* and hierarchical communion liturgically joining heaven and earth.

Hieratic Language

Etymologically speaking, the deep embedding of the Greek word *hiereus*—which we misleadingly translate as "priest"[2]—within a wider *hiera* discourse (that is, talk about temples and all that happens in and around them) must be carefully considered before broad conclusions are drawn about the New Testament's non-use of *hiereus* to describe Church leaders. Technically, *hiera* are simply "holy things," and this can embrace everything from ritual implements

---

1. Josephus, *Against Apion* 2.14. See https://penelope.uchicago.edu/josephus/apion-2.html.
2. See Mary Beard and John North, *Pagan Priests: Religion and Power in the Ancient World* (Ithaca, NY: Cornell University Press, 1990). In their introduction, Beard and North highlight the confusion created by calling ancient pagan *hiereis* and *sacerdotes* "priests"; they then employ the term nonetheless. It is perhaps best simply to transliterate *hiereus*, as I will do here. Otherwise one ought to highlight the variegated range of cultic technicians indiscriminately lumped in as "priests"—for example, the *sphageus* (slaughterer) and the *mageiroi* (butchers).

to the animal parts resulting from an act of sacrifice. The Greek *hiereus* is a man who handles and works with these *hiera*, just as a Latin *sacerdos* is one who deals with the similar *sacra*. This somewhat circular definition leaves plenty of options open, but in practice the *hiereus* was linked specifically to the offering of bloody animal sacrifice, though this did not exhaust his full identity or functions, which remain difficult to define in a comprehensive way.[3] Regardless, the point is clear. Had the New Testament adopted the language of *hiereis* with all its centuries of ancient socioreligious connotations, reflecting both the broad context of ancient Mediterranean culture and the particular reality of Second Temple Judaism, this would have inevitably risked misrepresenting the new socio-liturgical reality initiated by Jesus.

Linguists make an important but simple methodological distinction between strict and transferred senses, which is very useful for evaluating the lexical question at hand. As far as the authors of the New Testament were concerned, the word *hiereis* was in its strict sense already taken. It was a technical term that, in its specific Jewish application, unambiguously designated a dynastic group elaborately enmeshed in the sacrificial activities of the Jerusalem temple. When Acts 6:7 thus reports that "a great many of the priests [*tōn hiereōn*] became obedient to the faith," this is strict usage that can mean only one thing: an ethnically defined group of Jewish sacrificial agents. When, on the other hand, Clement and the *Didache* make mappings between Christian leaders and the tribe of Levi, they operate on the extended order of transferred meaning. Excursus 8 gives attention to the particular language that *was* adopted to speak more strictly about Christian ministers. Nevertheless, unless we for some reason expect that only ethnic Levites, like the Cypriote Barnabas (Acts 4:36), became leaders in the Christian congregations—a situation already excluded by Jesus' choice of the Twelve—there is no reason to await more than oblique (i.e., transferred) alignments with the imagery and word groups belonging to the sematic field of *hiera*: alignments that, in fact, are not at all wanting, as we shall presently see.

Personalizing the Hieratic Context

The New Testament's engagement with hieratic images and tropes is rather substantial, and several strategic texts will be considered below. A full survey is not necessary, however. More crucial is recognizing how the reorganization of Christian cultic life around the person of Jesus represents a major

3. See Albert Henrichs, "Introduction: What Is a Greek Priest?," in *Practitioners of the Divine: Greek Priests and Religious Officials from Homer to Heliodorus*, ed. Beate Dignas and Kai Trampedach, Hellenic Studies Series 33 (Washington, DC: Center for Hellenic Studies, 2008), https://chs.harvard.edu/chapter/introduction-what-is-a-greek-priest-albert-henrichs/.

transformation in the heart of this ancient field of temple/sacrifice language. This is an example of what in the rabbinic context Mira Balberg aptly calls a "discursive reform" in the understanding of the Jerusalem temple's sacrificial operations.[4] The primitive Christian reshaping was not merely restricted to a rhetorical recalibration, however, simply some new way of talking about sacrifice. The transformation of Christian hieratic conceptions transpired in living interaction with a transformed communion of cultic worship.

A New Temple

In the first place, as there is no priest without a temple (to repeat this central axiom one more time), the notion of temple itself had to be redefined in order to forge a distinctively Christian concept of priesthood.

The first step was that Church leaders broke with the basic structure of ancient Near Eastern religion, Judaism included, in which the class of *hiereis/kōhănim* was intimately bound to specific plots of sacred land. This does not simply imply a principled break with a chthonic notion of worship in favor of worship in "spirit and truth" (John 4:23). Nor is it simply a radical new commitment to the notion (already theoretically present in the Old Testament) that God cannot be contained in any sanctuary made by human hands (e.g., 1 Kings 8:27; 2 Chron. 2:6; Acts 7:48–50). There was an enormous economic corollary, with socially measurable implications, which directly touched those Christ commissioned to perpetuate cultic service in "spirit and truth."

Large temple estates, belonging to the deity but managed by *hiereis*, bound ancient cult personnel to vast agrarian enterprises. In the Jewish system, contoured around the theoretically landless status of the Levites, this included (1) land whose produce was meant to sustain the temple and its cultic staff; (2) land pledged to the Lord, via the *kōhănim*, in order to provide security against loans/debts (e.g., Lev. 27); and (3) *ḥērem* land, including the temple, which was viewed as the eternal holding of the Lord but was effectively held as the property of the *kōhănim*.[5] Within this Second Temple Jewish system, the (Greek) word *hiereus* thus pointed to Levitical clans and entailed all their hereditary tribal rights as a landless yet powerfully land-oriented *hierateia*. The *hiereis* were a social group very strictly bound to the temple and the promised land, which was itself viewed as a sort of vast temple plantation.

In the New Testament, of course, a new order of reflection on God's eschatological promises displaced the physical land and temple from their central

4. Mira Balberg, *Blood for Thought: The Reinvention of Sacrifice in Early Rabbinic Literature* (Oakland: University of California Press, 2017), 233.

5. See Benjamin D. Gordon, *Land and Temple: Field Sacralization and the Agrarian Priesthood of Second Temple Judaism*, Studia Judaica 87 (Berlin: de Gruyter, 2020).

position. At the ideological level, this efficiently disaggregates the power con-
glomerate of Israel's *hiereis* and, at the social level, it redefines the base of
the *ekklēsia*'s priestly operations. Under the New Covenant a post-tribal and
radically non-landed priestly class emerges. This dissolving of the Old Covenant's deeply entrenched soil-and-blood-based ethnic system of land-and-
temple religion is, in the end, as much at stake as anything in the question of
the New Testament's non-use of *hiereus* discourse.

In attestation of this sacred-land matrix of the *hiereus* concept, it is striking that one very early, extrabiblical passage where *hiereus* language *is* used
for Christian leaders is clearly still working within the traditional agrarian
context of cultic emoluments.

> Take, therefore, all the first fruits of the produce of the winepress and threshing
> floor, and of the cattle and sheep, and give these first fruits to the prophets, for
> they are your *high priests [archiereis]*. (*Did.* 13.3)[6]

It is obvious here, and from the loose Gospel logion that the "worker is worth
his food" cited just before in *Didache* 13.2 (cf. Luke 10:7; 1 Tim. 5:18), that
the Church did not simply abandon the notion of supporting its professional
ministerial class. Still, with the detachment from the temple, where food for
the priests derived essentially from animals offered on the altar, the situation
dramatically changed.

Paul's defense of his economic rights in 1 Corinthians 9:7–14 is illuminating to consider within this framework. After playing with a number of
agricultural examples with a suggestive biblical background—Who takes no
fruit from his own vineyard? Who tends a flock and gets no milk? (1 Cor.
9:7; cf. Isa. 5; Ezek. 34; Matt. 21; John 10)—Paul invokes the Mosaic law,
offering a clever exegetical application of Deuteronomy 25:4, "You shall not
muzzle an ox."

Paul's specific choice of all these agricultural images to defend his (un-
claimed) rights to be supported activates a "personalized' (rather than "spiritualized") strain of Old Testament thought. Paul identifies the Church community in Corinth as God's sacred farm: they are his holy vineyard, his holy
flock. And as the people are now the Lord's living (and exclusive) plantation,
their generosity must yield a fittingly generous harvest for those to whom it
is due, just as the earth richly gives forth its fruit in the land-temple system.
Paul's broad agricultural metaphor naturally echoes Jesus, John, and the
prophets, who all also employ the idea of the people as a vineyard that should
produce fruit. The agrarian discourse also returns to an idea that Paul used

6. Michael W. Holmes, ed. and trans., *The Apostolic Fathers: Greek Texts and English Translations*, 3rd ed. (Grand Rapids: Baker Academic, 2007), 365 (emphasis added).

earlier in the letter, however. He has planted, another has watered, and God has given the growth: "For we are God's servants, working together; *you are God's field*" (1 Cor. 3:9).

The unspoken logic behind Paul's thought is evidently that of hieratic land. Lest this be doubted and the submerged priestly resonance of his argument be missed, Paul concludes by likening himself to a *hiereus* in a temple.

> Nevertheless, we have not made use of this right, but we endure anything rather than put an obstacle in the way of the gospel of Christ. Do you not know that those who are employed in the temple service [*hoi ta hiera ergazomenoi*] get their food from the temple [*ek tou hierou*], and those who serve at the altar share in what is sacrificed on the altar [*tō thysiastēriō symmerizontai*]? In the same way, the Lord commanded that those who proclaim the gospel should get their living by the gospel. (1 Cor. 9:12–14)

"One is reminded," Joseph Fitzmyer says, "of the OT regulations about portions of sacrifices reserved for priests in the tent of meeting and later in the Jerusalem Temple (Num. 18:8–20) and also of tithes for the Levites (Num. 18:21–24)."[7] Similar regulations governed the rights of liturgical ministers in Greek and Roman sanctuaries. Paul assumed this wide cultural acceptance (even if the Levites were likely uppermost in his mind), and his identification of the congregation as the temple and himself as its priestly agent is quite revealing. It hints with rare clarity at Paul's ecclesial self-understanding as a proclaimer of the gospel. He sees himself as a sort of *hiereus*, "employed in the service of *ta hiera*," notably at the altar from which he deserves his portion.

One might object that this implicit comparison of himself to a temple minister holds no more ontological significance for Paul than the earlier vineyard and flock metaphors, which are used merely to make a point. This overlooks the biblical resonance of those agrarian metaphors, however, and the special prestige of the "shepherd" image in Christian leadership circles, as discussed in excursus 8.[8] Paul, in other words, is not speaking at random, hoping only to push his view. He is finding the most fitting and acceptable ways to talk about his self-understanding, describing his work in relation to the congregation. Besides this carefully chosen set of images, the objection also ignores several key points in the context of the letter. Above all, the implicit evocation of the people as a temple signals a subtle shift into a metaphysical, not merely metaphorical, plane of predication. For, in the end, there is little doubt that

7. Joseph Fitzmyer, *First Corinthians*, AYB 32 (New Haven: Yale University Press, 2008), 365.

8. A soldier metaphor is also used in 1 Cor. 9:7, but this could also carry a strong note of vocational self-identification, as in 2 Tim. 2:3–6 (cf. Phil. 2:25; Philem. 2), where Paul also tells Timothy to share in suffering "like a good soldier of Christ" and also adds that "it is the farmer who does the work who ought to have the first share of the crops."

Paul considered it ontologically and even physically true, not simply rhetorically forceful, to say that the eschatological indwelling of the Holy Spirit made believers into a temple. "Do you not know that you are God's temple? . . . God's temple is holy, and you are that temple" (1 Cor. 3:16–17). The people are not a field, as they are in truth a temple; nor is Paul a farmer, as he is in truth a ministering priest. And his priestly ministry—with all its natural rights, like the rights of any *hiereus*—is intimately bound to the people's identity as the living dwelling of God.

It follows that when in a text such as Philippians 4:18 Paul speaks about the gifts sent to him from the Philippian community, describing them cultically as "a fragrant offering, a sacrifice [*thysian*] acceptable and pleasing [*dektēn, euareston*] to God," he is not merely being poetic. The Apostle sees the economic support that believers put into his hands as somehow passing through his hands directly to God. Though Paul has taken his share of the gifts (at least from the Macedonian, if not the Achaean churches), he is, nevertheless, a living conduit through whom the Philippians interact directly with God. There are really only two possible reasons why Paul should speak and think in this manner. Either he sees himself as belonging to the poor or else he sees himself as a ministering priest. These were the two manners in which Second Temple Jews might imagine the economic support of mere mortals as taking on a sacrificial character pleasing to God.[9]

The case of Paul's collection for the "poor among the saints at Jerusalem" (Rom. 15:26) exemplifies his clear sacrificial understanding of charity for the poor; but it also shows equally clearly on which side Paul himself stands. In Romans 15:15–16, in discussing the collection, he speaks of "the grace given me by God to be a minister [*leitourgon*] of Christ Jesus to the Gentiles in the priestly service [*hierougounta*] of the gospel of God, so that the offering [*prosphora*] of the Gentiles may be acceptable [*euprosdektos*], sanctified by the Holy Spirit." By the grace of God, Paul is a liturgical minister, a mediator to whom are entrusted the people's gifts, which he somehow carries to God in an acceptable and sanctified fashion. It is not to be missed, moreover, just how this carrying to God is done. In the momentous last pilgrimage of Paul to Jerusalem, the most sacred of all sacred plots, his hands are filled with what is in effect an eschatological transformation of the old temple tax. Paul's collection remodels the conventional offering of those in the Diaspora for the support of Jerusalem's hieratic complex: the harvest by which the Levitical *hiereis* live and work. The "saints" themselves have now, in the Christian reformulation, taken the temple's place as the object of this offering, a new and living *hieron*, while Paul's ministry to the saints accomplishes his own priestly work of mediation

9. See Gary Anderson, *Charity: The Place of the Poor in the Biblical Tradition* (New Haven: Yale University Press, 2014).

on their behalf. The double meaning of the key genitive construction "offering of the Gentiles," which at once signifies the gifts offered *by* the Gentiles and the *Gentiles themselves* as a gift being offered by Paul, points to the double-sided nature of this ecclesial action. Through a corporate ecclesial work of charity, an interrelated *hieratic* identity clings to both Paul and people.

The wellspring of charity that ultimately fuels this new Christian system of "temple" support is of the most profound significance for defining the New Covenant's form of priestly ministry. Paul specifically instructed the Corinthians to put aside something for the poor every first day of the week, when they were liturgically assembled together (1 Cor. 16:1). This binds their work of charity directly to their celebration of the Lord's passion. *Love* (rather than animal parts) has, in the new configuration, become the specific form of their sacrifice: love not in any abstract way but in the most concrete and material way. Paul himself is the one entrusted with the task of "perfecting" the community's gift of love, by carrying it to the "temple" of the poor in Jerusalem. While Paul's collection was exceptional, it only manifests on a grand stage the dynamic at the heart of Christian worship. Thus, when Justin later describes in some detail the early Christian Eucharist, the so-called *agapē*, which takes place "on the day we call Sunday," we find the same Pauline model still at work—a cultic meal of blessed bread and wine, marked by an act of love for the poor, an act proceeding from the hands of the people through the hands of the priest. "What is collected is deposited with the president, who [helps] the orphans and widows and those who, through sickness or any other cause, are in want, and those who are in [prison] and the strangers . . . among us, and in a word takes care of all who are in need" (*1 Apol.* 67).[10] Significantly, however, in its most ancient and explicit form, we find this offering of love coming *after*, not before, the sacred meal. In other words, one first receives from the hands of the liturgical presider what Justin calls "the flesh and blood of that Jesus who was made flesh" (*1 Apol.* 66). Only thereafter is the community's collection made. Thus, the descending action of divine love, ministered to the congregation by the priest, is the *source*, not the *effect*, of that human charity that is also sanctified and returned to God via the poor and through the priest's hands. The grand movement is thus a ministry of simultaneously ascending and descending mediation. Love is communicated to and from the community, through Paul, to and from God.

A New Mode of Sacrifice

Paul avoids saying the word *hiereus*, even as he paints himself unmistakably in a hieratic position, bound to and in service of the community as a living

10. See https://www.newadvent.org/fathers/0126.htm.

hieron. Paul's attention to the altar and the language of sacrificial giving, communicating the community's cultic reconfiguration around an offering of love, points to the second, more central risk of adopting the direct language of *hiereis*. The character of the Christian altar has been radically redefined around the sacrifice of Jesus.

In 1 Corinthians 10, the chapter immediately following Paul's self-defense of his right to "share in what is sacrificed on the altar" (*tō thysiastēriō symmerizontai*), he speaks again, in a new connection, of being "communicants in the altar" (*koinōnoi tou thysiastēriou*), discoursing both on "spiritual food" (*to pneumatikon brōma*) and "food sacrificed to idols" (*eidōlothoton* and *hierothyton*). Clearly, Paul has not forgotten what he said in 1 Corinthians 9:12–14. In fact, this earlier passage about being entitled to a share in the sacrifice helps pull Paul back on track, for the entire defense in chapter 9 is actually a digression within a larger discussion concerning the question of meat sacrificed to idols, a topic occupying chapters 8 and 10. The discussion is quite intricate, but happily it is not necessary here to go down into the weeds. Two things suffice for our specific purpose.

First, at the most basic level, Paul's discussion about food sacrificed to idols is not, as it is so often treated, simply a point about the time-bound comportment of early Christians, with no appreciable modern interest—save, perhaps, in those parts of the world (e.g., India) where sacrificial paganism still survives. Yes, it is about Christianity's ethical rules of engagement with the surrounding pagan cults and culture. More fundamentally, however, the issue belongs to a larger discourse and articulation of the new faith's theological relationship to the bloody sacrificial system that ruled the ancient world, Judaism included. At the practical level, this rearticulation of the theology of the altar emerges through the idiom of eating meat.

If Paul in Corinth must troubleshoot this circumstance in a polytheistic Greco-Roman setting, a closely related question, with direct connection to the Mosaic law, appears in Acts 15. There the "Jerusalem Council" determines that believers must avoid *eidolōthyton*, food sacrificed to idols—the same issue we see in Corinth—as well as avoiding *haima*, "blood," and "what is strangled" (Acts 15:20, 29; 20:25).[11] These two latter, interrelated prohibitions complement the interdiction of eating meat sacrificed to idols/demons. Specifically, they disentangle the meat that one still *can* eat from the system of *Jewish* sacrifice and its cult to the one true God; meat sacrificed at the Jerusalem temple was in another category altogether from pagan sacrifice in Corinth and other such places. Briefly, then, by reaching back to the so-called

11. Animals that are strangled rather than slaughtered are killed while still having their blood within them (as do animals that die of themselves, which are also not to be eaten according to Deut. 14:21; cf. Lev. 17:15–16).

Noahide law in Genesis 9:4—"You shall not eat flesh with its life, that is, its blood"—the apostolic decision returns to a postlapsarian but pre-Mosaic dispensation obliging all righteous Gentiles: a typical New Testament move. This cultic return to a time before Moses effectively breaks the Priestly author's later binding of all animal blood to the life-saving work of the Jerusalem altar (Lev. 17:10–12).[12] Thus, whereas the Mosaic covenant carefully split the slaughter of animals between acts of consumption (related to the meat) and atonement (related to the blood), the eating of animals by Christians has been extricated from the entire ancient temple matrix. Consumption of flesh and altar sacrifice are neatly decoupled, with both a Jewish and a Gentile inflection, though the business of blood remains regulated on other grounds (cf. Gen. 9:5). Theologically, of course, this transformation in theory and daily praxis derives from the simple fact that for Christians the blood of atonement does not come from goats and bulls.

The replacement of the blood of animals by the blood of Christ points to the second key theme in 1 Corinthians 10. Paul contrasts *koinōnia*, communion meals at the altar of demons/idols, where animals are ritually slaughtered, with *koinōnia* in the blood and body of Christ. In contrasting these two types of participation, Paul at the same time implicitly compares them, setting both within a single sacrificial, hieratic frame: being "partakers in the table of the Lord" or in "the table of demons" (1 Cor. 10:14–21). Today, it is quite common to oppose domestic "meal" and "table" language applied to the Eucharist with a sacrificial understanding; but in the New Testament context reflected here, these two are inextricably one. The domestic language derives from the fact that a temple was the house of a god. A god's "table" (*trapeza*) was, thus, nothing other than an altar. Indeed, a *trapeza* was a specific sort of altar where unbloody and unburnt food offerings (e.g., bread, fruit, wine libations) could simply be laid.[13] The Jewish version of this was the golden tables of showbread. In 1 Corinthians 10 Paul is displacing the matrix of animal sacrifice with a new, unbloody cult—paradoxically identifying the "cup we bless," the Christian wine libation, as a "sharing in" the *blood* of Christ. This momentous change in the mode of Christian sacrifice, a "sacrifice of

12. The prohibition of ingesting blood is legislated in the Holiness Code in Lev. 17:10–12 (cf. Deut. 12:16, 23), where it applies to the resident alien (thus, by extension, to the Christian Gentile). At the center of this ordinance appears a clarification that the consumption of blood is to be avoided because blood is meant to be used for atonement (Lev. 17:11). For the Priestly author of the Holiness Code, avoiding blood thus goes hand in hand with the cultic function of the altar. The slaughter of animals, in other words, is split between acts of consumption (meat) and atonement (blood). As the rabbis saw, however, this link of animal slaughter to the altar *does not* extend to the alien, who remained free to kill animals privately at home.

13. See D. Gill, "The Greek Cult Table," *AJA* 69 (1965): 103–14; Gill, "Trapezomata: A Neglected Aspect of Greek Sacrifice," *HTR* 67 (1974): 117–37.

atonement by his blood" (Rom. 3:25), radically redefines the cultic character
of the presbyter/priest.

New Views of Sacrifice

A clear perception of the eucharistic meal as a sacrifice goes back as early as
we can see. In addition to the rather clear evidence from Paul, the *Didache*,
for example, makes as direct a use of the language of sacrifice as could
possibly be desired: "On the Lord's own day gather together and break
bread and give thanks [*eucharistēsate*], having first confessed your sins so
that your sacrifice [*hē thysia*] may be pure" (14.1; cf. 14.2–3).[14] Under the
Old Covenant, of course, Israel already knew of cereal offerings; primitive
Christian *thysia* discourse applied to the "breaking of the bread" arguably
derives straight from this LXX background.[15] Such a conceptual lineage
is strong evidence of the Church's innate sense of continuity between its
worship and the earlier Levitical regime. At the same time, it is impossible
not to note the flagrant lack of animal offerings in the exclusive cult of
bread and wine.

The creation of increasingly complex ways of speaking about Christianity's
new mode of worship assimilated elements of thought from beyond the Jewish
milieu. The notion of a "bloodless sacrifice" (*thysia anaimaktos*), for instance,
which ultimately attached itself not only to the eucharistic offering but also to
Christian prayer—and even the entire Christian way of life—borrows from a
type of Greco-Roman discourse with roots in Pythagorean philosophy and its
vegetarian views.[16] Philosophical critique of a sacrificial practice that came at
the cost of "ensouled" beings had an inevitable orientation toward vegetable
offerings, so that "bloodless" offerings gained a certain prestige as rational
(i.e., philosophically approved) worship. But this "rational" trajectory was not
understood as a retreat into a private and personal, interior liturgical space.
Pythagoreans were at times mocked for offering only figs, olive pomace, and
cheese—but the sacrifices were offered. As late as the fifth century AD, the
pagan author Nonnus of Panopolis could still employ the phrase "bloodless
table" (*anaimaktoio trapezēs*) to refer to the altar of Cybele, with its cereal
oblations (*Dion.* 17.58).

---

14. Translation from Holmes, *Apostolic Fathers*, 365.

15. So, e.g., Andrew McGowan, "Eucharist and Sacrifice: Cultic Tradition and Transforma-
tion in Early Christian Ritual Meals," in *Mahl und religiöse Identität im frühen Christentum—
Meals and Religious Identity in Early Christianity*, ed. Matthias Klinghardt and Hal Taussig
(Tübingen: Mohr Siebeck, 2012), 191–206.

16. See Benedikt Eckhardt, "'Bloodless Sacrifice': A Note on Greek Cultic Language in the
Imperial Era," *GRBS* 54 (2014): 255–73.

The formula "bloodless sacrifice" first appears in a Christian text in the *Legatio pro Christianis* of the second-century apologist Athenagoras, who must address the Christians' abstention from public animal sacrifice.

> First, as to our not sacrificing: the Framer and Father of this universe does not need blood, nor the odour of burnt-offerings. . . . What have I to do with holocausts, which God does not stand in need of?—though indeed it does behoove us to offer a bloodless sacrifice [*anaimakton thysian*] and "the service of our reason" [*tēn logikēn latreian*]. (*Legatio* 13.1–2)[17]

The notion of *logikē latreia*, "rational worship," used here in parallel to the idea of bloodless sacrifice, engages another established philosophical motif that reinforces the rational character of an unbloody offering. The particular phrasing of Athenagoras, however, is an allusion to Paul's usage in Romans 12:1: "I appeal to you therefore, brothers and sisters, by the mercies of God, to present your bodies as a living sacrifice [*thysian zōsan*], holy and acceptable to God, which is your spiritual [or rational/reasoning] worship [*tēn logikēn latreian*]." As commentators note, Paul's idea of reasonable worship here recalls the efforts of Greco-Roman philosophers, who "sought to transform cultic practices into intellectual and spiritual concepts."[18] Philo, to take a significant and particularly pertinent example, intertwines the concrete cultic imagery of the Jewish temple service with an intellectualization of sacrifice within the reasoning mind. The *logikē psychē*, the "rational soul," is thus for him one of the two temples of God (*hiera theou*) in which the divinity is worshiped. The high priest in this soul-sanctuary is "true human reason," whose ministry parallels the cosmic high priesthood of the "divine Word." The sacrifices of the Jerusalem temple, finally, reflect this rational liturgy in the soul, "so that soul, temple, and cosmos 'perform the liturgy together' [*synierougeō*] (*Somn.* 216)."[19]

Philo himself never dreamed of abolishing the system of bloody sacrifice in the Jerusalem temple; in fact he protested against any such thought (e.g., *On the Migration of Abraham* 89–93). To this extent it is actually somewhat misleading to say he attempted to *transform* and sublimate cultic practices into spiritual categories, as if he meant somehow to shed the cultic order like a cocoon. On the contrary, in his Middle Platonic version of Judaism, the great cosmic parallel that obtains between the whole Mosaic dispensation, temple and all, and the purely intellectual plane of existence of the *Logos*—a vast mirroring worked out in great detail throughout his oeuvre—was not

---

17. See https://www.newadvent.org/fathers/0205.htm.

18. Robert Jewett, *Romans*, Hermeneia (Minneapolis: Fortress, 2007), 730.

19. See Ian W. Scott, "'Your Reasoning Worship': ΛΟΓΙΚΟΣ in Romans 12:1 and Paul's Ethics of Rational Deliberation," *JTS* (2018): 528.

merely a provisional state of affairs. The Jerusalem cult was an incarnation of and theurgic participation in a world of spiritual realities: a terrestrial access point, in fact, to the celestial cosmic cult (on which more below). Contrast this perspective of a Hellenized Jew of the era with a recent, representative assertion about Paul's intended meaning with *logikē latreia* in Romans 12:1: "The worship of which God is worthy is not adequately accepted in symbols, rites rituals, and token offerings."[20] With Philo serving as a control on Paul, as another Hellenized Jew, one sees just how far many post-Reformation assumptions have strayed from actual first-century Jewish ritual thinking.[21]

Of course, Paul's relationship to the Jerusalem temple and Mosaic law is very different from Philo's. Yet our passage in Romans 12:1–2 follows immediately upon the Apostle's famous discussion in Romans 9–11. And here Paul, speaking of the Jewish covenants, concludes clearly that "the gifts and the calling of God are irrevocable" (Rom. 11:29). Paul unambiguously asserts the perduring goodness of the Mosaic law (he is working damage control against misunderstandings of certain ideas found in Galatians). Imagining that the Pauline ideal in Romans of "rational worship" is thus somehow essentially anti-ritual at its core is a major problem, to put it lightly. Very simply, this would make Paul anti-Moses. The charge is not new—it dates from Paul's own lifetime (e.g., Acts 21:28). Nevertheless, it mangles the Apostle's admittedly tangled thought and thereby mangles as well the hermeneutic of Christian newness.

"They are Israelites, and to them belong the adoption, the glory, the covenants, the giving of the law, *the worship* [*hē latreia*], and the promises; to them belong the patriarchs, and from them, according to the flesh, comes the Messiah, who is over all, God blessed forever. Amen" (Rom. 9:4–5). In short, Mosaic *latreia* is good. Nevertheless, "Christ is the end [*telos*] of the law" (Rom. 10:4): the endpoint and goal toward which it was always striving. Between Romans 11 and 12, two key motifs arise, which measure the discontinuity separating the old aeon and the new, thus distancing believers from the Mosaic regime. First, an eschatological experience of divine mercy, reversing the position of the Gentiles and Jews and described compactly in 11:30–32, prepares Paul's appeal in 12:1: "*by the mercies of God*, to offer [*parastēsai*; NRSV: "present"] your bodies as a living sacrifice." Second, the

20. Lesly Massey, "Paul and Christian Worship in Light of Romans 12:1," *Churchman* 130 (2016): 105.

21. Behind this, in part, is the irony of a philosophical/polemical commonplace adopted by the Church Fathers and used against their pagans rivals, which was later turned against the Church herself in the Christian Humanists' reading of Paul. See Kirk Summers, "The *logikē latreia* of Romans 12:1 and Its Interpretation among Christian Humanists," *Perichoresis* 15 (2017): 47–66.

unplumbable depths of the mind of the Lord, lauded in 11:34–36 and revealed precisely in his plan of mercy, demand the "renewal of the mind" evoked in 12:2. Together, what these two conjoined motifs imply is that Christians must not merely behold the law in the eschatological light of God's faithful work in Christ Jesus; they must thereby and in consequence offer a new mode of sacrifice. Indeed, offering this form of sacrifice is the very first imperative after the indicative of God's great deed in Christ: *logikē latreia* is the exhortation following Paul's exposition, appearing as its natural consequence ("therefore," 12:1).

Against this backdrop, the express *bodiliness* of acceptable sacrifice immediately stands out. "Immaterial" or purely "spiritual" ritual service is not and cannot be the character of the new eschatological order of worship, defined as it is by the "propitiatory offering" (*hilastērion*) of God's Son (Rom. 3:25).[22] The *reasonableness* of "rational worship" as it functions in Paul's vision is measured by the thoughts of new minds illumined in faith by divine wisdom—not by autonomous philosophical (and still less by post-Enlightenment) thought. The dynamism informing the pleasing sacrifice of Christians' own bodies begins thereby to become increasingly clear. It means cultic attunement to and participation in the bodily death of Christ Jesus, "whom God put forward as a sacrifice of atonement by his blood, effective through faith" (Rom. 3:25). This participation in Christ's sacrificial cult is defined by "the obedience of faith" (Rom. 1:5; 16:26), an inextricable nexus of belief and behavior that concretely implies ritually baptized bodies no longer obedient to sin, bodies such as Paul describes in his only other comment in Romans on the offering to God of one's bodily members. Namely, in Romans 6:14 he calls those "not under law but under grace" to (using the same verb as 12:1) "offer" (*parastēsate*) their members no longer as instruments of wickedness but as instruments of righteousness—in the obedience that leads to righteousness rather than the slavish obedience that leads to death—all on account of their baptismal death to sin in Christ Jesus (Rom. 6:12–17).

In Paul's view, then, the offering of Christian *latreia* is only in one sense a bloodless mode of worship. Baptized believers are no longer under the law, for in obedient faith they now enjoy freedom from sin. They thus have freedom from the bloody sacrificial slaughter by which the law worked to fend off sin's effects, above all death as sin's wages and the worst effect of all (Rom. 6:23). And yet the cost of this new Christian freedom is not free. Believers are "justified by *his* blood" (Rom. 5:9). Sharing in the blood of Christ through

---

22. A recent discussion about the meaning of *hilastērion* in Rom. 3:25 has introduced the possibility of understanding the word as a votive offering/propitiatory gift on the basis of parallel inscriptional material, rather than as a direct reference to Yom Kippur and Lev. 16, as it is very often understood. Either way, the text reorients the cultic world around the death of Jesus.

the cup of blessing and sharing in his body through the blessed bread (1 Cor. 10:16) mystically unites believers with Christ as his members. "Your bodies are members of Christ" (1 Cor. 6:15). And "anyone united to the Lord becomes one spirit with him" (6:17) and thereby a living temple, infused with God's Spirit: "Do you not know that your body is a temple of the Holy Spirit within you" (6:19). Here we see the full context of Pauline bodily *latreia*: "You were bought with a price: therefore glorify God in your body" (6:20). Christ's sacrificial blood is the dynamo of the pleasing worship of his mystical members.

Ritual communion in the death of the Lord, in baptism and eucharistic participation, leads to a moral communion of life in the Spirit in Paul's perception. To this degree, the expression "living sacrifice" that Paul employs in Romans 12:1 is not an idle description. The blood of Christ implies his death; yet like all blood (thinking from a Jewish perspective) Christ's blood is also the bearer of his life. And this Jesus who died on the cross is not like an animal victim, a dead carcass upon the altar. He is not made of dust like the first Adam. He is "a life-giving Spirit" (1 Cor. 15:45). Indeed, "we know that Christ, being raised from the dead, will never die again; death no longer has dominion over him" (Rom. 6:9); and "if the Spirit of him who raised Jesus from the dead dwells in you, he who raised Christ from the dead will give life to your mortal bodies also through his Spirit that dwells in you" (Rom. 8:11). The true and "living sacrifice" is measured by God's wisdom and stands simultaneously in a bloodless and bloody mystical relation to Christ. Paul's eschatological philosophy of truly rational worship is bound in this way to a theurgic cult of communion in the dying and rising of the atoning victim who lives forever.

The Liturgy of Heaven and Earth

What Paul's vision of the New Covenant's sacrificial cult does little to highlight becomes very clear in the Letter to the Hebrews. The illustration from Philo presented above of the two-tiered liturgy—the parallel spiritual and earthly temples—is a worldview clearly seen in Hebrews but also shared by the Judaism of the period more broadly. A striking illustration appears in *Testament of Levi* 3:6, for instance, where the celestial sacrifice of the angels is also described as being "a rational and bloodless oblation." Their sanctuary is located in a celestial holy of holies: the highest and seventh heaven (cf. 3:1–5).

In the uppermost heaven of all dwells the Great Glory in the Holy of Holies superior to all holiness. There with him are the archangels, who serve and offer propitiatory sacrifices to the Lord in behalf of all the sins of ignorance of the righteous ones. They present to the Lord a pleasing odor, a rational and bloodless oblation [*logikēn kai anaimakton thysian*]. (*Test. Levi* 3:4–6)[23]

The modeling of this celestial sanctuary on the earthly temple and cult in Jerusalem is quite plain.

At Qumran, in the *Songs of Sabbath Sacrifice*, the full picture of cosmic worship as a mirror linking heaven and earth comes into greater focus. Two parallel, ranked triads of ministers occupy the angelic and earthly realms; there are priests, Levites, and laymen among the angels in heaven, just like the corresponding three classes of Israelites on earth. Moreover, as Philip Alexander explains,

> within the order of priestly angels a distinction is made, as in the earthly Temple, between the ranks of high priest, and ordinary priest. . . . In its celestial hierarchy everything is multiplied sevenfold: there are seven angelic high priests, seven blessings, seven Merkabahs and so forth. . . . [Yet] confusingly Sabbath Songs also speak in the same breath of one Merkabah and one celestial high priest.[24]

This sevenfold character of the angelic realm is symbolic—"a way of asserting a qualitative difference between heaven and earth," he goes on.

> The terrestrial and celestial hierarchies clearly match: Israel on earth with its Temple, its terrestrial liturgy, and its three orders of Priests, Levites, and Israelites is the mirror image of the angels in heaven, with their Temple, their liturgy, and their three orders of priestly, Levitical, and lay angels. But there is also a hierarchical relationship between the two hierarchies: the celestial is the superior, because it is closer to God, and this is symbolized by its sevenfoldness, seven being numerologically the number of completeness and perfection.[25]

In the celestial, angelic liturgy represented in the book of Revelation, similar patterns of seven are found, such as the sevenfold doxologies of Revelation 5:12 and 7:12. Commentators have often speculated that the resurrected Jesus in Revelation 1:12–16 is depicted in high priestly garments in a heavenly temple, beside the seven-branched heavenly menorah. It is no incidental thing that John's rapture and vision occur precisely on "the Lord's day" (Rev. 1:10). There is a manifest link joining the earthly liturgy with the liturgy in heaven.

23. Translation by H. C. Kee in *OTP* 1:789.
24. Philip Alexander, "The Qumran Songs of the Sabbath Sacrifice and the Celestial Hierarchy of Dionysius the Areopagite: A Comparative Approach," *RevQ* 22, no. 87 (2006): 349–73 (here 364).
25. Alexander, "Qumran Songs," 364.

Indeed, the seven churches of Asia Minor somehow symbolically bind the sphere of the *ecclesia* on earth to the sevenfold perfection of heaven.

John's explicit temporal connection of the heavenly cult to the Christian eucharistic commemoration of the Lord's Day is made without fanfare, yet it is very telling. Rather than the Jerusalem temple as at Qumran and in Philo, the mirroring cult has become the worship of the Christian assembly. This shift is of immense theological importance. Moreover, positioning the risen Jesus in the place of the ministering angelic high priest(s) is not a detail of mere passing interest. In effect, the entire cultic axis of heavenly-*cum*-earthly worship has been radically reconceived. This is best seen in the Letter to the Hebrews.

The most crucial difference that becomes visible in Hebrews is that Jesus Christ, as the heavenly high priest, does not atone in a purely spiritual, bodiless, and angelic fashion. He is an earthly figure, though he is now raised to the heights of heaven. Suited to his human nature, he sacrifices not by offering the conventional angelic, bloodless offering; rather, he atones precisely *by means of his blood*. The shock of the heavenly cult being "stained" by blood in this way is an extraordinary novelty in the ancient context that is rarely if ever registered as it deserves. Homeric gods were famously "bloodless," and Jewish angels were equally unearthly, as we have seen. Yet Hebrews' heavenly cult, though presided over by God's Son, the *Logos*, who is higher than the angels, nevertheless has a graphically animal element to it, a fleshliness carried up to heaven from "the days of his flesh" (Heb. 5:7; cf. 2:14). We thus find in Hebrews a curious hybrid cult, fully proper to humankind as *to logikon zōon*, "rational animal": a simultaneous cult of obedience and blood, fit for the rational animal with his body and soul, and thus "better" than the Old Covenant's worship of *irrational* bulls and goats (*to alogon zōon*; cf. Heb. 10:4). Sacrifices and burnt offerings are in the new order replaced by "the offering of the body of Jesus once for all," the Son who learned obedience by suffering and so said, "I come to do your will" (Heb. 10:10).

In Hebrews, then, a new *interpenetration* of the formerly distinct earthly and celestial parallel cults has transpired—a fusion localized in the obedient flesh of Jesus, simultaneously crucified and glorified. Such blending of the heavenly with the earthly realm of liturgical sacrifice not only reaches up into the celestial holy of holies, where Jesus now intercedes forever at God's right hand, but also reaches down and pulls up Christians as if by rapture. Christ's participation in human flesh opens a way into heaven for those who "approach with boldness" (Heb. 4:16), those who have attained some manner of access to his blood. "Therefore, my friends, since we have confidence to enter the sanctuary by the blood of Jesus, by the new and living way that he opened for us through the curtain (that is, through his flesh), and since we have a great priest over the house of God, let us approach with a true heart in full assurance of faith, with our hearts sprinkled clean from an evil conscience and our bodies washed with pure water" (Heb. 10:19–22). For the author of Hebrews, baptismal sprinkling together with the blood of Jesus allows faithful believers to penetrate into the living presence of God, where Jesus serves as eternal and sinless high priest.

Hebrews' remarkably insistent cultic language of Jesus' blood need not be forever treated merely as an abstract symbol. In the light of early Christian

Heavenly Work on Earth

Like many ancient authors, John Chrysostom recognized the angelic character of the Church's priestly ministry and understood how the celestial imagery of the Old Covenant cult became a reality in the New. This cosmic vision permits him to behold the earthly priest acting in union with Christ as truly standing and ministering in the sanctuary in heaven.

> The work of the priesthood is done on earth, but it is ranked among heavenly ordinances. And this is only right, for no man, no angel, no archangel, no other created power, but the Paraclete himself ordained this succession, and persuaded men, while still remaining in the flesh to represent the ministry of angels. The priest, therefore, must be pure as if he were standing in heaven itself, in the midst of those powers.
>
> The symbols which existed before the ministry of grace were fearful and awe-inspiring: for example, the bells, the pomegranates, the stones on the breastplate, the stones on the ephod, the mitre, the diadem, the long robe, the golden crown, the Holy of Holies, the deep silence within. But if you consider the ministry of grace, you will find that those fearful and awe-inspiring symbols are only trivial. The statement about the Law is true here also: "The splendour that once was is now no splendour at all; it is outshone by a splendour greater still" [2 Cor. 3:10]. When you see the Lord sacrificed and lying before you, and the High Priest standing over the sacrifice and praying, and all who partake being tinctured with that precious blood, can you think that you are still among men and still standing on earth? Are you not at once transported to heaven, and, having driven out of your soul every carnal thought, do you not with soul naked and mind pure look round upon heavenly things? Oh, the wonder of it! Oh, the loving-kindness of God to men![a]

a. St. John Chrysostom, *Six Books on the Priesthood* 3.4, trans. Graham Neville (Crestwood, NY: St. Vladimir's Seminary Press, 1984 [orig. SPCK, 1964]), 70.

eucharistic praxis and discourse, there is no special difficulty in discerning, in the mention of Christ's sacrificial blood, a similarly "decodable" sacramental reference as that used in the transparent language of being sprinkled, with bodies washed in clean water.[26] Just as the motif of beholding Christ's blood, which appears in *1 Clement*, "is rooted in the eucharistic and corporate life of the early Christian community," so in Hebrews a real cult stands behind the recognizable cultic language.[27] In other words, access to the life-giving effects of Christ's passion and his risen glory is provided—for Hebrews as for Paul (and Clement)—by the twin sacraments of baptism and Holy Communion, the sprinkling and the blood. Access to God's mercy is open to those "who have once been enlightened [i.e., in baptism] and have tasted the heavenly gift [i.e., communion in Christ's body and blood]" (Heb. 6:4).

This mystical mingling of the heavenly and the earthly in the Christ-centered liturgy of Hebrews ultimately turns our attention to the celestial dimension of worship that already penetrates the Christian cult on the earth, in those ecclesial meetings that the author insists must not be neglected (Heb. 10:25). "We have an altar [*thysiastērion*] from which those who officiate in the tent have no right to eat," he says in an amazing and often overlooked remark at the conclusion of the letter (Heb. 13:10). Where is this altar and what is this food to which the priests of the Mosaic order have no right? It is the altar of Christ's sacrifice, which spans between and joins together heaven and earth. It is the celestial, angelic, unbloody food of the eucharistic sacrifice, which the priests in the old temple and covenant do not know.

There is only one altar and one sacrifice for sins, just as there is only one officiating, great high priest (cf. Eph. 4:4–5). The early Christians were keenly aware of this profound mystical unity of the single celestial-and-earthly liturgy of the Church. Ignatius of Antioch gives the sentiment its perfect and classical formulation.

---

26. The eucharistic resonance of Hebrews is widely ignored and often rejected but is importantly recognized by two Catholic scholars, Albert Vanhoye and James Swetnam. A Lutheran voice has also recently expressed very strong support for this minority approach to the letter. See Arthur A. Just Jr., "Entering Holiness: Christology and Eucharist in Hebrews," *CTQ* 69 (2005): 75–95. Just correctly concludes, "There is still much to be done in determining the full extent of Hebrews' eucharistic theology. More may be gained in this effort by taking a less defensive approach—that is, trying to prove through proof-texts that Hebrews is referring to the Eucharist—and instead demonstrate how a eucharistic interpretation provides answers to many of the questions Hebrews raises" (95). Swetnam ("Christology and Eucharist in the Epistle to the Hebrews," *Biblica* 70 [1989]: 84) rightly observes: "No reader of this epistle as it was first written would have been able to grasp this subtle [eucharistic] symbolism without the aid of an oral tradition against which the epistle would have been interpreted."

27. Edmund W. Fisher, "Let Us Look Upon the Blood-of-Christ (1 Clement 7:4)," *VC* 34 (1980): 218. Fisher highlights how the suggestive language of *atenizein*, "beholding, gazing upon" Christ's blood, is drawn from cultic language conventionally used for contemplating God and holy things in the temple.

Take care, therefore, to participate in one Eucharist (for there is one flesh of
our Lord Jesus Christ, and one cup that leads to unity through his blood; there
is one altar, just as there is one bishop, together with the council of presbyters
and the deacons, my fellow servants), in order that whatever you do, you do in
accordance with God. (*To the Philadelphians* 4.1)[28]

The one heavenly altar with its one sacrifice for sins is not imperiled or somehow multiplied by the Church's earthly share in Christ's flesh and blood—no
more than the seven churches in Revelation indicate a fracturing of heavenly
perfection. On the contrary! In every place where the Church is present and
gathered together as one at worship, united around its one bishop with his
presbyters and deacons, the single sacrifice of the one true high priest is
made mystically present on the one altar. This earthly liturgy of the new and
better covenant, like the liturgy of those who officiated in the Mosaic tent,
is powerfully linked and coordinated with the perfect liturgy in heaven. Yet
that worship above is now no longer mirrored in some second and separate
liturgical thing, a "shadow" as Hebrews calls it: a mere ritual echo from an
unbridgeable cosmic distance. Christ's flesh-and-blood priestly ministry on
earth opens up the community's participation in the Son of God's one act
of eternal worship.

A wonderful text from *Apostolic Constitutions* gives robust and synthetic
expression to the Church's perennial understanding of this dense mystery of
priestly service and sacrifice.

You, therefore, O bishops [*episkopoi*], are to your people priests [*hiereis*] and
Levites, ministering to the holy tabernacle, the holy Catholic Church; who stand
at the altar [*thysiastēriō*] of the Lord your God, and offer to Him reasonable
and unbloody sacrifices [*tas logikas kai anaimaktous thysias*] through Jesus
the great High Priest [*megalou archiereōs*]. You are to the laity prophets, rulers, governors, and kings; the mediators between God and His faithful people.
(*Apostolic Constitutions* 2.25)[29]

A Holy and Royal Priesthood

By an early date, the synthesis seen in the *Apostolic Constitutions* with its
various converging threads was well underway. And yet, obviously, nothing
so compact and overt is ever found in the New Testament itself. Reasons have
been given why the explicit use of *hiereus* applied to Church leaders was problematic in a time before this new conceptual synthesis was solidly in place.

28. Translation from Holmes, *Apostolic Fathers*, 239.
29. See https://www.newadvent.org/fathers/07152.htm.

The question remains, however: Why *is* the missing language of a *hierateuma* nevertheless applied unproblematically to the entire people by New Testament authors? The best way to approach this problem, the question of the common priesthood, is to consider briefly the key passage at issue, 1 Peter 2:4–10.

Come to him, a living stone, though rejected by mortals [cf. Ps. 118:22] yet chosen [*eklekton*] and precious [cf. Isa. 28:16] in God's sight, and like living stones, let yourselves be built into a spiritual house, to be a holy priesthood [*hierateuma hagion*], to offer spiritual sacrifices [*pneumatikas thysias*] acceptable to God through Jesus Christ. For it stands in scripture:

> "See, I am laying in Zion a stone,
>   a cornerstone chosen [*eklekton*] and precious;
> and whoever believes in him will not be put to shame [Isa. 28:16]."

To you then who believe, he is precious; but for those who do not believe,

> "The stone that the builders rejected
>   has become the very head of the corner [Ps. 118:22],"

and

> "A stone that makes them stumble,
>   and a rock that makes them fall [Isa. 8:14]."

They stumble because they disobey the word, as they were destined to do.
    But you are a chosen race [*genos eklekton*, Isa. 43:20], a royal priesthood [*basileion hierateuma*], a holy nation [Exod. 19:6], God's own people, in order that you may proclaim the mighty acts of him who called you out of darkness into his marvelous light.

> Once you were not a people,
>   but now you are God's people;
> once you had not received mercy,
>   but now you have received mercy. (1 Pet. 2:4–10; cf. Hosea 1:6, 9;
>   2:25)

The density of Old Testament citations and allusions is the first thing to observe about this complicated text. While variations on the stone motif, triggered by the conjunction of Psalm 118 and Isaiah 28, provide essential structure for the passage, the repeated language of election (*eklekton*) is no less central. It is this motif that drives the thought in the direction of the "royal priesthood" of Exodus 19:6; yet both ideas—the living stone and God's election—converge to create the concrete christological context for understanding 1 Peter's use of *hierateuma*. Like Christ, believers are "living stones," whose divine election finds expression in a priestly identity that, like Jesus' own, is at once holy and royal.

The theme of election is not a new idea at this point in 1 Peter's discourse. It was already announced in the tight thematic overture at the opening of the letter in 1 Peter 1:1–2.

> Peter, an apostle of Jesus Christ,
>   To the exiles of the Dispersion in Pontus, Galatia, Cappadocia, Asia, and Bithynia, who have been chosen [*eklektois*] and destined by God the Father and sanctified by the Spirit to be obedient to Jesus Christ and to be sprinkled with his blood:
>   May grace and peace be yours in abundance.

The sprinkling of Jesus' blood that appears in this greeting is a highly suggestive cultic allusion, which helps pry open 1 Peter's rich notion of election. It is a profound claim on Christian existence by the working of the triune God. The elect are foreknown by the Father, sanctified in the Spirit, and consecrated in the sprinkled blood of the Son.

In the Old Covenant, the sprinkling of blood directly recalls three things: the ordination of the priests in Leviticus 8:30, the Day of Atonement in Leviticus 16:14, and the covenant ceremony in Exodus 24:3–8. Obviously, an allusion to one of the high priestly sprinklings in Leviticus would be deeply revealing for the language of priestly status attributed to the Christian people in 1 Peter 2:9. An allusion to Exodus 24 is much more revealing, however. With good reason most scholars accept this as the likely allusion. A Passover perspective is betrayed, indeed, by the description of the "precious blood" of Christ as that of a spotless lamb in 1 Peter 1:18–19. According to the widespread early tradition of the Church, Jesus at his last Passover meal interpreted his own death through the covenant-making ceremony in Exodus 24. Accordingly, for the author of our letter, "the likelihood that this passage was in his mind as he wrote 1 Peter 1:2 is great."[30]

A *new* covenant-making ceremony, modeled on Moses' mediation at Sinai but now bound to Christ's final sacrifice, aptly illuminates the thrust of election in 1 Peter 2. First of all, the citation of Exodus 19:6 is explicitly tied to the Lord's sealing of a covenant with the people.

> If you obey my voice and keep my covenant, you shall be my treasured possession out of all the peoples. Indeed, the whole earth is mine, but you shall be for

30. Sydney H. T. Page, "Obedience and Blood Sprinkling in 1 Peter 1:2," *WTJ* 71 (2010): 297.

me a priestly kingdom and a holy nation. These are the words that you shall
speak to the Israelites. (Exod. 19:5–6)

The covenant foretold in Exodus 19 and sealed in Exodus 24 also explains
the climactic citation of Hosea in 1 Peter 2:10. The entire preoccupation
of the passage in 1 Peter 2 is the new covenantal creation of a holy people as
the Lord's divine possession out of what was a rejected, unholy nonpeople—
namely, the Gentiles. (Multiple explicit contacts link this dense passage in
1 Peter to Paul's discussion in Rom. 9–11.)

If the sprinkling with Christ's high priestly blood, which is a sign of participation in the New Covenant sacrifice, confers on all the faithful the dignity of
priestly election, this is manifestly no longer an ethnic and biological destiny,
as it was for the Jewish *hiereis*. The "spiritual temple" that is the Church is in
a landless state of worldly exile and "dispersion" (1 Pet. 1:1, 17; 2:11). It is by
nature a no-nation, made God's people by sheer grace. There is now no chosen
land, no sacred plantations, no tribal caste of ministers to slaughter animal
victims. And yet the whole Christian people—"saints from every tribe and
language and people and nation"—have been ransomed by the blood of the
Lamb that was slaughtered, to be together "a kingdom and priests [*hiereis*]"
for God (Rev. 5:9–10), offering spiritual sacrifice. The answer to the classic
question is thus clear. Why is the language of a *hierateuma* applied by New
Testament authors to the entire people but not to isolated leaders? In view
of the conceptual context evoked in 1 Peter 2, this choice begins to become
clear. Focus upon the specifically trans-ethnic and extraterritorial election
of the Gentiles enables the New Testament to comfortably employ hieratic
language without the risk of basic misperception. The fundamentally changed
New Covenant mechanics of divine election must be thematically in place to
speak accurately of a Christian identity as *hiereis*.

In securing this broad typological framework, the critical theological point
becomes clear. The status of Israel's *ministerial priesthood* is not being transferred in 1 Peter 1–2 and transposed in a blanket way onto all the individual
Christian faithful. Peter is not saying that the unique election and sprinkling
that once consecrated Aaron as high priest is now a description of the election of every believer. The message is rather about a corporate and covenantal
status, as the Greek word *hierateuma* implies. The letter speaks of a national
identity that coexisted in Israel alongside and not in competition with the
Aaronic priesthood.

By shifting the focus of 1 Peter's thought to the New Covenant people's
corporate election, it becomes possible at last to put the theological pieces
in their proper place. In the Second Temple mindset, Israel as a whole was
understood to stand relative to the other nations just as the elect tribe of Levi

stood relative to the other tribes. Or to express the notion in more universal terms, Philo says that Israel is for the world what the priest (*hiereus*) is for the polis (*On the Special Laws* 2.163; *On Giants* 61). A similar idea appears later in the *Letter to Diognetus*: "What the soul is to the body, Christians are to the world" (6.1).[31] As an identity specifically clarified in its relation to the world's non-elect peoples, this common Christian priesthood shows its special character by being a "spiritual house"—that is, a spiritual temple—designated "to offer spiritual sacrifices." Though the language is different from both Paul's *logikē latreia* (Rom. 12:1–2) and Hebrews' "sacrifice of praise" (*thysia aineseōs*, Heb. 13:15), the clear and common accent on the pleasing, rational nature of the unique Christian cult is clear. In contrast to the worship of those who stumble on Christ, the stone of scandal, those built up in union with him into a living and spiritual temple corporately offer the type of soulful sacrifice that God truly desires (cf. 1 Pet. 2:20–24). Temple, priesthood, and sacrifice are bound together in a single conceptual braid.

It would demand a curious leap in logic (albeit a leap indulged by Luther) to draw from the priestly character of the Christian people that their leaders should accordingly be denied the name of priests. In specifically appropriating Israel's priestly identity and status, would not priests reasonably be thought to come along as part of the package? Does Scripture permit picking apart the priestly charisms of Israel in this way? More directly: can the covenantal sprinkling in Exodus 24 be accepted, but not that same covenant's command for a subsequent sprinkling of Aaron and his sons in Leviticus 8? It is hard to see where the New Testament ever advances such a sifted, *this-but-not-that* teaching or reading of Israel's priestly character. Does it not, rather, appear to belong to the logic of the case that the baptismal *hierateuma*, as God's gracious gift and election, embraces and enables ministerial priestly service within the Church, in precise parallel to the way that the Mosaic covenant, by which Israel was made into a holy nation of priests, carried the implicit Aaronic priesthood within its bosom? The same thought might also be turned around and pressed from the other direction. Without the Aaronic priesthood of the altar, would or could Israel have been a priestly and holy people? In the ancient Near Eastern and biblical mindset, the priests in the temple were the crown and emblem of a nation's favor before their gods. Without priests, how exactly was Israel—or are the Christian people—priestly? "The layman is the light of the world, while clergy and religious are the light of the laity."[32] Shall the light of the body be darkness, but the body be nevertheless filled with light (Luke 11:35)? Without a revelation of God's sacred "set-apart-ness"

---

31. Translation from Holmes, *Apostolic Fathers*, 703.

32. Hans Urs von Balthasar, *Explorations in Theology*, vol. 2, *Spouse of the Word* (San Francisco: Ignatius, 1991), 340.

abiding within their very midst, how can an elect people themselves be holy, as the Lord is holy (1 Pet. 1:15; Lev. 11:45; 19:2; 20:7, 26; 21:6)?

However one tries to wiggle around such questions, it is manifest that organized structures of consecrated community leadership have not been leveled or abrogated in some sort of radical egalitarian vision in 1 Peter (see excursus 8), despite (or perhaps because of) its recognition of this common priesthood of the people. In 1 Peter 5:5 the author even offers a warning to submit to the authority of the *presbyters*: the Greek word, we can recall once more, for what we in English pronounce as "priests." The author of 1 Peter is far from alone within the New Testament in recognizing the gracious work of holy order, which organizes and arrays the Christian people like a great household (cf. 1 Pet. 2:13, 18; 3:1). He is likewise far from proposing that now, within the new Christian order, in full contrast to the Old Covenant that so deeply shapes his eschatological thinking, there can be no more act of priestly service animating the life of God's priestly people, no special election within the people's common election, no further mystery of grace hidden within the sphere of the Father's foreknowledge, no reception of a cooperative share in the Spirit's work of sanctification, no deeper consecration in union with the blood of the Son.

Conclusion

"You shall be called priests of the LORD [*kōhănê yhwh*], you shall be named ministers of our God" (Isa. 61:6). Isaiah's prophecy envisions a renewed and reestablished Jerusalem priesthood, ostensibly served by sacred farms that are tended by slaves from the Gentile nations. "Strangers shall stand and feed your flocks, foreigners shall till your land and dress your vines" (Isa. 61:5). The fulfillment of this eschatological vision takes an unexpected form, however, for the premise of the entire hieratic system, as it was known in the ancient world, has been radically broken in Christ. The divine promises and blessing symbolized by Israel's fruitful land will become a part of the Gentiles' share and spiritual fortune. The flock and farm of God will no longer be limited to Israel. The nations seen tilling the land of God's promise are not slaves but co-worshipers of the one true Lord. Indeed, the evangelization and incorporation of the Gentiles into the cult of the one true temple is the final surprise in the very last, parting verses of the book of Isaiah.

I am coming to gather all nations and tongues; and they shall come and shall see my glory, and I will set a sign among them. From them I will send survivors to the nations . . . to the coastlands far away that have not heard of my fame or seen my glory; and they shall declare my glory among the nations. They shall bring all your kindred from all the nations as an offering to the LORD, on horses, and in chariots, and in litters, and on mules, and on dromedaries, to my holy mountain Jerusalem, says the LORD, just as the Israelites bring a grain offering in a clean vessel to the house of the LORD. And *I will also take some of them as priests and as Levites*, says the LORD. (Isa. 66:18–21)

In the "new heavens and the new earth" that the Lord promises he will make (Isa. 66:22), those called and honored with the name of "priests," who offer a bloodless and clean grain offering, will include non-Jewish, non-Levite, non-Aaronite Gentiles.

The novelty of the New Testament cult over against ancient temple worship, both in Israel and in the pagan world, ultimately represents a kind of "christological mutation" tightly bound to God's triumphal victory in the gospel message. Indeed, a focus on the cross and the gospel comes closer to capturing the essence of the matter than words like "spiritualization," "eschatologization," "universalization," or "personalization," although all of these dynamics also describe different aspects of the process. The Old Covenant cult, through the power of the gospel and message of Christ's cross, is transposed to an elect and living temple, where spiritual sacrifice is constantly offered to God. A participation by grace in the unique sacrifice of Christ, the one high priest, stands at the very root of this mystery of Christian worship. The sacred blood of the sacrifice of the Father's only Son is the source and summit, the means and mode by which the Holy Trinity sanctifies the New Covenant priesthood.

SUMMARY OF KEY POINTS

1. A key measure of the "newness" of the gospel dispensation appears in the post-temple character of Christian sacrifice and cultic worship. Here a prominent differentiation from antecedent Jewish and Greco-Roman patterns of religion, centered upon ritual animal slaughter, is unmistakable and highly revealing.

2. The particular language that was both adopted and avoided by primitive Christian sources to speak of their communities' cultic leaders can only be understood against the background of ancient *hiera* discourse, with its concrete sociolinguistic connotations of established and landed priestly colleges and clans and their regular practice of bloody sacrifice. Obvious, undesirable associations prevented the simple assumption of this language in strict usage, without excluding its employment in transferred senses.

3. While never naming Christian ministers with technical hieratic taxonomy, New Testament texts, nevertheless, engage hieratic images and tropes in creative and often very expressive ways. A newly personalized vision of both temple and sacrifice is especially noteworthy in this connection; Paul's letters, especially the Corinthian correspondence, provide some extraordinary data for tracing the subtle ways early Christians renegotiated their relation to these essential priestly ideas.

4. Critical to the New Testament's view of priestly ministry is a special manner of understanding the sacrificial character of the Eucharist. The ancient motif of "unbloody" spiritual/rational sacrifice plays a decisive role here, both in clarifying the Christian manner of ritual participation in the sacrifice of Christ and in allowing some striking theological innovations in the Letter to the Hebrews to come into proper relief.

5. Hebrews depicts a unique form of hybrid cult, including both obedience and blood and thus proper to the nature of "the rational animal." A living interpenetration of the earthly and celestial realms is characteristic of this human mode of worship, presided over by Christ himself as high priest. One single heavenly altar and one sacrifice for sins are universally accessed through the earthly Church's cultic participation in this heavenly worship.

6. The application, finally, of the overt priestly language of *hierateuma* to describe the Christian people's common priesthood must not be construed with prejudice against a special ministerial priestly class. The force of the language lies in its covenantal register and allusions, which, far from excluding it, would seem to presuppose an elect priesthood at the heart of the priestly people.

The Laying On of Hands

After wavering long, Catholic sacramental theology (with the help of an intervention on the part of Pope Pius XII in *Sacramentum ordinis*) ultimately determined that the matter of the sacrament of Orders is the imposition of hands—not the handing over of the instruments of ministry (*traditio instrumentorum*). The fact that the Church took more than nineteen centuries to settle this question is a hint that the data is not easy to read.

It is a rude exegetical mistake, of course, to imagine or insist that every passing scriptural allusion to Holy Orders must provide an omnibus of sacramental and liturgical theology and information. This is especially true in garnering the New Testament's scattered hints to the ritual of transmission of office by the imposition of hands. Here, as much as anywhere in our study, the Church's living Tradition must be invoked and asserted as a heuristic yardstick. Without denying that the materials can also be viewed differently from alternative (even perfectly Catholic) angles, it bears saying that the firm resistance of many exegetes to any hint of office or ordination in the relevant texts is often no less theologically motivated than the perspective that is here suggested. The Church's hermeneutic of recognition has the advantage, in any event, of explaining not only the texts but also the roots of an immemorial Tradition, already remarkably codified by the time of Hippolytus and the *Apostolic Tradition*: a sprawling but critical body of liturgical data with an incontestable bearing on the subject.[1]

1. See Paul Bradshaw, Maxwell E. Johnson, and L. Edward Phillips, eds., *The Apostolic Tradition*, Hermeneia (Minneapolis: Fortress, 2002). Impressive ancient prayers are included for the hand-laying ceremonies provided for the ordination of bishops, presbyters, and

For reasons that might be challenged, it is not common to look to the witness of early ecclesial usage and the texts of so-called Church Orders—namely, early ritual manuals—for aid. In search of genealogical explanations, attention has instead been turned in alternative directions. The rabbinic *semikah*, a kind of ordination ceremony performed by "leaning on" a disciple's head with the hands with significant pressure, is the most important parallel point of reference, though the problems of appealing to this ritual have long been recognized.[2] It may accordingly be that the source of the gesture in the Christian context is to be sought rather in the several lurking and suggestive Old Testament allusions: Moses' impressive designation of Joshua as his successor in Numbers 27, for instance.

> Moses spoke to the LORD, saying, "Let the LORD, the God of the spirits of all flesh, appoint someone over the congregation who shall go out before them and come in before them, who shall lead them out and bring them in, so that the congregation of the LORD may not be like sheep without a shepherd." So the LORD said to Moses, "Take Joshua son of Nun, a man in whom is the spirit, and lay your hand upon him; have him stand before Eleazar the priest and all the congregation, and commission him in their sight." (Num. 27:15–19)

In effect, the primitive ecclesial practice must be seen as an act of ritual exegesis on the part of the Church, expressive of strong continuity with biblical Israel. In this regard, the fact that no positive evidence exists that Jesus himself laid hands on his apostles becomes revealing in its own right. The Church instinctively deferred to the Old Covenant to give expression to her self-understanding of ministerial life and her conviction that she was not to be left like sheep without shepherds.

Similar to any ritual gesture, the imposition of hands is a solemn but non-discursive action that can and does take on multiple meanings—for example, healing, reception of the Holy Spirit, and driving out evil spirits. Most of these biblical meanings are, in fact, still preserved in the wide ritual praxis of the Church. The laying on of hands is also the matter of confirmation, for instance, and the gesture is equally used in the sacrament of anointing and the rite of exorcism. While these distinct usages have their own foundations, easily linked to the life of Jesus, at least five times in the New Testament the expression "to lay hands upon" (*epitithenai tas cheiras*) can be construed as referring to an act of what we would call ordination (Acts 6:2–6; 13:1–3; 1 Tim. 4:14; 5:22; 2 Tim. 1:6).

---

deacons. According to the instructions, hands are *not* laid on confessors, lectors, subdeacons, virgins, widows, or healers, however.

2. See, e.g., Everett Ferguson, "Jewish and Christian Ordination: Some Observations," *HTR* 56 (1963): 13–19.

The text in Acts 6:2–6 highlights the establishment of distinct hierarchical orders, as seven men, overtly named as deacons at least since Irenaeus, are chosen by the community to be consecrated as helpers for the Twelve.

> The twelve called together the whole community of the disciples and said, "It is not right that we should neglect the word of God in order to wait on tables. Therefore, friends, select from among yourselves seven men of good standing, full of the Spirit and of wisdom, whom we may appoint to this task, while we, for our part, will devote ourselves to prayer and to serving the word." What they said pleased the whole community, and they chose Stephen, a man full of faith and the Holy Spirit, together with Philip, Prochorus, Nicanor, Timon, Parmenas, and Nicolaus, a proselyte of Antioch. They had these men stand [*estēsan*] before the apostles, who prayed and laid their hands on them [*epethēkan autois tas cheiras*]. (Acts 6:2–6)

The Greek grammar in this passage does not, as often claimed, suppose that hands are laid on these seven men by the "whole community." The apostles, though not the subject of the preceding verbs, "chose" and "stand," may be naturally taken as the subject of "prayed" and "laid hands," which follow. This understanding is unambiguously adopted in Codex Bezae, which, even if not original (though the so-called Western Text that it preserves very often is), is nevertheless the earliest interpretation of the passage that has been preserved. Either way, the whole community is clearly engaged in the dedication of these men, and it would be silly to imagine that the apostles' unique authority is somehow obscured for this reason. The word of the Twelve in verse 3, "whom we may appoint," already expresses their own special agency as representatives of the wider ecclesial "we," and it is only at their unilateral proposition and invitation that the whole community acts at all. As when Moses summoned the entire *ekklēsia* at the ordination of Aaron and his sons (Lev. 8:3–4 LXX), so the whole Church must be part of this moment in Acts. This role of the people in ritually approving and presenting the *ordinandi* to God has remained a crucial part of the rite from the most ancient times until today. *Apostolic Tradition* 2.1–2 witnesses to the same view: "Let him be ordained bishop who has been chosen by all the people, and when he has been named and accepted by all, let him assemble the people."[3]

With varying conviction scholars have observed an interesting parallel/ precedent to the ritual in Acts 6 that appears in Numbers 8, where the whole Israelite community sets apart the Levites as tabernacle servants in a sort of mini-ordination, centered upon the imposition of hands and modestly but unmistakably reminiscent of Leviticus 8–9.

---

3. Bradshaw, Johnson, and Phillips, *Apostolic Tradition*, 24.

The LORD spoke to Moses, saying: Take the Levites from among the Israelites and cleanse them. Thus you shall do to them, to cleanse them: sprinkle the water of purification on them, have them shave their whole body with a razor and wash their clothes, and so cleanse themselves. Then let them take a young bull and its grain offering of choice flour mixed with oil, and you shall take another young bull for a sin offering. You shall bring the Levites before the tent of meeting, and assemble the whole congregation of the Israelites. When you bring the Levites before the LORD, the Israelites shall lay their hands [wĕsāmkû . . . 'et-yĕdêhem] on the Levites, and Aaron shall present the Levites before the LORD as an elevation offering from the Israelites, that they may do the service of the LORD. The Levites shall lay their hands on the heads of the bulls, and he shall offer the one for a sin offering and the other for a burnt offering to the LORD, to make atonement for the Levites. Then you shall have the Levites stand [wĕha'ămadtā] before Aaron and his sons, and you shall present them as an elevation offering to the LORD. (Num. 8:5–13)

Acts 6, naturally, recounts nothing about ablutions. The possession of the Holy Spirit already accomplishes all the necessary cleansing—even as Joshua, already possessed of the Spirit, required no sprinkling, laundry service, or shaving in Numbers 27. As for the sacrificial offerings, though Acts is obviously silent, it is worthy of notice that the *Apostolic Tradition* 4 prescribes that the Eucharist is to be offered immediately after the hand-laying ceremony. Not merely that: the rubric reads, "Let the deacons offer him [i.e., the bishop being consecrated] the oblations, and let him, laying his hands on it with all the presbytery, say, giving thanks . . ."[4] This combined rite is openly modeled on the double hand-laying as recounted in Numbers 8—first on the Levites, then on the offerings—with the bloodless sacrifice taking the place of the bulls.

If a rite of ordination that in the old dispensation was proper specifically to the Levites became in the early Church used for deacons, presbyters, and bishops alike, one weighty reason might be sought precisely in the fact that the Christian clerical caste, in all its ranked orders, like the Levites, offered only spiritual sacrifice. A Christian bishop's hands could not be "filled," as were Aaron's, with all the fatty entrails of slaughtered animals for the altar (even if the *traditio* rite was, nevertheless, carried over and adapted). Instead, all Christian clerics are set apart in the simpler manner of Levites, in implicit subordination to the one heavenly high priest.

In Acts 6, of course, the subordination, even the menial role, of these seven ministers at table is quite apparent. Coupled with the sequence of a ceremonial laying on of hands (Acts 6:6b; cf. Num. 8:10; 27:18) and the ritual act of *standing* the Levites before Aaron (Acts 6:6a; cf. Num. 8:13; 27:19), this combines to create a highly suggestive, if admittedly unverifiable, echo

---

4. Bradshaw, Johnson, and Phillips, *Apostolic Tradition*, 38.

of Numbers 8. The apostles are implicitly understood in this picture to hold the priestly position of Aaron and his sons, while the Seven stand relative to them as Levitical servants. When read through this text in Numbers, Luke thus already anticipates (or at the very least his account invites) the systematic vision of Clement of Rome, who overtly classes the Christian community's leaders into the ancient ranks of high priest, priests, and Levites (1 Clem. 40.5; see excursus 2), in the same way that the Essenes at Qumran were also classed into priests, Levites, and laity, like Israel at large (e.g., 1QS 1:18–2:23; CD 14:4–5; 1QM).

Against those who observe that the Seven already possess the Spirit and remark that "there is no indication that any sacramental power, or more particularly the Holy Spirit, was conferred by the laying on of hands," it is necessary to recall what was said about the omnibus fallacy.[5] It is not necessary for every verse to say everything that must be said. The same holds for the observation that "unlike in Numbers 8 where the initiative belongs to God, in Acts it is the apostles who propose the appointment."[6] Luke characteristically builds up his picture block by block, and, with due respect for the intractable diversity of New Testament data, one must be prepared to pull together multiple passages if anything remotely like a coherent picture is to emerge.

In contrast to Acts 6, in Acts 13:1–3 the divine initiative is perfectly clear. So too is the Holy Spirit's dynamic presence in the form of a new, energizing divine *afflatus*: a grace revealed here to have an ecclesial and evangelical scope much wider than any private, personal strengthening of the consecrated men.

> Now in the church at Antioch there were prophets and teachers: Barnabas, Simeon who was called Niger, Lucius of Cyrene, Manaen a member of the court of Herod the ruler, and Saul. While they were worshiping the Lord and fasting, the Holy Spirit said, "Set apart [*aphorisate*] for me Barnabas and Saul for the work to which I have called them." Then after fasting and praying they laid their hands on them [*epithentes tas cheiras autois*] and sent them off [*apelysan*].

"No one takes this honor for himself" (Heb. 5:4 ESV), as we already discussed in chapter 1. The same combination of praying and the imposition of hands is seen here in Acts 13 as in Acts 6, this time with the addition of fasting. The presentation of the event as an action of the whole local church is once again strongly intoned. There is reason to class these two ritual reports together.

As a *sending-off* ceremony, it is often objected that the accomplishment of a single, circumscribed task is in view in Acts 13, not a lifetime appointment—a

5. So Everett Ferguson, "Laying On of Hands: Its Significance in Ordination," *JTS* 26 (1975): 1–12.

6. John Fleter Tipei, *The Laying On of Hands in the New Testament: Its Significance, Techniques, and Effects* (Lanham, MD: University Press of America, 2009), 250.

kind of liturgical bon voyage.[7] In answer to this, the prominence and weight of the "setting apart" motif might be stressed: this is priestly language, typical of Israel's holiness system, and again reminiscent of Numbers 8 (*aphoriei tous Leueitas*). That Paul's solemn, public consecration was not set simply to expire on his return home finds support in a subtle but plausible echo of this impressive opening moment in his apostolic career, when, in writing to the Romans much later, he proudly calls himself "an apostle, set apart [*aphōrismenos*] for the gospel" (Rom. 1:1). The text of Acts seems to make the same connection between apostleship and the Holy Spirit's command *aphorisate*, since Paul and Barnabas, subsequent to this ceremony, in Acts 14:4, 14, are strikingly described no longer as prophets and teachers but as "apostles." This is unlikely to be a slip of the pen, particularly in view of Luke's general reservation of this controverted title to the Twelve (Luke 6:12).

Given the mention of the "prophets" and "teachers" in Antioch in Acts 13:1, it is noteworthy that Paul ranks "apostles" in first place above these two in 1 Corinthians 12:28 (cf. Eph. 4:11), while in *Didache* 11.3–12 "apostle" is clearly a title describing wandering preachers who are evidently identical with itinerant "prophets." It is not unreasonable to hold, particularly given the likely Syrian and indeed Antiochene origin of the *Didache*, that Luke's shift in Acts 14 reflects this same, somewhat blurry regional usage. If so, it becomes immediately suggestive that in *Didache* 13.3 a tithe of firstfruits is stipulated for just such wandering preachers, who, on the typological model of the Old Covenant, are explicitly called "your high priests." These itinerant figures have an explicit cultic function, for they are invited to preside at the Eucharist. In any event, a number of scholars have rightly recognized in the early offices of "apostle" and "prophet" similar forms of translocal ministry, not tied down to a specific local church, as was the more grounded ministry of the *episkopoi/presbyteroi* and the teachers, who seemingly performed a key role as catechists and apologists. (The office of "teacher" in its original configuration is still visible, in its most mature early Christian form, in the great catechetical school of Alexandria. Clement and Origen ultimately pushed this primitive arrangement to its limit and opened the way for the charismatic "office" of the universal doctors of the Church.) Saul and Barnabas, prior to the moment of their new election, perfectly fit the profile of the teacher. Thus we find Saul debating and confounding nonbelieving Jews in the synagogues of Antioch after his conversion (Acts 9:20–22), while together the two men

---

7. By contrast, the comment of Joseph Fitzmyer is helpful: "The attempt to describe the laying on of hands solely as a blessing and not an ordination is meaningless. . . . The notion of office is not so developed in Lucan writings as it becomes in the Pastoral Epistles, but one should not deprive the action of its proper meaning" (Fitzmyer, *The Acts of the Apostles*, AB 31 [New York: Doubleday, 1997], 497).

are clearly devoted to the instruction of the community. "For an entire year they [i.e., Barnabas and Saul] met with the church and *taught* [*didaxai*] a great many people" (Acts 11:26). Given their new translocal apostolic field of action, the bon voyage of Barnabas and Saul is thus a sort of ecclesial farewell—but in the stronger sense of the Antiochian church handing these men over to a more universal mission and calling.

In specifically naming and accrediting Barnabas and Paul as *apostoloi*, Luke arguably means to recognize these two men as official—that is, authoritative— apostles, truly and legitimately commissioned, peers in some way to those originally called and sent out by Jesus and bearers of the same legitimacy, yet without thereby being members of the college of the Twelve. In this light, the famous two waves of disciples "sent out" in Luke's Gospel might very well presage Luke's interest in Acts to validate two successive modes of apostleship in the primitive Church: that of the original Twelve and that witnessed with Barnabas and Paul. The patterning of Jesus' sending out of the Seventy in Luke 10:1 on Moses' choice of the seventy *elders* who share the divine Spirit (Num. 11:24–25) introduces another Old Testament typological frame for understanding the ministerial organization of the primitive Church. The ancient prayer preserved in *Apostolic Tradition* 7 already appeals to this event of Moses' choice of elders in connection with the consecration of presbyters during the laying on of hands.[8]

The charismatic scene in Acts 13:1–3, with the "inspired designation" (as Everett Ferguson calls it) of those to be consecrated, a designation by the Holy Spirit surely vocalized through one or more of Antioch's prophets, puts vivid flesh on another relevant hand-laying text, closely connected to Paul's ecclesial circles. "Do not neglect the gift that is in you, which was given to you through prophecy with the laying on of hands [*epitheseōs tōn cheirōn*] by the council of elders [*tou presbyteriou*]" (1 Tim. 4:14). In this remark, several things otherwise hidden come into focus. First, the *charismatos*, the supernatural "gift" infused by the imposition of hands, is finally made quite explicit. The same gift is mentioned again in 2 Timothy 1:6–7, with still more attention to the God-given grace: "For this reason I remind you to rekindle the gift of God that is within you through the laying on of my hands; for God did not give us a spirit of cowardice, but rather a spirit of power and of love and of self-discipline." This is the most explicit textual evidence for what we would call the grace of the sacrament. Power (*dynamis*) is conferred upon the ordained to accomplish new things beyond his proper strength; love (*agapē*), to move by

---

8. "Impart the spirit of grace and of counsel of the presbyterate that he may help and govern your people with a pure heart, just as you looked upon your choice and commanded Moses that he should choose presbyters whom you filled with your Spirit that you gave your servant" (Bradshaw, Johnson, and Phillips, *Apostolic Tradition*, 56).

the sanctifying agency of the Holy Spirit; and self-discipline (*sophronismos*), to live uprightly according to the moral virtues.

A second aspect of the charismatic ceremony seen in Acts 13 that comes into focus in 1 and 2 Timothy is the revelation of who actually does the laying on of hands—namely, the council of presbyters. In Acts, one might often get the impression that the Church moves pneumatically, with no human instrumentality whatsoever. To the presbyters gathered in Miletus, for instance, Paul says, "Keep watch over yourselves and over all the flock, of which the Holy Spirit has made you overseers [*episkopous*], to shepherd the church of God" (Acts 20:28). The Holy Spirit is here the *episkopos/presbyteros*-maker. For Luke, Paul's point is an ecclesiological lesson, not a matter of ritual mechanics, of course. What the Church leaders do, the Spirit does, for they are moved by the Spirit. The fusion of office and charism are here on particularly impressive display (see excursus 10).

Naturally, certain authors refuse to see an ordination of Timothy envisioned in these two passages in 1 and 2 Timothy, which most, nevertheless, rightly take to refer to the same event. It is true that no title is specifically attached to either Timothy or Titus in the Pastoral Epistles. It is vain to pretend that the offices of bishops and deacons were unknown, however, even from the first generation (1 Tim. 3:1–12; Titus 1:7; cf. Phil. 1:1; *1 Clem.* 42.4–5). In 1 Timothy 5:22, Timothy is urged, "Do not ordain [*cheiras . . . epitithei*] anyone hastily," and, as in the later Church Orders, the Pastoral Epistles show themselves rather preoccupied with the qualities of candidates for office. The hortatory character of 1 Timothy 4:11–16, including its emphasis on teaching, fits squarely within these codes of Church officials' behavior, and it is natural to see Timothy as holding such a position. His power to lay hands on worthy candidates, moreover, puts him implicitly in the company of a presbyteral college ("council of elders"). The broad equation of *episkopos* and *presbyteros* as synonyms in the early Christian context has already been mentioned (see excursus 8).

In Acts 14:23, Paul and Barnabas, like a wandering, two-man council of elders, repeat the ritual of fasting and prayer as they "appoint elders" for every place where their preaching wins new believers. The phrase used here, *cheirotonēsantes presbyterous*, means simply "choosing" or else "appointing/installing presbyters," but etymologically it suggests doing so by the imposition of hands. With the fasting and praying of Acts 13:3 still in mind, the suggestion is all the stronger. The image of these itinerants leaving behind an institutional wake is powerful and poignant: the Holy Spirit blowing where it wills, through the lives of two men handing on what they themselves have received through the Church.

The delicate balance between choosing candidates on the basis of their qualities of upright moral character, on the one hand, and working charismatically by "inspired designation," on the other hand, is not a sign of the primitive Church's petrification into a degenerate "early Catholicism." To the contrary, it is the signal of what exactly is new in the New Testament. A concluding section of chapter 7 ("Charism and Office") will take up this theme directly. It is adequate here to note that the sacramental ritual as it is observed in the Scriptures in the laying on of hands is fittingly keyed to a double ecclesial-pneumatological movement. The Church acts with her own human powers, and the Spirit acts simultaneously with mysterious freedom.

EXCURSUS 10

Priests in the Letter
to the Hebrews

The Letter to the Hebrews contains what is obviously the most concentrated and complete theology of the priesthood in the Christian Bible. The letter's rich theological vision, itself a sort of canonical reading from within the canon, has already informed the orientation of this project in multiple ways. Although the main lines of the letter's vision are well known—Jesus' high priesthood "according to the order of Melchizedek" appears as a replacement for and improvement upon the old Levitical priesthood of Aaron—what is rarely considered in exposing the letter's doctrine is the way a ministerial priesthood on earth interacts with this priesthood of Christ in heaven. An important start to this wider understanding of Christ's sacerdotal service was offered in the preceding chapter, where we explored the way an angelic-yet-bloody cult belongs to the unique perspective of Hebrews. There are resources here that not only bind together heaven and earth but also bridge the sermonic and epistolary halves of the letter.

The concluding portion of Hebrews, particularly the hortatory end of chapter 13, is one of the most intriguing parts of the text.[1] It is in this chap-

---

1. The Pauline authorship of Hebrews has been questioned since ancient times—and not without some good reasons. The author never names himself, as Paul was accustomed to do, to mention only the most obvious problem. Still, Paul's authorship was also widely accepted since ancient times—as the majority tradition, in fact—again not without good reasons. Nowhere does the text have a more characteristically Pauline ring than in chap. 13, where the composition transitions from homiletic treatise to genuine missive. The most emphatically Pauline, final section, 13:(19)22–25, is today often taken to be a later addition, though many scholars

ter, with a tone vaguely reminiscent of the Pastoral Epistles, that we find the clearest hint of a sacramental share in that unique priesthood of Christ, which is so elaborately explored in the body of the letter.

> Remember your leaders, those who spoke the word of God to you; consider the outcome of their way of life, and imitate their faith. Jesus Christ is the same yesterday and today and forever. Do not be carried away by all kinds of strange teachings; for it is well for the heart to be strengthened by grace, not by regulations about food, which have not benefited those who observe them. We have an altar from which those who officiate in the tent have no right to eat. For the bodies of those animals whose blood is brought into the sanctuary by the high priest as a sacrifice for sin are burned outside the camp. Therefore Jesus also suffered outside the city gate in order to sanctify the people by his own blood. Let us then go to him outside the camp and bear the abuse he endured. For here we have no lasting city, but we are looking for the city that is to come. Through him, then, let us continually offer a sacrifice of praise to God, that is, the fruit of lips that confess his name. Do not neglect to do good and to share what you have, for such sacrifices are pleasing to God.
>
> Obey your leaders and submit to them, for they are keeping watch over your souls and will give an account. Let them do this with joy and not with sighing—for that would be harmful to you. (Heb. 13:7–17)

A double reference to "your leaders," uniting in one office those past and present, here surrounds a compact parenetic reflection with clear thematic contacts to the letter's main argument. The language of "leaders" is quite generic, but a clear expression of sober, structured authority in the community (cf. Luke 22:26). We are not facing an amorphous, radically egalitarian, or ecstatically charismatic group. The term "leader," interestingly, appears to have had a particular hold in the context of the primitive Roman church. In *1 Clement*, a (Roman) text with many strong connections to Hebrews, we seem to find "leaders" (*hēgoumenoi*) identified more precisely as *presbyteroi* (*1 Clem.* 1.3). It is thus not reckless to imagine a similar association/identification in Hebrews, especially given the likely Roman origin of the letter. The plausibility of a shared perspective is all the more compelling given the accent on obedience to the leaders in Hebrews 13:17, which finds a strong echo in the "rule of obedience" evoked in *1 Clement* 1.3. Briefly, *hēgoumenoi* appears to be an original, regional term for those exercising pastoral government in the Church, stressing specifically their possession of directive authority and the aspect of hierarchical order.

---

also accept the whole of the chapter as an integral and original part of the composition. See, e.g., A. J. M. Wedderburn, "The 'Letter' to the Hebrews and Its Thirteenth Chapter," *NTS* 50 (2004): 390–405; and Gert J. Steyn, "The Ending of Hebrews Reconsidered," *ZNW* 103 (2012): 235–53.

Church authority is never *authoritarian*, of course, as Jesus himself made quite clear (Mark 10:42). The description of the *hēgoumenoi* supplies an important description of the leaders' exercise of service. From Hebrews 13:7 it is clear that a defining behavior and duty of Church leaders is the proclamation of the "word of God": a ministry that can be imagined to include both initial evangelization and continued catechetical instruction. The warning about false teaching in 13:9 exposes the strong doctrinal content and character of this message, a content measured by an immutable christological rule of faith. Jesus himself, in fact, appears in the prologue as God's definitive act of speech to the human race. In chapter 2, he is presented again as the *initial* initial evangelizer: salvation was "declared at first through the Lord, and it was attested to us by those who heard him" (2:3). Proclamation of the word accordingly resounds through a living chain of witnesses, intimately conformed to what God has spoken once and for all in these last days through his Son. "Witness" is indeed the right word for this kerygmatic conformity to the revelation of Jesus, for the appeal to remember how the leaders' lives ended is widely recognized as an allusion to their *martyrdom*.

The exhortation in this context to "imitate their [the leaders'] faith," which recalls and recasts Paul's characteristic mimesis motif—"Be imitators of me, as I am of Christ" (1 Cor. 11:1)—is an expression of particular significance. This appeal to faith conjures up a major motif in the body of Hebrews. Not only does it hinge the leaders to the cloud of witnesses celebrated in Hebrews 11, coupling a contemporary example with the "many and various ways" (Heb. 1:1) that God worked in the past, but it also binds the leaders to Jesus himself, who is identified specifically as the "faithful high priest" (*pistos archiereus*, Heb. 2:17): a direct allusion to his fulfillment of the prophecy of the raising up of a "faithful priest" in 1 Samuel 2:35. To hammer home the point, in Hebrews 3:2–6, on the model of Moses, Christ repeatedly is called faithful (*pistos*) over God's house as Son. As a priestly trait, the leaders' own "faithfulness" reveals their explicitly *iconic* character as heads of the Church. The *hēgoumenoi* somehow manifest in their lives and in their deaths the defining character of Christ's eschatological priesthood. Through their own demonstration that they are "faithful in all God's house" (Heb. 3:2), they make the "merciful and faithful high priest" visible and effective "today" (like yesterday and forever) in the life of the contemporary community.

The faithful leaders are enjoined to keep a wakeful vigil over the souls of the believers and must render an account (Heb. 13:17). This is the duty that corresponds to the obedience they are due by virtue of their rank. The language of keeping unsleeping watch fits, though it does not strictly require, pastoral imagery. The similarity of the sentiment to 1 Peter 2:25, however, and to the "shepherd and *episkopos* of your souls"—notably this extraordinary notion of responsibility for souls (not a banal expression in the New Testament), a responsibility that in Hebrews, in contrast to 1 Peter, is strikingly extended from Christ himself to Church leaders—positions these same leaders once again in the place of the unique high priest, who is called, indeed, the "great shepherd of the sheep" (Heb. 13:20). To speak of Jesus as the "great shepherd" (*poimēn megas*; see excursus 8) in the final, solemn, doxological valediction of the Epistle to the Hebrews cannot help but recall his status as "great high priest" (*archiereus megas*, 4:14) and "great priest" (*hiereus megas*, 10:21). In other words, a parting play on words is at work here that equates Jesus' roles of *pastor* and *priest*. As a theological heuristic for the New Testament ensemble, this provides us a scriptural key of inestimable value.

As commentators note, at the climax of the letter the author speaks of Christ's priestly greatness in a pastoral way, full of rich biblical resonance that creates a final contrast with the figure of Moses, who in Isaiah 63:11 is explicitly called "the shepherd of the sheep." Isaiah's passage is, indeed, a remarkable fit; for God "*raises up* from the sea/earth the shepherd of the sheep" (MT/LXX). This expression is the clincher that many commentators somehow miss. The word for "raise up" is not the same as that in Deuteronomy 18:15, but the meaning is unmistakable and begging to be cleverly exploited as it is here, through the other connections built into the passage. The great shepherd Jesus is raised up like the shepherd Moses; Jesus is thus the "faithful priest" of the prophecy (1 Sam. 2:35). Jesus is raised up in a way much greater than Moses, however, for he is raised from the dead: "the God of peace, who brought back from the dead our Lord Jesus, the great shepherd of the sheep, by the blood of the eternal covenant" (Heb. 13:20).

Hebrews' allusion to Jesus' *resurrection/exaltation* as the fulfillment of Deuteronomy 18:15 and 1 Samuel 2:35 harmonizes perfectly with the letter's notion of Christ's heavenly priesthood. A cosmic elevation is taken to be the deep, prophetic meaning of the "raising up" of the faithful priest. "It was fitting that we should have such a high priest, holy, blameless, undefiled, separated from sinners, and exalted above the heavens" (Heb. 7:26). This perception of Christ's resurrection as a celestial journey and the special form of his eschatological priesthood presents a dense and forceful parallel to what we have seen in the *Testament of Levi*, yet with a remarkable reformulation and New Covenant paschal vision.

Hebrews' interest in Jesus' resurrected body conforms perfectly to what we already noted in chapter 5 about the physical metamorphosis that the Judaism of the period saw as necessary for a human to enter into the heavenly temple. In the case of Jesus' merciful priesthood in Hebrews, however, since it entails the Son's preexistence, there is both a descending and an ascending

movement: both kenosis and exaltation. James Swetnam has nicely expressed
Hebrews' rounded perspective.

> It is the transformation of the body which is crucial: just as Jesus needed a
> body of blood and flesh to overcome death by means of death (2, 14), so he
> needs a body which has overcome death to be forever available to those who
> need his intercession (7, 24–25). . . . At the resurrection Jesus was given a body
> commensurate with his high priestly need of immortality.[2]

Reading the text in this light, Swetnam keenly perceives that the "greater
and perfect tent" not made with hands in Hebrews 9:11 (a text that stands
structurally at the very heart of Hebrews) is, in fact, nothing else than Jesus'
own body. Both John and Paul also know this manner of speaking. Instead
of evoking the high priestly vestments to indicate Jesus' rank, as did the
Synoptic Gospels, Hebrews has fused together priest and temple—an easy
step for a scriptural thinker since the wilderness tabernacle was made of the
same materials as the priestly vestments (see chap. 1 above). Jesus himself is
now the living embodiment of divine $k\bar{a}b\hat{o}d$: his full humanity is the sacred
vestment and the holy dwelling place of YHWH.

The exegetical payoff of this identification is significant. Jesus' glorified
body is itself identified with the sanctuary that believers are exhorted to "approach" with confidence. It is, more precisely, an embodied cosmic threshold
uniting the separated realms of heaven and earth. The temple veil of Jesus'
flesh is, henceforth, "the new and living way" opened up into the holy of
holies of God's presence (cf. John 2:21; 10:9; 14:6).[3]

> Therefore, my friends, since we have confidence to enter the sanctuary by the
> blood of Jesus, by the new and living way that he opened for us through the
> curtain (that is, through his flesh), and since we have a great priest over the house
> of God, let us approach with a true heart in full assurance of faith, with our
> hearts sprinkled clean from an evil conscience and our bodies washed with
> pure water. (Heb. 10:19–22)

The motif of "approaching" derives from the cultic sphere, and it is plain
that, with this hortatory language, Hebrews has the Christian community's
own ritual life in view. The sacramental allusion to baptism in the washing
with pure water is uncontested. The dispute concerns the reference to the

2. James Swetnam, "Christology and Eucharist in the Epistle to the Hebrews," *Biblica* 70
(1989): 78, 79.
3. "What all this complicated imagery adds up to seems to be this: that for the addressees
the glorified body of Christ which they come into contact with as the eucharistic body is the
concrete means given to them by Christ the new high priest of entering the Holy of Holies, i.e.,
God's presence" (Swetnam, "Christology and the Eucharist," 82–84).

"sprinkling," which must be read in connection with the "sprinkled blood" in Hebrews 12:24 that speaks more eloquently than the blood of Abel. Unless everything we know about the ritual practice of the early Church is ignored, this allusion points us straight to the eucharistic cult. It passes by way of Moses' sprinkled "blood of the covenant" directly to the blood of the New Covenant announced by Jeremiah and invoked at Jesus' Last Supper (Exod. 24:5–8; Matt. 26:28). If Hebrews celebrates Christ the high priest as the mediator of the New Covenant (cf. Heb. 8:8–13; 9:15), like a new Moses, then the Eucharist is the place where Jesus reveals himself most clearly as such.

Protestant scholarship is disinclined to see this, acknowledging alone the baptismal allusion in Hebrews 10:22. From within this truncated ritual framework, Protestant scholarship is thus equally liable to see in Hebrews' "living way" to the holy of holies an absolute abrogation of the Old Testament priesthood and an extension of ungraded priestly rank to all individual baptized believers.[4] This is a very common but also a very bold reading. It is so bold, in fact, that it risks cutting off the interpretative branch on which it sits (not that a common priesthood is not a real New Testament teaching, of course). The view that for God's people the whole priestly system has somehow been abolished without remainder makes Hebrews' intensely priestly perspective quite a curious proposition. Rather than *purifying* the cult with its ministering priests, as foretold by the prophets, Jesus' sacrificial priesthood would simply put it all to an irremediable end. No cult of Jesus' body and blood would remain for the Church.

There is, naturally, textual support for this extreme position. In Hebrews 10:9, for instance, a strong Greek verb is used to express the disjunctive relation between the two contrasting covenant dispensations, nearly the opposite of Jesus' expression of continuity in Matthew 5:17. "He abolishes [*anairei*] the first in order to establish the second" (Heb. 10:9). The formulation is sharp, yet more than a few problematic assumptions shared with the antagonism hypothesis jeopardize a correct understanding of Hebrews' vision here. The risk of asserting an exaggerated supersessionism and a Church bereft of every form of sacrificial cult is accordingly quite real.

Through the evocation of the motif of *logikē latreia* in Hebrews 13:15–16, we see clearly that the work of Christian worship encompasses the entire life of all believers. The community's cult of spiritual worship takes a double form: a "sacrifice of praise" (the cult of the word, in hymnic confession) and the "pleasing" sacrifice of sharing one's goods (the cult of deeds of love). Does

---

4. For a formulation of these characteristically Protestant perspectives, see, e.g., Peter Leithart, "Womb of the World: Baptism and the Priesthood of the New Covenant in Hebrews 10:19–22," *JSNT* 78 (2000): 49–65.

this mean that from now on all sacrifice in the Church takes a purely ethical form? It is not clear why this should be the case if we think, for instance, of an example like Ben Sira, who also likens almsgiving to priestly offerings, which he nevertheless has no interest whatsoever in abrogating. That good deeds are somehow opposed to the Christians' ritual liturgical assembly seems to be a bad idea already openly rejected by Hebrews: "Let us consider how to provoke one another to love and good deeds, not neglecting to meet together, as is the habit of some" (Heb. 10:24–25).

As for Christ's own form of sacrificial service, it is far from being a simple ethical disposition. In this line, an important point of decision appears in the citation of Psalm 40:6–8 in Hebrews 10:5–7, which describes Jesus' offering and has often been read as a prophetic-style rejection of exterior cultic action in favor of interior obedience. In fact, this text is invoked in the letter as scriptural warrant for a new, eschatological form of sacrifice based in Jesus' *body*—corresponding, on the one hand, to the Levitical offerings and, on the other, to the new forms of covenant, priesthood, and sanctuary that the letter also finds foretold through scriptural texts.[5] Jesus' obedient body (*sōma*) is hence what he specifically offers as chief minister of the Church's reformed sacrificial life; it corresponds to the "gifts and sacrifices" that ever go with the business of being a priest and are thus "necessary for this priest also" (Heb. 8:3; cf. 5:1; 9:9).[6] Hebrews' contrast between this *sōma* offering of God's obedient Son and the Levitical sacrifices and holocausts offered up for sins never hints that the Levitical ceremonies were somehow erected to be an *obstacle* to communion with God—a barrier that had to be torn down and overcome. Rather, Hebrews embraces the narrative tension of claiming that God indeed commanded the Levitical system of sacrifice, yet he did not take pleasure in it—because, as we saw earlier in chapter 2, the law was added on account of Israel's sin.[7] The old Day of Atonement was never simply "plan A" as God had always desired it. *Sin,*

5. See Benjamin J. Ribbens, "The Sacrifice God Desired: Psalm 40:6–8 in Hebrews 10," *NTS* 67 (2021): 284–304 (here 289–90):

For the author, Ps 95.7–8 speaks of another rest (4.1–11), Ps 110.4 speaks of an eternal priesthood in the order of Melchizedek (5.5–6; 7.15–17), Jer 31.31–4 speaks of a new covenant (8.8–12; 10.16–17) and Exod 25.40 speaks of a heavenly sanctuary. Another rest, another priesthood, another covenant, another sanctuary. What is often left off these lists is Psalm 40 and another sacrifice. . . . Psalm 40 compares two kinds of cultic, bodily/bloody sacrifices. Yet, to affirm the cultic nature of Christ's offering, we have to address a number of competing claims. For instance, some see in Hebrews an extension and expansion of the cult criticism present in the Psalms and Prophets that pits sacrifice against acts of piety and obedience. Psalm 40 is often identified as one of the texts that affirm such a distinction, so that when the author of Hebrews uses Psalm 40, he is drawing a contrast between sacrifices of animals and sacrifices of obedience, between the bloody Levitical sacrifices and the obedience of Christ.

6. See Ribbens, "The Sacrifice God Desired," 291.

7. See Ribbens, "The Sacrifice God Desired," 290–95.

not priestly sacrifice, was what kept the people at a distance. Indeed, priestly service was precisely God's manner of showing his continued, awesome presence in his people's midst—in spite of their sins. This manifestation of glory continues and finds a new kind of perfection through the ensouled sacrifice of Jesus' sacred body and blood.

Ultimately for Hebrews, the relation established between the Old and the New is clear. It is between, on the one side, the prefiguration, "shadow," "sketch," or even "blueprint" (*hypodeigma*) and, on the other, the reality of the "true form" (*eikōn*). An exaggerated supersessionism, built on an excessively stark law and gospel opposition, ignores this concept of proportion. It also misapprehends the rhetorical character of the Greco-Roman *synkrisis* adopted by Hebrews, which makes a comparison between two laudable things (i.e., a double encomium) rather than a contrast between a good and an evil instance.[8] The conceptualization of Jesus' self-offering as a perfection of Yom Kippur prolongs and reconfigures something central of the priestly character of the Old Covenant's Levitical framework, while intoning the "better" order of things that Jesus has now established. Such an inner linkage of Old and New is so strong, in fact, that, in the estimation of a recent (Protestant) dissertation, we must recognize "an understanding of the levitical sacrifices in Hebrews as sacramental, Christological types."

> The levitical sacrifices are external rituals that themselves had no atoning efficacy. Yet, God promised that these external rituals would effect atonement and forgiveness, and they were able to be efficacious based on the sacrifice of Christ that would come later. His sacrifice would achieve atonement and forgiveness once-for-all-time, not only for the sins that would come after it but also for those that had preceded it. The levitical sacrifices, therefore, were external rituals sacramentally linked to the efficacy of Christ's sacrifice, and that efficacy was proleptically applied to the levitical sacrifices.[9]

Jesus is the great high priest of a single vast cult arching across the whole of salvation history and fusing law and gospel into one eternal dispensation of salvation.

In light of this asymmetrical yet profound unity of Old and New, and within Hebrews' shadow-reality system of correspondence, is it not right to expect to find some sacramental continuation of that Levitical "garland of brothers" that surrounds the high priest (Sir. 50:12)? Is it not a strange

---

8. On this positive mode and comprehensive project of comparison in Hebrews, see Michael Martin and Jason Whitlark, "The Encomiastic Topics of Syncrisis as the Key to the Structure and Argument of Hebrews," NTS 57 (2011): 415–39.

9. Benjamin J. Ribbens, *Levitical Sacrifice and Heavenly Cult in Hebrews*, BZNW 222 (Berlin: de Gruyter, 2016), 236.

suggestion that something as monumental and essential to the constitution of
Israel, so expressive of its unique holiness and election, as its whole immense
priestly ministry might be indeed recognized as a prophetic "blueprint" yet
vanish in the New Covenant without a trace: a *hypodeigma* without an *eikōn*?[10]
A sacrament of sacrificial priesthood is, indeed, a most central expression of
the bipartite but unified christological character of God's plan of salvation.

Priesthood according to the order of Melchizedek is not the only operative model of priesthood in Hebrews.[11] The figure of the faithful priest and
the Mosaic/Levitical order also shape the description of Jesus' priesthood
in countless powerful ways. Like Moses, Jesus is the priestly mediator who
stands above the priestly regime and who institutes a comprehensive covenantal system. In this light one might discern more clearly a *transfiguration*
of Israel's whole temple-*cum*-priesthood, not its simple collapse and rejection.
"We have an altar from which those who officiate in the tent have no right to
eat" (Heb. 13:10). The eucharistic food and the grace of this altar point to
Hebrews' hearers' embodied sacramental life, a lived ecclesial setting without
which an understanding of Christ's living high priesthood will always be
falsely perceived. Protestant readers may perhaps deny that the sacrifice of
Christ, our faithful high priest in heaven, is conjoined to the Church's altar
on earth, an altar tended faithfully by the leaders of the Christian assembly,
his icons—though Protestant scholars may, ironically, be perfectly open to
the retrojected, efficacious conjunction of Jesus' sacrifice with the sacramental rituals of the Old Law. But Catholic readers may then, in their turn, be
equally unconvinced by claims that Hebrews knows nothing whatsoever of
the Church's ritual life surrounding Jesus' body and blood. Catholics will be
still less convinced that, as many Protestants think, Hebrews actually also goes
a step further, rejecting this cult and the ecclesial knowledge of a mysterious
but perfectly incarnate and real priestly axis binding the twinned liturgies of
heaven and earth.

10. Hebrews' open interest to see the Church through the lens of Israel as the "people of
God" supports this idea of an isomorphism of old and new priestly ministry. For an effort to
sort through Hebrews' complex construction of Israel and the New Covenant people of God,
see Ole Jakub Filtvedt, *The Identity of God's People and the Paradox of Hebrews*, WUNT
2/400 (Tübingen: Mohr Siebeck, 2015).
11. On the multiple priestly models in Hebrews, see Michael Tait, *Too Many Priests? Melchizedek and the Others in Hebrews*, Scripturae 5 (Rome: Giacobbe, 2016).

7

Conclusion

Jesus as Charismatic Founder of a Hierarchical Church

In the preceding chapters and related excursuses I have attempted to present one possible—I think responsible and perhaps even compelling, however hasty and incomplete—biblical theology of the Catholic priesthood. The contours of the exposition have, I hope, diligently traced out an authentically scriptural course. The classical questions of sacramental theology—matter, form, minister, recipient, effects, and so on—although accepted for what they are, have been consciously set aside in an effort to permit the Scriptures to speak with optimal and integral clarity: as a unified chorus of individual canonical voices. As a concrete case study, the theme of priesthood, with its particularly acute problem of rightly relating the Old and the New, has provided good testing ground for an exegetical approach of wide-reaching theological interest. While the hermeneutical presuppositions guiding this broad experiment will not be universally shared, and while many questions still remain not only unanswered but even unasked, there is material here, I am convinced, to ground a solid reflection. No foolish ambition of providing a complete scriptural statement should be imputed to this necessarily narrow and selective sketch. Still, for those inclined to erect superstructures of systematic thought, building on these pages will, I think, not be building on sand.

Confronting the Crisis of Sin

As said at the outset, this book is animated largely as a response to what Benedict XVI called "the lasting crisis that the priesthood has been going through for many years."[1] The centrality of sin to the biblical data has become quite evident: from Aaron's sons in the wilderness to Peter in Caiaphas's courtyard, with the prophets fomenting and forecasting in between. This frank biblical facing of the fact of human failing allows a frontal approach to the issue that has led us directly to the answer of Jesus: indeed, Jesus himself as the answer. He is the solution promised by the prophets: the eschatological priest and purification and atoning sacrifice, through which all God's people, not only the priests, are made mystically spotless and clean. The Church's co-offering of this sacrifice, through the hands of her priests, has as its ultimate end a manifestation and mediation of the Lord's own glorious indwelling among his elect.

If this appears too much like a Sunday school kind of solution to a real and serious problem, and if I have given no ink to the issues that make all the headlines, notably women's ordination and priestly celibacy, it is not because there is no scriptural material to handle, and certainly not because there is nothing necessary or helpful to say. Even so, as biblical problems, these issues threaten to distort our exposition of the scriptural vision of the priesthood, which is preoccupied with other concerns. Frankly, a bit more Sunday school would probably do a great deal to address much internal dissatisfaction on these two fronts. To avoid the appearance of academic aloofness or pastoral negligence, however, a few brief points of orientation for confronting these issues can now be offered.

Ordination of Women

Contemporary agitation and advocacy, particularly for women's ordination, will obviously struggle to anchor various anachronistic commitments in a genuinely historical exegesis of the Bible, and thus in a biblical vision in full harmony with *Dei Verbum* 12. Whether we wish it or not, Scripture challenges and invites us to enter into a profoundly hieratic and patriarchal world. While this sits uneasily with many modern assumptions, it is also well worth observing that calls for the ordination of women are not a purely modern phenomenon. There is historical precedent among Gnostic groups in late antiquity.

This specific Gnostic context is itself highly revealing, for it indicates a theological universe having certain biblical contours, though of a most tenuous sort, planted in an alternative socio-ecclesial setting that stands in tension with the authoritative apostolic tradition. This apostolic tradition, rather early on, directly addressed and rejected the possibility of women priests in the

1. Benedict XVI and Robert Cardinal Sarah, *From the Depths of Our Hearts: Priesthood, Celibacy, and the Crisis of the Catholic Church* (San Francisco: Ignatius, 2019), 25.

Church.[2] It should be noted that an *explicit* negative judgment on the part of Tradition is different than an *ex silentio* situation and is thus apt material for the *positive* application of the Vincentian Canon as described in chapter 1.[3] At some level, the decision to accept or refuse this consistent judgment of Tradition is thus to take a simple stance for or against the Church's claim to exercise and bear apostolic authority. In any event, as its early viability in the Gnostic environment indicates, the question of ordaining women represents an ecclesiological question that touches the very roots of the Church's most basic claims and is of much broader import than speculation about any isolated sacramental discipline or practice.

If mainline Protestants have in recent years found the path wide open to the ordination of women, this only underscores the point being made. For, while the Protestant situation is entirely distinct from any ancient Gnostic setting, the character of ordained ministry in these Protestant communions is, nevertheless, inextricably bound up with a whole range of Reformation-era decisions and perspectives, including an open rejection of Tradition and a conscious option for different forms of communal government—all having profound consequences for the handling of the question. Ultimately, a theology of the priesthood and a complete, lived theology of the Church cannot be so easily disentangled, even for the artificial purposes of academic debate.

Where comprehensive attention to context is of such capital importance, the dangers of proof-texting are, naturally, unusually high. It is indeed noteworthy that the focal point in the discussions and arguments in favor of changing the Church's ancient practice has been the Pauline doctrine of a "new creation," and in a special way the text of Galatians 3:28 (themes also of special interest to the Gnostics). "There is no longer Jew or Greek, there is no longer slave or free, there is no longer male and female; for all of you are one in Christ." While in its historical and literary context this verse has nothing to do with priestly ordination, the principle Paul enunciates is indeed of great importance. At the same time, however, it is vital to measure well this fragment of Pauline thought, which is polemically stated and thus rhetorically

---

2. The *Apostolic Church Order*, a pre-Constantinian Egyptian document, dated around AD 300, reflects this situation: "When the Master prayed over the bread and the cup and blessed them saying: This is my Body and Blood, he did not allow women to stand with us." For the citation and information about the text edition and translation, see Aidan Nichols, *Holy Order: Apostolic Priesthood from the New Testament to the Second Vatican Council* (Eugene, OR: Wipf & Stock, 1990), 144.

3. "If ever there was a practice that contravened the Vincentian canon, it is certainly the ordination of women to the priesthood" (Kallistos Ware, "Man, Woman and the Priesthood of Christ," in *Women and the Priesthood*, ed. T. Hopko [Crestwood, NY: St. Vladimir's Seminary Press, 1983], 9–38 [here 12]).

extreme. One must ultimately integrate into an adequately expansive synthesis of broad scriptural teaching the entire motif of "freedom in Christ."

The impossible tension sensed by some between Galatians 3:28 and a very direct comment like 1 Timothy 2:12—"I permit no woman to teach or have authority over a man"—as well as Paul's statement in 1 Corinthians 14:34 and the obscure argumentation in 1 Corinthians 11:2–16, is only the beginning of the challenge to find the right canonical and theological balance.[4] Careful attention to the wider and controlling anthropological paradigm in which these biblical statements are made must also be cultivated. That a biblically based doctrine of the Church will quickly yield a gendered ecclesiology with very deep Old Testament roots—Christ as head and spouse, the Church as his bride—will not make it easier, or desirable, to erase all gender distinctions in the symbolically charged and socially grounded shape of ecclesial life. For the "household of God" is inevitably a case of grace building on nature.[5] The sacrament of marriage as an emblem of Paul's great ecclesial *mystērion* (Eph. 5) will thus quickly be pulled into this discussion—as is proven through the mainline Protestant context, where the traditional spousal/christological icon no longer meaningfully functions in a theological praxis that now admits both women and those in active same-sex unions to ordained ministry.[6]

At stake, of course, in a fundamental way, is the existence of hierarchical structures in Christ's mystical body and a cleansing of "patriarchal" abuses in the pejorative sense of that word. The dangerous proximity of the priestly establishment (and of the entire Church) to congenital sources of sin, including manifold forms of abuse of power, obviously not excluding multiple forms of misogyny, should by this point be quite apparent. It is precisely into this situation of sin, however, that Christ enters to *re-create* a priestly apparatus of grace, grounded upon and animated by the immaculate holiness of his

4. A basic issue concerning 1 Tim. 2:12 is determining how context-specific this statement is. Is it presented as Paul's own personal disciplinary opinion, as in 1 Cor. 7? Is it confined to this particular local church (Ephesus?), where women appear especially implicated in the propagation of some sort of (proto-Gnostic?) heresy? And so forth. Of course, even if the statement is circumscribed in a considerable way by various circumstances and qualifications, it remains quite a forceful expression and an early appeal to apostolic authority in the prudential handling of a very relevant question.

5. It is important not to entertain false impressions about how ancient "patriarchy" actually worked, for it was not uniformly oppressive. For a useful exploration of the household context of early Christianity and the sometimes surprising ways women functioned as leaders in this social world, see Carolyn Osiek and Margaret Y. MacDonald, eds., *A Woman's Place: House Churches in Earliest Christianity* (Minneapolis: Fortress, 2006).

6. Although it is culturally treated as the next logical civil-rights issue, theologically the question of admitting to ordained ministry persons publicly living in a sexual union with a partner of the same sex is obviously a different sort of problem than the ordination of women—a problem directly touching on the relation of the priesthood to the messy problem of human sin. As a disruption of the traditional spousal icon of the priest, there is an important affinity, however.

own celestial priesthood. Dogmatic constructions like the concept *ex opere operato* and a special sacramental character that supernaturally renders one a suitable minister of Christ are ultimately explanations of and not premises for this biblical belief that Christ is the universal high priestly agent. While this remains a truth known and accepted firmly by faith—Christ himself acts directly in and through the priestly ministry of his Church—and while unstinting efforts must be made to conform ordained ministers to this objective holiness (as well as to prune away epiphenomenal dysfunctions—*semper reformanda*), utopian illusions about systemic reform and untainted human exercise of priestly power must be avoided as naïve and unhelpful distractions. The hierarchical constitution of the Church, with its episcopal and "patriarchal" organization (in the positive sense of that word), is instituted by Christ the Son, the revealed face of the Father, and not open to alteration, though it is entrusted on earth to the custody of sinners: sinners in constant need of that same reconciliation with God of which they themselves have been made the ambassadors and stewards (2 Cor. 5:20). Balthasar exposed the traditional ecclesiology undergirding this view in the paradoxical and biblically sourced image of the Church as *casta meretrix*, the chaste whore.

In the end, the mystical action of Christ, the living sacrament of God, in and through his chosen priests implies an *iconic* aspect that is inherent to the embodied logic proper to all the sacraments as such and is in many ways the decisive consideration. For this reason, it is entirely correct when Protestant objectors to the traditional reservation of priestly ordination to males demand not a simple change in practice but a fundamental change in the Church's entire sacramental claim.

> As long as a male priest claims that he re-enacts in a sacramental form the sacrifice of Jesus on the Cross and is thereby identified mystically with the living Christ—the Bridegroom of the Church—any discussion on the ordination of women will remain sterile.[7]

This insightful statement captures with great accuracy and concision exactly what is at stake in the conversation about ordaining women. If the Church first forfeits its belief in the sacramental mediation of Christ in the eucharistic sacrifice, its intense identification of the earthly and heavenly priest, if it forgoes a mystic transparency of the man at the altar to the exalted incarnate bridegroom, the gender of the minister will indeed no longer be such a sensitive topic. Another consequence—and a grave one—of breaking this identification, however, will be a resurfacing of the ancient problem of priestly (and

---

7. Samuel Terrien, *Till the Heart Sings: A Biblical Theology of Manhood and Womanhood* (Philadelphia: Fortress, 1985), quoted in Nichols, *Holy Order*, 152.

indeed human) sin, for Christ's immediate high priestly action through the Church's ministers will be directly called into question. An alternate solution must in this case be found, different from the Church's sacramental partaking in the high priest's sanctifying and sacrificial flesh: an alternate solution like a private form of salvation by faith alone, a salvation for individuals reckoned to be *simul justus et peccator*. It is not a coincidence that, in contrast to the Protestant setting, no "women priests" exist in those same churches (Catholic and Orthodox) that have maintained precisely this strong sacrificial and sacramental understanding of the offering of the ordained priest as being the selfsame offering of Jesus. It is perhaps also no coincidence that precisely in the Gnostic context, an anti-Evangelium like the Coptic *Gospel of Judas* portrays Jesus openly laughing at his apostles' eucharistic theology of sacrifice, rejecting their vision of themselves as twelve priests standing at the altar, making offerings and invoking his (Jesus') name. They remain in their sins, Jesus says—"sleeping with other men, murdering, committing many sins and criminal acts"—for salvation comes not through sacrifice, which leads only to death, but from gaining the hidden gnosis leading them back to the twelve androgynous luminaries. This "enlightened" critique of the apostolic tradition and of the theology of priestly service that characterized the so-called Great Church is bound to a soteriological vision quite incompatible with the gospel that the countered apostolic Church proclaims. For the alternative proto-Manichean, anti-apostle theology, transcending the body as an ultimate aim leads equally to a docetic Christology, an ungendered cosmology, and a rejection of cultic sacrifice. It is a mythopoeic bundle of ideas, but there is a definite coherence to this whole pattern of thought. Without wishing to overstate the point, therefore, or insist on a similarity on every point, we find here an unflattering but helpful heuristic for penetrating to the heterodox heart of the matter.

If at base a major part of the debate about the ordination of women comes down to a judgment about apostolic tradition and the sacrificial interpretation of the Church's cult, the foregoing chapters, while presenting no direct theology of the Eucharist, have hopefully made a useful contribution to the elaboration of a more biblically coherent and well-grounded New Testament doctrine. The result should be a more resolute commitment to the sacrificial and iconic understanding of priestly service as a divinely revealed apostolic teaching.

Priestly Celibacy

Priestly celibacy is a rather different but not unrelated question, particularly as it touches the sexual/spousal and broad ecclesial dimensions of the priesthood.

Apostolic tradition is, likewise, an important point of reference, and thorough studies of this aspect of the problem have been made.[8] The unbroken, primitive tradition not only that Jesus and Paul were themselves unmarried but also that they openly recommended the unmarried state is of enormous authority and significance (Matt. 19:10–12; 1 Cor. 7:7–8). Also of special interest is the very early conviction that the apostles regulated their marriages by refraining from conjugal union and living "as sister and brother" in a state of perpetual continence with their wives.[9] This conviction accords, in fact, with the rule given to Timothy about bishops: "Now a bishop must be above reproach, married only once [*mias gynaikos andra*], temperate, sensible, respectable, hospitable, an apt teacher," and so on (1 Tim. 3:2). The Greek phrase used here and translated as "married only once" is more literally rendered as "the husband of one wife" (cf. 1 Tim. 5:9). The particular force of the phrase is debated, but it very likely corresponds to the expression's frequent appearance as a formula on ancient funerary inscriptions, where it lauds the tender devotion and sexual self-control of widowers who never remarried after the death of their first and only wives. As an indication of a man's capacity for virtuously embracing a state of sustained sexual abstinence, the "one wife man" was thus a particularly apt candidate for episcopal office, ready to observe a practice of prolonged continence.

To this ecclesial dossier, which includes also revealing legislation from various early local councils, it is worth adding a word about the Second Temple Jewish setting, which deserves more attention than it has received in this connection. This pre-Christian material demonstrates the genuine antiquity of a link between priesthood and sexual abstinence and so challenges the misinformed but common perception that the practice of periodic or perpetual clerical celibacy is a late ecclesiastical ideal, ultimately traceable to medieval Gregorian reforms. The historical reality is actually quite different. In his first-century *Life of Moses*, for instance, "Philo incorporates the tradition of Moses' celibacy into the preparatory process Moses undergoes to become high priest and the prophet of God."[10]

In the first place, before assuming that office of priest, it was necessary for him [Moses] to purify not only his soul but also his body, so that it should be connected with and defiled by no passion, but should be pure from everything which is of a mortal nature, from all meat and drink, and from any connection with women. And this last thing, indeed, he had despised for a long time,

8. See, most notably, Christian Cochini, *The Apostolic Origins of Priestly Celibacy* (San Francisco: Ignatius, 1990).

9. Cochini, *Apostolic Origins*, 65–83.

10. Naomi Koltun-Fromm, *Hermeneutics of Holiness: Ancient Jewish and Christian Notions of Sexuality and Religious Community* (Oxford: Oxford University Press, 2010), 177.

and almost from the first moment that he began to prophesy and to feel divine inspiration, thinking that it was proper that he should at all times be ready to give his whole attention to God's commands. (*Mos.* 2.68–69)[11]

The firm linkage between priestly (and prophetic) service and celibacy could not be more explicit. If the ascetic image of Moses that Philo constructs admittedly has little to do with the Pentateuch in its original context, it has everything to do with the world of the New Testament writings. The matrix of these ascetical ideas in a Greco-Roman moral philosophy of the passions does not discount its significance, moreover, though it has become popular to reduce and reject this whole perspective as a form of body-hating Platonism.

Presuppositions about the perennial (or merely time-bound?) philosophy that has so deeply shaped the Catholic Tradition are revealed here as unavoidable and very important, though often neglected, aspects of the celibacy discussion. As with the ordination of women, there is more on the table than just a few Bible verses. No convincing presentation of the Church's position can be made without a clear decision about an anthropological vision and about the holistic good of the human person that, while affirming the essential goodness of sexuality as such, is also less dangerously naïve than many contemporary currents are about the highly disruptive power of human libido and unmoderated sexual expression.

Even if a positive or neutral view can be taken of the anthropology informing the Church's practice historically, it is also important to state that Greek moral philosophy alone lacks what is necessary to generate anything like the living cult of virginity that arose with early Christianity. Indeed, in countless ways, the sexual practices and premises of Greco-Roman society, whatever its elite ideals, presented a direct obstacle to the promotion of widespread Christian celibacy.[12] Even in the Jewish setting, it is difficult to determine what, if any, real-world influence Greek ideals about controlling sexual passions had on embracing the radical option of celibacy. It has been proposed, for instance, that the ancient literary witnesses attesting to a celibate community at Qumran are in fact a fiction and fantasy of Hellenistic writers like Josephus and that no such community actually ever existed.[13] This is an unnecessarily skeptical view, however, that hardly commands a consensus. Most scholars would agree that there was in reality an elite branch of the broader Essene

11. Quoted in Koltun-Fromm, *Hermeneutics of Holiness*, 177.

12. See Christian Laes, "Male Virgins in Latin Inscriptions from Rome," in *Religious Participation in Ancient and Medieval Societies: Rituals, Interaction and Identity*, ed. Sari Katajala-Peltomaa and Ville Vuolanto, Acta Instituti Romani Finlandiae 41 (Rome: Institutum Romanum Finlandiae, 2013), 105–19.

13. See Paul Heger, "Celibacy in Qumran: Hellenistic Fiction or Reality? Qumran's Attitude towards Sex," *RevQ* 26 (2013): 53–90.

movement, a group of celibate members who formally renounced marriage (cf. CD 7:4–8).

What is striking in this decision on the part of a self-consciously priestly Jewish movement, openly critical of the official temple priesthood's pedigree, is the direct threat their practice of celibacy posed to Israel's whole system of pure priestly descent. The group described its members as "the sons of Zadok" yet took no care to raise up heirs from the wellborn priests among them. Is this due simply to an eschatological perspective like Paul's in 1 Corinthians 7:31, that the world as we know it is passing away? Eschatology certainly plays a role, but as with Paul, eschatology alone does not explain all their patterns of behavior.

The many reasons proffered by scholars as explanations for the phenomenon of celibacy at Qumran consistently fail in this regard: they are inevitably equally applicable to both the celibate and the married members of the community.[14] Both groups were considered to be configured to the special purity of the temple, to be participants in the heavenly angelic cult, to be preparing for a holy war, and so on. The whole community was reckoned as being the priestly "sons of Zadok," even while there were also priests in a stricter sense recognized among them—another clear instance of the coexistence of a common and ministerial priesthood. The important lesson to be derived from this is that Jewish celibacy in the New Testament period is a phenomenon that is firmly embedded in communal identity; it is not, in fact, the performance of individual ascetic virtuosos. In this sense, the distinctive practice of celibacy by certain members of the group is rather like the distinction of a special priestly service: it somehow crystalizes and brings to visible, focused expression a truth about the special holiness of the entire community. And it somehow does this without jeopardizing the delicate balance between what is proper to an inner elect and what is held in common.

Against this communal background, which is central to the Jewish ideal, Ezra's notion of the "holy seed" is revealed as central to the celibacy question.[15] Of the many things that might be said here, perhaps the most important is simply to insist that regulating the purity of the priests' sexual lives is viewed, within the Old Testament, as an inextricable part of a broader program aiming at communal holiness and freedom from sin.

In addition to this, on the inner-canonical order, Mary Douglas has made an enticing (if also uncertain) suggestion. She posits that Ezra's nationalistic

---

14. Cecilia Wassen, "Women, Worship, Wilderness, and War: Celibacy and the Constructions of Identity in the Dead Sea Scrolls," in *Sibyls, Scriptures, and Scrolls*, vol. 2, ed. Joel Baden, Hindy Najman, and Eibert Tigchelaar, JSJSup 175 (Leiden: Brill, 2017), 1385.

15. See Koltun-Fromm, *Hermeneutics of Holiness*, 53–96.

notion of holiness by means of enforced endogamy was directly countered by an alternative Levitical understanding of the purity-impurity problem: an understanding focused upon protecting the tabernacle through zones of graded holiness and consecration.[16] In other words, the Priestly school's response to Ezra's state-sponsored program for the creation—on entirely ethnic/racial grounds—of a perfectly pure Israel (a "holy seed") was to reorient the holiness of the people of God strictly around the work of the altar. Ezra's aspiration for a definitive purification was accordingly recentered, shifting from the priests themselves and their private lives to the temple they served. A ritual/sacrificial, not dynastic, resolution was thereby proposed as the official priestly answer to the stain of the sins of the exile.

There is an implicit lesson here countering a distinct Pelagian and Donatist danger. With Ezra, one might imagine Israel's holiness to be a thing accomplished by programs of reform. One might attempt to establish purity on the level of priestly behavior and good order, rather than (with the priests themselves) through the Lord's own sovereign action on the altar. Sociohistorically, of course, a lax position toward their own established practice of intermarriage may well lie behind the layer of Priestly tradition that seemingly throws cold water on Ezra's program. This is indeed hinted at by a text like Numbers 12:1–11, where Moses' marriage to the Cushite woman is criticized, but then the criticism is divinely rejected. On the other hand, this may be taken as a doctrinal object lesson; it would be wrong to imagine that Leviticus and Numbers simply scuttled Ezra's elevation of the marriage issue. Moses is affirmed by God not because his marriage with a Cushite was right but simply because he was chosen. "He is entrusted with all my house. With him I speak face to face" (Num. 12:7–8). The story of Phinehas, of course, is the most direct evidence against a simple Priestly disinterest in Ezra's question. (On the implicit Mushite critique in the Phinehas story, see excursus 2.) Yet precisely this pentateuchal account of Phinehas reinserts the intermarriage issue into its more properly cultic context, where the motif functions in harmony with its parallel deployment in the prophets, as explored in chapter 3. The sexual issue is a matter of fidelity to the covenant, demonstrated in fidelity to the Lord's altar. In this light, a practice like perpetual continence is less about asserting a heroic priestly morality—married priests can be perfectly orderly and upright—than it is about visibly manifesting an absolute covenant/cultic fidelity to God.

---

16. Mary Douglas, "Responding to Ezra: The Priests and the Foreign Wives," *BibInt* 10 (2002): 1–23. Douglas contends that "the best way to interpret their [the Priestly editors'] strong interest in the laws of impurity, and the peculiar twist these laws receive in Leviticus, is to assume that the books are written as a riposte to the Governor's use of the idea of defilement as a political weapon" (2).

When Luther, the former monk, married Katharina von Bora, the former nun—a step Melanchthon reckoned as "an unlucky deed"—one must recognize the protest against what was viewed as a Pelagian ideal rampant in the Catholic Church. Luther's decision to break his vows was at the same time based on an extreme pessimism about the ability to live in a state of chastity, even by the power of God's grace, a theological position and personal conviction admittedly corroborated by flagrant immorality among clerics. In any case, it was not obviously a biblical argument that governed this momentous break with ancient Church Tradition. Indeed, the Reformers' eradication of clerical and consecrated celibacy was, for a self-consciously scripturally based system, embarrassingly insensitive to Paul's perspicuous counsel in 1 Corinthians 7 in favor of remaining unmarried and so bound to the Lord.

For the Tradition, the difficulty of fallen humanity to live in a holy state of chastity was part of the demonstration of supernatural power that early Christians celebrated in the charism of perpetual continence. The veritable explosion of consecrated virginity in the experience of the early Church exceeds anything that Second Temple Judaism, not to say the pagan world, ever saw or imagined. The Fathers were convinced that it could be explained only as an extraordinary outpouring of the Holy Spirit, and a pneumatic infusion remains a convincing explanation for believers. If a new era thus dawned, the Second Temple Jewish perspective was, nevertheless, critical theological background for this explosion. As at Qumran, the Church as a whole perceived its deepest, collective identity reflected in the special holiness and charism of perfect chastity, even if not all Christians were equal participants in this unique gift of the Spirit. In this regard, the female virgin martyr, much more than the priest, quickly became an icon for the Church as the spotless bride of Christ. Paul already prepares this conception when he speaks of espousing the community as "a chaste virgin to Christ" (2 Cor. 11:2). The Pauline notion of the body of Christ represents the classical Christian framework, moreover, for understanding the corporate identification of the whole ecclesial community with the spiritual gifts given to its individual members.

Paul's body-of-Christ ecclesiology is ultimately decisive. The priesthood belongs to all; it stands in the service of all; it brings honor and shame to the whole body in various ways; for the special role accorded to the priest is rightly understood on the model of a Pauline charism. In this light, the Council of Trent's appeal to 1 Corinthians 12 as a shorthand scriptural statement of the Church's essential hierarchical constitution, and the existence of a special ministerial priesthood therein, remains a compelling biblical point of reference. Above all, the logic of the Pauline text implicitly suggests the essentially *charismatic* character of priestly office. Such an identification of hierarchical offices as gifts/grace (*dorea/charis*) is particularly clear in Ephesians 4:11–12, where the connection to the good of the whole body is also clearly seen: "The gifts he gave were that some would be apostles, some prophets, some evangelists, some pastors and teachers, to equip the saints for the work of ministry, for building up the body of Christ." The Pauline expression in 2 Timothy 1:6 is likewise entirely apt in this connection: "I remind you to rekindle *the gift of God* [*ta charisma tou theou*] that is within you through the laying on of my hands." Priestly office is a special charism and gift of the Holy Spirit: a "Spirit of power and of love and of self-discipline" (2 Tim. 1:7). That "self-discipline," the self-control of prudent moderation, should be singled out and named as constitutive of the priestly charism is not without interest for the celibacy question, particularly in view of the Pastoral Epistles' wider interest in the temperance and control of the passions proper to the *episkopoi*.

Seen in this light, as a work of the Spirit, the Church's intimate binding together of celibacy and sacramental ordination helpfully accentuates the uniquely pneumatic aspect at work in Christ's new order of priestly service. In the New Covenant one is not born into the priesthood, called according to the flesh and as a simple matter of familial descent, as were the Levites under the law of Moses. Entrance into Jesus' new charismatic form of priestly life has much more the character of a personal conversion: a direct work of the Holy Spirit reorienting the destiny of an individual Christian. Bound to a celibate charism, such pneumatic priesthood is not a self-perpetuating establishment invested in assuring its own worldly success through a biological line of physical heirs. While everything under the sun obviously lies open to sinful abuse, including this new priestly institution, the adventitious *charismatic* element, the constant dependence on the alighting of the Holy Spirit, serves as a most important *systemic* safeguard for the Church. The future of the priesthood—yes, the very existence of an ongoing share in the gift of priestly office—is constantly invested in the simple and direct working of God's grace. Coupled with the force of the priests' own spiritual fruitfulness as living branches on the vine—the ordained ministers' concurrent witness of holiness and gospel preaching—it remains the Lord's own prerogative to assure for his Church the blessing of priestly descendants: to *raise up faithful priests* who live according to his heart, gifted with a Spirit of power, love, and self-control.

Charism and Office

"Follow me." Jesus' call of the Twelve to follow him and participate in a special way in the unique mission given to him by his Father was not a call extended to all. This is true despite the fact that the message of the kingdom was a universal invitation made to any and all who would listen. This special call to follow and the radical response that it repeatedly provoked demonstrate the extraordinary power and attractive force of Christ's persona.

Martin Hengel, an important New Testament scholar, wrote a well-known book entirely focused on this theme of Jesus' charisma, *The Charismatic Leader and His Followers*.[17] The title (especially in its German version) hints at the influence of Max Weber, the German sociologist whose notion of "charisma" has had an immense impact on biblical studies in a kind of feedback loop, for Weber himself acknowledged borrowing the language of "charisma" from Christian theology (notably from Rudolf Sohm).[18] The impact of this interpretative cycle has not always been benign. An oversimplified sociological paradigm strongly opposing charisma and institution, in ways that Weber himself did not intend, ultimately filtered back into biblical studies, where it was loaded up with theological value judgments.

Charisma thus very quickly became a key category in a common narrative of "d/evolution" describing how the structures of office and authority, tradition and law, emerged out of the originally unregulated spontaneity of Christian communities. This perspective is conveniently captured in the contrast between the "historical" Paul of the Corinthian correspondence, where we meet communities in which supposedly "there was nobody ultimately in charge,"[19] and the "Deutero-Pauline" tradition behind the Pastoral Letters, where we find instead clear offices like bishop and deacon. According to this Deutero-Pauline schema, so-called *Frühkatholizismus*, "early Catholicism," with its rituals and structured hierarchy, displaced a primitive regime of charismatic leaders and "wandering radicals."[20]

Weber's influence and insights are at once both helpful and problematic. The estimate of Justin Taylor is quite sound on this point.

> Weber's model of "routinisation of charisma" probably can be applied to certain aspects of the origins of Christianity. On the other hand, the way that model is often understood and applied to the origins of Christianity—as a process of degeneration and even a betrayal, though perhaps an unavoidable betrayal, of Jesus and his message—is not adequate to the New Testament data. Furthermore, it seems to misrepresent Weber's own thought. In particular, the institutional features of the Church should not be regarded as secondary. Rite, office, tradition belong to the very origins of Christianity and were inherited

17. Martin Hengel, *The Charismatic Leader and His Followers*, Studies of the New Testament and Its World 1 (Edinburgh: T&T Clark, 1981).
18. Max Weber, *Economy and Society: An Outline of Interpretive Sociology*, ed. Guenther Roth and Claus Wittich, 2 vols. (Berkeley: University of California Press, 1978).
19. So Bart Ehrman, *The New Testament: A Historical Introduction to the Early Christian Writings* (Oxford: Oxford University Press, 2012), 416.
20. The "wandering radical" thesis is especially associated with Gerd Theissen, *The First Followers of Jesus: A Sociological Analysis of Earliest Christianity* (London: SCM, 1978).

from the original Jewish environment from which Christianity emerged. Indeed, the Christian gospel can be seen as breathing new life and meaning into existing structures. . . . Perhaps the emergence of Christianity involved not simply the "routinisation of charisma," but also the "charismatisation of routine."[21]

Office and ritual are indeed original features, with ample attestation in Second Temple and New Testament data. What we find is the infusion of a new life force: an élan centered entirely on the person of Jesus Christ.

Jesus is indeed the charismatic leader. It thus becomes quite revealing to observe, as Weber does, that the disintegration of social order in times of acute crisis and stress permits the emergence of charismatic personas, extraordinary leaders possessed of exceptional power, who arrive somehow from *outside*, excite among others the effect of devoted discipleship, and so engender a following. At the extreme, this following entails an experience of vocation, a radical freedom from normal social ties coupled with a profound personal commitment. From this perspective, the Church is simply the new social order built up around the organizing power of a single, living person—Jesus—who appears bearing a new source of legitimacy and convicting power: "What is this? A new teaching—with authority!" (Mark 1:27). Theologically speaking, Jesus' ecclesial following is the new creation of the divine outsider, who by the communication of his Spirit unifies and enlivens a body of devoted adherents. The sustained charismatic magnetism of the risen Lord, by which the Church is thus continually animated and held in being, operates at a level higher than any crisis in first-century Judea, ultimately fitting within the whole disordering catastrophe of human sin. It is from this position that Christ also animates a new and spiritualized priesthood.

Super hanc Petram

At the beginning of this study we took a hint from Karl Rahner and agreed on the importance of plotting the institution of the sacraments within a broader ecclesial frame. Here at the end we now confront a promising model for this ecclesial vision in a highly personalized perspective on the Church as the body of Christ energized by his own Holy Spirit. Such a head-and-members perspective is evocative of the organic *communio* style of ecclesiology that developed in the nineteenth and twentieth centuries. If a mystical tinge clings

21. See Justin Taylor, "Max Weber Resisted: Charisma and Institution at the Origins of Christianity," *Australian eJournal of Theology* 19 (2012): 195–208 (here 207–8). "Certain aspects of Weber's theory can be applied to Jesus himself, to his disciples and to the first believers. On the other hand, they have to be applied carefully and with discrimination. For they do not provide a complete explanation of the data as represented in the New Testament" (201).

to this vision, a vital interpersonal energy suited to the character of sacramental life, it is also possible and profitable to think in a more historical way about Christ's influence in generating and enlivening the Church.

To the classic question "Did Jesus found the Church?" the modern (and Modernist) answer is unmistakably no. "Jesus announced the Kingdom and it was the Church that arrived." These famous words, uttered by the Modernist scholar Alfred Loisy, are often used to suggest the Church's stupendous betrayal of Jesus. The kingdom was God's plan, while the Church is a human affair. Jesus awaited the imminent, cataclysmic end of the world. The Church is an institution comfortably settled in time: a political power and religious regime that has nothing to do with Jesus' apocalyptic vision.

What estimation should be given to this prevalent and influential view? Did Jesus really found the Church? The debates are clearly complex. The question is critical, however. Did Jesus truly (that is to say, *falsely*) announce that the end of the world was palpably near, thereby excluding all thought of the establishment of a Church, not to say a hierarchy of priestly office?

The case of St. Paul is enlightening in this respect. It testifies to a first-century Jew who somehow both held the conviction that "the ends of the ages have come" (1 Cor. 10:11) and advanced a plan to propagate the Church of God everywhere and among all peoples. Far from dissuading him, this eschatological urgency prompted Paul to gather together the end-time community of believers: a great assembly of God's people, saved by faith and through the mystical liturgical rites of baptism and Eucharist. Spreading the Church, with its worship and beliefs, was in fact a direct response to the threat of "the wrath that is coming" (1 Thess. 1:10).

The Dead Sea Scrolls offer another illuminating point of comparison. In the same way that today we find doomsday preppers preparing for an impending apocalypse, the Essenes of Qumran prepared for the final battle—not with generators, guns, and piled-up cans of Spam but with carefully studied religious rites and regulations. To oppose the establishment of a structured religious community, with an elaborately ritualized cultic liturgy and hierarchy functioning as custodian of its own praxis and teachings, to the feverish expectation of the manifestation of the reign of God is not only anachronistic; it stands in flagrant contradiction with all we know about Judaism at the time of Jesus. The preaching and rituals in the ministry of John the Baptist, who was the contemporary of Jesus and who displayed some tantalizing links to the group at Qumran, again illustrate the central role that liturgical rites can play in the gathering together of a holy remnant, especially from an intensely eschatological perspective.

This is all quite natural insofar as the Jewish religion is deeply ritualistic. It must be emphasized against a standing modern prejudice, however, which imagines that interior and subjective (charismatic/prophetic/Pauline) religion is superior to externalized, public (ritualized/priestly/Jewish) gestures and that it would therefore have been logical for Jesus to have founded a proto-Protestant religion. Here as elsewhere, behind modern reconstructions of the so-called Jesus of history often lurks the anti-Catholicism (which is also an anti-Judaism) of the Reformation.

According to the Gospels, Jesus borrowed his kingdom preaching directly from the Baptist: "Repent, for the kingdom of heaven has come near" (Matt. 3:1; 4:17). It is therefore not surprising that the Gospel of John relates that Jesus himself, by the hands of his disciples, baptized believers, even before Easter (John 3:2–23; 4:2). A significant difference separates John the Baptist from Jesus, however. Jesus identified himself in various ways with the "mightier one" who came after John, showing his strength by all kinds of signs (Matt. 11:2–6; Luke 7:18–23). Jesus was aware that he had been anointed by the Spirit (Mark 1:10; Luke 4:18), and he knew that he was the one who would baptize, not with water, but with the Holy Spirit (Mark 1:6–8; John 10:41). The Baptist himself would not dare to touch the dressing of the one who is announced as coming with fire. It is a passing of the baton already evident in Jesus and John's common announcement of the kingdom, but which here turns dramatically from the message to the *messenger*.

The relationship between John and Jesus, between the baptism of the former and the baptism of the latter, is crucial in assessing the religious movement initiated by Jesus. For Jesus did not start his ministry from scratch. The diarchic messianism discussed in chapter 5 seems to shape Jesus' own understanding of his connection to John. Jesus seems to have accepted an eschatological scenario something broadly like that of the Essenes: two chief agents, twinned priestly and royal messiahs of Aaron and Judah. Jesus, and likely not Jesus alone, recognized John as a priestly/Aaronic, Elijah/Phinehas figure.[22] Jesus read John's martyr's fate to have taken an unexpected but prophesied turn: John *tasted death* as was fitting for God's messenger and servant. As the Davidic Son-of-Man Messiah, Jesus placidly discerned his own mission to be taking up John's mantle in order to share his fate and complete

22. On the subject of John's priestly background, see Joel Marcus, *John the Baptist in History and Theology* (Columbia: University of South Carolina Press, 2018), appendix 4, 133–34. Luke alone of the Synoptic Gospels mentions John's priestly pedigree (Luke 1:5). Marcus determines that this information is not a Lukan invention but comes from preexisting sources. John's likely association with Qumran similarly points in a priestly direction. "John's association of himself with Elijah," finally, leads Marcus to the following remark: "If the equation of Elijah with Phineas was already existent in the first century, Phineas' strong objection to an illicit union is an interesting and perhaps significant parallel to John's repudiation of Herod Antipas' marriage to Herodias (Mark 6:17–18; see chap. 6). John's action may have reflected his sense of himself as Elijah = Phineas returned from the dead" (134).

the priestly purification of Israel. The resulting fusion of priestly and royal identities is, in some sense, what ceremonially transpires at the transfiguration. The Davidic Messiah, identified by Peter, is promptly identified with the priestly role earlier accorded to the now-departed John.

The "Jesus movement"—a modern scholarly neologism crafted to avoid the authentic New Testament word "Church," but a phrase which, despite that, highlights the real importance of Jesus' person—was an apocalyptic Jewish movement in the special mode initiated by John yet reoriented entirely around the person of Jesus. It was a christological novelty rooted in a formidable continuity, profoundly Jewish in content.

Jesus' own christological reconfiguration of Israel is visible in multiple ways. The choice of the Twelve is entirely symbolic of a re-created Israel, with the twelve tribes united and gathered around the Messiah. The transformation of the Passover into the Eucharist illustrates even more brilliantly this reconfiguration. Out of the feast that stood at the heart of the identity of the Jewish people, of its entire history of salvation and its future hope, Jesus creates a rite that represents and makes present his own personal passion. The announcement, made during this meal, of a New Covenant that would replace the Old, a testament sealed "*in my blood*," as Jesus says, is presented as the fulfillment of Jeremiah's prophecy and the mediation of a new Moses. "See, days are coming—oracle of the LORD—when I will make a new covenant with the house of Israel and the house of Judah" (Jer. 31:31 NABRE). The institution of the Eucharist thus illustrates, perhaps more clearly than any other gesture of Jesus, his intention to inaugurate a new economy of salvation from within the old regime. To this extent, nothing could be more accurate than to locate Jesus' institution of the priesthood at this key moment.

Theologically, the priestly character of Holy Thursday is a direct function of Jesus' *anamnesis* command—"Do this in remembrance of me." A share in his own high priestly action is entailed in the identification of the eucharistic bread and wine with his action on the altar of the cross. The moment this mystical conjunction is embraced for the sacramental reality that it claims to be, a priestly service is established, binding Jesus' own priesthood to the earthly continuation of the cult he inaugurated.

Christ's founding of the Church and his institution of its priesthood are inextricably intertwined events. In fact, there is not one without the other. If for various reasons I opted to highlight Jesus' commissioning of Peter as an iconic moment in the institution of pastoral office, the ecclesiological pendant to this sacerdotal scene is easily seen. "You are Peter, and on this rock I will build my church" (Matt. 16:18). Jesus builds his Church upon the one to whom he entrusts the keys and whom he also entrusts with feeding and tending his flock. That Peter's special position is also thematized at the Last

Supper binds the whole complex to Jesus' solemn act of covenant-making (Luke 22:32).

Matthew assures us that Jesus explicitly wanted to found a church, but exegetes are quick to notice that the word "church" is extraordinarily rare in the mouth of Jesus (only three occurrences, all in Matthew, whereas Paul uses the word fifty-nine times). Jesus did not speak to Peter in Greek, of course. (The pun on Peter's name makes more sense in Aramaic, suggesting, of course, a tradition that predates our Gospel.) It seems that the use of the Greek word *ekklēsia* to denote the assembly of disciples of Jesus (like the name "Christian" as well) dates from the time of the Hellenists mentioned in Acts 6. But the word chosen by these Greek-speaking Christians, *ekklēsia*, translates a Hebrew word, *qāhāl*, which in the Old Testament means the holy liturgical assembly of YHWH. It thus had a meaning very close to another Greek term, "synagogue," in the same way that the two groups behind those two words were also quite close. Both etymologically and historically, "the church" and "the synagogue" were defined side by side: two competitors for the right to be the legitimate heir of the people formed by Moses.

To fully appreciate this point, it is necessary to listen to Luke and Matthew in stereo, for together they recapitulate the delicate balance between what is old and what is new. Jesus does not found the Church in Luke as he does in Matthew, quite simply because, for Luke, the *ekklēsia*, the assembly of God's elect, has existed uninterruptedly since Sinai (Acts 7:38). Thus, Jesus "acquires" this Church by the purchase price of his own blood (Acts 20:28): he makes it his own, as YHWH tore his people from Egypt, redeeming them from the hand of Pharaoh by the blood of the Passover lamb. For Luke then, who has the distinct advantage over Matthew of having two full volumes to tell his story, the Church does not spring fully formed from the mouth of Christ. Jesus instead acquires a people—it is a work that he began with his first disciples and that continues by his gift of the Spirit after Pentecost (Acts 2:33) and by all the conquests and conversions until today by which pagans and Jews return "from the power of Satan to God" (Acts 26:18).

Modern scholars often suspect that Matthew simply invented Christ's words to Peter. But their doubt arises from the doubtful premise of a Jewish Jesus who has nothing particularly new to accomplish or promise. Even if Matthew did indulge in mere storytelling here (which remains to be proven), the verse would still be impressive. Faced with the modern scholars who give Paul the credit for having created Christianity, Matthew shows that in the first century this work was unambiguously attributed to Jesus. Paul himself says nothing different when he takes up Matthew's/Jesus' image, not without a certain irony with regard to the partisans of *Cephas*, and shifts the "rock" of Peter over to Christ: "No one can lay any foundation other than the one that has been laid; that foundation is Jesus Christ" (1 Cor. 3:11; cf. 1:12; 3:22). The Apostle and builder of churches is even more insistent than the evangelist: the Church has her only foundation stone in Jesus Christ.

Did Jesus found the Church? Did he institute the priesthood? The answers to these questions require acknowledging the fruitful tension between what is new and what is old in Christ's ministry. Historically, he emerged from a booming apocalyptic Judaism, swollen with the hope that God was about to do "a new thing" (Isa. 43:19). Paradoxically, the principle of continuity thereby invites a sort of quantum leap: the dynamics of the old open themselves up to the new. The gift of the Spirit and the New Covenant, although they belong to the old prophecies, burst the old wineskins by their sheer power (Matt. 9:17). The desire to see in Jesus only a first-century Jew leads to a dead end insofar as this same first-century Judaism claimed an eschatological break with the sinful bondage of Israel's past. The rupture therefore did not occur between Jesus and the Church, as Loisy thought. It separates the Judaism of Jesus from all that came before it. The new creation of Jesus' eschatological priesthood is just such a bursting of the old Levitical wineskins. Or, better, it is a new vessel: a new *garment*—a high priestly vestment—rather than a mere patching of the old. From this perspective, one might perhaps dare to offer an answer to the thorny questions. The proclamation of the kingdom of God in the words and actions of Jesus aroused a surge of bracing novelty, a wave of astonishment palpable in the entire primitive tradition: "a new teaching— with authority" (Mark 1:27), "a new commandment" (John 13:34), "a new creation" (Gal. 6:15). These novelties were—and are—for those who believe, nothing other than the *good news*. The Church, sanctified and governed by the purified priesthood of our high priest and great shepherd of the sheep, served by a ministry binding together heaven and earth, is this prophesied and foreshadowed newness, a living "grace in place of grace" (John 1:16 NABRE).

Suggested Resources

Balthasar, Hans Urs von. *The Office of Peter and the Structure of the Church*. San Francisco: Ignatius, 1985.

Benedict XVI, and Robert Cardinal Sarah. *From the Depths of Our Hearts: Priesthood, Celibacy, and the Crisis of the Catholic Church*. San Francisco: Ignatius, 2019.

Cody, Aelred. *A History of the Old Testament Priesthood*. AnB 35. Rome: Pontifical Biblical Institute, 1969.

Kirk, Kenneth, ed. *The Apostolic Ministry: Essays on the History and the Doctrine of Episcopacy*. London: Hodder & Stoughton, 1957.

Nichols, Aidan. *Holy Order: Apostolic Priesthood from the New Testament to the Second Vatican Council*. Eugene, OR: Wipf & Stock, 1990.

O'Collins, Gerald, and Michael Keenan Jones. *Jesus Our Priest: A Christian Approach to the Priesthood of Christ*. Oxford: Oxford University Press, 2010.

Selected Bibliography

Alexander, Philip. "The Qumran Songs of the Sabbath Sacrifice and the Celestial Hierarchy of Dionysius the Areopagite: A Comparative Approach." *RevQ* 22, no. 87 (2006): 349–73.

Altmann, Peter. "What Do the 'Levites in Your Gates' Have to Do with the 'Levitical Priests'? An Attempt at European–North American Dialogue on the Levites in the Deuteronomic Law Corpus." In *Levites and Priests in Biblical History and Tradition*, edited by Mark Leuchter and Jeremy M. Hutton, 135–54. AIL 9. Atlanta: Society of Biblical Literature, 2011.

Andersen, Francis I., and David Noel Freedman. *Amos*. AB 24A. New York: Doubleday, 1989.

Anderson, Gary. "Original Sin: The Fall of Humanity and the Golden Calf." In *Christian Doctrine and the Old Testament: Theology in the Service of Biblical Exegesis*, 59–73. Grand Rapids: Baker Academic, 2017.

———. "'Through Those Who Are Near to Me, I Will Show Myself Holy': Nadab and Abihu and Apophatic Theology." *CBQ* 77 (2015): 1–19.

Anderson, Gary, and Saul M. Olyan. *Priesthood and Cult in Ancient Israel*. JSOTSup 125. Sheffield: Sheffield Academic, 1991.

Attridge, Harold. "How Priestly Is the 'High Priestly Prayer' of John 17?" *CBQ* 75 (2013): 1–14.

Balberg, Mira. *Blood for Thought: The Reinvention of Sacrifice in Early Rabbinic Literature*. Oakland: University of California Press, 2017.

Balthasar, Hans Urs von. *Explorations in Theology*. Vol. 2, *Spouse of the Word*. San Francisco: Ignatius, 1991.

———. *The Office of Peter and the Structure of the Church*. San Francisco: Ignatius, 1985.

Barber, Michael. "Jesus as the Living Temple Builder and Peter's Priestly Role in Matt 16:16–19." *JBL* 132 (2013): 935–53.

Bautch, Richard J. "The Formulary of Atonement (Lev 16:21) in Penitential Prayers of the Second Temple Period." In *The Day of Atonement: Its Interpretations in Early Jewish and Christian Traditions*, edited by Thomas Hieke and Tobias Nicklas, 33–48. TBN 15. Leiden: Brill, 2012.

Beard, Mary, and John North. *Pagan Priests: Religion and Power in the Ancient World*. Ithaca, NY: Cornell University Press, 1990.

Benedict XVI, and Robert Cardinal Sarah. *From the Depths of Our Hearts: Priesthood, Celibacy, and the Crisis of the Catholic Church*. San Francisco: Ignatius, 2019.

Blankenhorn, Bernhard. "The Instrumental Causality of the Sacraments: Thomas Aquinas and Louis-Marie Chauvet." *Nova et Vetera* 4 (2006): 255–94.

Bockmuehl, Markus. *The Remembered Peter in Ancient Reception and Modern Debate*. WUNT 262. Tübingen: Mohr Siebeck, 2010.

———. "Scripture's Pope Meets von Balthasar's Peter." In Bond and Hurtado, *Peter in Early Christianity*, 321–40.

Bond, Helen, and Larry Hurtado, eds. *Peter in Early Christianity*. Grand Rapids: Eerdmans, 2015.

Campbell, R. Alastair. *The Elders: Seniority within Earliest Christianity*. Studies of the New Testament and Its World. Edinburgh: T&T Clark, 1994.

Childs, Brevard. *Biblical Theology of the Old and New Testaments: Theological Reflection on the Christian Bible*. Minneapolis: Fortress, 2011.

———. *Introduction to the Old Testament as Scripture*. Philadelphia: Fortress, 1979.

Cochini, Christian. *The Apostolic Origins of Priestly Celibacy*. San Francisco: Ignatius, 1990.

Cody, Aelred. *A History of the Old Testament Priesthood*. AnB 35. Rome: Pontifical Biblical Institute, 1969.

Congar, Yves. *Lay People in the Church*. Westminster, MD: Newman, 1965.

Conrad, Edgar. "The End of Prophecy and the Appearance of Angels/Messengers in the Book of the Twelve." *JSOT* 22, no. 73 (1997): 65–79.

Cook, Stephen L. "Ezekiel's God Incarnate! The God That the Temple Blueprint Creates." In *The God Ezekiel Creates*, edited by Paul M. Joyce and Dalit Rom-Shiloni, 132–49. LHBOTS 607. London: Bloomsbury, 2015.

Corley, Jeremy. "Seeds of Messianism in Hebrew Ben Sira and Greek Sirach." In *The Septuagint and Messianism*, edited by Michael Knibb, 301–12. BETL 195. Leuven: Leuven University Press, 2006.

Cross, Frank Moore. *Canaanite Myth and Hebrew Epic: Essays in the History of the Religion of Israel*. Cambridge, MA: Harvard University Press, 1973.

De Andrado, Paba Nidhani. "Ḥesed and Sacrifice: The Prophetic Critique in Hosea." *CBQ* 78 (2016): 47–67.

de La Potterie, Ignace. *The Hour of Jesus: The Passion and the Resurrection of Jesus according to John*. New York: Alba House, 1989.

Dequeker, L. "1 Chronicles xxiv and the Royal Priesthood of the Hasmoneans." In *Crises and Perspectives: Studies in Ancient Near Eastern Polytheism, Biblical Theology,*

Palestinian Archaeology and Intertestamental Literature, edited by A. S. van der Woude, 94–106. Oudtestamentische Studiën 24. Leiden: Brill, 1986.

Dix, Dom Gregory. "Ministry in the Early Church." In *The Apostolic Ministry: Essays on the History and the Doctrine of Episcopacy*, edited by Kenneth Kirk, 274–87. London: Hodder & Stoughton, 1957.

Douglas, Mary. *Purity and Danger: An Analysis of Concepts of Pollution and Taboo*. New York: Routledge, 2002 [1966].

———. "Responding to Ezra: The Priests and the Foreign Wives." *BibInt* 10 (2002): 1–23.

Eckhardt, Benedikt. "'Bloodless Sacrifice': A Note on Greek Cultic Language in the Imperial Era." *GRBS* 54 (2014): 255–73.

Eidevall, Göran. "A Farewell to the Anticultic Prophet: Attitudes towards the Cult in the Book of Amos." In *Priests and Cults in the Book of the Twelve*, edited by Lena-Sofia Tiemeyer, 99–114. ANEM 14. Atlanta: SBL Press, 2016.

Faust, Avraham. "The World of P: The Material Realm of Priestly Writings." *VT* 69 (2019): 173–218.

Ferguson, Everett. "Jewish and Christian Ordination: Some Observations." *HTR* 56 (1963): 13–19.

———. "Laying On of Hands: Its Significance in Ordination." *JTS* 26 (1975): 1–12.

Fisher, Edmund W. "Let Us Look Upon the Blood-of-Christ (1 Clement 7:4)." *VC* 34 (1980): 218–36.

Giambrone, Anthony. *A Quest for the Historical Christ: Scientia Christi and the Modern Study of Jesus*. Washington, DC: Catholic University of America Press, 2022.

———. "Revelation in Christian Scripture." In *The Oxford Handbook of Divine Revelation*, edited by Balázs M. Mezei, Francesca Aran Murphy, and Kenneth Oakes, 68–84. Oxford: Oxford University Press, 2021.

Gill, D. "The Greek Cult Table." *AJA* 69 (1965): 103–14.

———. "Trapezomata: A Neglected Aspect of Greek Sacrifice." *HTR* 67 (1974): 117–37.

Glaim, Aaron. "'I Will Not Accept Them': Sacrifice and Reciprocity in the Prophetic Literature." In *Sacrifice, Cult, and Atonement in Early Judaism and Christianity: Constituents and Critique*, edited by Henrietta L. Wiley and Christian A. Eberhart, 125–50. RBS 85. Atlanta: SBL Press, 2017.

Gordon, Benjamin D. *Land and Temple: Field Sacralization and the Agrarian Priesthood of Second Temple Judaism*. Studia Judaica 87. Berlin: de Gruyter, 2020.

Gorman, Frank H. "Pagans and Priests: Critical Reflections on Method." In *Perspectives on Purity and Purification in the Bible*, edited by Naphtali S. Meshel, Jeffrey Stackert, David P. Wright, and Baruch J. Schwartz, 96–110. LHBOTS 474. New York: T&T Clark, 2008.

Grabbe, Lester. "The Scapegoat Tradition: A Study in Early Jewish Interpretation." *JSJ* 18 (1987): 152–67.

Greer, Jonathan. "The 'Priestly Portion' in the Hebrew Bible: Its Ancient Near Eastern Context and Implications for the Composition of P." *JBL* 138 (2019): 263–84.

Hahn, Scott. *The Kingdom of God as Liturgical Empire: A Theological Commentary on 1–2 Chronicles.* Grand Rapids: Baker Academic, 2012.

Hanson, Paul D. *The Dawn of Apocalyptic: The Historical and Sociological Roots of Jewish Apocalyptic Eschatology.* Philadelphia: Fortress, 1984.

Hays, Nathan. "The Redactional Assertion of the Priestly Role in Leviticus 10–16." *ZAW* 130 (2018): 175–88.

Hayward, Robert. "Phinehas—the Same Is Elijah: The Origins of a Rabbinic Tradition." *JJS* 29 (1978): 22–34.

Heger, Paul. "Celibacy in Qumran: Hellenistic Fiction or Reality? Qumran's Attitude towards Sex." *RevQ* 26 (2013): 53–90.

Heil, John Paul. "Jesus as the Unique High Priest in the Gospel of John." *CBQ* 57 (1995): 729–45.

Hendel, Ronald S. "Away from Ritual: The Prophetic Critique." In *Social Theory and the Study of Israelite Religion: Essays in Retrospect and Prospect,* edited by Saul M. Olyan, 59–80. RBS 71. Atlanta: Society of Biblical Literature, 2012.

Hengel, Martin. *The Charismatic Leader and His Followers.* Studies of the New Testament and Its World 1. Edinburgh: T&T Clark, 1981.

Henrichs, Albert. "Introduction: What Is a Greek Priest?" In *Practitioners of the Divine: Greek Priests and Religious Officials from Homer to Heliodorus,* edited by Beate Dignas and Kai Trampedach. Hellenic Studies Series 33. Washington, DC: Center for Hellenic Studies, 2008. https://chs.harvard.edu/chapter/introduction -what-is-a-greek-priest-albert-henrichs/.

Himmelfarb, Martha. *Ascent to Heaven in Jewish and Christian Apocalypses.* New York: Oxford University Press, 1993.

———. "Levi, Phineas, and the Problem of Intermarriage at the Time of the Maccabean Revolt." *JSQ* 6 (1999): 1–24.

Hof, Otto. "Luther's Exegetical Principle of the Analogy of Faith." *CTM* 38 (1967): 242–57.

Holmén, Tom. "Caught in the Act: Jesus Starts the New Temple—A Continuum Study of Jesus as the Founder of the *Ecclesia.*" In *The Identity of Jesus: Nordic Voices,* edited by Samuel Byrskog, Tom Holmén, and Matti Kankaanniemi, 181–231. WUNT 2/373. Tübingen: Mohr Siebeck, 2014.

Hurtado, Larry W. "The Apostle Peter in Protestant Scholarship: Cullmann, Hengel, and Bockmuehl." In Bond and Hurtado, *Peter in Early Christianity,* 1–15.

Hutton, R. R. *Charisma and Authority in Ancient Israelite Society.* Minneapolis: Fortress, 1994.

Ishida, Tomoo. *The Royal Dynasties in Ancient Israel: A Study on the Formation and Development of Royal-Dynastic Ideology.* BZAW 142. New York: de Gruyter, 1977.

Johnson, Nathan C. "The Messianic Temple Builder in the Dead Sea Scrolls, Midrash Rabbah, and Targum Jonathan." *AncJud* 8 (2020): 199–232.

Just, Arthur A., Jr. "Entering Holiness: Christology and Eucharist in Hebrews." *CTQ* 69 (2005): 75–95.

Kasper, Walter. "Ministry in the Church: Taking Issue with Edward Schillebeeckx." *Communio* 10 (1983): 185–95.

Klawans, Jonathan. *Impurity and Sin in Ancient Judaism.* Oxford: Oxford University Press, 2000.

Knohl, Israel. "Melchizedek: A Model for the Union of Kingship and Priesthood in the Hebrew Bible, *11QMelchizedek*, and the Epistle to the Hebrews." In *Text, Thought, and Practice in Qumran and Early Christianity*, edited by Ruth Clements and Daniel Schwartz, 255–66. STDJ 84. Leiden: Brill, 2009.

———. *The Sanctuary of Silence: Priestly Torah and the Holiness School.* Minneapolis: Fortress, 1995.

Knoppers, Gary. *1 Chronicles 10–29.* AB 12A. New York: Doubleday, 2004.

Kratz, Reinhard G. "The Teacher of Righteousness and His Enemies." In *Is There a Text in This Cave? Studies in the Textuality of the Dead Sea Scrolls in Honour of George J. Brooke*, edited by Ariel Feldman, Maria Cioata, and Charlotte Hempel, 515–32. STDJ 119. Leiden: Brill, 2017.

Krispenz, Jutta. "Idolatry, Apostasy, Prostitution: Hosea's Struggle against the Cult." In *Priests and Cults in the Book of the Twelve*, edited by Lena-Sofia Tiemeyer, 9–30. ANEM 14. Atlanta: SBL Press, 2016.

Kugel, James. "Levi's Elevation to the Priesthood in Second Temple Writings." *HTR* 86 (1993): 1–64.

Kugler, Robert. *From Patriarch to Priest: The Levi-Priestly Tradition from "Aramaic Levi" to "Testament of Levi."* EJL 9. Atlanta: Scholars Press, 1996.

Leithart, Peter. "Womb of the World: Baptism and the Priesthood of the New Covenant in Hebrews 10:19–22." *JSNT* 78 (2000): 49–65.

Leuchter, Mark. "Samuel: A Prophet or a Priest like Moses?" In *Israelite Prophecy and the Deuteronomistic History: Portrait, Reality, and the Formation of a History*, edited by Mignon R. Jacobs and Raymond F. Person Jr., 147–68. AIL 14. Atlanta: Society of Biblical Literature, 2013.

Levenson, Jon D. *Creation and the Persistence of Evil: The Jewish Drama of Divine Omnipotence.* San Francisco: HarperCollins, 1988.

———. *Theology of the Program of Restoration of Ezekiel 40–48.* HSM 10. Missoula, MT: Scholars Press, 1976.

Lundbom, Jack. "Contentious Priests and Contentious People in Hosea IV 1–10." *VT* 36 (1986): 52–70.

MacDonald, Nathan. *Priestly Rule: Polemic and Biblical Interpretation in Ezekiel 44.* BZAW 476. Berlin: de Gruyter, 2015.

Malchow, B. "The Messenger of the Covenant in Mal. 3:1." *JBL* 103 (1984): 252–55.

Marcus, Joel. *John the Baptist in History and Theology.* Columbia: University of South Carolina Press, 2018.

Mason, Rex. "The Prophets of the Restoration." In *Israel's Prophetic Tradition: Essays in Honour of Peter R. Ackroyd*, edited by Richard Coggins, Anthony Phillips, and Michael Knibb, 137–54. Cambridge: Cambridge University Press, 1982.

McGowan, Andrew. "Eucharist and Sacrifice: Cultic Tradition and Transformation in Early Christian Ritual Meals." In *Mahl und religiöse Identität im frühen Christentum—Meals and Religious Identity in Early Christianity*, edited by Matthias Klinghardt and Hal Taussig, 191–206. Tübingen: Mohr Siebeck, 2012.

Meyers, Carol, and Eric Meyers. *Haggai, Zechariah 1–8*. AB 25B. New York: Doubleday, 1987.

Meyers, Eric. "Messianism in First and Second Zechariah and the 'End' of Biblical Prophecy." In *"Go to the Land I Will Show You": Studies in Honor of Dwight W. Young*, edited by Joseph E. Coleson and Victor H. Matthews, 127–42. Winona Lake, IN: Eisenbrauns, 1996.

Milgrom, Jacob. "Israel's Sanctuary: The Priestly 'Picture of Dorian Gray.'" *RB* 83 (1976): 390–99.

———. *Leviticus 1–16*. AB 3. New York: Doubleday, 1991.

———. *Leviticus 23–27*. AB 3B. New York: Doubleday, 2001.

Möhler, Johann Adam. *Symbolism: Exposition of the Doctrinal Differences between Catholics and Protestants as Evidenced by Their Symbolic Writings*. New York: Herder & Herder, 1997.

Monson, Andrew. "The Jewish High Priesthood for Sale: Farming Out Temples in the Hellenistic East." *JJS* 67 (2016): 15–35.

Mulder, Otto. *Simon the High Priest in Sirach 50: An Exegetical Study of the Significance of Simon the High Priest as Climax to the Praise of the Fathers in Ben Sira's Concept of the History of Israel*. JSJSup 78. Leiden: Brill, 2003.

Naiden, Fred. "Rejected Sacrifice in Greek and Hebrew Religion." *JANER* 6 (2006): 189–223.

———. *Smoke Signals for the Gods: Ancient Greek Sacrifice from the Archaic through Roman Periods*. Oxford: Oxford University Press, 2013.

Nichols, Aidan. *Holy Order: Apostolic Priesthood from the New Testament to the Second Vatican Council*. Eugene, OR: Wipf & Stock, 1990.

Nihan, Christophe, and Julia Rhyder. "Aaron's Vestments in Exodus 28 and Priestly Leadership." In *Debating Authority: Concepts of Leadership in the Pentateuch and the Former Prophets*, edited by Katharina Pyschny and Sarah Schulz, 45–67. BZAW 507. Berlin: de Gruyter, 2018.

O'Brien, Julia M. *Priest and Levite in Malachi*. Atlanta: Scholars Press, 1990.

O'Collins, Gerald, and Michael Keenan Jones. *Jesus Our Priest: A Christian Approach to the Priesthood of Christ*. Oxford: Oxford University Press, 2010.

Olyan, Saul M. "Ben Sira's Relationship to the Priesthood." *HTR* 80 (1987): 261–86.

O'Neill, Colman E. *Meeting Christ in the Sacraments*. New York: Alba House, 1990 [1964].

———. *Sacramental Realism*. Wilmington, DE: Michael Glazier, 1983.

Orpana, Jessi. "Awareness of Nudity in Jubilees 3: Adam Portrayed as a Priest in the Garden." In *Crossing Imaginary Boundaries: The Dead Sea Scrolls in the Context of Second Temple Judaism*, edited by Mika S. Pajunen and Hanna Tervanotko, 241–58. PFES 108. Helsinki: Finnish Exegetical Society, 2015.

Petersen, David L. *Haggai and Zechariah 1–8*. OTL. Philadelphia: Westminster, 1984.

Poirier, John C. "The Endtime Return of Elijah and Moses at Qumran." *DSD* 10 (2003): 221–42.

Poorthuis, Marcel, and Joshua Schwartz, eds. *Purity and Holiness: The Heritage of Leviticus*. Jewish and Christian Perspectives 2. Leiden: Brill, 2000.

Purcell, Richard Anthony. "The King as Priest? Royal Imagery in Psalm 110 and Ancient Near Eastern Iconography." *JBL* 139 (2020): 275–300.

Rahner, Karl. *The Church and the Sacraments*. New York: Herder & Herder, 1963.

————. "Theology of Symbol." In *Theological Investigations IV*, 221–52. New York: Seabury, 1973.

Rainbow, Paul. "The Last Oniad and the Teacher of Righteousness." *JJS* 48 (1997): 30–52.

Reif, S. C. "What Enraged Phineas? A Study of Numbers 25:8." *JBL* 90 (1971): 200–206.

Ribbens, Benjamin J. *Levitical Sacrifice and Heavenly Cult in Hebrews*. BZNW 222. Berlin: de Gruyter, 2016.

————. "The Sacrifice God Desired: Psalm 40:6–8 in Hebrews 10." *NTS* 67 (2021): 284–304.

Rooke, Deborah. "The Day of Atonement as a Ritual of Validation for the High Priest." In *Temple and Worship in Biblical Israel*, edited by John Day, 342–64. New York: T&T Clark, 2007.

Schmidt, A. Jordan. *Wisdom, Cosmos, and Cultus in the Book of Sirach*. DCLS 42. Berlin: de Gruyter, 2019.

Schwartz, Baruch J. "Israel's Holiness: The Torah Traditions." In Poorthuis and Schwartz, *Purity and Holiness*, 54.

Scott, Ian W. "'Your Reasoning Worship': ΛΟΓΙΚΟΣ in Romans 12:1 and Paul's Ethics of Rational Deliberation." *JTS* 69, no. 2 (2018): 500–532.

Shea, C. Michael. "Father Giovanni Perrone and Doctrinal Development in Rome: An Overlooked Legacy of Newman's *Essay on Development*." *JHMTh/ZNThG* 20 (2013): 85–116.

Silverman, Jason M. "Vetting the Priest in Zechariah 3: The Satan between Divine and Achaemenid Administrations." *JHebS* 14 (2014): 1–27.

Söhngen, Gottlieb. "The Analogy of Faith: Likeness to God from Faith Alone?" and "The Analogy of Faith: Unity in the Science of Faith." *Pro Ecclesia* 21 (2012): 56–76, 169–94.

Sommer, Benjamin. "Did Prophecy Cease? Evaluating a Reevaluation." *JBL* 115 (1996): 31–47.

Starling, David. "The Analogy of Faith in the Theology of Luther and Calvin." *RTR* 72 (2013): 5–19.

Stewart, Bryan A. *Priests of My People: Levitical Paradigms for Early Christian Ministers*. Patristic Studies 11. New York: Peter Lang, 2015.

Stripling, Scott. "The Israelite Tabernacle at Shiloh." *Bible and Spade* 29 (2016): 89–94.

Summers, Kirk. "The *logikē latreia* of Romans 12:1 and Its Interpretation among Christian Humanists." *Perichoresis* 15 (2017): 47–66.

Swetnam, James. "Christology and Eucharist in the Epistle to the Hebrews." *Biblica* 70 (1989): 74–95.

Tait, Michael. *Too Many Priests? Melchizedek and the Others in Hebrews*. Scripturae 5. Rome: Giacobbe, 2016.

Taylor, Justin. "Max Weber Resisted: Charisma and Institution at the Origins of Christianity." *Australian eJournal of Theology* 19 (2012): 195–208.

Thiering, B. E. "*Mebaqqer* and *Episkopos* in the Light of the Temple Scroll." *JBL* 100 (1981): 59–74.

Tiemeyer, Lena-Sofia. "The Guilty Priesthood (Zech 3)." In *The Book of Zechariah and Its Influence*, edited by Christopher Tuckett, 1–20. Aldershot: Ashgate, 2003.

———. *Priestly Rites and Prophetic Rage*. FAT 2/19. Tübingen: Mohr Siebeck, 2006.

Tipei, John Fleter. *The Laying On of Hands in the New Testament: Its Significance, Techniques, and Effects*. Lanham, MD: University Press of America, 2009.

Valve, Lotta. *Early Modes of Exegesis: Ideal Figures in Malachi as a Test Case*. Åbo: Åbo Akademis, 2014.

VanderKam, James C. *From Joshua to Caiaphas: High Priests after the Exile*. Minneapolis: Fortress, 2004.

Voitila, Anssi. "The End of the High Priestly Family of Simon and the Conclusion of the Book of Ben Sira." *BN* 179 (2018): 69–84.

Vonier, Dom Anscar. *A Key to the Doctrine of the Eucharist*. Bethesda, MD: Zaccheus, 2003.

Ware, Kallistos. "Man, Woman and the Priesthood of Christ." In *Women and the Priesthood*, edited by T. Hopko, 9–38. Crestwood, NY: St. Vladimir's Seminary Press, 1983.

Wassen, Cecilia. "Women, Worship, Wilderness, and War: Celibacy and the Constructions of Identity in the Dead Sea Scrolls." In *Sibyls, Scriptures, and Scrolls*, vol. 2, edited by Joel Baden, Hindy Najman, and Eibert Tigchelaar, 1361–85. JSJSup 175. Leiden: Brill, 2017.

Watts, James. "Aaron and the Golden Calf in the Rhetoric of the Pentateuch." *JBL* 130 (2011): 417–30.

———. *Leviticus 1–10*. HCOT. Leuven: Peeters, 2013.

Wellhausen, Julius. *Prolegomena to the History of Israel*. Atlanta: Scholars Press, 1994.

Weyde, Karl William. "Ezra's Penitential Prayer: Priestly Vocabulary and Concepts in Ezra 9." In *Houses Full of All Good Things: Essays in Memory of Timo Veijola*, edited by Juha Pakkala and Martti Nissinen, 238–50. PFES 95. Göttingen: Vandenhoeck & Ruprecht, 2008.

Wolff, Hans Walter. *Hosea*. Hermeneia. Philadelphia: Fortress, 1974.

Wright, Benjamin G., III. "Ben Sira and the *Book of the Watchers* on the Legitimate Priesthood." In *Intertextual Studies in Ben Sira and Tobit*, edited by Jeremy Corley and Vincent Skemp, 241–54. CBQMS 38. Washington, DC: Catholic Biblical Association of America, 2005.

Zeron, Alexander. "The Martyrdom of Phineas-Elijah." *JBL* 98 (1979): 99–100.

Zevit, Ziony. "The Prophet versus Priest Antagonism Hypothesis: Its History and Origin." In *The Priests in the Prophets: The Portrayal of Priests, Prophets and Other Religious Specialists in the Latter Prophets*, edited by Lester L. Grabbe and Alice Ogden Bellis, 189–216. LHBOTS 408. Sheffield: Sheffield Academic, 2004.

Subject Index

abstinence, sexual, 63, 260–66
Akitu festival, Mesopotamian, 126
altar, 46–47, 193–95, 228–29
analogy of faith, the, 28–35
Andersen, Francis, 86, 92–94, 96, 100
Anderson, Gary, 59–60
anointing, priestly, 46–47
antagonism hypothesis, the, 82–83, 89, 94, 103,
 192, 195, 251
Apocalypse of Abraham, 172, 172n24
Apocalypse of Peter, 175
apostles, sending of, 241–43
Apostolic Tradition, 18, 237, 239–40, 243
apparel. *See* vestments, priestly
Appeal to the German Nobility (Luther), 16
Atonement, Day of, 34, 47, 64–66, 73, 102, 109,
 122, 124–26, 153, 157, 174, 231, 252. *See
 also* Yom Kippur
Augustine, 10, 22, 25, 58, 115, 188
authority
 ordination and, 51–56
 priesthood and, 175–81, 183–84, 187–90,
 246–54
 See also ordination, priestly

Babylonian Captivity of the Church, The (Luther), 4n2, 189
Balberg, Mira, 213
Balthasar, Hans Urs von, 189, 259
baptism, 4, 6–8, 12, 14, 16–20, 122, 224, 228,
 250, 269–70
Barth, Karl, 30
beloved disciple, the, 177, 185
Benedict XVI, 3–4, 25, 255

Ben Sira, 135–43, 145
Berlin, Adele, 149
Bethel, sanctuary at, 86
Blenkinsopp, Joseph, 21
blood, sacrifice and, 218–24, 226–29, 231–32,
 251
Booths, Feast of, 174–75, 199
bread, offering of, 49–51
Brown, Raymond, 176
bulls, sacrificial, 47–48

Caiaphas, 178–80
Calvin, John, 29
Campenhausen, Hans von, 206
canon, the, 28, 129–31, 135
causality, sacramental, 13–14
celibacy, priestly, 63, 260–66
Charismatic Leader and His Followers, The
 (Hengel), 267
Childs, Brevard, 26, 130
chrism. *See* oil, anointing
Chrysostom, John, 10, 61, 227
clothing. *See* vestments, priestly
Congar, Yves, 9, 26–27, 189
consecration, priestly, 43–51
consuming fire, 56–62
Cook, Stephen, 154
corruption, priestly. *See* sin
creation, 42–43, 74–75, 257–58
Cross, Frank Moore, 112
cult, ethics and the, 82–84, 87–91, 251–53
Cyril of Alexandria, 101
Cyril of Jerusalem, 54

Scripture and Other Ancient Sources Index